THE ESSENTIAL WAYNE BOOTH

*The Essential*
# WAYNE BOOTH

||||||||||||||||||||||||||||||||||||||||||||||||||||||||||||||||||||||||||

*Edited and with an Introduction by*
*Walter Jost*

THE UNIVERSITY OF CHICAGO PRESS
CHICAGO AND LONDON

Wayne C. Booth (1921–2005) was the George M. Pullman Distinguished Service Professor Emeritus at the University of Chicago. His many books include *The Rhetoric of Fiction* and *For the Love of It: Amateuring and Its Rivals*, both published by the University of Chicago Press.

Walter Jost is professor of English at the University of Virginia. He is the author of *Rhetorical Investigations: Studies in Ordinary Language Criticism* and *Rhetorical Thought in John Henry Newman* and the coeditor of four books, most recently *A Companion to Rhetoric and Rhetorical Criticism*.

The University of Chicago Press, Chicago 60637
The University of Chicago Press, Ltd., London
© 2006 by The University of Chicago
All rights reserved. Published 2006
Printed in the United States of America

15 14 13 12 11 10 09 08 07 06    1 2 3 4 5

ISBN: 0-226-06592-8 (cloth)

Library of Congress Cataloging-in-Publication Data

Booth, Wayne C.
   The essential Wayne Booth / edited and with an introduction by Walter Jost.
     p. cm.
   Includes bibliographical references and index.
   ISBN 0-226-06592-8 (cloth : alk. paper)
   1. Literature—History and criticism.  2. Rhetoric.  3. Criticism.  I. Jost, Walter,
   1951–  II. Title.
   PN511.B56 2006
   809—dc22

                                   2005032417

# Contents

# Introduction

*Walter Jost*

Readers unfamiliar with Wayne C. Booth's full authorship—both his numerous books and his nearly innumerable essays and occasional writings—may not be aware of how engagingly and unassumingly, yet with what authority, he has written about such a great variety of matters: narrative fiction, ethics in and out of literature, irony, literary and cultural criticism, higher education, the need for methodological pluralism in intellectual inquiry of all kinds, rhetoric, teaching, religion. In truth Booth's writings are more than enough to reinvigorate the phrases "the examined life" and "the life of the mind," but far more than will fit into any familiar set of genres or convenient academic categories.

Readers familiar with Booth, on the other hand, and attracted by just such breadth of interests, who happen to glance at the table of contents of the present volume purporting to offer an "essential" Wayne Booth, are, I fear, destined to suffer the fate of disappointment in not finding this or that particular Booth essay or chapter, perhaps a special favorite, included within its covers. Indeed, I cannot help placing myself in this group. Where is Booth's fine essay on Bakhtin and feminist criticism? I have complained on more than one occasion. What did I do with that interesting early piece on the ontological proof? Where are the more choice satires and spoofs from the desktop of this supreme ironist? Why—in short—haven't we been granted more essays, more of the multicolored facets of the literary outpouring over the previous five and a half decades of this myriad-minded thinker?

As editor working in collaboration with this book's author, I solved this problem for the both of us—many times, only to discover, after each turn of the screw, that I had merely re-created the difficulty in another guise. My approach was sometimes to drop, say, this rhetoric piece, or that ethics essay, in order to make room for some other indispensable chapter, but more often I added "just one more" essay to the bunch, waving aside the customary editorial considerations of size, cost, and marketing. Nothing worked—just because Booth has succeeded in his intellectual pursuits so well. Had he written fewer pieces most worth saving, the rest of us might have been spared the disappointment of not having them all neatly packaged in one handsome, affordable, slim volume. There is nothing for it: we must blame Booth.

And it gets worse. For it is not only his distinguished career but a genuinely estimable life that deserves, even while it must forgo here, a proper accounting. Family, colleagues, friends of Wayne Booth, including those like myself fortunate enough to have been one of his students, will already know that readers would appreciate hearing about his generosity with his time and talents, his seemingly boundless vitality, his sense of social justice, and his broad understanding of human life and the anxious creatures (fictional and real) responsible both for making a mess of things and for making them hum. Booth initiates will assert their general readers' rights to be informed of his numerous, richly deserved awards, ranging from the University of Chicago's prestigious Quantrell Award for Excellence in Undergraduate Teaching to Fulbright, Rockefeller, and National Endowment for the Humanities grants, to his being elected a member of the American Academy of Arts and Letters and president of the Modern Language Association, his having had bestowed upon him honorary doctorates by several colleges and universities, and his being invited to serve on untold numbers of scholarly and educational committees and to give many hundreds of talks and lectures in the United States and around the world. Some readers, it is true, may not think that it qualifies strictly as a moral or even an intellectual virtue that Booth began playing the cello at age thirty-one and has diligently practiced and played—not at all well, to hear him tell it—in countless amateur ensembles ever since. But even that passing fact of his biography says something important about a deep desire that we all share with him, namely, that of living well by filling our time not only with things that we love but with what is truly worthy of our love.[1]

Such a life well-loved is not easily summed up. Booth himself says as much in an early collection of essays of his own and of others that he edited, whose title, *The Knowledge Most Worth Having* (1967), identifies important subjects that he twice returned to in later essays. In our present cultural context, however, "most worth having" seems to me too confining a phrase and "knowledge" too inflexible a concept to do justice to the way Booth himself has lived, and pondered, and written. In my experience, at least, reading Booth is more like encountering "the knowing most worth doing and sharing," than fixed knowledge most worth possessing, and it is that *activity*—of learning and teaching, however haltingly, together—in which these essays especially invite us to engage.

In fact, putting my thesis about Booth as concisely as possible up front, "character-as-textual-activities" has always been his central substantive preoccupation, and in the second half of this introduction I try to clarify what I mean as well as address the related questions of what we might make of Booth's own character-as-activity in his writings and of how he encourages us to shape what we bring to his texts into resources for our own character-as-active-readers. But all of this first calls for some contextual background about Professor Booth's lifelong commitment to rhetoric to help us appreciate the nature of his intellectual contributions.

## Listening to Rhetoric

Re-reading most of Booth's work as he and I selected and edited the essays included here, I was genuinely struck (again) at just how lightly Booth has worn his considerable learning over the decades. Booth does not show off his knowledge; he uses it. It is only later that one begins to realize how carefully yet with what ease of familiarity he moves from Samuel Johnson to Shakespeare to Homer to Ovid to Chaucer, from Fielding to Yeats to Beckett, from Plato and Aristotle to Weber to Freud to Jacques Derrida. Such a list may be airily dismissed by some as merely the usual suspects of canonical, Western, dead, white males; but to that list could easily be added Booth's broad and deep reading in world literature, especially in world fiction, by men *and* women (he has been a lifelong Janeite). Immediately after graduate school Booth spent a Fulbright year in Germany—reading Kant. And it shows, not in any macaronic leavings from the *Critique of Pure Reason* littering his texts, nor in the professional Kantian's erudition that Booth himself never professed, but only on the occasions when Kant can be of real use to him in helping to develop a certain line of argument or in reminding his readers of a neglected possibility of thought. And it shows more subtly when one really leans on one of Booth's arguments and finds that it holds its own in any company—critical, theoretical, or philosophical. One may disagree—perhaps vehemently—with any given argument, but the argument itself will require and often invite you to think hard in order to do so.

Consider the massive amount of reading, for example, that stands behind, or rather flanks (like flying buttresses), *The Rhetoric of Fiction*, a book that remains to many a kind of Proustian church-cathedral seen from afar and from which one gets one's bearings even in a rapidly moving intellectual landscape. When you are ready for a change of scale, scrutinize the inductive theorizing from his own experience that makes *A Rhetoric of Irony* (1974) the tightly written, useful study it is to this day (no small feat). Or take one of Booth's earliest published essays, "Macbeth as Tragic Hero," which opens the present collection. Here, even in his salad days, the new Ph.D. and Laurence Sterne scholar unfolds, as though it were a personal, well-creased map, a nuanced account of the treatment of "character" in one of Shakespeare's plays. Booth illuminates Macbeth's ethical physiognomy with the diverse lights of Aristotle's *Poetics* and Fitzgerald's Dick Diver and Arthur Miller's Willy Loman. On reflection, this kind of thing is impressive, but it can come in stealthily through the literary radar, its many-sided achievement easy to overlook, in the way, for example, that the philosophy of William James can look—deceptively—easy to do.

There is, come to think of it, an engaging, Jamesian informality, as well as a pronounced philosophical bent, to Booth's own attitude toward literature and learning in general, but a better term than *philosophical* or *theoretical* is *rhetorical*, or—if we follow to the end Booth's most recent promptings—*rhetorological*. It is a pity that *rhetoric* as a term of general usage still has trailing behind it clouds of whatever on two legs is corrupt and corrupting, what, of late, Booth wittily labels "rhetrickery." The opprobrium that *rhetoric* as a term of art continues to elicit unthinkingly throughout the academy is nothing short of dismaying, in view of all that Booth and the likes of I. A. Richards, Richard McKeon, Kenneth Burke, and many, many others during the past hundred years have done to recover and rethink what was, in ancient Greece, the first intellectual discipline established as such, preceding even philosophy itself.

As for rhetoric in our own time, and particularly now, in light of better-moderated understandings of the influential work of (for example) Roland Barthes, Paul de Man, and Jacques Derrida,[2] and of post-structuralism and its earlier uses in new historicism and later uses in cultural studies generally, it is becoming clearer that their many, quite different, often Nietzsche-inflected accounts of "rhetoric" *could* have joined forces with American accounts of philosophy and rhetoric, such as Richard McKeon's, and Booth's, and (especially) Kenneth Burke's—in the way, for example, that Nietzsche is known to have read and admired Ralph Waldo Emerson—and the term *rhetoric* at last taken hold as the more appropriate marker for so-called interdisciplinarity in the academy.[3] As Booth puts it in *Modern Dogma and the Rhetoric of Assent* (1974), "Rhetoric is the art of discovering warrantable beliefs and improving those beliefs in shared discourse," no matter what the subject matter. But, alas, no. Even while rhetoric has long been practiced under many names by critics and scholars in all fields, the age-old contempt or reduction of the term continues to appear obligatory in and out of academe. Why should this be, or, more pointedly, what does Wayne Booth care, and why should we? Why cleave to the term *rhetoric* as he (sometimes fitfully, but finally and emphatically) has done?

Booth's own high argument for rhetoric, undertaken throughout all of his writings, suggests part of the reason: Much good rhetoric, really worthwhile persuasion of oneself and others, not only involves "warrantable assent" (John Dewey's phrase, borrowed by Booth), but also requires looking for common intellectual ground among competing factions, in part by really *listening* to what others have to say. And how many of us do that, how often, and how intently? In his most recent book, *The Rhetoric of Rhetoric: The Quest for Effective Communication*,[4] Booth calls this sort of continuing communicative effort "listening-rhetoric," an ongoing exchange in which one considers others' purposes, principles, and perspectives with eyes and ears open for what might be of genuine worth in human life. As Booth has written, in what was once a characteristically American-ameliorative (some will insist "naive") attitude, "Here both sides join in a trusting dispute, determined to listen to the opponent's arguments, while persuading the opponent to listen in exchange. Each side attempts to think about the arguments presented by the other side. Neither side surrenders merely to be tactful or friendly. . . . Both sides are pursuing not just victory but a new reality, a new agreement about what is real" (46–47).

At a time when intellectual argument across disciplines (*argument*, not only inquiry) seems to many to be thriving, Booth has suggested that, on the contrary, comparatively few of the contestants ever pause to check that they are even on the same page, discussing the same issues as others— much less working toward locating premises they might share and develop competitively together. Booth's point is that such an enterprise is not, after all, impossible, that in fact there are known ways in which we do on occasion manage it, and that as an ideal for critique as well as construction it is *universally* to be desired. Far from being himself naive about the difficulties of engaging in real inquiry and achieving assent with others, Booth would have us return in some humility to our own intellectual dispositions and practices to ask ourselves to what extent we, not only personally but professionally and culturally, are naive, co-opted, closed-minded, narrow, impatient, prematurely (or immaturely) judgmental.

Such a clarion call to conscience may not quicken the pulse with the drumbeat of a Foucault, an Althusser, or a Judith Butler against the System, but then it may be all the more difficult to dodge than certain grand abstractions of Theory, freely cited by many who seem to feel little personal responsibility to if not for them. I myself feel some affinity between Booth and someone whom Booth (like many others) initially regarded with great skepticism, but whom he came over time to admire, namely, Jacques Derrida, regarding both their common interest in situating their generalizations in highly individualized particularities and the latter's remark, after 9/11, that "I would be tempted to call philosophers those who, in the future, reflect in a responsible fashion on these [inter alia political] questions and *demand accountability* from those in charge of public discourse."[5] Booth never called himself a philosopher, but he has, from the beginning of his career, performed in just the way Derrida himself came only over time to describe. Recently the contemporary feminist theorist Toril Moi, whom I have occasion to quote below, in her own recent turn to a Wittgensteinian-Cavellian, ordinary-language philosophy, has also come to share with Booth and others just this concern with a rhetorical (as well as grammatical or philosophical) accountability to community, real or envisioned.[6]

Just such cautious inquiry into, inventive discovery of, and demand for accountability regarding public arguments, as well as the study of the theory and practice of how these are undertaken ("rhetorology"[7]), have always constituted Booth's intellectual home-away-from-home (the rubric of "English Department" could never quite contain him): "It is clear to me now that rhetorical matters [have] been at the center of most of my thinking . . . from adolescence on. . . . At every moment in my teaching, at every moment in my writing, I was trying to think of ways of improving communication: by studying those ways and by training students in distinctions between defensible and indefensible forms of rhetoric."[8] This is not quite the place, of course, for a primer on rhetoric, but rhetoric as Booth defines it offers insight both into the coherence of the professional and personal life he has led and, more immediately, into the corresponding integrity of the present volume.

Booth's latest formulation of rhetoric has the virtue of underlining the scope of his lifelong concerns: "[R]hetoric [involves] *the entire range of resources that human beings share for producing effects on one another*: effects ethical (including everything about character), practical (including political), emotional (including aesthetic), and intellectual (including every academic field). It is the entire range of our use of 'signs' for communicating, effectively or sloppily, ethically or immorally."[9] Rhetoric for him might be said to be not "principled" subject matters or knowledge per se but the human mode of apprehension, formulation, and understanding of any and all knowledge in and out of disciplinary fields—always partial, always value-laden, always "interested," and for just those reasons always our own—but knowledge, no less (however provisional), of the only world or cosmos at present it is ours to know.

This most recent sense of rhetoric is consistent with (though of course more capacious than) Booth's project in *The Rhetoric of Fiction* more than forty years earlier, in which he was interested in "finding [authorial] techniques of expression that will make the [literary] work accessible in the highest possible degree."[10] Indeed, we can think of Booth's whole corpus of work as a continuum, comprising overlapping sets of interests in communicative exchange and accessibility to a nondogmatic, nonreductive variety of perspectives on the world, suitable for all who are willing to defer closure on truth.

## Vicissitudes of Character

Booth's abiding interest in character—in narrators dramatized or undramatized, in implied authors, in communities real and readerly, and in the aesthetics, ethics, and politics of all of these—is, as I have indicated, his own most important issue, rhetorically the "logos" of his lifelong studies. To be sure, Booth's discussion of character is also connected with his own ethos, inasmuch as his discussions also reveal his own character as he manifests it in his writings. But inquiries about the character of others are at the center of much of his work, and that centrality tells us what Booth understood to be the chief substantive center of *any* life—namely, one's ethical character as it shapes, and is shaped in and by, action (not "knowledge" per se, then, or even "knowing," so much as knowledgeable *acting* has been his lifelong concern).[11] This is a way of insisting that, back in the day of the "death of the author," and, before that, of "authorial objectivity," Booth foresaw the return of the repressed sources of the self in the revivals of rhetoric and ethical criticism that he himself helped instaurate. Such a sense of Booth's center of gravity leads me to group *The Rhetoric of Fiction*, *A Rhetoric of Irony*, and *The Company We Keep: An Ethics of Fiction* together to organize and explore certain aspects of this theme.[12] Allow me to give several short examples of what I mean.

*The Rhetoric of Fiction* remains justly famous for the many contributions it makes to narrative studies, foremost of which has been Booth's development of the notion of the author's "second self," or what he called the "implied author," and of the unreliable narrator (a teller whose evaluations and reports are not endorsed by the implied author). In this first systematic book Booth was working against the then-widespread literary dogma that there was, or in any case should be, no modern "rhetoric of fiction" at all. To be good, this dogma held, novels must be "realistic," and to be realistic, novels must eschew any authorial intrusion into the tale or any signs of a writer's crassly worrying about his or her readers.

Incautiously seeking to generalize an attitude or a theory, many critics re-duced the complexity of the writer's craft by privileging formal "purity" and personal dispassionateness over all other values, stripping the novel of any possible norms of authorial commentary or any sort of "telling" over "showing." For these critics, realism entailed not only an "unsentimental" but a value-free fiction disdainful of all undue emphasis on action (plot) or even of human presence (recall Ortega's "dehumanization of art")—a fiction, in sum, that loftily "ignored the audience."

Booth's distinction of the flesh-and-blood writer from the implied author—"an implicit picture of an author who stands behind the scenes, whether as stage manager, as puppeteer, or as an indifferent God, silently paring his fingernails"—allowed him to open up and fill in new topoi to show the almost innumerable ways in which an author becomes present in his or her text,[13] all the while "imposing [a] fictional world upon the reader" ("Preface to the First Edition," xiii). Whether the writer dramatizes him- or herself in a reliable narrator who represents the author's own val-ues and views in the tale—a narrator perhaps even self-conscious about his own role *as* a writer of the story—or, instead, creates an undrama-tized and even unreliable narrator; whether the author intrudes with overt commentary and other forms of telling rather than showing, or works in-stead entirely without such intrusions, allowing the characters (and even the plot) to parade before the reader without guiding lights of any kind—nevertheless *all* writers, whether they speak directly or indirectly, appear implicitly as partners in a dialogue with the reader "that is at the heart of all experience with fiction" (272). By way of both careful close reading and an astonishing ability to generalize from his own reading without losing the particular case, Booth fully earns his claim, mid-book, that "[w]e have seen that the author cannot choose to avoid rhetoric; he can choose only the kind of rhetoric he will employ" (149).

While *The Rhetoric Fiction* was obviously focused on authorial control of rhetorical techniques, the notion of the implied author enabled Booth to explore a corresponding range of narrative effects while sidestepping any need for naive deterministic attributions of "intentions" to writers (the pretense that we can know, or even need to know, what a real-life author was thinking in order to share the world he or she has created), a fallacy he elsewhere rightly condemns as one kind of "motivism" (the erroneous belief that the causes of an action or a text explain it without remainder). For the same reason, the complexity of the concept of an implied author allowed his treatment of the "morality of fiction" to avoid flatfooted accounts of what is moral or immoral. Such accounts by others often featured reductive value-propositions and moralizing summaries or even sought to inculcate "the right values," as if authors or critics can itemize such things without regard to particular circumstances and purposes and readers.

Booth's discussion of morality worked not as an imposition from the outside in—deductively requiring narratives to conform to "our" moral expectations—but from the inside out. That is, Booth noted that rhetorical techniques had *consequences* for our judgments of characters, and that these judgments had consequences for our emotional and ethical engagements with those characters and the narrative worlds they inhabited. In this way, Booth at his best achieved extremely subtle and nuanced analyses of narrative undreamed of by most other "moral" critics at the time. Nevertheless, Booth's discussion was controversial in the early 1960s, and he himself came to recognize that he sometimes worked from the outside in, leading him later to devote a whole book (*The Company We Keep*) to the ethics of fiction.[14]

Moreover, in the notion of the implied author was the germ of several ideas that exfoliate over subsequent works, among which is the insight—hardly unique to Booth but deftly used by him[15]—that any author, any character or person at all, *always* comes in multiple versions, that any self (as he puts it in *Modern Dogma and the Rhetoric of Assent*) is "a field of selves."[16] Not only is (say) "Nabokov" incarnated in innumerable ways throughout a given novel, but Nabokov's own implied authors (plural) have perforce changed from book to book according to each book's aims and effects. Among other things, this entails that the reader's (the real as well as implied reader's) experience of an author is *itself* always changing and multiple, a dialogue, perhaps, but a multivocal one (Booth bends one of Bakhtin's terms, making "heteroglossia" a "polyglossia")—call it a polylogue of many selves, both those of the author (as well as the characters) and not least those of the reader.

These ideas become clearer in *A Rhetoric of Irony*, another breakthrough book in its field on at least two counts. First, even while fully allowing for the destabilization of the reading and writing self, Booth provides a complex set of topoi to explore how a fully intended, fully stable irony is one of the richest and most efficient ways that authors share their views of the (or a fictional) world with readers. Second, far from being strictly, much less exclusively, a corrosive or subverting trope of language, irony can be a great builder of textual community, sometimes small but often very large indeed. As he writes in "The Empire of Irony" (chapter 6 of this volume),

> Whenever a piece of intended irony works, when a clever ironist manages to hook us, we come closer than at any other time to a full *identification of two minds*. The only figure that can rival irony in achieving this effect is

metaphor, but I think that the bonding is even tighter with irony.... In the moment of identification, the receiver loses his or her private identity in a way that is more dramatic than in our ordinary surrender to other people's meanings. (111)

This essentially moral or ethical interest in the identification of (implied) author(s) and (implied) reader(s) comes to a kind of culmination in *The Company We Keep: An Ethics of Fiction*. Begun during the time when Booth wrote his afterword to the 1983 edition of *The Rhetoric of Fiction*, *The Company We Keep* more than makes good on what he had come to recognize over the years, namely, the complexity involved in reading (and in readers) that follows from his embrace of the divided or multiple self, as he admits in the afterword:

> I am shocked at the confidence my younger self sometimes shows in reporting how "we" respond [to certain novels]. Who *are* we, here? ... Fortunately, much of what the book says about "us" can be simply translated into talk about the relatively stable audience postulated by the implied author—the readers the text asks us to become. In making that translation, I now would underline the inherently, inescapably creative role we play in every act of reading. Recent "reader-critics" are quite right in insisting that the actual reader must "make" whatever story gets made, including, of course, its teller. And since we are such diverse creatures, actual readings will always to some degree diverge. (420)

One way Booth follows through on this self-correction is by focusing his ethics of fiction on the various *activities* offered in a text by an author. He does this at length throughout *The Company We Keep*, but its most focused expression occurs in his employment of "friendship" as a metaphor for one kind of relationship between authors and readers.[17] Not articulable "beliefs" alone, or even primarily (as given, for instance, in what a character or reliable narrator says or does), but the full, active experience of reading understood as one (or more) of Aristotle's three kinds of friendship—the pleasurable, the useful, and the virtuous (these terms need not be mutually exclusive)—circumscribes a beginning, and in Booth a very rich vocabulary, for ethical criticism as Booth presents it.

Booth is inventive in his metaphorizing of friendship. Obviously he professes his own (Aristotelian) hierarchy of values, with virtuous friendships on top. As he puts it in "'The Way I Loved George Eliot': Friendship with Books as a Neglected Critical Metaphor" (chapter 9 of this volume), "The fullest friendship arises whenever two people not only offer each other pleasure or utilities but believe that they are equals in all their as-pirations and thus are good for and with each other" (159). But Booth also notes that one must distinguish the gifts that are offered by a text, perhaps with great fanfare, from what is actually delivered or (better) achieved in it by author and reader together. Thus a book of "mere" plea-sures may in fact outweigh in moral value the false promises of edification offered by some well-intentioned, high-toned pretender. Booth details sev-eral qualities of such pleasures: a fair *quantity* of them (e.g., suspense, wry humor, likable criminals, hapless cops—I am thinking of the delicious Dortmunder capers by Donald E. Westlake); pleasures that challenge the reader with intellectual responsibilities of different intensities; those that exhibit a more or less limited *range* and *kind* and make few, or many, se-rious claims to virtue: these are among the things that we go to fiction *for*. Bearing in mind, moreover, that virtuous activity is itself always pleasur-able, and may also be useful, such ethical talk of "pleasure" or "utility" can (though it need not) fully inform what is virtuous about an implied author, while virtuous friendships offered by books afford pleasures whose discriminations require yet further complex vocabulary. For Booth as for Aristotle, pleasure is not passive enjoyment but involves *active desire*, the wish to move from A to B (most fully realized in plot),[18] and hence a range of possible active engagements, from the near-zero of activity (Booth in-stances literary anecdotes; one might go lower and think of most television and Internet pop-up ads) to the nearly humanly impossible (*Finnegans Wake*).

Booth himself gives many examples of such ethical criticism in *The Company We Keep*, and there are several examples throughout the essays in this volume. But rather than repeat or summarize one of his efforts, it might be more illuminating to elicit what I take to be the chief (not the only) ethical activity that Booth himself affords in all of his books—I mean the virtuous pleasures of reciprocal and responsible inquiry and argument.

Given, in other words, that pleasurable, useful, virtuous "character-as-textual-activities" is Booth's chief issue, what can we make briefly of his *own* character-as-activity, his own ethos? To be sure, if I were attempting here particular studies of how Booth's ethos changes from work to work, I might very well begin to speak of personae like Uncle Wayne, Brother Wayne, Reverend Wayne, the neo-Aristotelian Booth, Booth the Educator, Booth the Satirist, and so on. Instead, I invite us to think of Boothian ethos not as a fairly determinate set of qualities (e.g., Aristotle's triad of intelligence, virtue, and good will) that the "real" Wayne Booth himself at one time and another possessed or expressed, but as something that we ourselves, rhetorically, figure out or "pose" as the authorial Wayne

Booth, and specifically *as* multiform thinker and writer. In other words, I want to ask, not only what Wayne Booth cares about (his "beliefs"), but how in his writings he went about performing his tasks of thinking and writing (his ethical "activities"). In this way character becomes a question of general intellectual method, and we can, accordingly, invent a second grouping of his works: his early collections, *The Knowledge Most Worth Having* (1967) and *Now Don't Try to Reason with Me* (1970), both of which focus on reasoning and intellectual inquiry; his three "pedagogical" books (my term: all his books are pedagogical), two of them coauthored with Marshall Gregory, *The Harper & Row Reader* (1984) and *The Harper & Row Rhetoric* (1987), and one with Joseph Williams and Gregory Colomb, *The Craft of Research* (1995); and, most important, *Modern Dogma and the Rhetoric of Assent* (1974) and especially *Critical Understanding: The Powers and Limits of Pluralism* (1979).[19]

It is in these latter two inquiries in particular that Booth most fully lays out not only who he is, methodologically speaking, but also how his own intellectual ideal functions—I mean, specifically, just how one goes about "thinking like a rhetorician." Regrettably, again, I cannot pursue in any detail the kind of ethical criticism of particulars that Booth asks of us and that he himself deserves. Instead, I content myself with putting my own implied reader, avid to learn more from and about Booth, on the lookout for two interlocking intellectual virtues that Booth (real and implied) always professed: rhetorical inquiry as a communal activity of understanding and argument, and a nonrelativistic "pluralism" of intellectual methods.

### Tools of the Trade

The first virtue I have perhaps already said enough about, namely, Booth's "topical" method of rhetoric and rhetorology, richly displayed and discussed in *Modern Dogma and the Rhetoric of Assent* and evident in almost all of his writings, failing to appear only when Booth himself becomes, on a bad day, himself dogmatic or otherwise preemptory. The signature of this method is the use of intellectual tools—concepts, arguments, cases, examples, hypotheticals, tropes like irony and metaphor, analogies, imagined conversations, even fictional characters and entire works of art—as resources, that is, as "openings" (to use Booth's term) to explore what it is he takes to be a more or less indeterminate matter. Since not all texts and problems are *equally* indeterminate across contexts, the method mandates a kind of intent *listening* to the particular case. To be sure, to contrast the transparency of a method of openness of concepts and arguments with, for example, that of shouting heads on cable "news" programs is a no-brainer for any Booth reader. But to discriminate how the better literary, cultural, and critical Theorists-with-a-capital-T *themselves* turn more or less determinate principles into their own inventive tools for rhetorical employment—that is, to discriminate those thinkers from the more dogmatic, who "lock in" a fixed rate of return on their intellectual investments (namely, zero, for they get no more out of their first principles than they put into them)—such discrimination *itself* requires topical rhetoric, just what Toril Moi (my own example of one of the better contemporary thinkers) has herself come to appreciate in Simone de Beauvoir and other theorists (Freud, Bourdieu, Wittgenstein, Austin, Cavell). In *What Is a Woman?* Moi writes,

> The point made by Cavell and others is that we cannot even have struggle and disagreement unless we speak to each other on the basis of some common understanding (a shared practice) of what counts as political conflict or disagreement. If there is no such shared practice, we would not understand each other sufficiently to disagree. . . .
>
> By examining two different situations—one in which a man begins a work of philosophy and one in which a woman does so—Beauvoir demonstrates that there are cases where the sex of the speaker has decisive influence on what "we" would say, so that there cannot be any question of what "we" would say *in general.*[20]

This should sound familiarly Boothian. One of the insights that follows from such a line of thought is that in doing philosophy, or in doing some kinds of literary theory and criticism and most other things besides, our terms, claims, arguments, conclusions, "all depend." In fact, just the common saying "It all depends" may be taken as the architectonic principle of trans-disciplinary Boothian rhetoric—I mean the dependence of intellectual inquirers on time, place, occasion, audience, purpose, circumstances, institutional constraints, and a great deal more to make a genuine case. Just as Moi finds Bourdieu's call for sociological thick description to be a welcome tonic, and a considerable challenge, for contemporary literary critics, Booth has always championed, usually against the current, the patient accumulation of detail, himself acknowledging more and more the need for just such contextual detail as Bourdieu demands. Like Booth's, Moi's message (like her practice) is not "No Theoretical Generalizations," but rather "No Unyielding Generalizations without Exceptions"—or, in short, "Experience Required." In *The Company We Keep*, Booth called this kind of attitude and logic "coduction": "I suggest that we arrive at our sense of value in narratives in precisely the way we arrive at our sense of value in persons: by *experiencing* them in an immeasurably rich context of others that are both like and unlike them":

> [T]he logic we depend on as we arrive at our particular appraisals is neither deduction from clear premises, even of the most complex kind, nor induction from a series of precisely defined and isolated instances. Rather it is always the result of a direct sense that something now before us has yielded an experience that we find *comparatively* desirable, admirable, lovable or, on the other hand, comparatively repugnant, contemptible or hateful.[21]

This logic, again, is rhetoric, and rhetoric is a significant but (still!) far too neglected dimension of philosophy, theory, and criticism across all fields.

### Principles and Possibilities

My quoting the feminist theorist Toril Moi is not a mere gesture in the direction of fashionable theorizing but a respectful acknowledgment of her and others' considerable rhetorical insights and achievements as well as (more to the point) my own suggestion that it is Booth's (and others') rhetorical studies that are now bearing fruit in vineyards in which he himself did not labor (at least not for any length of time: one cannot do everything). In her recent work, Moi, dealing with critical theory that Booth did not himself espouse (e.g., Freud's, Irigaray's), is nevertheless in my view an exemplary *Boothian* theorist and ethical critic. To say this another way, Booth has from the beginning *already* implicitly or explicitly welcomed the kinds of principled enterprise that she and others undertake. I can explain what I mean by alluding, again all too briefly, to two of Booth's works, one an essay from this volume, the other *Critical Understanding: The Powers and Limits of Pluralism*.

In chapter 7 of this volume, "Richard McKeon's Pluralism: The Path between Dogmatism and Relativism," Booth, with both fondness and lingering residual terror, recalls his first collegiate philosophy course, on Plato's *Republic* (there was only one other student in this "class"), under the tutelage of Richard McKeon. Asked after a time by another professor how his studies in Plato were going, Booth made small talk and then, youthfully, complained about finding McKeon's "dogmatic Platonism weird." To which the professor responds, "Oh, is that so? Have you not heard that Richard McKeon is thought to be a dogmatic Aristotelian?" Booth had not heard. But in time he certainly came to hear and learn much more about the "kind of mind" that he was dealing with in McKeon: "[I]t was the same kind that I met in a later course,"

> that of an absolutely dogmatic Humeian, not just eager to defend Hume from every conceivable attack but brilliant at exposing the stupidities of any of us who raised what seemed to us obvious objections to Hume. It was a mind that had earlier produced a "dogmatically Spinozist" book on Spinoza, that obviously heroic geometrist of ethics who cannot easily be fitted under the umbrella of either a Platonist or an Aristotelian or a Humeian. As any reader of McKeon might predict, I later met in him an equally persuasive dogmatic defender of Democritus, of Cicero, of Kant, of Dewey. (122–23)

Now, obviously, such "dogmatism" is by definition no dogmatism at all; we might call it "understanding-in-motion" (note the practical, moral concern with action again). What kept such a mind (I mean McKeon's, but also Booth's) from succumbing, on the other hand, to "mere relativism," were his moral and intellectual values, Booth calls them "universals," *adjusted*, in the most sophisticated philosophical ways, to just that plurality of philosophers and their philosophies indicated above. Booth writes,

> For McKeon, the major philosophies are irrefutable in the sense that they each reveal ONE true path to ONE vision of ONE genuine aspect of truth.... The list of the fully *comprehensive* philosophies, in contrast to the fragmented ones, was never very long for him, but there was never a moment, after his twenties, when he offered the hope, either to himself or to any future philosopher, of developing a single philosophy that would genuinely refute or encompass all those others. (124)

I have quoted at some length because the passages capture much of the attitude and spirit of Booth's travels on his own winding, sometimes arduous path between relativism and dogmatism. *Critical Understanding* details his own conclusion that, while no pluralism can genuinely refute or encompass all other positions, including the pluralism he himself set out to construct and test, nevertheless we are all far richer as critics, and as human beings, if we first allow for, then tirelessly seek, "vitality, justice, and understanding"[22] among critical positions—even when such pluralism cannot be intellectually "proved" in any way that would satisfy all those who occupy different positions on the critical spectrum. I cannot hope here to save such values as vitality, justice, and understanding from their inevitable ring of banality in the way that Booth himself so powerfully does in his book, but I might hazard a paraphrase of his own defense of them: Far better is it to launch out on critical principles of one's own choice, diverse and conflicting as they will inevitably be with regard to someone else's choices, than either to cling, dogmatically, to some determinate and unyielding set of principles (however broad) or, relativistically, to surrender one's power to *try* to understand, do justice to, and honor the vitality of "the Other," merely because that "Other" cannot be folded neatly into hard-and-fast rules of argument and debate. In sum: Better to *act virtuously* (morally and intellectually) than to wait for an impossible, final metapluralism of pluralistic absolute truth.

I need hardly warn that my paraphrase is a poor thing; but if taken as the pointer it is meant to be, the reader will, I hope, want to return to the larger context of Booth's works to make fuller sense of the wonderful essays here. Booth's own model of pluralism is itself (no surprise) rhetorical, a rich deployment of more or less indeterminate topoi in an attempt to account for the pluralisms of R. S. Crane, M. H. Abrams, and Kenneth Burke. But saying so does not defeat, it rather furthers his aim of understanding others, precisely because it encourages others (like Moi) to pursue their own principled theories as fully as possible, even as others can treat them as yet further "openings" (not fixed answers or even principles) to new thought and experience.

This leads me, finally, to consider Booth's various handlings of his "audience"—not as we might try to think of ourselves empirically but *as the audience gets shaped rhetorically in and through Booth's writings*. Specifically, how does Booth handle our "mood" (to use an unlikely but appropriate Heideggerian term), our emotional disposition, our "state of mind"? Into what emotional disposition does Booth most commonly seek to place us, his readers? Naturally the answer to this question is rhetorically open to interpretation and argument, and naturally it "all depends," once more, on the Booth book or essay we are referring to, its provenance, its purpose, and so on. And once again I cannot enlarge on these matters in the way that I wish to here. But I can modestly suggest the following.

Booth has always chosen to "pose" his implied readers, much as he poses himself, as *genuine learners*, leading us by example to want to emulate those who inquire well, rhetorically and ethically, including making an example of himself. He does not achieve this by merely talking about himself autobiographically, though he sometimes does that, but by drawing on his own experience and claiming it as "representative" (after Kant's idea of "reflective," not determinant, judgment, that is, judgment that is both non-rule-governed and universal in intent). Toril Moi gets at what I am tracking here: "'The problem of the critic, as of the artist,' Cavell writes, 'is not to discount his subjectivity, but to include it; not to overcome it in agreement, but to master it in exemplary ways.'" And, having just quoted Cavell, she explains him and herself in a way that I believe fits Booth's own attitude and practice perfectly:

> If my subjectivity—my experience—is to be of any use in my criticism or my philosophy, Cavell seems to say, I have to be able to make it exemplary. Otherwise it will remain staunchly particular, and so of no interest to anybody but myself. To make it exemplary is to show what light it can shed on a general question, not to claim that it is itself general, [but] that it in some mysterious way already subsumes that of others.[23]

But if this holds for the critic who successfully exemplifies it in his or her writing, then his or her readership, too, is required to make an example of itself—that is, to risk reading in a way that actively engages the activities of the text sympathetically and critically. Hence the "mood" Booth asks us to assume is always attended by the anxiety (Heidegger's *Angst*) that I may fail both myself and others as an example of the ideal active reader, at once sympathetic and critical. In Booth, however, this primordial anxiety is rhetorically orchestrated toward a continued growth through *education* in the broadest sense of that term, in line with Aristotle's claim that, by nature, we desire to know. Booth might call his posing of us our own call to wonder, and even to joy. If I am right, we are then in a position to group together Booth's remaining books: *The Art of Growing Older: Writers on Living and Aging* (1992), and (speaking of the cello) *For the Love of It: Amateuring and Its Rivals* (1999); but also, and more importantly (even culminatingly), *The Vocation of a Teacher: Rhetorical Occasions, 1967–1988*.[24]

By now, however, if I myself have provided any kind of example or guide, new as well as seasoned Booth readers will want to pursue these additional books and the others on their own, as inquirers and learners ready to transform their own expectations and questions into personal resources, that is, more or less indeterminate topoi useful for uncovering circumstances for their own inquiry, interpretation, argument, and judgment. I have tried to suggest that just this is what Booth invites us all to do—that the rhetorical occasions of reading his books and essays are, above all, education in action.

In addition, some such formulation as the preceding ought, I think, to clarify the organization of this book, though it is roughly chronological, as more importantly thematic. That is, while all of the essays are at once rhetorical arguments themselves, in addition to being *about* the many aspects and levels of rhetoric, they also cluster around Booth's abiding concerns with character, intellectual methods of inquiry, and the desire to learn by doing.

Among the first six essays, the first two, "Macbeth as Tragic Hero" and "Control of Distance in Jane Austen's *Emma*," showcase Booth's lifelong (and "Aristotelian") concern with formal considerations of ethos in fiction. The following two, "The Rhetorical Stance" and "The Revival of Rhetoric," extend those same interests in character and its representations to the forms of rhetoric of undergraduate writing and the revival of an art that extends, we now understand, from freshman comp to Shakespeare to Derrida and indefinitely beyond. And the next two, "Metaphor as Rhetoric: The Problem of Evaluation (with Ten Literal 'Theses')" and "The Empire of Irony," similarly extend and turn that art to the commanding tropes of metaphor and irony, by which (among other things) we communicate our own characters and build, or fail to build, communities.

Chapters 7 and 8 interrupt the chronological progression of the essays followed thus far. Chapter 7, "Richard McKeon's Pluralism: The Path between Dogmatism and Relativism," and chapter 8, "How Bakhtin Woke Me Up," Booth's introduction to Mikhail Bakhtin's *Problems of Dostoyevsky's Poetics*, discuss two of Booth's more significant intellectual heroes. The essays' anachronistic placement may seem also to constitute a rather random pairing, but their appearance in the middle of the book is intended as a means to pause and reflect, forward and back, on Booth's catholicity as a critic and theorist, and as an aid in measuring the depth and extent of his achievement in all the essays. For these two essays at once argue for and celebrate that "listening-rhetoric" mentioned above, in the form of Bakhtin's theorizing of the many voices, the "dialogism," "polyphony," and "heteroglossia," of fiction; and, more broadly, in Richard McKeon's investigations of philosophic semantics as a (rhetorical) means for managing the exchange of ideas and methods in and across *all* disciplines. To see Booth in the preferred company of these two thinkers is to appreciate better his own focus on communication amid diversity.

The following five essays return to a chronological order after the break, taking up different aspects of practicing ethical criticism. Chapter 9, "'The Way I Loved George Eliot': Friendship with Books as a Neglected Critical Metaphor," proposes the powerful metaphor of "friendship with books" later developed in Booth's *The Company We Keep: An Ethics of Fiction*, while chapter 10, "On Relocating Ethical Criticism," establishes new coordinates for the practice of ethical criticism in light of responses to *The Company We Keep*. Chapter 11, "The Ethics of Forms: Taking Flight with *The Wings of the Dove*," enacts Booth's own complex friendship with

Henry James, revisiting his long-standing preoccupations with rhetoric, ethics, and formal design in that very complex novel. Chapters 12 and 13, "The Ethics of Teaching Literature" and "'Of the Standard of Moral Taste': Literary Criticism as Moral Inquiry," are sophisticated inquiries into the meanings of "moral" and "ethical" as deserving constituents of the "aims" of education, aims that can reflect a "standard of moral taste" that is neither deductively imposed from philosophy or theory nor relativistically exposed to any and every opinion that blows down the street. With help from David Hume, Booth's inquiry characteristically turns to concrete examples—Goethe, Kafka, and (once again) Shakespeare—to test his hypotheses. This latter essay is a particularly impressive example of Booth's strengths as rhetorical theorist and ethical critic.

Chapters 14 through 16 are synoptic. Chapter 14, "Rhetoric, Science, Religion," bridges the two cultures of science and religion in ways that have intrigued Booth from his earliest writings. Chapter 15, "The Idea of a University—as Seen by a Rhetorician," considers how academics in their institutional labors, and by extension all of us in our respective activities, manage to get their collective work done. And chapter 16, "For the Love of It: Spending, Wasting, and Redeeming Time," is a personal meditation on a life worth living.

In music a coda is a passage at the end of a movement that brings it to a formal close. Chapter 17, "Mere Rhetoric, Rhetorology, and the Search for a Common Learning," is a fitting close, in my judgment, to the trajectory of this book, for it reaches out one last time, as Booth always has done, to address matters of character, rhetorical inquiry, and education. For more than half a century, Professor Booth unflaggingly pursued the activities of knowledge, insight, and intellectual pleasure of all kinds—his own critical understanding of that which, just *because* it changes, abides. Call that understanding "The Rhetoric of Wayne Booth."

Most of the essays included here have been shortened somewhat from their originally published forms. Most have had phrases or sentences added, usually for purposes of greater clarity, and some few have had new comments interpolated by Booth (these latter are placed in brackets and italics). Headnotes in italics offer Booth's current perspective on the essays; those in roman are my own comments and include original publication information.

I wish to thank Alan Thomas at the University of Chicago Press for his abiding interest and support, and my graduate assistants, Jake Heil, Casa Wilson, and Mollie Sledd for their attentive and careful work on the manuscript. My colleague at the University of Virginia, Professor Alison

Booth, has encouraged and helped me (and her father) along the way, as have Michael Hyde at Wake Forest University, Wendy Olmsted and David Smigelskis at the University of Chicago, and James Phelan at the Ohio State University. Their collective advice on the project as a whole and this introduction in particular was needed and welcomed.

My deepest gratitude goes to the late Wayne C. Booth. Among my teachers and fellow students at the University of Chicago, he was not my only role model in moral and intellectual virtues, but he continues to remain a central one. I am grateful for his trust of these essays into my care; it is my hope that they experience renewed life among longtime Booth readers and that they continue to give further openings to new readers in search of a common, and uncommon, learning.

*This essay was published more than fifty years ago, twelve years before any of the others in this anthology. It began as a term paper, when I was strongly under the influence of the so-called Chicago School, or neo-Aristotelian formalists. The leader of that "school," Ronald Crane, considered it "brilliant" and urged me to polish (and polish), and then publish, which I did—to my thrilled surprise—in the* Journal of General Education *(1951). That was one year after I finished my dissertation "proving" the "unity" of* Tristram Shandy, *and ten years before publishing my first book—also based on close reading.*

*Since formal analysis and close reading are now widely ignored, the essay may strike many readers as absurdly outdated—while my Vanity Self insists it is not. We are now flooded with "criticism" based on quick readings conducted in search of evidence for this or that ideological conclusion: "Ah, I've found proof that X was a homosexual" or "that Y was a sexist" or "that Z was a racist." Pursuing what Crane called the "high-priori road," critics too often simply ignore the artistic structure that the author intended to create, thrilled when they find the evidence that they knew in advance they wanted—and thus often escaping the deeper thrill offered by the work itself.*

This first chapter is not Professor Booth's first published academic essay, having been preceded by two somewhat slighter pieces and, on the heels of his dissertation, an essay entitled "Did Sterne Complete *Tristram Shandy*?" (*Modern Philology*, 1951). The essay is, however, a fine example of why he was in such good standing as a junior member of the so-called Chicago neo-Aristotelians, whose concern with literary parts and wholes did not preclude (any more than it did for Aristotle) close attention to questions of ethics and rhetoric.

The essay was originally published in the *Journal of General Education* 6, no. 1 (October 1951): 17–25. It was revised and reprinted as "Shakespeare's Tragic Villain," in *Shakespeare's Tragedies: An Anthology of Modern Criticism*, ed. Lawrence Lerner (Harmondsworth, UK: Penguin, 1963), 180–90.

## Macbeth as Tragic Hero

Put even in its simplest terms, the problem Shakespeare gave himself in *Macbeth* was a tremendous one. Take a good man, a noble man, a man admired by all who know him—and destroy him, not only physically and emotionally, as the Greeks destroyed their heroes, but also morally and intellectually. As if this were not difficult enough as a dramatic hurdle, while you are transforming him into one of the most despicable mortals conceivable, maintain him as a tragic hero—that is, keep him so sympathetic that, when he comes to his death, the audience will pity rather than detest him; they must feel relieved to see him out of his misery rather than pleased to see him destroyed. Put in Shakespeare's own terms: take a "noble" man, full of "conscience" and "the milk of human kindness," and make of him a "dead butcher," yet keep him an object of pity rather than hatred.

If we thus artificially reconstruct the problem as it might have existed before the play was written, we see that, in choosing these "terminal points" and these terminal intentions, Shakespeare makes almost impossible demands on his dramatic skill, although at the same time he insures that, if he succeeds at all, he will succeed magnificently. If the trick can be turned, it will inevitably be a great one.

One need only consider the many relative failures in attempts at similar "plots" and effects to realize the difficulties involved. When dramatists or novelists attempt the sympathetic-degenerative plot, almost always one or another of the following failures or transformations occurs:

1. The feeling of abhorrence for the protagonist becomes so strong that all sympathy is lost, and the play or novel becomes "punitive"—that is, the reader's or spectator's chief pleasure depends on his satisfaction in revenge or punishment.

2. The protagonist is never really made very wicked, after all; he only seems wicked by conventional (and, by implication, unsound) standards and is really a highly admirable reform-candidate.
3. The protagonist reforms in the end and avoids his proper punishment.
4. The book or play itself becomes a "wicked" work; that is, either deliberately or unconsciously the artist makes us side with his degenerated hero against "morality."

If it is deliberate, we have propaganda works of one kind or another, often resembling the second type above; if it is unconscious, we get works whose immorality (as in pornographic or sadistic treatments of the good-girl-turned-whore, thief, or murderess) makes them unenjoyable as literature unless the reader or spectator temporarily or permanently relaxes his own standards of moral judgment. Any of these failures or transformations can be found in conjunction with the most frequent failure of all: the degeneration remains finally unexplained, unmotivated; the forces employed to destroy the noble man are found pitifully inadequate to make his fall seem credible.

Even in works that are somewhat successful, there is almost always some shrinking from a fully responsible engagement with the inherent difficulties. For example, in *Tender Is the Night*, which is in many ways strikingly similar to *Macbeth*, Fitzgerald waters down the effect in several ways. Dick Diver, Fitzgerald's "noble" man, is destroyed, but he is destroyed only to helplessness—to unpopularity and drunkenness and poverty; he becomes a "failure." The signs of his destruction are never grotesque acts of cruelty or wickedness of the kind committed by Macbeth or of a kind which, for the modern reader, would be analogous in their unsympathetic quality. Rather, he speaks more sharply to people than he used to; he is no longer charming. This is indeed pitiful enough, in its own way, but it is easy enough, too, especially when the artist chooses, as Fitzgerald does, to report the final demoralization of the hero only vaguely and from a great distance: one never sees Dick Diver's final horrible moments as one sees Macbeth's. The result is that, at the end of his downward path, Diver has been more sinned against than sinning, and we have no obstacles to our pity. On the other hand, since the fall has not been nearly so great, our pity that the fall should have occurred at all is attenuated, compared with the awfulness of the last hours of Macbeth. Other attenuations follow from this one. If the fall is not a very great one, the forces needed to produce it need not be great (although one might argue that even in *Tender Is the Night* they should have been greater, for credibility).

Nicole and a general atmosphere of gloom and decay are made to do a job which, in *Macbeth*, requires some of the richest degenerative forces ever employed.

If, then, comparison on these structural points is just, in spite of the strong differences between the works, it indicates that in point of the difficulties created, Shakespeare in *Macbeth* has it all over Fitzgerald, as he has it all over anyone else I know of who has attempted this form.

## I

A complete study of how *Macbeth* succeeds in spite of—or rather because of—the difficulties is beyond the capacities of any one reader. But the major devices employed by Shakespeare—one never knows how "consciously"—can be enumerated and discussed quite simply.

The first step in convincing us that Macbeth's fall is a genuinely tragic occurrence is to convince us that there was, in reality, a fall: we must believe that Macbeth was once a man whom we could admire, a man with great potential. One way to convince us would have been to show him, as Fitzgerald shows Dick Diver, in action as an admirable man. But, although this is possible in a leisurely novel, in a play it would have wasted time needed for the important events, which begin only with Macbeth's great temptation at the conclusion of the opening battle. Thus the superior choice in this case (although it would not necessarily always be so) is to begin your representation of the action with the first real temptation to the fall and to use testimony by other characters to establish your protagonist's prior goodness. We are thus given, from the beginning, sign after sign that Macbeth's greatest nobility was reached at a point just prior to the opening. When the play begins, he already covets the crown, as is shown by his excessively nervous reaction to the witches' prophecy; it is indeed likely that he has already considered foul means of obtaining it. But, in spite of this wickedness already present to his mind as a possibility, we have ample reason to think Macbeth a man worthy of our admiration. He is "brave" and "valiant," a "worthy gentleman"; Duncan calls him "noble Macbeth." These epithets have an ironic quality only in retrospect; when they are first applied, one has no reason to doubt them. Indeed, they are true epithets, or they would have been true if applied, say, only a few days or months earlier.

Of course, this testimony to his prior virtue given by his friends in the midst of other business would not carry the spectators for long with any sympathy for Macbeth if it were not continued in several other forms. We have the testimony of Lady Macbeth (the unimpeachable testimony of a "bad" person castigating the goodness of a "good" person):

> Yet do I fear thy nature;
> It is too full o' the milk of human kindness
> To catch the nearest way. Thou wouldst be great,
> Art not without ambition, but without
> The illness should attend it. What thou wouldst highly,
> That wouldst thou holily; wouldst not play false,
> And yet wouldst wrongly win.

No such verbal evidence would be enough, however, if we did not see in Macbeth himself signs of its validity, since we have already seen many signs that he is not the good man that the witnesses seem to believe. Thus the best evidence we have of his essential goodness is his vacillation before the murder. Just as Raskolnikov is tormented and just as we ourselves—virtuous theater viewers—would be tormented, so Macbeth is tormented before the prospect of his own crime. Indeed, much as he wants the kingship, he decides in Scene 3 against the murder:

> If chance will have me King, why, chance may crown me,
> Without my stir...

So when he first meets Lady Macbeth, he is resolved not to murder Duncan. In fact, as powerful a rhetorician as she is, she has all she can do to get him back on the course of murder.[1]

In addition, Macbeth's ensuing soliloquy not only weighs the possible bad practical consequences of his act but shows him perfectly aware, in a way an evil man would not be, of the moral values involved:

> He's here in double trust:
> First, as I am his kinsman and his subject,
> Strong both against the deed; then, as his host,
> Who should against murderer shut the door,
> Not bear the knife myself. Besides, this Duncan
> Hath borne his faculties so meek, hath been
> So clear in his great office, that his virtues
> Will plead like angels, trumpet-tongued, against
> The deep damnation of his taking-off...

In this speech we see again Shakespeare's wonderful economy, as we saw in the opening of the play: the very speech which shows Macbeth to best advantage is the one which shows the audience how very bad his contemplated act is, since Duncan is blameless. One need only think of the same speech if it were dealing with a king who deserved to be assassinated, or if it were given by another character commenting on Macbeth's action, to see how right it is as it stands.

After this soliloquy Macbeth announces again to Lady Macbeth that he will not go on ("We will proceed no further in this business"), but her eloquence is too much for him. Under her jibes at his "unmanliness," he progresses from a kind of petulant, though still honorable, boasting ("I dare do all that may become a man; / Who dares do more is none"), through a state of amoral consideration of mere expediency ("If I should fail?"), to complete resolution, but still with a full understanding of the wickedness of his act ("I am settled . . . this terrible feat"). There is never any doubt, first, that he is bludgeoned into the deed by Lady Macbeth's superior rhetoric and by the pressure of unfamiliar circumstances (including the witches) and, second, that even in the final decision to go through with it he is extremely troubled by a guilty conscience ("False face must hide what the false heart doth know"). In the entire dagger soliloquy he is clearly suffering from the realization of the horror of the "bloody business" ahead. He sees fully and painfully the wickedness of the course he has chosen, but not until after the deed, when the knocking has commenced, do we realize how terrifyingly alive his conscience is: "To know my deed, 't were best not know myself. / Wake Duncan with thy knocking! I would thou couldst!" This is the wish of a "good" man who, though he has become a "bad" man, still thinks and feels as a good man would.

To cite one last example of Shakespeare's pains in this matter, we have the testimony of Macbeth's character offered by Hecate (III, 5):

> And which is worse, all you have done
> Hath been but for a wayward son,
> Spiteful and wrathful, who, as others do,
> Loves for his own ends, not for you.

This reaffirmation that Macbeth is not a true son of evil comes, interestingly enough, immediately after the murder of Banquo, at a time when the audience needs a reminder of Macbeth's fundamental nobility.

The evil of his acts is thus built upon the knowledge that he is not a naturally evil man but a man who has every potentiality for goodness. This potentiality and its frustration are the chief ingredients of the tragedy of Macbeth. He is a man whose progressive external misfortunes seem to produce, and at the same time to be produced by, his parallel progression from great goodness to great wickedness. Our emotional involvement (which perhaps should not be simplified under the term "pity" or "pity and fear") is thus a combination of two kinds of regret: (1) We regret that any potentially good man should come to such a bad end: "What a pity that things should have gone this way, that things should be this way!" (2) We regret even more the destruction of this particular man, a man who is not only morally sympathetic but also intellectually and emotionally interesting. In eliciting both these kinds of regret to such a high degree, Shakespeare goes beyond his predecessors and establishes trends which are still working themselves out in literature.

The first kind—never used at all by classical dramatists, who never employed a genuinely degenerative plot—has been attempted again and again by modern novelists. Their difficulty has usually been that they have relied too completely on a general humane response in the reader and too little on a realized prior height or potentiality from which to fall. The protagonists are shown succumbing to their environment—or, as in so many "sociological" novels, as already succumbed—and the reader is left to himself to infer that something worth bothering about has gone to waste, that things might have been otherwise—that there is any real reason to react emotionally to the final destruction. The second kind—almost unknown to classical dramatists, whose characters are never "original" or "fresh" in the modern sense—has been attempted in even greater extremes since Shakespeare, until one finds many works in which mere interest in particular characteristics completely supplants emotional response to events involving men with interesting characteristics. The pathos of Bloom in *Ulysses*, for example, is an attenuated pathos, just as the comedy of Bloom is an attenuated comedy; one is not primarily moved to laughter or tears by events involving great characters, as in Macbeth, but rather one is primarily interested in details about characters. It can be argued whether this is a gain or a loss to literature, when considered in general. Certainly, one would rather read a modern novel like *Ulysses*, with all its faults on its head, than many of the older dramas or epics involving "great" characters in "great" events. But it can hardly be denied that one of Shakespeare's triumphs is his success in doing many things at once which lesser writers have since done only one at a time. He does produce the general effect of classical tragedy: catharsis of pity and fear. We do lament the "bad fortune" of a great man who has known good fortune. But to this he adds the much more poignant (at least to us) pity one feels in observing the moral destruction of a great man who has once known goodness.

Thus one major difference between watching Macbeth go to destruction and watching the destruction of a typical modern hero, whether in drama (say, Willy Loman [in *Death of a Salesman*]) or novels (say, Jake or any other of Hemingway's heroes) is that in *Macbeth* there is some "going." Willy Loman doesn't have very far to fall; he begins the play on the verge of suicide, and at the end of the play he has committed suicide. Even if we assume that the "beginning" is the time covered in the earliest of the flashbacks, we have not "far to go" from there to Willy's destruction.

It is true that our contemporary willingness to exalt the potentialities of the average man makes Willy's fall seem to us a greater one than it really is, dramatically. But the reliance on convention will, of course, sooner or later dictate a decline in the play's effectiveness. Macbeth continues to be effective at least in part because everything necessary for a complete response to a complete action is given to us. A highly individualized, noble man is sent to complete moral, intellectual, and physical destruction.

## II

But no matter how carefully the terminal points of the drama are selected and impressed on the spectator's mind, the major problem of how to represent such a "plot" still remains. Shakespeare has the tremendous task of trying to keep two contradictory dynamic streams moving simultaneously: the stream of events showing Macbeth's growing wickedness and the stream of circumstances producing and maintaining our sympathy for him. In effect, each succeeding atrocity, marking another step toward complete depravity, must be so surrounded by contradictory circumstances as to make us feel that, in spite of the evidence before our eyes, Macbeth is still somehow admirable.

The first instance of this is the method of treating Duncan's murder. The chief point here is Shakespeare's care in avoiding any "rendering" or representation of the murder itself. It is, in fact, not even narrated. We hear only the details of how the guards reacted and how Macbeth reacted to their cries. We see nothing. There is nothing about the actual dagger strokes; there is no report of the dying cries of the good old king. We have only Macbeth's conscience-stricken lament for having committed the deed. Thus what would be an intolerable act if depicted with any vividness becomes relatively bearable when seen only afterward in the light of Macbeth's suffering and remorse. This may seem ordinary enough; it is always convenient to have murders take place offstage. But if one compares the handling of this scene, where the perpetrator must remain sympathetic, with the handling of the blinding of Gloucester in *King Lear*, where the perpetrators must be hated, one can see how important such a detail can be. The blinding of Gloucester is not so wicked an act, in itself, as murder. If we had seen, say, a properly motivated Goneril come in from offstage wringing her hands for nearly a full scene, and crying, "Methought I heard a voice cry, 'Sleep no more.' Goneril does put out the eyes of sleep . . . I am afraid to think what I have done . . . Goneril shall sleep no more," and on thus, our reaction to the whole episode would, needless to say, be exactly contrary to what it now is.

A second precaution is the highly general portrayal of Duncan before his murder. It is necessary only that he be known as a "good king," the murder of whom will be a wicked act. He must be the type of benevolent monarch. But more particular characteristics are carefully kept from him. There is nothing for us to love, nothing for us to "want further existence for," within the play. We hear of his goodness; we do not see it. We know practically no details about him, and we have little, if any, personal interest in him at the time of his death. All the personal interest is reserved for Macbeth and Lady Macbeth. So, again, the wickedness is played up in the narration but played down in the representation. We must identify Macbeth with the murder of a blameless king, but only intellectually; emotionally we should be concerned as far as is possible only with the effects on Macbeth. We know that he has done the deed, but we feel primarily only his own suffering.

Banquo is considerably more "particularized" than was Duncan. Not only is he a good man, but we have also seen him acting as a good man, and we know quite a lot about him. We saw his reaction to the witches, and we know that he has resisted temptations similar to those of Macbeth. We have seen him in conversation with Macbeth. We have heard him in soliloquy. We know him to be very much like Macbeth, both in valor and in being the subject of prophecy. He thus has our lively sympathy; his death is a personal, rather than a general, loss.

Perhaps more important, his murder is actually shown on the stage. His dying words are spoken in our presence, and they are unselfishly directed to saving his son. We are forced to the proper, though illogical, inference: It is more wicked to kill Banquo than to have killed Duncan.

But we must still not lose our sympathy for Macbeth. This is partially provided for by the fact that the deed is much more necessary than the previous murder; Banquo is a real political danger. But the important thing is again the choice of what is represented. The murder is done by accomplices, so that Macbeth is never shown in any real act of wickedness. When we see him, he is suffering the torments of the banquet table. In our incorrect emotional inference, the self-torture has already expiated the guilt of the crime.

The same devices work in the murder of Lady Macduff and her children, the third and last atrocity explicitly shown in the play (except for the killing of young Siward, which, being military, is hardly an atrocity in this sense). Lady Macduff is more vividly portrayed even than Banquo, although she appears on the stage for a much briefer time. Her complaints against the absence of her husband, her loving banter with her son, and her stand against the murderers make her as admirable as the little boy himself, who dies in defense of his father's name. The audience is made to feel that the murder of women and children of such quality is wicked indeed. And when we move to England and see the effect of the atrocity on Macduff, our active pity for Macbeth's victims is at the high point of the play. For the first time, perhaps, pity for Macbeth's victims really wars with pity for him, and consequently our desire for his downfall, to protect others and to protect himself from his own further misdeeds, begins to mount.

Yet even here Macbeth is kept as little "to blame" as possible. He does not do the deed himself, and we can believe that he would have been unable to, had he seen the wife and child as we have seen them. (The Orson Welles movie version contains many grotesque errors of reading, but none worse than showing Macbeth actively engaged in the scene portraying this crime.) He is much further removed from them than from his other victims; as far as we know, he has never seen them. They are as remote and impersonal to him as they are immediate and personal to the audience, and personal blame against him is thus attenuated. More important, however, is that immediately after Macduff's tears, we shift to Lady Macbeth's scene—the effect being again to impress on us the fact that the punishment for these crimes is always as great as, or greater than, the crimes themselves.

Thus all three crimes are followed immediately by scenes of suffering and self-torture. Shakespeare works almost as if he were following a master-rulebook: By your choice of what to represent from the materials provided in your story, insure that each step in your protagonist's degeneration will be counteracted by mounting pity for him.

All this would certainly suffice to keep Macbeth at the center of our interest and sympathy, even with all our mounting concern for his victims. But it is reinforced by qualities in his character distinct from his moral qualities. Perhaps the most important of these is his gift (indirectly Shakespeare's gift, it is true, but we should remember that in his maturer work Shakespeare does not bestow it indiscriminately on all his characters) of expressing himself in great poetry. We naturally tend to feel with whatever character speaks the best poetry of the play, no matter what his deeds (Iago would never be misplayed as the protagonist—as he sometimes is—if his poetry did not rival, and sometimes surpass, Othello's). When we add to this poetic gift an extremely rich and concrete set of characteristics, over and above his moral qualities, we have a character who is in his own way more sympathetic than any character portrayed in only moral colors could be. Even the powers of virtue gathering about his castle to destroy him seem petty compared with his mammoth sensitivity, his rich despair. When he says,

> my way of life
> Is fall'n into the sere, the yellow leaf;
> And that which should accompany old age,
> As honour, love, obedience, troops of friends,
> I must not look to have,

we feel that he wants these things quite as honestly and a good deal more passionately than even the most virtuous man could want them. And we regret deeply the truth of his conclusion that he "must not look to have" them.

## III

If Macbeth's initial nobility, the manner of representation of his atrocities, and his rich poetic gift are all calculated to create and sustain our sympathy for him throughout his movement toward destruction, the kind of mistake he makes in initiating his own destruction is equally well calculated to heighten our willingness to forgive while deploring. On one level it could, of course, be said that he errs simply in being overambitious and underscrupulous. But this is only partly true. What allows him to sacrifice his moral beliefs to his ambition is a mistake of another kind—of a kind which is, at least to modern spectators, more probable or credible than any conventional tragic flaw or any traditional tragic effort, such as Iphigenia's mistaking the identity of a brother or Oedipus's not knowing that his wife is his mother. Macbeth knows what he is doing; yet he does not know. He knows the immorality of the act, but he has no conception of the effects of the act on himself or on his surroundings. Accustomed to murder of a "moral" sort, in battle, and having valorously and successfully "carv'd out his passage" with "bloody execution" many times previously, he misunderstands completely what will be the devastating effect on his own character if he tries to carve out his passage in civil life.

Macbeth's tragic error, then, is at least threefold: he does not understand the forces working upon him to make him commit the deed, neither his wife nor the weird sisters; he does not understand the differences between "bloody execution" in civilian life and his past military life; and he does not understand his own character—he does not know what will be the effects of the evil act on his own future happiness. Only one of these—the misunderstanding of the witches' prophecy—can be considered similar to, say, Iphigenia's ignorance of her brother's identity. Shakespeare has realized that simple ignorance of that sort will not do for the richly complex degenerative plot. The hero here must be really aware of the wickedness of his act, in advance. The more aware he can be—and still commit the act convincingly—the greater the regret felt by the reader or spectator. Being thus aware, he must act under a special kind of misunderstanding: it must be a misunderstanding caused by such powerful forces that even a good man might credibly be deceived by them into "knowingly" performing an atrocious deed.

All these points are illustrated powerfully in the contrast between the final words of Malcolm concerning Macbeth—"This dead butcher and his fiendlike queen"—and the spectator's own feelings toward Macbeth at the same point. One judges Macbeth, as Shakespeare intends, not merely for his wicked acts but in the light of the total impression of all the incidents of the play. Malcolm and Macduff do not know Macbeth and the forces that have worked on him; the spectator does know him and, knowing him, can feel great pity that a man with so much potential for greatness should have fallen so low. The pity is that everything was not otherwise, since it so easily could have been otherwise. Macbeth's whole life, from the time of the first visitation of the witches, is felt to be itself a tragic error, one big pitiful mistake. And the conclusion brings a flood of relief that the awful blunder has played itself out, that Macbeth has at last been able to die, still valiant, and is forced no longer to go on enduring the knowledge of the consequences of his own misdeeds.

While a number of other chapters might have been chosen from *The Rhetoric of Fiction* to represent its wide range of ideas and methods, Professor Booth and I readily agreed on this one. It stands perfectly well by itself, it bespeaks his (and others') deep love of Jane Austen, and it deepens and enriches the kind of analysis given in the preceding chapter. Booth might have been speaking in terms of his later metaphor of "friendships" with real and implied authors when he concludes this essay: "We can find love scenes in almost any novelist's works, but only here can we find a mind and heart that can give us clarity without oversimplification, sympathy and romance without sentimentality, and biting irony without cynicism."

This essay was originally published in *The Rhetoric of Fiction* (Chicago: University of Chicago Press, 1961; 2nd ed., 1983), 243–66.

# Control of Distance in Jane Austen's *Emma*

> Jane Austen was instinctive and charming.... For signal examples of what composition, distribution, arrangement can do, of how they intensify the life of a work of art, we have to go elsewhere.
>
> —Henry James

> A heroine whom no one but myself will much like.
>
> —Jane Austen describing Emma

## Sympathy and Judgment in *Emma*

Henry James once described Jane Austen as an instinctive novelist whose effects, some of which are admittedly fine, can best be explained as "part of her unconsciousness." It is as if she "fell-a-musing" over her work-basket, he said, lapsed into "wool-gathering," and afterward picked up "her dropped stitches" as "little masterstrokes of imagination."[1] The amiable accusation has been repeated in various forms, most recently as a claim that Jane Austen creates characters toward whom we cannot react as she consciously intends.[2]

Although we cannot hope to decide whether Jane Austen was entirely conscious of her own artistry, a careful look at the technique of any of her novels reveals a rather different picture from that of the unconscious spinster with her knitting needles. In *Emma* especially, where the chances for technical failure are great indeed, we find at work one of the unquestionable masters of the rhetoric of narration.

At the beginning of *Emma*, the young heroine has every requirement for deserved happiness but one. She has intelligence, wit, beauty, wealth, and position, and she has the love of those around her. Indeed, she thinks herself completely happy. The only threat to her happiness, a threat of which she is unaware, is herself: charming as she is, she can neither see her own excessive pride honestly nor resist imposing herself on the lives of others. She is deficient both in generosity and in self-knowledge. She discovers and corrects her faults only after she has almost ruined herself and her closest friends. But with the reform in her character, she is ready for marriage with the man she loves, the man who throughout the book has stood in the reader's mind for what she lacks.

It is clear that with a general plot of this kind Jane Austen gave herself difficulties of a high order. Though Emma's faults are comic, they constantly threaten to produce serious harm. Yet she must remain sympathetic, or the reader will not wish for and delight sufficiently in her reform.

Obviously, the problem with a plot like this is to find some way to allow the reader to laugh at the mistakes committed by the heroine and at her punishment, without reducing the desire to see her reform and thus earn happiness. In *Tom Jones* this double attitude is achieved [*in chapter 8 of* The Rhetoric of Fiction], partly through the invention of episodes producing sympathy and relieving any serious anxiety we might have, and partly through the direct and sympathetic commentary. In *Emma*, since most of the episodes must illustrate the heroine's faults and thus increase either our emotional distance or our anxiety, a different method is required. If we fail to see Emma's faults as revealed in the ironic texture from line to line, we cannot savor to the full the comedy as it is prepared for us. On the other hand, if we fail to love her, as Jane Austen herself predicted we would[3]—if we fail to love her more and more as the book progresses—we can neither hope for the conclusion, a happy and deserved marriage with Knightley following upon her reform, nor accept it as an honest one when it comes.[4] Any attempt to solve the problem by reducing either the love or the clear view of her faults would have been fatal.

### Sympathy through Control of Inside Views

The solution to the problem of maintaining sympathy despite almost crippling faults was primarily to use the heroine herself as a kind of narrator, though in third person, reporting on her own experience. So far as we know, Jane Austen never formulated any theory to cover her own practice; she invented no term like James's "central intelligence" or "lucid reflector" to describe her method of viewing the world of the book primarily through Emma's own eyes. We can thus never know for sure to what extent James's accusation of "unconsciousness" was right. But whether she was inclined to speculate about her method scarcely matters; her solution was clearly a brilliant one. By showing most of the story through Emma's eyes, the author insures that we shall travel with Emma rather than stand against her. It is not simply that Emma provides, in the unimpeachable evidence of her own conscience, proof that she has many redeeming qualities that do not appear on the surface; such evidence could be given with authorial commentary, though perhaps not with such force and conviction. Much more important, the sustained inside view leads the reader to hope for good fortune for the character with whom he travels, quite independently of the qualities revealed.

Seen from the outside, Emma would be an unpleasant person, unless, like Mr. Woodhouse and Knightley, we knew her well enough to infer her true worth. Though we might easily be led to laugh at her, we could never be made to laugh sympathetically. While the final unmasking of her faults and her humiliation would make artistic sense to an unsympathetic reader, her marriage with Knightley would become irrelevant if not meaningless. Unless we desire Emma's happiness and her reform, which alone can make that happiness possible, a good third of this book will seem irredeemably dull.

Yet sympathetic laughter is never easily achieved. It is much easier to set up a separate fool for comic effects and to preserve your heroine for finer things. Sympathetic laughter is especially difficult with characters whose faults do not spring from sympathetic virtues. The grasping but witty Volpone can keep us on his side so long as his victims are more grasping and less witty than he, but as soon as the innocent victims, Celia and Bonario, come on stage, the quality of the humor changes; we no longer delight unambiguously in his triumphs. In contrast to this, the great sympathetic comic heroes often are comic largely because their faults, like Uncle Toby's sentimentality, spring from an excess of some virtue. Don Quixote's madness is partly caused by an excess of idealism, an excess of loving concern for the unfortunate. Every crazy gesture he makes gives further reason for loving the well-meaning old fool, and we can thus laugh at him in somewhat the same spirit in which we laugh at our own faults—in a benign, forgiving spirit. We may be contemptible for doing so; to persons without a sense of humor, such laughter often seems a wicked escape. But self-love being what it is, we laugh at ourselves in a thoroughly forgiving way, and we laugh in the same way at Don Quixote: we are convinced that his heart, like ours, is in the right place.

Nothing in Emma's comic misunderstandings can serve for the same effect. Her faults are not excesses of virtue. She attempts to manipulate Harriet not from an excess of kindness but from a desire for power and admiration. She flirts with Frank Churchill out of vanity and irresponsibility.

She mistreats Jane Fairfax because of Jane's *good* qualities. She abuses Miss Bates because of her own essential lack of "tenderness" and "good will." We have only to think of what Emma's story would be if seen through Jane Fairfax's or Mrs. Elton's or Robert Martin's eyes to recognize how little our sympathy springs from any natural view, and to see how inescapable is the decision to use Emma's mind as a reflector of events—however beclouded her vision must be. To Jane Fairfax, who embodies throughout the book most of the values which Emma discovers only at the end, the early Emma is intolerable.

But Jane Austen never lets us forget that Emma is not what she might appear to be. For every section devoted to her misdeeds—and even they are seen for the most part through her own eyes—there is a section devoted to her self-reproach. We see her rudeness to poor, foolish Miss Bates, and we see it vividly. But her remorse and act of penance in visiting Miss Bates after Knightley's rebuke are experienced even more vividly. We see her successive attempts to mislead Harriet, but we see at great length and in high color her self-castigation (chaps. 16–18). We see her boasting proudly that she does not need marriage, boasting almost as blatantly of her "resources," as does Mrs. Elton (chap. 10). But we know her too intimately to take her conscious thoughts at face value. And we see her, thirty-eight chapters later, chastened to an admission of what we have known all along to be her true human need for love. "If all took place that might take place among the circle of her friends, Hartfield must be comparatively deserted; and she left to cheer her father with the spirits only of ruined happiness. The child to be born at Randalls must be a tie there even dearer than herself; and Mrs. Weston's heart and time would be occupied by it. . . . All that were good would be withdrawn" (chap. 48).

Perhaps the most delightful effects from our sustained inside view of a very confused and very charming young woman come from her frequent thoughts about Knightley. She is basically right all along about his preeminent wisdom and virtue, and she is our chief authority for taking *his* authority so seriously. And yet in every thought about him she is misled. Knightley rebukes her; the reader knows that Knightley is in the right. But Emma?

> Emma made no answer, and tried to look cheerfully unconcerned, but was really feeling uncomfortable, and wanting him very much to be gone. She did not repent what she had done; she still thought herself a better judge of such a point of female right and refinement than he could be; but yet she had a sort of habitual respect for his judgment in general, which made her

dislike having it so loudly against her; and to have him sitting just opposite to her in angry state, was very disagreeable. (chap. 8)

Even more striking is the lack of self-knowledge shown when Mrs. Weston suggests that Knightley might marry Jane Fairfax.

> Her objections to Mr. Knightley's marrying did not in the least subside. She could see nothing but evil in it. It would be a great disappointment to Mr. John Knightley [Knightley's brother]; consequently to Isabella. A real injury to the children—a most mortifying change, and material loss to them all; a very great deduction from her father's daily comfort—and, as to herself, she could not at all endure the idea of Jane Fairfax at Donwell Abbey. A Mrs. Knightley for them all to give way to!—No, Mr. Knightley must never marry. Little Henry must remain the heir of Donwell. (chap. 26)

Self-deception could hardly be carried further, at least in a person of high intelligence and sensitivity.

Yet the effect of all this is what our tolerance for our own faults produces in our own lives. While only immature readers ever really identify with any character, losing all sense of distance and hence all chance of an artistic experience, our emotional reaction to every event concerning Emma tends to become like her own. When she feels anxiety or shame, we feel analogous emotions. Our modern awareness that such "feelings" are not identical with those we feel in our own lives in similar circumstances has tended to blind us to the fact that aesthetic form can be built out of patterned emotions as well as out of other materials. It is absurd to pretend that because our emotions and desires in responding to fiction are in a very real sense disinterested, they do not or should not exist. Jane Austen, in developing the sustained use of a sympathetic inside view, has mastered one of the most successful of all devices for inducing a parallel emotional response between the deficient heroine and the reader.

Sympathy for Emma can be heightened by withholding inside views of others as well as by granting them of her. The author knew, for example, that it would be fatal to grant any extended inside view of Jane Fairfax. The inadequacies of impressionistic criticism are nowhere revealed more clearly than in the suggestion often made about such minor characters that their authors would have liked to make them vivid but didn't know how.[5] Jane Austen knew perfectly well how to make such a character vivid; Anne in *Persuasion* is a kind of Jane Fairfax turned into heroine. But in *Emma*, Emma must shine supreme. It is not only that the slightest glance inside

Jane's mind would be fatal to all of the author's plans for mystification about Frank Churchill, though this is important. The major problem is that any extended view of her would reveal her as a more sympathetic person than Emma herself. Jane is superior to Emma in most respects except the stroke of good fortune that made Emma the heroine of the book. In matters of taste and ability, of head and of heart, she is Emma's superior, and Jane Austen, always in danger of losing our sympathy for Emma, cannot risk any degree of distraction. Jane could, it is true, be granted fewer virtues, and then made more vivid. But to do so would greatly weaken the force of Emma's mistakes of heart and head in her treatment of the almost faultless Jane.

## Control of Judgment

But the very effectiveness of the rhetoric designed to produce sympathy might in itself lead to a serious misreading of the book. In reducing the emotional distance, the natural tendency is to reduce—willy-nilly—moral and intellectual distance as well. In reacting to Emma's faults from the inside out, as if they were our own, we may very well not only forgive them but overlook them.[6]

There is, of course, no danger that readers who persist to the end will overlook Emma's serious mistakes; since she sees and reports those mistakes herself, everything becomes crystal clear at the end. The real danger inherent in the experiment is that readers will overlook the mistakes as they are committed and thus miss much of the comedy that depends on Emma's distorted view from page to page. If readers who dislike Emma cannot enjoy the preparation for the marriage to Knightley, readers who do not recognize her faults with absolute precision cannot enjoy the details of the preparation for the comic abasement which must precede that marriage.

It might be argued that there is no real problem, since the conventions of her time allowed for reliable commentary whenever it was needed to place Emma's faults precisely. But Jane Austen is not operating according to the conventions, most of which she had long since parodied and outgrown; her technique is determined by the needs of the novel she is writing. We can see this clearly by contrasting the manner of *Emma* with that of *Persuasion*, the next, and last-completed, work. In *Emma* there are many breaks in the point of view, because Emma's beclouded mind cannot do the whole job. In *Persuasion*, where the heroine's viewpoint is faulty only in her ignorance of Captain Wentworth's love, there are very few. Anne Elliot's consciousness is sufficient, as Emma's is not, for most of the needs of the novel which she dominates. Once the ethical and intellectual framework has been established by the narrator's introduction, we enter Anne's consciousness and remain bound to it much more rigorously than we are bound to Emma's. It is still true that whenever something must be shown that Anne's consciousness cannot show, we move to another center; but since her consciousness can do much more for us than Emma's, there need be few departures from it.

The most notable shift for rhetorical purposes in *Persuasion* comes fairly early. When Anne first meets Captain Wentworth after their years of separation that follow her refusal to marry him, she is convinced that he is indifferent. The major movement of *Persuasion* is toward her final discovery that he still loves her; her suspense is thus strong and inevitable from the beginning. The reader, however, is likely to believe that Wentworth is still interested. All the conventions of art favor such a belief: the emphasis is clearly on Anne and her unhappiness; the lover has returned; we have only to wait, perhaps with some tedium, for the inevitable outcome. Anne learns (chap. 7) that he has spoken of her as so altered "he should not have known her again!" "These were words which could not but dwell with her. Yet she soon began to rejoice that she had heard them. They were of sobering tendency; they allayed agitation; they composed, and consequently must make her happier." And suddenly we enter Wentworth's mind for one time only: "Frederick Wentworth had used such words, or something like them, but without an idea that they would be carried round to her. He had thought her wretchedly altered, and, in the first moment of appeal, had spoken as he felt. He had not forgiven Anne Elliot. She had used him ill"—and so he goes on, for five more paragraphs. The necessary point, the fact that Frederick believes himself to be indifferent, has been made, and it could not have been made without some kind of shift from Anne's consciousness.

At the end of the novel, we learn that Wentworth was himself deceived in this momentary inside view: "He had meant to forget her, and believed it to be done. He had imagined himself indifferent, when he had only been angry." We may want to protest against the earlier suppression as unfair, but we can hardly believe it to be what Miss Lascelles calls "an oversight."[7] It is deliberate manipulation of inside views in order to destroy our conventional security. We are thus made ready to go along with Anne on her long and painful road to the discovery that Frederick loves her after all.

The only other important breaks in the angle of vision of *Persuasion* come at the beginning and at the end. Chapter 1 is an excellent example of how a skillful novelist can, by the use of her own direct voice, accomplish in a few pages what even the best novelist must take chapters to do if he uses nothing but dramatized action. Again at the conclusion the author enters with a resounding reaffirmation that the Wentworth-Elliot marriage is as good a thing as we have felt it to be from the beginning.

> Who can be in doubt of what followed? When any two young people take it into their heads to marry, they are pretty sure by perseverence to carry their point, be they ever so poor, or ever so impudent, or ever so little likely to be necessary to each other's ultimate comfort. This may be bad morality to conclude with, but I believe it to be the truth; and if such parties succeed, how should a Captain Wentworth and an Anne Elliot, with the advantage of maturity in mind, consciousness of right, and one independent fortune between them, fail of bearing down every opposition?[8]

Except for these few intrusions and one in chapter 19, Anne's own mind is sufficient in *Persuasion*, but we can never rely completely on Emma. It is hardly surprising that Jane Austen has provided many correctives to insure our placing her errors with precision.

The chief corrective is Knightley. His commentary on Emma's errors is a natural expression of his love; he can tell the reader and Emma at the same time precisely how she is mistaken. Thus, nothing Knightley says can be beside the point. Each affirmation of a value, each accusation of error is in itself an action in the plot. When he rebukes Emma for manipulating Harriet, when he condemns her for gossiping and flirting with Frank Churchill, and finally when he attacks her for being "insolent" and "unfeeling" in her treatment of Miss Bates, we have Jane Austen's judgment on Emma, rendered dramatically. But it has come from someone who is essentially sympathetic toward Emma, so that his judgments against her are presumed to be temporary. His sympathy reinforces ours even as he criticizes, and her respect for his opinion, shown in her self-abasement after he has criticized, is one of our main reasons for expecting her to reform.

If Henry James had tried to write a novel about Emma, and had cogitated at length on the problem of getting her story told dramatically, he could not have done better than this. It is possible, of course, to think of *Emma* without Knightley as *raisonneur*, just as it is possible to think of *The Golden Bowl*, say, without the Assinghams as *ficelles* to reflect something not seen by the Prince or Princess. But Knightley, though he receives less independent space than the Assinghams and is almost never seen in an inside view, is clearly more useful for Jane Austen's purposes than any realistically limited *ficelle* could possibly be. By combining the role of commentator with the role of hero, Jane Austen has worked more economically than James, and though economy is as dangerous as any other criterion when applied universally, even James might have profited from a closer study of the economies that a character like Knightley can be made to achieve. It is as if James had dared to make one of the four main characters, say the Prince, into a thoroughly good, wise, perceptive man, a thoroughly clear rather than a partly confused "reflector."

Since Knightley is established early as completely reliable, we need no views of his secret thoughts. He has no secret thoughts, except for the unacknowledged depths of his love for Emma and his jealousy of Frank Churchill. The other main characters have more to hide, and Jane Austen moves in and out of their minds with great freedom, choosing for her own purposes what to reveal and what to withhold. Always the seeming violation of consistency is in the consistent service of the particular needs of Emma's story. Sometimes a shift is made simply to direct our suspense, as when Mrs. Weston suggests a possible union of Emma and Frank Churchill, at the end of her conversation with Knightley about the harmful effects of Emma's friendship with Harriet (chap. 5). "Part of her meaning was to conceal some favourite thoughts of her own and Mr. Weston's on the subject, as much as possible. There were wishes at Randalls respecting Emma's destiny, but it was not desirable to have them suspected."

One objection to this selective dipping into whatever mind best serves our immediate purposes is that it suggests mere trickery and inevitably spoils the illusion of reality. If Jane Austen can tell us what Mrs. Weston is thinking, why not what Frank Churchill and Jane Fairfax are thinking? Obviously, because she chooses to build a mystery, and to do so she must refuse, arbitrarily and obtrusively, to grant the privilege of an inside view to characters whose minds would reveal too much. But is not the mystery purchased at the price of shaking the reader's faith in Jane Austen's integrity? If she simply withholds until later what she might as well relate now—if her procedure is not dictated by the very nature of her materials, why should we take her seriously?

If a natural surface were required in all fiction, then this objection would hold. But if we want to read *Emma* in its own terms, the real question about these shifts cannot be answered by an easy appeal to general principles. Every author withholds until later what he "might as well" relate now. The question is always one of desired effects, and the choice of any one effect always bans innumerable other effects. There is, indeed, a question to be raised about the use of mystery in *Emma*, but the conflict is not between an abstract end that Jane Austen never worried about and a shoddy mystification that she allowed to betray her. The conflict is between two effects, both of which she cares about a good deal. On the one hand, she cares about maintaining some sense of mystery as long as she can. On the other, she works at all points to heighten the reader's sense of dramatic irony, usually in the form of a contrast between what Emma knows and what the reader knows.

As in most novels, whatever steps are taken to mystify inevitably decrease the dramatic irony, and, whenever dramatic irony is increased by telling the reader secrets the characters have not yet suspected, mystery is inevitably destroyed. The longer we are in doubt about Frank Churchill, the weaker our sense of ironic contrast between Emma's views and the truth. The sooner we see through Frank Churchill's secret plot, the greater our pleasure in observing Emma's innumerable misreadings of his behavior, and the less interest we have in the mere mystery of the situation. And we all find that on second reading we discover new intensities of dramatic irony resulting from the complete loss of mystery; knowing what abysses of error Emma is preparing for herself, even those of us who may on first reading have deciphered nearly all the details of the Churchill mystery find additional ironies.

But it is obvious that these ironies could have been offered even on a first reading if Jane Austen had been willing to sacrifice her mystery. A single phrase in her own name—"his secret engagement to Jane Fairfax"— or a short inside view of either of the lovers could have made us aware of every ironic touch.

The author must, then, choose whether to purchase mystery at the expense of irony. For many of us, Jane Austen's choice here is perhaps the weakest aspect of this novel. It is a commonplace of our criticism that significant literature arouses suspense not about the "what" but about the "how." Mere mystification has been mastered by so many second-rate writers that her efforts at mystification seem second-rate.

But again we must ask whether criticism can be conducted effectively by balancing one abstract quality against another. Is there a norm of dramatic irony for all works, or even for all works of a given kind? Has anyone ever formulated a "law of first and second readings" that will tell us just how many of our pleasures on page 1 should depend on our knowledge of what happens on page the last? We quite properly ask that the books we call great be able to stand up under repeated reading, but we need not ask that they yield identical pleasures on each reading. The modern works whose authors pride themselves on the fact that they can never be read but only re-read may be very good indeed, but they are not made good by the fact that their secret pleasures can only be wrested from them by repeated readings. In any case, even if one accepted the criticism of Jane Austen's efforts at mystification, the larger service of the inside views is clear: The crosslights thrown by other minds prevent our being blinded by Emma's radiance.

### The Reliable Narrator and the Norms of *Emma*

If mere intellectual clarity about Emma were the goal in this work, we should be forced to say that the manipulation of inside views and the extensive commentary of the reliable Knightley are more than is necessary. But for maximum intensity of the comedy and romance, even these are not enough. The "author herself"—not necessarily the real Jane Austen but an implied author, represented in this book by a reliable narrator—heightens the effects by directing our intellectual, moral, and emotional progress. She performs, of course, most of the functions described in chapter 7 [*of* The Rhetoric of Fiction]. But her most important role is to reinforce both aspects of the double vision that operates throughout the book: our inside view of Emma's worth and our objective view of her great faults.

The narrator opens *Emma* with a masterful simultaneous presentation of Emma and of the values against which she must be judged: "Emma Woodhouse, handsome, clever, and rich, with a comfortable home and happy disposition, seemed to unite some of the best blessings of existence; and had lived nearly twenty-one years in the world with very little to distress or vex her." This "seemed" is immediately reinforced by more directly stated reservations. "The real evils of Emma's situation were the power of having rather too much her own way, and a disposition to think a little too well of herself; these were the disadvantages which threatened alloy to her many enjoyments. The danger, however, was at present so unperceived, that they did not by any means rank as misfortunes with her."

None of this could have been said by Emma, and if shown through her consciousness, it could not be accepted, as it must be, without question. Like most of the first three chapters, it is nondramatic summary, building up, through the ostensible business of getting the characters introduced, to Emma's initial blunder with Harriet and Mr. Elton. Throughout these chapters, we learn much of what we must know from the narrator, but she turns over more and more of the job of summary to Emma as she feels more and more sure of our seeing precisely to what degree Emma is to be trusted. Whenever we leave the "real evils" we have been warned against in Emma, the narrator's and Emma's views coincide: we cannot tell which of them, for example, offers the judgment on Mr. Woodhouse that "his talents could not have recommended him at any time," or the judgment on Mr. Knightley that he is "a sensible man," "always welcome" at Hartfield, or even that "Mr. Knightley, in fact, was one of the few people who could see faults in Emma Woodhouse, and the only one who ever told her of them."

But there are times when Emma and her author are far apart, and the author's direct guidance aids the reader in his own break with Emma. The beautiful irony of the first description of Harriet, given through Emma's eyes (chap. 3), could no doubt be grasped intellectually by many readers without all of the preliminary commentary. But even for the most perceptive, its effect is heightened, surely, by the sense of standing with the author and observing with her precisely how Emma's judgment is going astray. Perhaps more important, we ordinary, less perceptive readers have by now been raised to a level suited to grasp the ironies. Certainly, most readers would overlook some of the barbs directed against Emma if the novel began, as a serious modern novelist might well begin it, with this description:

> [Emma] was not struck by anything remarkably clever in Miss Smith's conversation, but she found her altogether very engaging—not inconveniently shy, not unwilling to talk—and yet so far from pushing, shewing so proper and becoming a deference, seeming so pleasantly grateful for being admitted to Hartfield, and so artlessly impressed by the appearance of every thing in so superior a style to what she had been used to, that she must have good sense and deserve encouragement. Encouragement should be given. Those soft blue eyes . . . should not be wasted on the inferior society of Highbury.

And so Emma goes on, giving herself away with every word, pouring out her sense of her own beneficence and general value. Harriet's past friends, "though very good sort of people, must be doing her harm." Without knowing them, Emma knows that they "must be coarse and unpolished, and very unfit to be the intimates of a girl who wanted only a little more knowledge and elegance to be quite perfect." And she concludes with a beautiful burst of egotism: "She would notice her; she would improve her; she would detach her from her bad acquaintance, and introduce her into good society; she would form her opinions and her manners. It would be an interesting, and certainly a very kind undertaking; highly becoming her own situation in life, her leisure, and powers." Even the most skillful reader might not easily plot an absolutely true course through these ironies without the prior direct assistance we have been given. Emma's views are not so outlandish that they could never have been held by a female novelist writing in her time. They cannot serve effectively as signs of her character unless they are clearly disavowed as signs of Jane Austen's views. Emma's unconscious catalogue of her egotistical uses for Harriet, given under the pretense of listing the services *she* will perform, is thus given its full force by being framed explicitly in a world of values which Emma herself cannot discover until the conclusion of the book.

The full importance of the author's direct imposition of an elaborate scale of norms can be seen by considering that conclusion. The sequence of events is a simple one: Emma's faults and mistakes are brought home to her in a rapid and humiliating chain of rebukes from Knightley and blows from hard fact. These blows to her self-esteem produce at last a genuine reform (for example, she brings herself to apologize to Miss Bates, something she could never have done earlier in the novel). The change in her character removes the only obstacle in the way of Knightley's proposal, and the marriage follows. "The wishes, the hopes, the confidence, the predictions of the small band of true friends who witnessed the ceremony, were fully answered in the perfect happiness of the union."

It may be that if we look at Emma and Knightley as real people, this ending will seem false. G. B. Stern laments, in *Speaking of Jane Austen*, "Oh, Miss Austen, it was not a good solution; it was a bad solution, an unhappy ending, could we see beyond the last pages of the book." Edmund Wilson predicts that Emma will find a new protégée like Harriet, since she has not been cured of her inclination to "infatuations with women." Marvin Mudrick even more emphatically rejects Jane Austen's explicit rhetoric; he believes that Emma is still a "confirmed exploiter," and for him the ending must be read as ironic.[9]

But it is precisely because this ending is neither life itself nor a simple bit of literary irony that it can serve so well to heighten our sense of a complete and indeed perfect resolution to all that has gone before. If we look at the values that have been realized in this marriage and compare them with those realized in conventional marriage plots, we see that Jane Austen means what she says: this will be a happy marriage because there is simply nothing left to make it anything less than perfectly happy. It fulfills every value embodied in the world of the book—with the possible exception that Emma may never learn to apply herself as she ought to her reading and her piano! It is a union of intelligence: of "reason," of "sense," of "judgment." It is a union of virtue: of "good will," of generosity, of unselfishness. It is a union of feeling: of "taste," "tenderness," "love," "beauty."[10]

In a general way, then, this plot offers us an experience superficially like that offered by most tragicomedy as well as by much of the cheapest popular art: we are made to desire certain good things for certain good characters, and then our desires are gratified. If we depended on general criteria derived from our justified boredom with such works, we should reject this one. But the critical difference lies in the precise quality of the values appealed to and the precise quality of the characters who violate or realize them. All of the cheap marriage plots in the world should not lead us to be embarrassed about our pleasure in Emma and Knightley's marriage. It is more than just the marriage: it is the rightness of *this* marriage, as a conclusion to all of the comic wrongness that has gone before. The good for Emma includes both her necessary reform and the resulting marriage. Marriage to an intelligent, amiable, good, and attractive man is the best thing that can happen to this heroine, and the readers who do not experience it as such are, I am convinced, far from knowing what Jane Austen is about—whatever they may say about the "bitter spinster's" attitude toward marriage.

Our modern sensibilities are likely to be rasped by any such formulation. We do not ordinarily like to encounter perfect endings in our novels—even in the sense of "perfectedness" or completion, the sense obviously intended by Jane Austen. We refuse to accept it when we see it: witness the many attempts to deny Dostoevski's success with Alyosha and Father Zossima in *The Brothers Karamazov*. Many of us find it embarrassing to talk of emotions based on moral judgment at all, particularly when the emotions have any kind of affirmative cast. Emma herself is something of a "modern" in this regard throughout most of the book. Her self-deception about marriage is as great as about most other important matters. Emma boasts to Harriet of her indifference to marriage, at the same time unconsciously betraying her totally inadequate view of the sources of human happiness.

> If I know myself, Harriet, mine is an active, busy mind, with a great many independent resources; and I do not perceive why I should be more in want of employment at forty or fifty than one-and-twenty. Woman's usual occupations of eye and hand and mind will be as open to me then, as they are now; or with no important variation. If I draw less, I shall read more; if I give up music, I shall take to carpet-work.

Emma at carpet-work! If she knows herself indeed.

> And as for objects of interest, objects for the affections, which is, in truth, the great point of inferiority, the want of which is really the great evil to be avoided in *not* marrying [a magnificent concession, this] I shall be very well off, with all the children of a sister I love so much, to care about. There will be enough of them, in all probability, to supply every sort of sensation that declining life can need. There will be enough for every hope and every fear; and though my attachment to none can equal that of a parent, it suits my ideas of comfort better than what is warmer and blinder. My nephews and nieces!—I shall often have a niece with me. (chap. 10)

Without growing solemn about it—it is wonderfully comic—we can recognize that the humor springs here from very deep sources indeed. It can be fully enjoyed, in fact, only by the reader who has attained to a vision of human felicity far more profound than Emma's "comfort" and "want" and "need." It is a vision that includes not simply marriage, but a kind of loving converse not based, as is Emma's here, on whether the "loved" person will serve one's irreducible needs.

The comic effect of this repudiation of marriage is considerably increased by the fact that Emma always thinks of marriage for others as *their* highest good, and in fact unconsciously encourages her friend Harriet to fall in love with the very man she herself loves without knowing it. The delightful denouement is thus what we want not only because it is a supremely good thing for Emma, but because it is a supremely comic outcome of Emma's profound misunderstanding of herself and of the human condition. In the schematic language of chapter 5 [*of* The Rhetoric of Fiction], it satisfies both our practical desire for Emma's well-being and our appetite for the qualities proper to these artistic materials. It is thus a more resounding resolution than either of these elements separately could provide. The other major resolution of the work—Harriet's marriage with her farmer—reinforces this interpretation. Emma's sin against Harriet has been something far worse than the mere meddling of a busybody. To destroy Harriet's chances for happiness—chances that depend entirely on her marriage—is as close to viciousness as any author could dare to take a heroine designed to be loved. We can laugh with Emma at this mistake (chap. 54) only because Harriet's chance for happiness is restored.

Other values, like money, blood, and "consequence," are real enough in Emma, but only as they contribute to or are mastered by good taste, good judgment, and good morality. Money alone can make a Mrs. Churchill, but a man or woman "is silly to marry without it." Consequence untouched by sense can make a very inconsequential Mr. Woodhouse; untouched by sense or virtue it can make the much more contemptible Mr. and Miss Elliot of *Persuasion*. But it is a pleasant thing to have, and it does no harm unless, like the early Emma, one takes it too seriously. Charm and elegance without sufficient moral force can make a Frank Churchill; unschooled by morality it can lead to the baseness of Henry Crawford in *Mansfield Park* or of Wickham in *Pride and Prejudice*. Even the supreme virtues are inadequate in isolation: good will alone will make a comic Miss Bates or a Mr. Weston, judgment with insufficient good will a comic Mr. John Knightley, and so on.

I am willing to risk the commonplace in such a listing because it is only thus that the full force of Jane Austen's comprehensive view can be seen. There is clearly at work here a much more detailed ordering of values than any conventional public philosophy of her time could provide. Obviously, few readers in her own time, and far fewer in our own, have ever approached this novel in full and detailed agreement with the author's norms. But they were led to join her as they read, and so are we.

### Explicit Judgments on Emma Woodhouse

We have said in passing almost enough of the other side of the coin—the judgment of particular actions as they relate to the general norms. But something must be said of the detailed "placing" of Emma, by direct commentary, in the hierarchy of values established by the novel. I must be convinced, for example, not only that tenderness for other people's feelings is an important trait but also that Emma's particular behavior violates the true standards of tenderness, if I am to savor to the full the episode of Emma's insult to Miss Bates and Knightley's reproach which follows. If I refuse to blame Emma, I may discover a kind of intellectual enjoyment in the episode, and I will probably think that any critic who talks of "belief" in tenderness as operating in such a context is taking things too seriously. But I can never enjoy the episode in its full intensity or grasp its formal coherence. Similarly, I must agree not only that to be dreadfully boring is a minor fault compared with the major virtue of "good will," but also that Miss Bates's exemplification of this fault and of this virtue entitle her to the respect which Emma denies. If I do not—while yet being able to laugh at Miss Bates—I can hardly understand, let alone enjoy, Emma's mistreatment of her.

But these negative judgments must be counteracted by a larger approval, and, as we would expect, the novel is full of direct apologies for Emma. Her chief fault, lack of good will or tenderness, must be read not only in relationship to the code of values provided by the book as a whole—a code which judges her as seriously deficient; it must also be judged in relationship to the harsh facts of the world around her, a world made up of human beings ranging in degree of selfishness and egotism from Knightley, who lapses from perfection when he tries to judge Frank Churchill, his rival, down to Mrs. Elton, who has most of Emma's faults and none of her virtues. In such a setting, Emma is easily forgiven. When she insults Miss Bates, for example, we remember that Miss Bates lives in a world where many others are insensitive and cruel. "Miss Bates, neither young, handsome, rich, nor married, stood in the very worst predicament in the world for having much of the public favour; and she had no intellectual superiority to make atonement to herself, or frighten those who might hate her, into outward respect." While it would be a mistake to see only this "regulated hatred" in Jane Austen's world, overlooking the tenderness and generosity, the hatred of viciousness is there, and there is enough vice in evidence to make Emma almost shine by comparison.

Often, Jane Austen makes this apology-by-comparison explicit. When Emma lies to Knightley about Harriet, very close to the end of the book, she is excused with a generalization about human nature: "Seldom, very seldom, does complete truth belong to any human disclosure; seldom can it happen that something is not a little disguised, or a little mistaken; but where, as in this case, though the conduct is mistaken, the feelings are not, it may not be very material.—Mr. Knightley could not impute to Emma a more relenting heart than she possessed, or a heart more disposed to accept of his."

## The Implied Author as Friend and Guide

With all of this said about the masterful use of the narrator in *Emma*, there remain some "intrusions" unaccounted for by strict service to the story itself. "What did she say?" the narrator asks, at the crucial moment in the major love scene. "Just what she ought, of course. A lady always does.—She said enough to show there need not be despair—and to invite him to say more himself." To some readers this has seemed to demonstrate the author's inability to write a love scene, since it sacrifices "the illusion of reality."[11] But who has ever read this far in *Emma* under the delusion that he is reading a realistic portrayal which is suddenly shattered by the unnatural appearance of the narrator? If the narrator's superabundant wit is destructive of the kind of illusion proper to this work, the novel has been ruined long before.

But we should now be in a position to see precisely why the narrator's wit is not in the least out of place at the emotional climax of the novel. We have seen how the inside views of the characters and the author's commentary have been used from the beginning to get the values straight and to keep them straight and to help direct our reactions to Emma. But we also see here a beautiful case of the dramatized author as friend and guide. "Jane Austen," like "Henry Fielding," is a paragon of wit, wisdom, and virtue. She does not talk about her qualities; unlike Fielding, she does not in *Emma* call direct attention to her artistic skill. But we are seldom allowed to forget about her for all that. When we read this novel, we accept her as representing everything we admire most. She is as generous and wise as Knightley; in fact, she is a shade more penetrating in her judgment. She is as subtle and witty as Emma would like to think herself. Without being sentimental, she is in favor of tenderness. She is able to put an adequate but not excessive value on wealth and rank. She recognizes a fool when she sees one, but unlike Emma she knows that it is both immoral and foolish to be rude to fools. She is, in short, a perfect human being, within the concept of perfection established by the book she writes; she even recognizes that human perfection of the kind she exemplifies is not quite attainable in real life. The process of her domination is of course circular; her character establishes the values for us according to which her character is then found to be perfect. But this circularity does not affect the success of her endeavor; in fact it insures it.

Her "omniscience" is thus a much more remarkable thing than is ordinarily implied by the term. All good novelists know all about their characters—all that they need to know. And the question of how their narrators are to find out all that they need to know, the question of "authority," is a relatively simple one. The real choice is much more profound than this would imply. It is a choice of the moral, not merely the technical, angle of vision from which the story is to be told.

Unlike the central intelligences of James and his successors, "Jane Austen" has learned nothing at the end of the novel that she did not know at the beginning. She needed to learn nothing. She knew everything of importance already. We have been privileged to watch with her as she observes her favorite character climb from a considerably lower platform to join the exalted company of Knightley, "Jane Austen," and those of us readers who are wise enough, good enough, and perceptive enough to belong up there too. As Katherine Mansfield says, "The truth is that every true admirer of the novels cherishes the happy thought that he alone—reading between the lines—has become the secret friend of their author."[12] Those who love "gentle Jane" as a secret friend may undervalue the irony and wit; those who see her in effect as the greatest of Shaw's heroines, flashing about her with the weapons of irony, may undervalue the emphasis on tenderness and good will. But only a very few can resist her.

The dramatic illusion of her presence as a character is thus fully as important as any other element in the story. When she intrudes, the illusion is not shattered. The only illusion we care about, the illusion of traveling intimately with a hardy little band of readers whose heads are screwed on tight and whose hearts are in the right place, is actually strengthened when we are refused the romantic love scene. Like the author herself, we don't care about the love scene. We can find love scenes in almost any novelist's works, but only here can we find a mind and heart that can give us clarity without oversimplification, sympathy and romance without sentimentality, and biting irony without cynicism.

*This essay, originally a conference talk, was "commissioned" by the CCCC (College Conference on Composition and Communication) in 1963. As I re-read it now, I find its definition of rhetoric much narrower than the one I embrace today. Rhetoric is no longer for me the successful or failed imparting of information derived elsewhere, "the art of persuading" someone to believe a truth discovered somewhere else by some form of "genuine thought." It is in itself one form of genuine thought. I feel tempted to quarrel with that forty-two-year-old ignoramus.*

*But my disagreement with that earlier self does not undermine the importance of the points he made; indeed, I detect in the essay the subtle emergence of the later definition.*

Together with both "The Revival of Rhetoric" (chapter 4 in this volume) and "Boring from Within: The Art of the Freshman Essay" (not included in this volume), "The Rhetorical Stance" has surely been one of Booth's most widely read and influential essays—though I am inclined to believe that its account of rhetoric is not so narrow as Booth suggests.

The essay was originally published in *College Composition and Communication* 14 (1963): 139–45 (copyright 1963 by the National Council of Teachers of English; reprinted with permission). It was reprinted in *Now Don't Try to Reason with Me: Essays and Ironies for a Credulous Age* (Chicago: University of Chicago Press, 1970), 25–33.

# The Rhetorical Stance

Last fall I had an advanced graduate student, bright, energetic, well-informed, whose papers were almost unreadable. He managed to be pretentious, dull, and disorganized in his paper on *Emma*, and pretentious, dull, and disorganized on *Madame Bovary*. On *The Golden Bowl* he was all these and obscure as well. Then one day, toward the end of term, he cornered me after class and said, "You know, I think you were all wrong about Robbe-Grillet's *Jealousy* today." We didn't have time to discuss it, so I suggested that he write me a note about it. Five hours later I found in my faculty box a four-page essay, polemical, unpretentious, stimulating, organized, and surprisingly convincing. Here was a man who had taught freshman composition for several years, and who was incapable of committing any of the more obvious errors that we think of as characteristic of bad writing. Yet he could not write a decent sentence, paragraph, or paper until his rhetorical problem was solved—until, that is, he had found a definition of his audience, which then focused his argument, and his own proper tone of voice.

The word *rhetoric* is one of those catchall terms that can easily raise trouble when our backs are turned. As it regains a popularity that it once seemed permanently to have lost, its meanings seem to range all the way from something like "the whole art of writing on any subject," as in Kenneth Burke's *The Rhetoric of Religion*, through "the special arts of persuasion," on down to fairly narrow notions about rhetorical figures and devices. And of course we still have with us the flood of pejorative meanings, as in "empty bombast," "mere propaganda," and the phrase "merely rhetorical."

I suppose that the question of the role of rhetoric in the English course is meaningless if we think of rhetoric in either its broadest or its narrowest meanings. No English course could avoid dealing with rhetoric in

Burke's sense, under whatever name, and on the other hand nobody would ever advocate anything so questionable as teaching "mere rhetoric." But if we settle on the following, traditional, definition, some real questions are raised: "Rhetoric is the art of finding and employing the most effective means of persuasion on any subject, considered independently of intellectual mastery of that subject." As the students say, "Prof. X knows his stuff, but he doesn't know how to put it across." If rhetoric is thought of as the art of "putting it across," considered as quite distinct from mastering an "it" in the first place, we are immediately landed in a bramble bush of controversy. Is there such an art? If so, what does it consist of? Does it have a content of its own? Can it be taught? Should it be taught? If it should be, how do we go about it, head-on or obliquely?

Obviously, it would be foolish to try to deal with many of these issues in twenty minutes. But I wish that there were more signs of our taking all of them seriously. I wish that along with our new passion for structural linguistics, for example, we could point to the development of a rhetorical theory that would show just how knowledge of structural linguistics can be useful to anyone interested in the art of persuasion. I wish there were more freshman texts that related every principle and every rule to functional principles of rhetoric, or, where this proves impossible, I wish one found more systematic discussion of why it is impossible. But for today, I must content myself with a brief look at the charge that there is nothing distinctive and teachable about the art of rhetoric.

The case against the isolability and teachability of rhetoric may look at first like a good one. Nobody writes rhetoric, just as nobody ever writes writing.[1] What we write and speak is always *this* discussion of the decline of railroading and *that* discussion of Pope's couplets and the other argument for abolishing the poll tax or for getting rhetoric back into English studies.

We can also admit that like all the arts, the art of rhetoric is at best very chancy, only partly amenable to systematic teaching; as we are all painfully aware when our one o'clock section goes miserably and our two o'clock section of the same course is a delight. Our own rhetoric is not entirely under control. Successful rhetoricians are to some extent like poets, born, not made. They are also dependent on years of practice and experience. And we can finally admit that even the firmest of principles about writing cannot be taught in the same sense that elementary logic or arithmetic or French can be taught. In my first year of teaching, I had a student who started his first two essays with a swear word. When I suggested that perhaps the third paper ought to start with something else, he protested that his high school teacher had taught him always to catch the reader's attention. Now the teacher was right, but the application of even such a firm principle requires reserves of tact that were somewhat beyond my freshman.

But with all of the reservations made, surely the charge that the art of persuasion cannot in any sense be taught is baseless. I cannot think that anyone who has ever read Aristotle's *Rhetoric* or, say, Whately's *Elements of Rhetoric* could seriously make the charge. There is more than enough in these and the other traditional rhetorics to provide structure and content for a year-long course. I believe that such a course, when planned and carried through with intelligence and flexibility, can be one of the most important of all educational experiences. But it seems obvious that the arts of persuasion cannot be learned in one year, that a good teacher will continue to teach them regardless of his subject matter, and that we as English teachers have a special responsibility at all levels to get certain basic rhetorical principles into all of our writing assignments. When I think back over the experiences that have had any actual effect on my writing, I find the great good fortune of a splendid freshman course, taught by a man who believed in what he was doing, but I also find a collection of other experiences quite unconnected with a specific writing course. I remember the instructor in psychology who penciled one word after a peculiarly pretentious paper of mine: *bull.* I remember the day when P. A. Christensen talked with me about my Chaucer paper and made me understand that my failure to use effective transitions was not simply a technical fault but a fundamental block in my effort to get him to see my meaning. His off-the-cuff pronouncement that I should never let myself write a sentence that was not in some way explicitly attached to the preceding and following sentences meant far more to me at that moment, when I had something I wanted to say, than it could have meant as part of a pattern of such rules offered in a writing course. Similarly, I can remember the devastating lessons about my bad writing that Ronald Crane taught me, with a simple question mark on a graduate seminar paper, or a penciled "Evidence for this?" or "Why this section here?" or "Everybody says so. Is it true?"

Such experiences are not, I like to think, simply the result of my being a late bloomer. At least I find my colleagues saying such things as "I didn't learn to write until I became a newspaper reporter," or "The most important training in writing I had was doing a dissertation under old *Blank.*" Sometimes they go on to say that the freshman course was useless; sometimes they say that it was an indispensable preparation for the later experience. The diversity of such replies is so great as to suggest that before we try to reorganize the freshman course, with or without explicit confrontations with rhetorical categories, we ought to look for whatever there is in common among our experiences, both of good writing and of good writing instruction. Whatever we discover in such an enterprise ought to be useful to us at any level of our teaching. It will not, presumably, decide once and for all what should be the content of the freshman course, if there should be such a course. But it might serve as a guideline for the development of widely different programs in the widely differing institutional circumstances in which we must work.

The common ingredient that I find in all of the writing I admire—excluding for now novels, plays, and poems—is something that I shall reluctantly call the rhetorical stance,[2] a stance which depends on discovering and maintaining in any writing situation a proper balance among the three elements that are at work in any communicative effort: the available arguments about the subject itself, the interests and peculiarities of the audience, and the voice, the implied character, of the speaker. I suggest that it is this balance, this rhetorical stance, difficult as it is to describe, that is our main goal as teachers of rhetoric. Our ideal graduate will strike this balance automatically in any writing that he considers finished. Though he may never come to the point of finding the balance easily, he will know that it is what makes the difference between effective communication and mere wasted effort.

What I mean by the true rhetorician's stance can perhaps best be seen by contrasting it with two or three corruptions, unbalanced stances often assumed by people who think they are practicing the arts of persuasion.

The first I'll call the pedant's stance; it consists of ignoring or underplaying the personal relationship of speaker and audience and depending entirely on statements about a subject—that is, the notion of a job to be done for a particular audience is left out. It is a virtue, of course, to respect the bare truth of one's subject, and there may even be some subjects which in their very nature define an audience and a rhetorical purpose so that adequacy to the subject can be the whole art of presentation. For example, an article on "the relation of the ontological and teleological proofs," in a recent *Journal of Religion*, requires a minimum of adaptation of argument to audience; the audience is predetermined. But most subjects do not in themselves imply in any necessary way a purpose and an audience and hence a speaker's tone. The writer who assumes that it is enough merely to write an exposition of what he happens to know on the subject will produce the kind of essay that soils our scholarly journals, written not for readers but for bibliographies.

In my first year of teaching I taught a whole unit on "exposition" without ever suggesting, so far as I can remember, that the students ask themselves what their expositions were *for*. So they wrote expositions like this one—I've saved it, to teach me toleration of my colleagues: the title is "Family

Relations in More's *Utopia*." "In this theme I would like to discuss some of the relationships with the family which Thomas More elaborates and sets forth in his book, *Utopia*. The first thing that I would like to discuss about family relations is that overpopulation, according to More, is a just cause of war." And so on. Can you hear that student sneering at me, in this opening? What he is saying is something like "You ask for a meaningless paper, I give you a meaningless paper." He knows that he has no audience except me. He knows that I don't want to read his summary of family relations in *Utopia*, and he knows that I know that he therefore has no rhetorical purpose. Because he has not been led to see a question which he considers worth answering, or an audience that could possibly care one way or the other, the paper is worse than no paper at all, even though it has no grammatical or spelling errors and is organized right down to the line, one, two, three.

An extreme case, you may say. Most of us would never allow ourselves that kind of empty fencing? Perhaps. But if some carefree foundation is willing to finance a statistical study, I'm willing to wager a month's salary that we'd find at least half of the suggested topics in our freshman texts as pointless as mine was. And we'd find a good deal more than half of the discussions of grammar, punctuation, spelling, and style totally divorced from any notion that rhetorical purpose to some degree controls all such matters. We can offer objective descriptions of levels of usage from now until graduation, but unless the student discovers a desire to say something to somebody and learns to control his diction for a purpose, we've gained very little. I once gave an assignment asking students to describe the same classroom in three different statements, one for each level of usage. They were obedient, but the only ones who got anything from the assignment were those who intuitively imported the rhetorical instructions I had overlooked—such purposes as "Make fun of your scholarly surroundings by describing this classroom in extremely elevated style," or "Imagine a kid from the slums accidentally trapped in these surroundings and forced to write a description of this room." A little thought might have shown me how to give the whole assignment some human point, and therefore some educative value.

Just how confused we can allow ourselves to be about such matters is shown in a recent publication of the Educational Testing Service, called "Factors in Judgments of Writing Ability." In order to isolate those factors that affect differences in grading standards, the ETS set six groups of readers—businessmen, writers and editors, lawyers, and teachers of English, social science, and natural science—to reading the same batch of papers. Then the ETS did a hundred-page "factor analysis" of the amount of agreement and disagreement, and of the elements which different kinds of graders emphasized. The authors of the report express a certain amount of shock at the discovery that the median correlation was only .31 and that 94 percent of the papers received either 7, 8, or 9 of the 9 possible grades.

But what *could* they have expected? In the first place, the students were given no purpose and no audience when the essays were assigned. And then all these editors and businessmen and academics were asked to judge the papers in a complete vacuum, using only whatever intuitive standards they cared to use. I'm surprised that there was any correlation at all. Lacking instructions, some of the students undoubtedly wrote polemical essays, suitable for the popular press; others no doubt imagined an audience, say, of *Reader's Digest* readers, and others wrote with the English teachers as implied audience; an occasional student with a real philosophical bent would no doubt do a careful analysis of the pros and cons of the case. This would be graded low, of course, by the magazine editors, even though they would have graded it high if they had been asked to judge it as a speculative contribution to the analysis of the problem. Similarly, a creative student who has been getting As for his personal essays will write an amusing, colorful piece, failed by all the social scientists present, though they would have graded it high if asked to judge it for what it was.

I find it shocking that tens of thousands of dollars and endless hours should have been spent by students, graders, and professional testers analyzing essays and grading results totally abstracted from any notion of purposeful human communication. Did nobody protest? One might as well assemble a group of citizens to judge students' capacity to throw balls, say, without telling the students or the graders whether altitude, speed, accuracy, or form was to be judged. The judges would be drawn from football coaches, jai alai experts, lawyers, and English teachers, and asked to apply whatever standards they intuitively apply to ball throwing. Then we could express astonishment that the judgments did not correlate very well, and we could do a factor analysis to discover, lo and behold, that some readers concentrated on altitude, some on speed, some on accuracy, some on form—and the English teachers were simply confused.

One effective way to combat the pedantic stance is to arrange for weekly confrontations of groups of students over their own papers. We have done far too little experimenting with arrangements for providing a genuine audience in this way. Short of such developments, it remains true that a good teacher can convince his students that he is a true audience, if his comments on the papers show that some sort of dialogue is taking place. As Jacques Barzun says in *Teacher in America*, students should be made to feel that unless they have said something to someone, they have failed; to bore the teacher is a worse form of failure than to anger him. From this point of view we can see that the charts of grading symbols that mar even the best freshman texts are not the innocent time-savers that we pretend. Plausible as it may seem to arrange for more corrections with less time, they inevitably reduce the student's sense of purpose in writing.[3] When he sees innumerable W18s and P19s in the margin, he cannot possibly feel that the art of persuasion is as important to his instructor as when he reads personal comments, however few.

This first perversion, then, springs from ignoring the audience, or over-reliance on the pure subject. The second, which might be called the advertiser's stance, comes from undervaluing the subject and overvaluing pure effect: how to win friends and influence people.

Some of our best freshman texts—Sheridan Baker's *The Practical Stylist*, for example—allow themselves on occasion to suggest that to be controversial or argumentative, to stir up an audience, is an end in itself. Sharpen the controversial edge, one of them says, and the clear implication is that one should do so even if the truth of the subject is honed off in the process. This perversion is probably in the long run a more serious threat in our society than the danger of ignoring the audience. In the time of audience-reaction meters and pretested plays and novels, it is not easy to convince students of the old Platonic truth that good persuasion is honest persuasion, or even of the old Aristotelian truth that the good rhetorician must be master of his subject, no matter how dishonest he may decide ultimately to be. Having told them that good writers always to some degree accommodate their arguments to the audience, it is hard to explain the difference between justified accommodation—say changing *point one* to the final position—and the kind of accommodation that fills our popular magazines, in which the very substance of what is said is accommodated to some preconception of what will sell. "The publication of *Eros* [magazine] represents a major breakthrough in the battle for the liberation of the human spirit."

At a dinner about a month ago I sat between the wife of a famous civil rights lawyer and an advertising consultant. "I saw the article on your book yesterday in the *Daily News*," she said, "but I didn't even finish it. The title of your book [*The Rhetoric of Fiction*] scared me off. Why did you choose such a terrible title? Nobody would buy a book with a title like that." The man on my right, whom I'll call Mr. Kinches, overhearing my feeble reply, plunged into a conversation with her, over my torn and bleeding corpse. "Now with my *last* book," he said, "I listed twenty possible titles and then tested them out on four hundred businessmen. The one I chose was voted for by 90 percent of the businessmen." "That's what I was just saying to

Mr. Booth," she said. "A book title ought to grab you, and *rhetoric* is not going to grab anybody." "Right," he said. "My *last* book sold fifty thousand copies already; I don't know how this one will do, but I polled two hundred businessmen on the table of contents, and ..."

At one point I did manage to ask him whether the title he chose really fit the book. "Not quite as well as one or two of the others," he admitted, "but that doesn't matter, you know. If the book is designed right, so that the first chapter pulls them in, and you *keep* 'em in, who's going to gripe about a little inaccuracy in the title?"

Well, rhetoric is the art of persuading, not the art of *seeming* to persuade by giving everything away at the start. It presupposes that one has a purpose concerning a subject which itself cannot be fundamentally modified by the desire to persuade. If Edmund Burke had decided that he could win more votes in Parliament by choosing the other side—as he most certainly could have done—we would hardly hail this party-switch as a master-stroke of rhetoric. If Churchill had offered the British "peace in our time," with some laughs thrown in, because opinion polls had shown that more Britishers were "grabbed" by these than by blood, sweat, and tears, we could hardly call his decision a sign of rhetorical skill.

One could easily discover other perversions of the rhetorician's balance—most obviously what might be called the entertainer's stance—the willingness to sacrifice substance to personality and charm. I admire Walker Gibson's efforts to startle us out of dry pedantry, but I know from experience that his exhortations to find and develop the speaker's voice can lead to empty colorfulness. A student once said to me, complaining about a colleague, "I soon learned that all I had to do to get an A was imitate Thurber."

Perhaps this is more than enough about the perversions of the rhetorical stance. Balance itself is always harder to describe than the clumsy poses that result when it is destroyed. But we all experience the balance whenever we find an author who succeeds in changing our minds. He can do so only if he knows more about the subject than we do, and if he then engages us in the process of thinking—and feeling—it through. What makes the rhetoric of Milton and Burke and Churchill great is that each presents us with the spectacle of a man passionately involved in thinking an important question through, in the company of an audience. Though each of them did everything in his power to make his point persuasive, including a pervasive use of the many emotional appeals that have been falsely scorned by many a freshman composition text, none would have allowed himself the advertiser's stance; none would have polled the audience in advance to discover which position would get the votes. Nor is the highly individual personality that springs out at us from their speeches and essays present for the sake of selling itself. The rhetorical balance among speakers, audience, and argument is with all three men habitual, as we see if we look at their nonpolitical writings. Burke's work *On the Sublime and Beautiful* is a relatively unimpassioned philosophical treatise, but one finds there again a delicate balance: though the implied author of this work is a far different person, far less obtrusive, far more objective, than the man who later cried "Sursum corda!" to the British Parliament, he permeates his philosophical work with his philosophical personality. And though the signs of his awareness of his audience are far more subdued, they are still here: every effort is made to involve the *proper* audience, the audience of philosophical minds, in a fundamentally interesting inquiry and to lead them through to the end. In short, because he was a man engaged with men in the effort to solve a human problem, one could never call what he wrote dull, however difficult or abstruse.[4]

Now, obviously, the habit of seeking this balance is not the only thing we have to teach under the heading of rhetoric. But I think that everything worth teaching under that heading finds its justification finally in that balance. Much of what is now considered irrelevant or dull can, in fact, be brought to life when teachers and students know what they are seeking. Churchill reports that the most valuable training he ever received in rhetoric was in the diagramming of sentences. Think of it! Yet the diagramming of a sentence, regardless of the grammatical system, can be a live subject as soon as one asks not simply "How is this sentence put together," but rather "Why is it put together in this way?" or "Could the rhetorical balance and hence the desired persuasion be better achieved by writing it differently?"

As a nation we are reputed to write very badly. As a nation, I would say, we are more inclined to the perversions of rhetoric than to the rhetorical balance. Regardless of what we do about this or that course in the curriculum, our mandate would seem to be, then, to lead more of our students than we now do to care about and practice the true arts of persuasion.

*Re-reading the following speech, delivered at the General Meeting on English in New York, December 29, 1964, I am a bit startled by how much of it echoes my most recent book,* The Rhetoric of Rhetoric: The Quest for Effective Communication. *It is obvious to me now that I was already embarked on a lifelong effort to elevate rhetorical studies to their proper status—not quite queen of all the sciences, as one image portrayed her in the Renaissance, but certainly among the most important of all subjects. In* The Rhetoric of Rhetoric, *I offer a long chapter on the explosion—or flowering—of rhetoric study, including a report of works with titles like "The Rhetoric of——(this or that academic discipline)." The Library of Congress reveals only nineteen before 1950 and almost seven hundred since then.*

In this essay Booth asks, and ventures an answer to, a fundamental question, one that is even more pressing today: "Why is it . . . that so much that is done in the name of advertising, of news reporting, of political campaigning, of education, is so cheap, so obviously aimed at persuasion without justification?"

This essay was originally published in *PMLA* 80, no. 2 (1965): 8–12 (reprinted by permission of the Modern Language Association of America). It was reprinted in *Now Don't Try to Reason with Me: Essays and Ironies for a Credulous Age* (Chicago: University of Chicago Press, 1970), 35–46.

# The Revival of Rhetoric

As teachers of language and literature, you have all noticed that my title is even more ambiguous than most. Those of you who are amiably disposed may even have called it "too general," in the old style, rather than "too ambiguous," in the new. The word *rhetoric* has for a long time served both for the *study* of the art of persuasion and for the *art* itself; Aristotle's *Rhetoric*, uppercase, is still unsurpassed, but take away the capital letter and Aristotle's actual practice of rhetoric is often very bad indeed, at least as we view it. In the second sense, that of the art, rhetoric has never had a real quantitative revival because it has *always* thrived; but in the first sense—the study of it—we seem to be in the midst of a revival of rhetoric unmatched for more than two centuries.

Unfortunately, in spite of some very good work, there are signs that it may prove a very shoddy revival indeed, with no more lasting effect than the rhetorically oriented "communications" movement of a decade ago, unless we take more thought about what we are doing. Judging from some of the recent freshman texts I have seen, I would not be surprised to find in my box tomorrow when I return a new work entitled *A Speller's Rhetoric*.

What, exactly, are we reviving? As applied to art, the term is today given every conceivable degree of narrowness and generality. It means anything from mere ornamental figures that can be tacked onto a discourse or subtracted at will to the whole range of all possible forms of discourse. As systematic study, rhetoric may be anything from a classification of ornamental figures to the theory of man as a logos-possessing animal. What is worse, one cannot even now, after nearly a decade of revived popularity, predict whether the term will be used to refer to something good or something bad. In publications for freshmen it has recently been an OK term. Yet in the media it is still used in ways that might well deter us from calling ourselves "Professors of Rhetoric." Listen to Malcolm Muggeridge, in a recent *Esquire* article: "Like a man in a dark place without a lantern, Churchill in his war memoirs has to fall back on shouting—that is, rhetoric, which is a factor of power rather than of understanding."

Here, as in much of current usage, rhetoric is still bombast, mere propaganda, perhaps necessary for the affairs of men but necessarily tainted, antiliterary. Now obviously I did not come here to plead for a revival of such stuff. But I might well have come to describe how it feels to live in an age dominated by it. A case could be made for the claim that we live in the most rhetorical age of all time, *if* by *rhetoric* we mean whatever men do to change each other's minds without giving good reasons for change. I am thinking not only of our fantabulous annual expenditures on advertising and public relations and political campaigns, though these alone might brand us, quantitatively, as having no previous rivals. I am thinking even more about how image building and propaganda have come to dominate fields where traditionally one could expect to find not blandishment or trickery but either solid action or genuine argument. The hand that used to guide the plow now pens the Agricultural Association Press Release. The warrior's sword is now either literally a typewriter [*yes, typewriter!*—*WCB, 2004*] or, if still in fact a destructive weapon, one that is wielded not so much to win battles as to change men's minds. The whole affair in South Vietnam, as President Johnson has said, is carried on in order to prevent Peking and Hanoi "from *thinking* that their current policy of military force will pay dividends" (emphasis added). Our nuclear deterrent power is not discussed much any more in terms of its superior strength—nobody doubts that—but in terms of its "credibility." But surely *credibility* is a rhetorical term. We ask not whether our weapons will destroy you but whether you *believe* that they will destroy you.

I could go on through almost every part of our lives and show a similar reliance on mere persuasion rather than substance. In journalism we find traditional notions of news accuracy replaced more and more, especially in the news magazines, by standards of rhetorical effectiveness; in place of the facts we are titillated and aroused by weekly collections of little short stories, rhetorically organized to sell an editorial point of view. Or again, our notions of personal worth, once decided by such hard substantive matters as moral virtue, or family history, or money in the bank, are now settled rhetorically. The new annual publication *Celebrity Register*, as Daniel Boorstin has pointed out, says of itself, "We think we have a better yardstick than the *Social Register*, or *Who's Who*, or any such book. . . . It's impossible to list accurately the success or value of men; but you *can* judge a man as a celebrity—all you have to do is weigh his press clippings." But of course *Who's Who* is not much different. Its criterion is announced under the exalted phrase "subjectivity of reference," which, after long puzzlement, I take to mean simply the number of times people are likely to want to look you up.

More significant to us here, perhaps, is the transformation of intellectual disciplines to mere rhetorical uses—to continue to think of rhetoric as divorced from genuine argument. I have a strong conviction, difficult to prove, that standards of controversy in history, philosophy, and literary criticism—to name only three—have become less and less substantive throughout this century; irrelevant blandishment, name-calling, sheer one-upmanship have increased, while solid argument has diminished— sometimes to the point of disappearing altogether.[1] There are, of course, splendid exceptions in all disciplines; if there were not, the disciplines would themselves disappear as genuine disciplines. But I invite you to examine your favorite journal—even if it is one of those few that have tried to maintain serious standards—and count the number of solid reasons offered for conclusions as compared with irrelevant ploys like guilt-by-association, old-hatism, and so's-your-old-thesis-chairman. Wherever one looks, one is likely to find, in place of a coherent effort to move from evidence to conclusions, an outpouring of what one of my colleagues calls a mere "rhetoric of conclusions." Controversy is conducted as if all strong effects were equally valuable; to shock or simply to win is more important than the discovery of truth. I announce no secrets here, of course; many of our most prominent controversialists have explicitly repudiated reason in the name of rhetorical effects like shock or outrage.

In short, it is not difficult to find signs that we are a rhetorical age, if we mean by that—once again—an age in which men try to change each other's minds without giving good reasons for change. I know of no past culture where power was so persistently thought of as power to manipulate men's minds; where beauty was so persistently tested by mere popularity or salability; where the truth of propositions was so persistently judged by whether this or that group accepts them; where notions of human greatness were so persistently reduced to the question of fame or "national luminosity"; where, finally, educational goals and methods were so persistently reduced to the notion of conditioning or the imposition of already formed ideas or practices upon an infinitely malleable material.

I might very well, then, have come here to plead for a further revival of rhetorical studies in order to protect ourselves and our students from rhetoric as a bad thing. Many popular prophets have in fact, like David Riesman in his portrayal of the other-directed man, implored us to find a mode of guidance for our lives somewhat more substantive than a perpetually operating radar set turned to receive rhetorical directions from other members of the lonely crowd.

But I have played too long with a definition that I don't accept. Rhetoric can mean good things, too. All of the critics who have taken part in the revival of rhetorical studies that began in the mid-1950s have defined the term in ways that would require us to speak of "*bad* rhetoric" when we refer to the perversions I have just described. The definition of *good* rhetoric, or of rhetoric in general, good *and* bad, varies from critic to critic.[2] But beneath the differences there is general agreement that to engage with one's fellow men in acts of mutual persuasion, that is, of mutual inquiry, is potentially a noble thing. Indeed, none of the corruptions found in our rhetorical time would even be possible in a society which had not also laid itself open to the great virtues of moral and intellectual suasion when properly used. Consider once again my summary description of our rhetorical age. One can easily translate it, proposition by proposition, into a description of a kind of utopia.

Suppose I could say of our society the following: I can think of no previous society in which questions of political power were so persistently referred to the people for consultation and decision; where questions of beauty were so often decided not by arbitrary rules imposed by an elite but by reference to a genuine capacity of art works to please those who experience them; where questions of truth were so often tested by debate rather than settled by decree; where notions of human greatness were so consistently determined not by fiat of a hereditary aristocracy or plutocracy but by reference to standards testable on the popular pulse; where, finally, educational goals and methods were tested so constantly against practical experience, and where it was unfailingly assumed that, since all men are educable—that is, subject to good rhetoric—there is no limit to the good that can be done through improving the rhetoric of education. Would not such a society—fully as rhetorical as the earlier one—be a noble thing indeed?

All of the evils of our rhetorical age are thus corruptions of tendencies that might be ennobling, or at least liberating. Or, to put it again in terms of Riesman's radar set owned by the other-directed man, everything depends on how the radar set is aimed and on the quality of the messages received. An other-directed society would be an ideal society if the "others" were in fact bearers of truth, goodness, and beauty.

Why is it, then, that so much of what we see about us, so much that is done in the name of advertising, of news reporting, of political campaigning, of education, is so cheap, so obviously aimed at persuasion without justification? If I thought I could get away with it here, I might intone an answer something like this: The bad rhetoric of our rhetorical time can be blamed on our almost total failure to develop good rhetorical theory adequate to our needs. I could not get away with such oversimplification, because you are all aware of how little can be changed, directly, by *any* theory, good or bad. But perhaps I *can* get away with a statement only slightly less forceful: Of all the causes of our rhetorical shoddiness, the only one that you and I have much chance of doing anything about is our shoddy rhetorical theory and our shoddier teaching thereof. To our nonmajors we have offered a collection of high school and freshman textbooks that, with a few exceptions, are as shameful as any of the ills they purport to cure. To our majors, graduate and undergraduate, we have offered even less: at most universities still a student cannot undertake serious rhetorical study even if he wants to, for lack of teachers, courses, or library facilities. [*Again I am struck by how much better things are now than they were in 1964.*]

Finally, what have we offered to the public? That the American public wants rhetorical assistance in an age of rhetoric is shown by the almost incredible success of a popular rhetorician like Rudolf Flesch. Flesch's sophistries about achieving an interesting style by using short words, short sentences, and a personal tone are dangerous, but it is hard to think of what guide to recommend to a literate adult in their place. If someone asks me for works that will help him in reading poetry, I can suggest dozens of respectable works, some of them very good indeed. But if I am asked for guidance in distinguishing good controversial argument from bad, or in constructing a really powerful argument on one's own, or even in constructing an effective—not just a passable—staff report, what do I say? Where, in all of our textbooks about how to write, do we send an intelligent adult for guidance in the true arts of transferring ideas, motives, intentions from his mind to other men's minds?

Please don't try to fob me off with the title of your favorite freshman text. There are some good ones, but we must be quite clear about what is needed, and it is not to be found in works designed, for the most part, for semiliterates. What is needed can be seen clearly if we ask where I might turn, in the available rhetorics, for help in improving this talk. I can get help in improving my diction and sentence structure, help of a general kind, from most freshman texts. But where is the theory, where are the practical rules for ensuring that this talk will not only grab you, as the Madison Avenue rhetoricians say, but keep you grabbed and send you away determined to behave differently?

Most of the rhetorical advice I find, even in texts that go beyond simple formulae for correctness, is entirely general. Be brief. Be clear. Be forceful. Revise carefully. Use short words. Such advice is not plainly wrong. It can even be useful. But since it is general, it gives me no help in deciding what arguments might appeal to you, sitting out there in all your particularity on a particular occasion. What appeals are available to me? What order should I give them? Brevity, clarity, unity, coherence, emphasis—none of these will be worth a brass farthing with you unless somehow I have managed to invent an organized chain of arguments about *this* subject for *this* audience that will bridge the gap between what you believed when you came and what I want you to believe when you depart. But you will look a long while in the available modern rhetorics before you will find much that could possibly help me in this central task.

Are you surprised that I do find considerable help about such matters in Aristotle and the many traditional rhetorics fathered by him? They all tell me to look to my arguments and to make sure that there is at least a semblance of genuine connection between them and my conclusions. They all tell me, more importantly, that what will *be* a semblance of sound connection can be decided only by considering my audience, and they all give me, by implication, some notion of what a large gathering of more-or-less-middle-aged and thoroughly fatigued teachers of language and literature will demand or allow as a ratio of real proof to other, incidental appeals. They all suggest ways of handling emotional appeals and those essential, disguised claims that I am a citizen of good standing in the world of letters.

I find it interesting, incidentally, that with all our modern passion for inventing new studies with proper labels, we do not even have words in our language for the sciences of invention and arrangement or for the study of emotional and ethical appeal. With all our new grammars and new stylistics, with our proxemics and tagmemics, surely it is time for someone to make himself a professor of inventionics or arrangementistics.

The traditional rhetorics had terms for such matters, and they can still give us more help than most of us suspect. We would be in much better condition if everyone now reviving rhetoric took at least the trouble to learn one traditional rhetoric thoroughly.

But it would be naive to think that reviving Aristotle or Quintilian or Campbell or Whately could solve our problems if we only studied them carefully. For one thing, our rhetorical age has invented forms of persuasion that earlier ages knew not of. Much, perhaps most, of our rhetoric occurs in informal situations; we need a rhetoric of the symposium, of the conference room—I would hope somewhat more respectable intellectually than what is now offered the public under terms like "group dynamics" and "conference techniques."

Perhaps more important, we cannot take for granted, as most traditional rhetoricians felt that *they* could, a systematic coverage under other categories of such matters as logic and dialectic. Our students are not trained, as they could assume of their students, in the analysis of serious argument. Whether we choose to extend the term *rhetoric* to include the whole art of meaningful discourse or confine it to nonbelletristic, obviously persuasive forms, or confine it even further to the paralogical elements in such persuasive forms, we must find some place in our revived rhetorical studies for training in how to build arguments that coerce, by their cogency, the agreement of all who will attend to them. Traditional logics and grammars will help us here, but I suspect that modern logics and semantics and grammars will prove indispensable. The revival, here again, must do more than echo the past.

But this leads to a final reason for rejecting the notion that the revival of rhetoric can mean only the revival of earlier rhetorics. It is simply that none of them can possibly give us the comprehensive rhetorical theory we seek. Living in a new kind of rhetorical age, surrounded by, indeed practicing daily, forms of persuasion their authors never dreamed of, we inevitably hunger for a theory that will do justice to *our* manifold rhetorical experiences, and we do not find that the categories used by earlier theorists quite do the job. I can illustrate this point by asking if you have not felt impatient, so far in my talk, by my omission of the rhetoric of literature. I have talked as if the whole problem were that of finding a theory of rhetoric for the teaching of composition. But you and I are groping for much more than that, as we work at reviving this old, magical term.

Why have some of the greatest theorists of our time—men like Richard McKeon and Kenneth Burke—found themselves trying to construct unified rhetorical views of *all* the verbal arts? Obviously, I cannot answer this rhetorical question about rhetoric in our time, but I can suggest an answer by asking another: Why do we find ourselves gathered here engaged in rhetoric about rhetoric and literature? Whatever answer we give must include, I think, a recognition that we are a rhetorical age in a sense far more profound than the one I began with. We believe in mutual persuasion as a way of life; we live from conference to conference. More significantly, the intellectual inquiries of our time, even at their most responsible level, have tended to be inquiries that can best be called rhetorical. In philosophy we do not begin with metaphysical questions and pursue *being* and *substance* to the bitter end; rather, we begin with existentialist commitment, induced by rhetorical works in philosophical garb, or we analyze the uses of language. We *do* philosophy on each other, as it were, rather than pursue truth as if it were a thing to be obtained. In literary criticism, similarly, we have constructed innumerable semantics and rhetorics and stylistics and linguistics. Even our histories tend to be histories of linguistic or rhetorical fashion. New sciences like cybernetics are invented to unite all human in-quiry under one science of information. Even the so-called hard sciences are discussed in terms of information theory. Last month a new interde-partmental committee was formed at Chicago, to supervise information studies—I assume that they will be studying the rhetoric of genes, atoms, and computers.

To try to deal with such a profusion of sciences of communication with traditional theories would be folly. We hunger, or at least I hunger, for a comprehensive view of the arts and sciences of man, a view at least as comprehensive, say, as the two radically different but equally thorough-going views of Plato and Aristotle. What we have instead is a logomachy, a rhetorical babel about forms of rhetoric. And the warring factions wage their battles without generals and without having had their basic infantry training.

It is time now for me to come out from behind that feeble metaphor and make my main plea quite openly. My rhetorical point to a group of rhetori-cians is twofold: first, that in a rhetorical age rhetorical studies should have a major, respected place in the training of all teachers at all levels; and sec-ond, that in such an age, specialization in rhetorical studies of all kinds, narrow and broad, should carry at least as much professional respectability as literary history or as literary criticism in nonrhetorical modes. Whether we restore the old chairs of rhetoric by name or not, chairs in rhetorical studies ought to exist in every department, to provide visible proof that to dirty one's hands in rhetorical studies is not a sure way to professional oblivion.

If I had made such a plea for a genuine revival of advanced rhetorical studies ten years ago, I would have had to base my appeal almost entirely on your sense of duty: "The condition of our writing courses demands that we sacrifice ourselves by doing the unpopular thing." But in 1964 one can indulge in that appeal dear to the hearts of all rhetoricians, namely: "Here for once duty and profit and pleasure are reconciled." The fashionable demand for rhetorical studies is such that even the worst textbook profits from the word *rhetoric* in the title. (I speak from experience: whatever the faults or merits of *The Rhetoric of Fiction*, it has profited from my having used a fad term, quite unwittingly, in the title. . . .) If, as I am assuming, you want to do serious intellectual work without undue penalties from society, and if—like most of us—you want your work to have some relevance to the real needs of society, you need neither to blush nor to tighten your belt when you turn from *belles lettres* to rhetoric.

To those of you who feel that your present research is trivial though respected, I would say: drop that study of Phineas Fletcher or of Suckling's imitators and take up the great rhetorical theorists and the great rhetoricians who helped to mold our age. Those of you, on the other hand, who are doing seemingly nonrhetorical literary study that you know to be not in the least trivial can find both fun and profit in discovering what happens if you grasp your subject by a rhetorician's handle. Best of all, you might in the process even discover how to make literary studies genuinely relevant to the literate and semiliterate public of a rhetorical age.

*This essay was first a talk for a conference entitled "Metaphor: The Conceptual Leap," sponsored by the University of Chicago Extension in 1978. Mine was the only presentation that dealt directly with judgments of quality, but anyone listening closely would have found implicit judgments in almost every paper delivered.*

Later this essay appeared in the journal *Critical Inquiry* that Booth cofounded with colleagues Sheldon Sacks and Arthur Heiserman in 1974 and coedited for many years. The essay provides a good example of Booth's rhetorical method of inquiry in its use of open-ended terms (topoi) to "invent," rather than impose, a definition of metaphor persuasive to his audience.

The essay was originally published in *Critical Inquiry* 5, no. 1 (autumn 1978): 49–72, 175–76. It was reprinted in *On Metaphor*, ed. Sheldon Sacks (Chicago: University of Chicago Press, 1979), 47–70, 173–74.

## Metaphor as Rhetoric

The Problem of Evaluation (with Ten Literal "Theses")

I

There were no conferences on metaphor, ever, in any culture, until our own century was already middle-aged. As late as 1927, John Middleton Murry, complaining about the superficiality of most discussions of metaphor, could say, "There are not many of them."[1] If we take what he said at face value, what we are doing in this symposium appears as part of an intellectual movement that is—to use the word that Thucydides uses to set things up for his history—one of the "greatest" in the history of thought. Explicit discussions of something called metaphor have multiplied astronomically in the past fifty years. This increase is not simply parallel to the vast general increase in scholarly and critical writing. Shakespeareans have multiplied too, as have scholars of Homer, of Dickens, and of Charles the Second. But students of metaphor have positively pullulated. The bibliographies show more titles for 1977, for example, than for—well, the truth is that I refuse to do the counting to make this point, but I'll wager a good deal that the year 1977 produced more titles than the entire history of thought before 1940. We shall soon no doubt have more metaphoricians than metaphysicians— or should that be metamorticians, the embalmers of dead metaphor? I have in fact extrapolated with my pocket calculator to the year 2039; at that point there will be more students of metaphor than people.

But of course we can never take such explosions at face value. We must discount this one in at least two ways. First, there have been many more discussions of what people from the Greek philosophers on *called* metaphor than any bibliography could show. Almost all such discussions before this century were either short sections in treatises on rhetoric or style or incidental complaints and warnings by philosophers seeking an unequivocal language. For almost everyone, *metaphor* was one kind of figurative device among many, not the generic term for all similitudes. The total number of discussions must be almost as great as the total number of treatises on the resources available to the rhetorician or poet. And that would make a fair number of "titles."

On the other hand, if we take metaphor to be what people *now* call metaphor, we must discount even more. Along with the immense increase in bibliography about something previously *called* metaphor, there has been an immense explosion of meanings for the word. If I listed what was said about metaphor before Murry's statement, defining it as "whatever people *now* mean by the word," I would in fact be forced to list pages from every philosopher, grammarian, rhetorician, and logician from the pre-Socratics on.

Even when we do all the discounting possible, however, the fact remains that all of us here are part of a very curious, perhaps finally inexplicable, intellectual movement. No matter how we define it, metaphor seems to be taking over not only the world of humanists but the world of the social and natural sciences as well.[2]

Perhaps this broadening of meanings and explosion of interest are all to the good. If we love metaphor, we surely should not complain when we find thousands of students taking it seriously. But there is a problem for students of any subject when the word for that subject expands to cover everything. And that is precisely what has happened to this word. *Metaphor* has by now been defined in so many ways that there is no human expression, whether in language or any other medium, that would not be metaphoric in *someone's* definition. This could mean that the word has become useless and that we should all take up some other line of inquiry. Surely when a word can mean everything, it risks meaning nothing.

But what's interesting is that in spite of differences in the scope of our definitions, we all meet every day certain statements that everyone recognizes as metaphor and calls by that name. We seem to have a kind of commonsense agreement about a fairly narrow definition, one that survives even while our theory expands the original concept beyond recognition.

In a seminar that I cannot claim to be running—rather, it runs me—the students and I have so far not found any one definition of *metaphor* that we all could possibly agree on. But we have found innumerable instances of what all of us happily *call* metaphors regardless of our definitions. In Paul Ricoeur's metaphoric definition, they are "full-fledged": "Man is a wolf to man"; "Chicago is a dungheap"; "You're the cream in my coffee." We have also found many that are metaphors only in definitions that are not universally accepted: "I'll defend that position"; "God is love." And of course there are many that look metaphoric but that could in some contexts be quite literal: "Mary is an elephant"; "Jeffrey is a rat"; "Something's rotten in the state of Denmark."

If I said, "We have here three different breeds of cat," everyone would agree that I had attempted a metaphor. But we would begin to dispute if I asked for a clear vote about whether this sentence I am now delivering contains no metaphors. Some of us would note that "delivering" and "contains" and "clear" still have some metaphoric sense whether I intended it or not. Others would want to add further words, like "sentence" itself or "metaphor," that I did not intend metaphorically.

Classical rhetoricians—if by an odd chance we had any among us— would say that the sentence contains *no* metaphors; dead ones are not just dead, they are no longer metaphors. Metaphor for them is generally not contrasted with literal speech but with normal or ordinary or usual, *un*twisted, speech. Since the words *delivery* and *contain* have become one usual way of saying what I wanted to say, they are not dead metaphors but nonmetaphors. At the postmodernist extreme, some would claim that all my terms were metaphors, and they would seek, though not always find, philological evidence to prove that the metaphors were originally "motivated." Or they might, like Paul de Man, seek to show the inescapable metaphorical quality of all human discourse. We might even find among us someone who would want to argue for the once popular theological view that not only is all language metaphorical but that the whole of our life is but a metaphor—what used to be called an analogy—for God's truth.

## II

Suppose we confine our attention for a while to examples that we would all call metaphors and ask the question that would have occurred first to Demetrius, say, or Quintilian: Which are the good ones?

Most writers on metaphor imply that they know how to answer that question; some actually give their criteria. But why is it that so few give any real help to the writer or reader of metaphor? Where would you send me now for assistance in determining which metaphors should be celebrated and which should be hanged from the neck until dead? Donald Davidson might say that to ask the question is to pursue a wild goose or will-o'-the-wisp. There are no unsuccessful metaphors, he says, only tasteless ones. If he wishes, we can change the question to "Where do I go for help in improving my taste?"

Let's choose an easy metaphor for a close look. A lawyer friend of mine was hired to defend a large southern utility against a suit by a small one, and he thought at first that he was doing fine. All of the law seemed to be on his side, and he felt that he had presented his case well. Then the lawyer for the small utility said, speaking to the jury, almost as if incidentally to his legal case, "So now we see what it is. They got us where they want us. They holding us up with one hand, their good sharp fishin' knife in the other, and they sayin', 'You jes' set still, little catfish, we're *jes'* going to *gut* ya.'" At that moment, my friend reports, he knew he had lost the case. "I was in the hands of a genius of metaphor."

It is not too difficult to figure out ways of talking about why this metaphor is a good one. Our sense of its mastery is indeed quick and intuitive, but it is useful to slow down a bit and see if we can discover the grounds of our assurance.

In the first place, we have isolated a particular kind of metaphor from all the other things called metaphor. We are thus forced to put aside a variety of definitions that we may for other occasions want to use. For the purpose of explaining the power of "catfish," we get no help from classing it (1) with all symbolic expressions that claim similarity or likeness or, narrowing down a bit, (2) with all nonliteral language, whether intended to be recognized as "figured" or "troped" or "twisted" or not, or, still narrowing, (3) with all symbolic inventions, whether in language or other media, that *are* intended to be taken nonliterally. Our catfish does belong, of course, in all these increasingly smaller classes, but the classes are still so large that they cannot, in themselves, lead us toward discriminations of quality among their members. Even the notion of human intention, added in the third class, does not help us much, until we take the obvious next step and ask *"What* intention?"—thus importing the rhetorical notion of *purpose* into the philosophical problem of intentions. If the lawyer's purpose was to tell the truth in a new and interesting way, then we might discover the metaphor's work by inquiring into its truth, and we might try to decide whether his metaphor said anything more than "They're trying to cheat us." Or if his purpose was to be accurate and clear, we might, as many modern guides to writing tell us to do, find fault with his mixed metaphors, pointing out that catfish don't set, or even sit. But his purpose is obviously to forge a weapon in order to win, and that weapon is thus in a class of metaphors that classical rhetorical treatises took as a large part of their province.

Suppose that, instead of attempting a formal definition of the class, we simply list the marks of this beast, so that we can then judge its "points," in the hope that the same procedure may enable us to mark off other kinds that will yield different criteria. Whether or not we finally decide that the various species of what we call metaphor belong to a single genus or simply bear family resemblances to each other will not matter much for our various special inquiries into quality, though it will of course continue to matter to us in our philosophical endeavors. (Since most of the papers at the symposium seem to assume that metaphor is, finally, a single determinate concept, I suppose I should, without providing argument, declare myself on that issue. I am pretty sure that the many things we call metaphor are not mutually compatible under a single determinate definition; at most they bear family resemblances to some other members of the family, and some of them are in fact essentially different from some others. One obvious clash, for example, is that between any "weapon metaphor" chosen to produce the greatest possible shock, with heightened contempt for the victim, and any "sublime metaphor" embodied in a culture [not chosen by a particular author] and expressing the greatest possible spiritual heightening: for example, all myths and rituals. We may all want to legislate against certain uses of the word in order to distinguish what true metaphor is. But in fact people will go on calling these disparate things metaphors, and we should not use the word without acknowledging its inescapable indeterminacy.)

Here, then, are some marks of the catfish metaphor:

1. It is a part of an intended rhetorical communication, not primarily a piece of self-expression or an attempt at formal beauty.
2. What is being communicated is context-dependent: the full meaning of the metaphor cannot be determined without reference to the rhetorical situation. *That* it is a metaphor everyone will see without a context. *What* it says or does depends on a rhetorical situation.
3. That context reveals to everyone a clear persuasive purpose: to win.
4. That *purpose* can be paraphrased regardless of what theorists say about whether the *metaphor* can be. There are many different synonymous ways of describing the lawyer's intent to win his case.
5. The metaphor is itself also *largely* paraphrasable, but the contrast is not necessarily with some literal meaning but rather with some less striking or more everyday way of putting the point. Other metaphors might be invented, more or less effective for the same purpose.
6. What is being compared are two things, not just two words. In this case they are two *situations* which could be unpacked as an elaborate analogy: large utility is to fisherman as small utility is to catfish; knife is to catfish's vital center as large utilities' measures are to small utility's vital center; and so on.
7. Unlike the metaphors Paul Ricoeur prefers to talk about, this one is stable, in the sense that once the jury has recognized the comparison, no further act of interpretation is required, no further underminings of

normal readings invited. Though analysis will reveal immense complexity in the rhetorical moment, the invitation to reconstruct one comparison out of another comparison is sharply limited by implicit standards of relevance. Hundreds of associations with fish, knives, fishermen, gutting, and utilities are simply and flatly declared irrelevant. To pursue them would be a mistaken extension of the metaphorical process.

8. It is thus local or finite. There is no direct invitation to speculate about meanings, profound or otherwise: about metaphor, about life, about the universe, not even about capitalist exploitation. Our attention is held to the battle of utilities. The metaphor adds no new truth, not in any obvious way. (This does not mean that a probing thinker cannot see how the metaphor is "really" related to larger matters, just as he can render the metaphor's stability unstable without half trying.)

9. Yet implicit in all this is a mark that this kind of metaphor shares with all other deliberate rhetorical deviations: more is communicated than the words literally say. What the "more" is cannot be easily described. Aristotle and others called it energy, which does point us in the right direction. Whether the metaphor communicates more than the nonmetaphor is not mainly a question of cognitive content or meaning, though we might still want to debate about that. What is unquestionable is that when weapon metaphors succeed, more passes from speaker to hearer than would have passed otherwise. I shall return in a few moments to look at what that "more" might be, but for now it is enough to repeat what Ted Cohen has said in his talk here: part of what is communicated does not depend on the metaphor succeeding in the sense of winning or even in the sense of being thought good. The speaker has performed a task by yoking what the hearer had not yoked before, and the hearer simply cannot resist joining him; they thus perform an identical dance step, and the metaphor accomplishes at least part of its work, even if the hearer then draws back and says, "I shouldn't have allowed that!"

10. Finally, we find a mark that clearly distinguishes this figure from what I have elsewhere called stable irony. It is true that the act of reconstruction begins, as it does with irony, in a recognition that literal, discrete, or "ordinary" meanings alone will not make sense of the passage—a new relation must be actively sought. But after the auditor has reconstructed such acceptable meanings, they are not, with this kind of metaphor, separated from the *stated* meanings and then in some sense repudiated, as they must be in receiving irony. Having moved from the gutting of catfish to the gutting of small utilities, the mind is not then asked to rule out what it first saw, a wrong reading. The original meaning, what might

be called the uninterpreted picture, remains as part of the final picture in a way that is not true of stable ironies. The big utility is forever a knife-wielding threat.

These seem the marks that are essential in the sense that whenever I find them applicable, I will be able to derive criteria for success with weapon metaphors: an unusual or surprising comparison of two things, part of a communication in a context that reveals a predetermined purpose that can be paraphrased, intended to be recognized and reconstructed with stable, localized meanings that can thus be evaluated as contributing to that purpose.

It is curious that the difference between metaphor and simile, essential in the study of some kinds of metaphor, seems here to become extremely unimportant. It is perhaps true that adding a "like" or "as" to the catfish picture will weaken it somewhat. But this addition does not change the nature of the picture, and one is not surprised to find that classical theorists, unlike many modern philosophers with different purposes in view, have seen the choice between simile and metaphor as minor, as depending simply on whether the speaker profits from seeming more or less daring.[3]

## III

Once we have a metaphoric species clearly in mind—and I remind you that I have begun with one of the simplest kinds—we can easily discover criteria for effectiveness. In fact, we can invent other metaphors designed for the same purpose and then judge their relative quality. Suppose the lawyer had said, "And so the big utilities are proceeding to disembowel the company I represent, right before our eyes." Or "The big utilities just expect us stand looking on helplessly while they sap our vital forces." Or, finally, to make one that is a closer rival: "They got us where they want us. They holding us up with one hand, their good sharp fishin' knife in the other, and they sayin', 'You jes' hang quiet, little bass, we're *jes'* going to *gut* ya.'"

Where can I go for help in choosing between "bass" and "catfish"? Philosophical discussions seldom deal with any metaphor more complex than "Man is a wolf," "My sweetheart is my Schopenhauer," and "Smith is a pig." And they almost never give me a rhetorical context that would determine my standards of success. Even when such discussions deal with complexities and offer evaluations, they seem to reduce all criteria to two, truth and coherence, sometimes adding novelty, or a novel truth that reveals new incoherence. And I find the same poverty, somewhat surprisingly, when I turn to authors who explicitly promise to be helpful about such matters. All modern guides to writing have a word to say about metaphor, or at most two: *cliché* and *mixed*. That is to say, most modern writing guides that fall into the hands of the young have only two standards to be applied to my examples: novelty and coherence. (Note that they tend to drop the philosopher's concern for truth.) New metaphors are good, the newer the better; old ones are clichés, if they are not so old that they are actually dead, in which case they don't matter unless we happen to remember the etymology. At this point the second criterion comes in: metaphors should be coherent, that is, metaphors should not be mixed.

Well, I have made my bass metaphor more coherent, with "hang quiet" instead of "set still." Have I improved it? And as for novelty, surely it is just as novel to talk of gutting a bass in that situation as gutting a catfish. It is not even clear to me that it matters, for those on the jury, whether they have all heard that comparison before: so much depends on *other* qualities.

One of the subtlest of modern guides, H. W. Fowler, in his book *The King's English*, adds two criteria. He is against "overdone" metaphors no matter how coherent, and he quotes Samuel Richardson's long passage with disapproval: "Tost to and fro by the high winds of passionate control, I behold the desired port, the single state, into which I would fain steer."[4] And on for eight lines of sailing to the right country. Second, he is against "spoilt metaphors," by which he means that our metaphors should be accurate: "Yet Jaurès was the Samson who upheld the pillars of the Bloc"— Samson, you may or may not remember, did not exactly *uphold* pillars.

It would take the rest of this paper to describe the criteria that leap to mind to be added to or subtracted from these, now that we know what we are looking for. But they need not leap to mind unaided. The classical rhetoricians are a rich source of suggestions about such matters, and it is a pity that because rhetoric has so often been degraded into mere lists of shoddy devices we have let ourselves lose what it could teach. Here is a short list that one could dig out of almost any rhetoric text from Aristotle to Whately.

1.  Good metaphors of this kind are *active*, lending the energy of animated things to whatever is less energetic or more abstract. As Demetrius says, they introduce "inanimate things in a state of activity as though they were animate." "Catfish" and "bass" both win easily here over my other versions.

2.  Good weapon metaphors are *concise*. All the rhetoricians had a strong sense of what Herbert Spencer later described, at length, as a law of stylistic economy: the more you can convey in a given number of words,

the better. Indeed, that is one reason for using metaphor rather than ordinary language: it says more with less. If I try to unpack "catfish" I find that a full paragraph or two will be required to describe what it manages to convey. "Bass" is as economical, but my "disembowel" version is less economical (though shorter) because it says so much less. Even it is better, however, than simply saying, "They're trying to destroy us."

3. Good metaphors are *appropriate*, in their grandeur or triviality, to the task in hand. If the point is to heighten sublimity, then trivial metaphors must be avoided. But if diminishment is desired, vice versa. Now in our example what is needed is a heightening of powerful, hypocritical destructiveness on the one hand, and of helpless innocence on the other. On the face of it neither a catfish nor a bass is an *especially* good metaphor for innocence. But both are innocent enough, and catfish is a bit better than bass for squirming helplessness, since it is not a game fish but an easily caught, harmless scavenger.

4. It is not enough that the metaphor be appropriate to the task, and thus to other elements in the text. It must be properly *accommodated to the audience*, in this case a southern jury. It is not hard to think of hearers for whom some other innocent victim would be preferable, and there might even be some juries for whom the very vulgarity that makes "catfish" so powerful should be diminished.

5. Finally such a metaphor should build a proper *ethos* for the speaker, building or sustaining his character as someone to be trusted. Here we approach something difficult to talk about indeed. But once we think about it, we realize that every speaker who uses any figure with the intent that it be recognized *as* figure, instead of using it as an art that disguises art, calls attention to himself in ways that the user of "ordinary, usual," untwisted language does not. It's true that every speaker makes a character, an ethos for himself, whether he is using figurative language or not. He may even choose to build a character like the Jonathan Swift Samuel Johnson described—the sort of "rogue" who "never hazards a metaphor." But this kind of metaphor, like all kinds that invite recognition, builds a character in a further sense: the ethos of what we call a "real character," in this case a colorful jester who identifies, in a kind of humorous helplessness, with the little fellow. He makes us almost forget that the little fellow is actually a utility, something that cannot suffer, and that the lawyer is paid to invent metaphors like this.

This by no means exhausts the criteria we could discover and apply to weapon metaphors. I think that with a year or two of thought one might work out those criteria, and it would be worth doing in a world that for want of rhetorical attention writes and speaks mainly blobs of verbal spaghetti. But it is time to turn to even more complicated matters. I want first to suggest larger and more important relations between metaphor and character than were implied in my final mark of weapon metaphors, larger in fact than even the classical rhetoricians seem to have recognized.

I invite you a second time to ask where, in all that you have read about metaphor, you would go for assistance in deciding not whether any part of the following is good or bad as craft but whether the whole passage is an admirable conclusion to a book. The one-page final chapter, "The Metaphor Delivered," concludes a book about the protest march on Washington during the Vietnam War:

> Whole crisis of Christianity in America that the military heroes were on one side, and the unnamed saints on the other! Let the bugle blow. The death of America rides in on the smog. America—the land where a new kind of man was born from the idea that God was present in every man not only as compassion but as power, and so the country belonged to the people; for the will of the people—if the locks of their life could be given the art to turn—was then the will of God. Great and dangerous idea! If the locks did not turn, then the will of the people was the will of the Devil. Who by now could know where was what? Liars controlled the locks.
>
> Brood on that country who expresses our will. She is America, once a beauty of magnificence unparalleled, now a beauty with a leprous skin. She is heavy with child—no one knows if legitimate—and languishes in a dungeon whose walls are never seen. Now the first contractions of her fearsome labor begin—it will go on: no doctor exists to tell the hour. It is only known that false labor is not likely on her now, no, she will probably give birth, and to what?—the most fearsome totalitarianism the world has ever known? or can she, poor giant, tormented lovely girl, deliver a babe of a new world brave and tender, artful and wild? Rush to the locks. God writhes in his bonds. Rush to the locks. Deliver us from our curse. For we must end on the road to that mystery where courage, death, and the dream of love give promise of sleep.[5]

Now it may at first appear that Norman Mailer's passage uses several metaphors of the catfish kind: weapons designed to win adherents and destroy enemies. "Let the bugle blow." "Bugle" is to "U.S. Army troops" as "my plea" to "the army of saints." "Vietnam protesters" are to "saints" as "military heroes" to—well, we must be careful, because it is not clear that Mailer means "heroes" to be turned into "devils." Can we say that

America, the "beauty with the leprous skin" is to "unpredictable future" as "pregnant woman languishing in prison" is to "unpredictable, perhaps illegitimate babe"? Already things are getting too complicated for literal analysis. And suddenly the leprous woman becomes a lovely giant, who, though lacking a doctor, is sure to deliver either a fearsome totalitarianism or a "babe of a new world brave and tender, artful and wild," a babe that may or may not be identified with the God who is writhing in his bonds— no doubt suffering in the smog on which the death of America rides. The last sentence alone defies close analysis, because if it is true that we must end on the road where there is promise of sleep, it is not at all clear why we should rush to what locks, or who is to deliver us from our curse.

I cannot know, of course, how readers will respond to this passage out of context. But it may be useful to underline its intensities by reporting on a contrast between my expectations in reading this paper to the original audience and the actual response. I had written for delivery, immediately following my attempt at a neutral reading, the following: "I cannot know, of course, how you feel about the passage by now. But I should be much surprised if most of you do not think it a terrible piece of metaphoric jumbling. . . . I shall not try to reverse your judgment completely, but I do want to think a bit about the grounds for that judgment."

My actual surprise was of a different kind. The audience began laughing much too early and too hard for my own comfort. At "tormented lovely girl" I interrupted the reading, with a plea for a fair hearing: "You're spoiling the pleasure for those who like the passage." But the laughter continued to mount. When I said, at the end, "I tried very hard to read that neutrally, so that I would not give an opinion about it in advance, and I was surprised by the laughter," the comment itself produced *more* laughter. Finally, in something of a flurry, I asked: "Was there anyone who *resented* the laughter?" The question was first met with silence.

"Not a single person in this room thinks that the passage is a good way to end a book?"

At that point a voice said "Yes," and I said, "At last! Who is it? Ah, Mr. Strier [my colleague Richard Strier]. Well, we'll hear from you later."

In the discussion after the talk, Strier said that "if Booth had wanted to, he could have made this audience laugh at *any* author. His reading was *not* neutral. He did not let us know that the author was Mailer, and the passage was thus wrenched out of its context, taken out of its historical moment and put into a new context, where attention was focused on deliberately scrambled metaphor as a thing in itself."

I welcomed the rather warm discussion that followed, and I accept Strier's point—it is in fact one of my theses about metaphor that it cannot be judged without reference to a context. The interchange is worth re-porting here, however, primarily because it illustrated the high emotional involvement we display in our judgments of metaphor. Having laughed in contempt at the passage, many in the audience reported themselves ex-tremely uncomfortable. When they learned that the author was Mailer and that I thought the passage really quite skillful ["much better than I could have managed if I had attempted a book like that"], they were left confused, their emotional investment without a clear object.

In any case, even if we finally decide that Mailer's attempt is not as successful as he would have hoped, the reason can surely not be that Mailer has mixed his metaphors as aggressively as Shakespeare often did. It would not be hard to find passages in many great authors which, as Strier said, would make an audience laugh if read out of context.

In judging a passage of this intricate kind, then, we must think hard about what the kind really is and about how contexts work. Almost all of the marks that we found in "catfish" have here been changed. It is true that we still have metaphors that are clearly intended and that seem to serve *some* rhetorical purpose. But everything else is different. I won't bore you this time by running through all of the marks, but we must note that whatever was covert about "catfish" is not only overt here but positively brandished, as a stage magician would brandish his saw before hacking his assistant to pieces. Trumpets blaring, Mailer openly promises his metaphor and proclaims its "delivery" with a blaring pun on the woman's delivery.

Note secondly that the metaphors are so grotesquely scrambled that one cannot believe that the scrambling is accidental. Our schoolteacherly norms are deliberately violated, and we cannot easily tell whether, or at what point, the naughty boy is writing with his pen in his cheek. As it were.

Such metaphor, we should not forget as we analyze, has proved itself to have great power in our time. *Armies of the Night* received mostly rave reviews, and you may remember that the world on the whole palpitated to what was said—quite inaccurately—to be Mailer's invention of a new literary genre: the novel as history, history as a novel. Richard Gilman, re-viewing for the *New Republic*, wrote, "All the rough force of his imagination, his brilliant gifts of observation, his ravishing if often calculating honesty, his daring and his *chutzpah* are able to flourish on the steady ground of a newly coherent subject . . . history and personality confront each other with a new sense of liberation."

The key word here is *personality*. Such metaphoric muddlings, "rough," "brilliant," "ravishing," "calculating," "honest," "daring," are designed to flaunt personality—that is, a special ethos. The "character of the speaker" is flaunted to a degree that prevents our determining whether the passage is designed to win members to the antiwar camp or to construct another of Mailer's "advertisements" for himself. We have no way of knowing how many converts to the [antiwar] cause Mailer's book made, but we have plenty of evidence that it was immensely successful in selling Mailer.

I can remember trying to convince a student when the book first came out that it was cheaply self-serving, though it was for me on the "right side." I got nowhere, of course, because to her my judgment against Mailer's art meant that I was not really committed to opposing the war. Another graduate student confessed last week that when he first read the book years ago he found the experience overwhelmingly moving and that when he re-reads this page now he feels embarrassed about his earlier gullibility.

What kind of creature is it that can shift like that under our gaze? And how could we ever arrive at defensible judgments of its quality, not simply expressions of our prejudice? One possible answer to the first question is that Mailer has turned the ethos, which in "catfish" was a means to practical ends, into an end in itself. You will note that if we accepted that answer, we would have transported the passage out of the domains of rhetoric into the clear pure air of poetry—at least we would have done so according to one traditional way of distinguishing the two. Obviously the means-end distinction doesn't help us very much; if it is true that Mailer is making and advertising a self in such passages, he would surely have a right to insist that such a project is an essential part of his effort to attack the warlords.

To complicate things further, it is clear that Mailer is attempting, however desperately, to remake the ethos of America; though his metaphors call attention to him when we look at them critically, they are explicitly addressed to the reader's view of America's rebirth. Read uncritically, as my graduate student originally read them, the metaphors did their work, and their work was an inextricable mixture of argument about the war, portraiture of Mailer, and promise-threat about a glorious-gruesome future society.

Such metaphors are far more obviously constitutive of characters and societies than are the catfish kind. It is true that even the simplest weapon metaphor of the catfish kind will reveal to the perceptive critic the constitution of characters, both of the speaker and of the victim. But metaphors of Mailer's kind do not simply allow the critic to think of such matters; they require every reader to do so.

I needn't tell you that Mailer was not the first rhetor to attempt such immense metaphoric identifications of a constituted self and a constituted cause. Every great political speech or pamphlet reveals similar grand fusions. Toward the end of Edmund Burke's *Reflections on the Revolution in France*, for example, he attempts a metaphoric heightening appropriate to his antirevolutionary cause (I italicize some of the metaphors):

> Our people will find employment enough for a truly patriotic, free, and in-
> dependent spirit, in guarding what they possess [the British constitution]
> from violation. I would not exclude alteration, neither; but even when I
> changed, it should be to preserve. I should be led to *my remedy by a great
> grievance*. In what I did, I should follow the example of our ancestors. I
> would make the reparation as nearly as possible in *the style of the building*.
> A politic caution, a guarded circumspection, a moral rather than a com-
> plexional timidity, were among the ruling principles of our forefathers in
> their most decided conduct. Not being *illuminated with the light* of which
> gentlemen of France tell us they have got so abundant a share, they acted
> under a strong impression of the ignorance and fallibility of mankind. He
> that had made them thus fallible, rewarded them for having in their conduct
> attended to their nature. Let us imitate their caution, if we wish to deserve
> their fortune, or to retain their bequests. Let us add, if we please, but let us
> preserve what they have left; and *standing on the firm ground* of the British
> constitution, let us be satisfied to admire, rather than attempt to follow in
> their desperate flights, the *aëronauts of France*.
>
> I have told you [the ostensible French correspondent receiving Burke's
> "reflections"] candidly my sentiments. I think they are not likely to alter
> yours. I do not know that they ought. You are young; you cannot guide, but
> must follow the fortune of your country. But hereafter they may be of some
> use to you, in some future form which your commonwealth may take. In
> the present it can hardly remain; but before its final settlement it may be
> obliged to pass, as one of our poets says, "through great varieties of untried
> being," and in all its transmigrations to *be purified by fire and blood*.
>
> I have little to recommend my opinions but long observation and much
> impartiality. They come from one who has been no *tool of power*, no flatterer
> of greatness; and who in his last acts does not wish to belie the *tenor* of
> his life. They come from one, almost the whole of whose public exertion
> has been a struggle for the liberty of others; from one in whose breast *no
> anger durable or vehement has ever been kindled*, but by what he considered
> as tyranny; and who snatches from his share in the endeavors which are
> used by good men to discredit opulent oppression, . . . and [who], when *the
> equipoise of the vessel in which he sails may be endangered by overloading
> it upon one side*, is desirous of carrying *the small weight of his reasons* to
> that which may preserve its equipoise.

Despite the obvious differences between that and the Mailer quote, the similarities are close enough to justify comparison. Burke's metaphors are also mixed, though less wildly than Mailer's: remodelled buildings, lights, bequests, firm ground, desperate flights, fire and blood, steady tenors, kindled fires, overloaded vessels. The tone of self-advertisement as a passionately concerned, distressed citizen is thus similar, though Burke calls attention to himself much more explicitly. And, like Mailer, Burke implies that the fate of the whole nation depends on embracing a *national* character that will match the *personal* ethos of the speaker.

If we feel a difference in quality between them, we cannot, then, explain it with general rules of metaphoric practice. We cannot even employ that old and useful criterion, decorum: though Mailer's style might be considered indecorous according to general standards, it is entirely appropriate to its context. There is nothing out of keeping, either with the book that has preceded the passage or with the situation as Mailer has portrayed it: any reader who has followed Mailer this far will be offended if the speaker does *not* come close to losing control; only shouting, perhaps even shrieking, can do justice to the total vision he has tried to portray.

With a phrase like "total vision" I betray the immensity of the tasks concealed behind the search for a way to appraise metaphors. The metaphors we care for most are always embedded in metaphoric structures that finally both depend on and constitute selves and societies; any critic who presumes to say that Burke's concluding passage is superior to Mailer's, not just as a matter of "personal preference" but for reasons testable in public discourse, must claim to practice a criticism adequate to differences of quality among selves and societies.

What might such a criticism of metaphorical worlds conceivably be? Most obviously, it will not be peculiar to what we ordinarily call metaphor. It is likely, on the face of it, to make use of every art we have for criticizing cultures and it is certain to reveal that special kind of reflexivity that all cultural criticism reveals: the quality of the culture that produces the criticism. But if this is so, the dual criticism of metaphor that we seek—of the self-created characters and of the cultures made by metaphorists—will itself be a mode of preserving and improving our culture. Thus I am moving toward a grand thesis: *The quality of any culture will in part be measured both by the quality of the metaphors it induces or allows and the quality of the judges of metaphor that it educates and rewards.*[6] Such a thesis obviously suggests several lifetimes of inquiry, but since I seem to be stuck with it, let me now suggest, without attempting demonstration, some of the consequences we face if we take it seriously.

## IV

Whatever you may think about the implausibility of the quest for a reasoned discourse about metaphoric selves and cultures, it should be obvious from the word *quest* that I am shifting consciously to a radically different kind of inquiry. Studies of metaphor can themselves be thought about under at least four basic metaphors. We can *wield a scalpel* to analyze the *nature of the beast* regardless of whether it lives or dies. (If that seems too hostile a way of putting it, find your own metaphoric tool for what one does when specific metaphors are isolated from daily life and literary culture and probed for what or how they mean.) Moving to a slightly "warmer" classroom, study of metaphor can be the *solving of a puzzle*, taking literally Aristotle's statement that metaphors are like enigmas or riddles. Study of this kind will differ greatly, of course, depending on whether the puzzle solver expects what he finds to fit what he knew when he began or hopes for something new. If the former, he is like an explorer or anthropologist or missionary who has his conclusions fixed in advance and merely seeks new data to support predetermined causes; if the latter, he is more like a third kind of student, an explorer hoping to find *a better way to live*, or an anthropologist who, like Lévi-Strauss in *Tristes tropiques*, hopes that somehow his quest will allow him *to return a wiser if not a better man.*

In spite of an obvious hierarchy among these three, I see no reason to assume any of them to be illegitimate. But the study of metaphor is for me better described by a fourth kind of metaphor: *a quest for ways to improve my culture and myself*; that is, a search for a cure. And I am acutely aware that this might suggest Mailer's own way of employing metaphor. It is thus not hard to think of metaphoric ridicule for what I am suggesting: you are, I can hear a mocking voice say, turning the library into a spiritual culture emporium; or, you want to be both athletic coach and referee of the game. You will turn the critic and scholar into hollow prophetic voices rivaling the already too plentiful prophets on our scene. Let the bugle blow! God writhes in his bonds! Rush to the locks!

Let us take the point as a warning, but then remind ourselves that we are, if I am right, forced into something like this kind of talk whenever we study metaphor seriously. Mailer's extravagant style has forced us to bring into the open a mark of all figurative language. It is fairly easy to ignore this mark when dealing with metaphors out of context. But nobody can read Mailer's two paragraphs without discovering that, regardless of whatever subject is ostensibly being aggrandized or diminished, they call Norman Mailer on stage and demand of us that we deal with him personally, as we say, deal with him as a larger figure than he would have seemed had he followed any "normal" stylistic path. And we cannot claim to deal with him if we avoid judging his actual "size."

We may detest or love or fear or emulate the giant figure that emerges; we may indeed conclude that his effort to appear large has in fact turned him into a ridiculous dwarf or imp. But we cannot ignore his character, not only his character as a writer who aspires to special effects but his ethos as a human being who writes. Once we have as much attention called to the writer as these metaphors demand of us, we cannot stop our inferences about the person who has been responsible for all this. He will either bond us to him or alienate us, the very intimacy of the bonding increasing our distress. And immense consequences for our psyches, and hence for our culture, will result from our choices.

In short, the question is not *whether* we will judge the character of metaphorists and the societies that produce and sustain them. We all are forced to do that all the time, consciously or unconsciously—as the responses to Mailer illustrate. To *understand* a metaphor is by its very nature to *decide* whether to join the metaphorist or reject him, and that is simultaneously to decide either to be shaped in the shape his metaphor requires or to resist. The only remaining question is thus whether to attempt reasoned critical discourse about such judgments.


## V

My guess is that modern Western society is the only one in the history of mankind in which many thinkers, perhaps a majority, have assumed that criticism of character, and of cultures as they feed or destroy characters, is inherently nonrational. We are the first to have proclaimed that since we cannot use Locke's recommended scientific language for judgments of Mailer's or Burke's ethos, we can do no more than express our feelings and preferences about it. I have not, of course, proved here that we have been wrong in that assumption. But suppose we assume, as many inquirers have recently claimed, that we have been.[7] *If* we have been wrong, *if* rational criticism of values is possible, however difficult, then we have an immense obligation to build and improve our repertory of standards and of our ways of talking about standards. In this perspective, criticism of metaphoric worlds, or visions, becomes one clear and important—perhaps the clearest and most important—instance of a general human project of improving life by criticizing it. And it is a project that will necessarily entail the use of metaphor; literal propositions will not be adequate to convey many of the judgments that our criticism must attempt. I can now only hint at what such a claim for a metaphorical criticism of metaphor might mean.

What I am calling for is not as radically new as it may sound to ears that are still tuned to positivist frequencies. A very large part of what we value as our cultural monuments can be thought of as metaphoric criticism of metaphors and the characters who make them. The point is perhaps most easily made about the major philosophies. Stephen Pepper has argued, in *World Hypotheses*,[8] that the great philosophies all depend on one of four "root metaphors," formism, mechanism, organicism, and contextualism, and they are great precisely because they have so far survived the criticism of rival metaphors. Each view of the totality of things claims supremacy, but none has been able to annihilate the others. They all thus survive as still plausible, pending further criticism through further philosophical inquiry. In this view, even the great would-be literalists like Hobbes and Locke are finally metaphorists—simply committed to another kind of metaphor, one that to them seems literal. Without grossly oversimplifying, we could say that the whole work of each philosopher amounts to an elaborate critique of the inadequacy of all other philosophers' metaphors. What is more, the very existence of a tradition of a small group of great philosophies is a sign that hundreds of lesser metaphors for the life of mankind have been tested in the great philosophical—that is, critical—wars and found wanting.

In fact, we find in every major philosophy not just this implicit critique of all rival metaphors but quite explicit consideration of the validity of particular metaphors. When Thrasymachus, for example, tries to take over the inquiry in *The Republic* by offering as a metaphor for justice the relation of shepherd and sheep, Socrates (and Plato) are much too wise to dismiss him, as many moderns might do, by claiming that metaphors prove nothing. Instead, the dialogue painstakingly explores what such a picture means, gradually substitutes rival metaphors, and argues for their superiority. If we think of justice, for example, as like the relation of pilot to ship and passengers, we can suggest thereby that the pilot has a personal stake binding him to the welfare of the passengers: if the ship goes down, he goes with it, and serious consequences for the course of the inquiry follow. That metaphor in turn can be criticized by inventing others, until, by the end of *The Republic*, the parts of the soul, the parts of the state, and the organization of the universe itself have been richly analogized and illuminated. No one who has ever seriously pursued justice with Socrates through *The Republic* could ever again defend Thrasymachus's position, at least not in the simple form that has been permanently unmasked by Plato's critique of metaphor.

One can conceive, then, of a philosophical critique of Mailer's entire metaphoric effort, one that would place his implied embattled "self" onstage shouting his view of justice and injustice in the world, and then subject that self to steady questioning in the light of alternative metaphors. Such a critique would, no doubt, convince only those with a taste for philosophical argument; the Mailers of the world might ignore it. I obviously hope that all or most of us here would be receptive to it.

Perhaps more pertinent to the audience that was originally swayed by Mailer's pregnant giant and all that preceded her in the book would be a second kind of critique, the kind practiced by all good historians when they attempt to tell rival stories. I have several times implied that the effectiveness of Mailer's final page cannot really be determined aside from the whole of the work that leads to it. Another way of saying the same thing is to say that the adequacy of Mailer's metaphors is in part tested by their capacity to serve as a conclusion to an account of *these* events treated in *this* way. The fact that an intelligent and gifted author could face these events and build a relatively coherent and persuasive work about them, a work that moves with some success toward this deliberate jumble of metaphors at the end, is in itself evidence for some pertinence in the view that emerges. Many a metaphoric view of the Vietnam crisis could not survive the "proving" applied by this interesting (and exasperating) mind: "The national conflict about Vietnam is a tempest in a teapot"; "American intervention in Vietnam has been a Sunday school picnic"; "The marchers on Washington were a pack of self-serving, mercenary lackeys." Anyone who tries to write so much as three pages about that march, leading to any one of these three metaphors as climax, will see that Mailer's effort has, by its very existence, already earned the right to a serious critique. Thus any historical critique that is to offer a genuine challenge must be equally serious in attempting adequacy to the magnitude of the events.

It is entirely beyond my competence to suggest what such a rival history would contain, let alone to invent a final metaphoric page to surpass Mailer's; the difficulties in such a task are precisely the mark of why accomplishing it, or failing to, would constitute a valid kind of criticism of Mailer's own achievement.

For most of us, a more plausible direction would be a third kind of critique, a literary history that would tell the story not of the protest march itself but of this kind of literary work, describing it in careful detail and placing it with its siblings in the history of apocalyptic protest. My reference to Burke's final pages is only a hint toward what such a history would look for: the range of devices and effects achieved by similar rhetors attempting to produce a similar sense of political crisis. As Samuel Johnson insisted, all criticism of human achievements must at some point be comparative: What have other authors been able to accomplish with similar tasks? What have been the advantages and disadvantages of jumbling metaphors at the moment of greatest passion? What are the uses of explicit avowals of one's own character, as in Burke's climax and in so many pages of Mailer's? Which specific metaphors for a nation in agony have shown the greatest power to survive the criticism provided by other metaphors? M. H. Abrams's great literary history *Natural Supernaturalism* might be a kind of model for anyone seeking to place Mailer's vision in the history of apocalyptic and revolutionary metaphor.[9]

It should be clear from these three examples that almost every discipline can provide some of the criticism of metaphor that we are calling for. Every theology entails a metaphor for man's relation to God, and the great theologies are those that have survived after generations of criticism. Every anthropology entails metaphors for man's relation to man and to nature and culture, and a great deal of anthropological writing is devoted to criticizing bad metaphors. Marshall Sahlins's recent *Culture and Practical Reason*, for example, can be viewed as an extended critique of functional metaphors for how we invent our cultures.[10]

Similarly, most important literary critics have a good deal to say about how to distinguish the pusillanimous from the magnanimous, the metaphors that diminish us from those that enlarge us. And the major psychologists all develop ways of criticizing each other's metaphors for the soul. Why have Freud's metaphors for the soul's working parts proved so much more appealing to the modern world than, say, a psychology of the four humors? And why, at the other extreme, has the metaphor of the conditioned response, or operant conditioning, appealed to thousands of inquirers as the only truly literal way of talking about human behavior? It is interesting that those who advocate the simplest metaphors for man's soul are likely to prove most simplistic when they turn to criticism of souls and societies. B. F. Skinner, for example, lays about him freely with charges against our society's way of making its citizens; though he doesn't use the word *soul*, which for him would be a metaphoric disguise for *behavior*, his program, as announced most popularly in *Beyond Freedom and Dignity*, could be described as an aggressive critique both of freedom and autonomy metaphors for individual people and of the social measures that such metaphors lead us to practice.

## VI

The study of metaphor would, as I have said, be only one part of any revived practice of the two ethical criticisms: of characters and of societies that make characters. But there is one important fact about our society that makes metaphor an even more important part of such criticism for us than for any previous culture. For the first time in history, society finds itself offering immense rewards to a vast number of hired metaphorists, hired to make metaphors that will accomplish a predetermined end regardless of what they say about our character or do to it. Advertisers are hired to make some possession stand for happiness or well-being. I am of course not neutral on the question of whether we are on the whole harmed by their ministrations. There is an essentially corrupting, diminishing process in inducing desire for a predetermined happiness, a happiness that depends on possessing something, anything: some drug or exercise program. But one needn't accept my particular judgment, which would take some tall arguing to prove, to see that we have a totally new cultural situation that invites an army of critics to study and judge its effects.

It's true that all metaphorists in all cultures have hoped to be rewarded for their successes. Patronage and sometimes immense wealth have been freely given to those who could invent metaphoric visions of human life and happiness in that life. But those metaphorists were not paid to keep their visions small and precisely centered on possession. What they invented to *stand for* human happiness could best be described as having a kind of reflexive quality. All of the great poets seem to be saying something like this: my vision of what *stands for* human happiness is itself the activity of sharing pictures of what human life is or can be. Metaphor in this view is not a means to other ends but one of the main ends of life; sharing metaphors becomes one of the experiences we live for.

From this point of view, the great plays and narratives, like the great lyric poems, are themselves metaphors for what life is or can be; and they are thus a further great resource of criticism of what life is and of what other poets' metaphors say it is. We need not have explicit statements that "life is" this or that.

> Our birth is but a sleep and a forgetting:
> The Soul that rises with us, our life's Star,
>     Hath had elsewhere its setting,
>         And cometh from afar: . . .

Taken as a literal statement about preexistence, such comments are too easily rejected with counterstatements: no, our birth is much more (or less) than a sleep and a forgetting; the soul did *not* have elsewhere its setting; and so on. To argue with Wordsworth in that way would be like attempting to say to Mailer, "No, America is not much like a pregnant giant lost in the fog." Rather than such direct debate about propositions, good literature, whether or not it presents either literal or allegorical *statements* about life, provides an *experience* that takes place literally and yet somehow stands for or represents what life might be or ought to be.

I don't pretend to know what Aristotle really had in mind when he called poetry more philosophical than history because it is more "universal." But there is a sense in which every poem, whether overtly didactic or not, presents a claim to universal truth by implying a prologue for itself: "If you ask what life *is*, the best answer I can give at the moment is this representative slice of what it feels like—not a slice of life itself, as in the old formula, but a slice of representation, a metonymic bit":

> What shall I do with this absurdity—
> Oh heart, O troubled heart—this caricature,
> Decrepit age that has been tied to me
> As to a dog's tail?

The truth in Yeats's metaphoric vision of old age is, to be sure, of a kind that cannot be placed into direct contradiction with Wordsworth's radically different vision of childhood and youth. But that does not mean that the two visions claim no truth value. The metaphors criticize each other, in a sense contradict each other, but without the effort at mutual annihilation that logical contradictions imply.

No doubt it is this inherent aspiration of all literature to metaphoric truth that accounts for our tendency in modern times, as the old religious metaphors have weakened their hold on us, to turn literature to overt religious uses. When critics like Matthew Arnold found themselves treating poetry as the religion of the future, they were in fact simply expressing a kind of rivalry that was implicit in all secular metaphoric enterprises from the beginning: My story, though it may present no visible Gods and no expressions of piety, inevitably rivals yours that begins, "In the beginning was the Word." Our stories criticize each other as expressions of how life is.

The enduring religions have survived, one could argue, because the narrated metaphors that represent them have proved invulnerable to the criticism offered by rival metaphors. And the literary works that become classics are precisely those that have survived the unrelenting criticism presented by the literature of each new generation. Viewed in this perspective, even the most secular literary work is engaged in the religious exchange. The most innocent nonsense poem or nonreferential aleatoric verbal game says to us, "Life as it is, or as it ought to be, is best known as you experience me. I stand for bigger things." And every such work is in turn criticized by every other work. Bellow's *Herzog* says to Robbe-Grillet's *Project for a Revolution in New York*, "Your absurdist view is absurd and immoral, negatively sentimental." *Project* replies, "Your affirmation is a sentimental lie."

In calling for a criticism that would take such matters seriously I am, of course, violating the aesthetic presuppositions of many modern literary critics. I am saying that there can be no "innocent" art, no art that can be considered free of ethical responsibility. Since every work of art will, to the degree that it succeeds, change the character of individuals and thus of cultures, and since culture will, to the degree that it is viable, determine the production of this or that kind of art, critics cannot honestly dodge the task of attempting to judge, dangerous and difficult as that task will always be. And the judgment will always entail criticism of metaphor.

The great critics have all accepted this responsibility, in one form or another. The great artists have all known it. And from the beginning they have often, though not always, dramatized within their works their awareness of how their art presented a metaphoric vision of life and thus a critique of life without art and of other artists' visions.

Metaphors as courtroom weapons; metaphors as advertisements for myself; metaphors as sales pitches, or as potential firebombs capable of destroying entire cultures overnight in prime time; metaphors as love letters to readers; metaphors as visions of how making metaphor itself redeems our lives. . . . Any criticism that attempts to discriminate among the problems and possibilities in such an assemblage will not be easy and it will not be precise. It will be neither univocal in its methods nor certain in its conclusions. It will itself be a part of the process it studies.

All serious study of anything is, no doubt, life-justifying. But there might be a special flowering about a criticism that pursued the two kinds of ethical criticism I have adumbrated: discriminating among the characters and cultures that metaphors build, in the belief that the quality of any culture is in large part the quality of the metaphorists that it creates and sustains.

[*Addendum: After the conference we were asked to add further speculation about metaphor. Here is what I added.*]

## Ten Literal "Theses"

Because my paper was often metaphorical, some participants in the symposium expressed puzzlement about my literal meaning, especially about the passage from Mailer. Here are ten *literal* "theses" that the paper either argues for, implies, or depends on.

1. What metaphor *is* can never be determined with a single answer. Because the word has now become subject to all of the ambiguities of our notions about similarity and difference, the irreducible plurality of philosophical views of how similarities and differences relate will always produce conflicting definitions that will in turn produce different borderlines between what is metaphor and what is not. We thus need taxonomies, not frozen single definitions, of this "essentially contested concept."

2. What any metaphor *says* or *means* or *does* will always be to some degree alterable by altering its context. Every metaphor cited in any of the symposium papers could be made to communicate various shades of meaning; each of them could even be made, by employing the easy terms of irony, to say the reverse of what it seems to say.

3. Whether or not such transformations occur, the receiver's process of interpretation is itself part of what is communicated; the activity of interpretation, performed at the speaker's command, produces a "bonding" which is part of the "meaning." Thus the act of interpreting metaphor will always be more intense ("other things being equal") than engagement with whatever we take to be nonmetaphoric (for some, what is *literal*; for others, what is *normal*).

4. The question of what a metaphor *means* is thus actually many different questions. If by "meaning" we mean "all that is effected by an utterance," or "all that is communicated by a speaker," then the meaning of most metaphors is far richer than most accounts have acknowledged, even those that claim that metaphoric meanings are mysterious or ineffable.

5. It follows that whether any metaphor is judged to be *good* is inescapably dependent on its context: what surrounds it in the text, spoken or written, and who speaks it to whom for what purpose. But "context" is another essentially contested concept: different critical purposes will discover and impose different contexts.

6. For those who agree upon a given purpose in a given social context, judgments of value can be simple, unambiguous, and as nearly certain as anyone could reasonably ask in this vale of uncertainties.

7. Even such judgments are not, however, simple judgments of craft in any usual sense, because the deliberate use of a recognizable metaphor (a special case of the deliberate use of any abnormality, any figuring) inevitably invites judgments of the speaker's character. No jury member can resist engagement with the character of the metaphorist. Any critic

can carry the engagement to further levels of judgment by making explicit what a given metaphor implies about its maker.

8. Thus judgments of skill are always complicated, or complicatable, with questions of intent, and judgments of intent entail judgments of characters working in the cultures that both produce and are produced by them. Most of the metaphors we care about are, like Mailer's, immensely complicated, and they are embedded in contexts that force us to think about questions that go beyond matters of "craft."

9. The resources available to the critic who would judge characters and cultures are far richer than is suggested by our usual notions of "literary criticism." The best criticism of Mailer might well be another history of the same events, a history laden with alternative metaphors; or it might be a philosophical inquiry or a religious tract or an epic poem.

10. A good measure of our culture would be our capacity to produce such criticism, that is, to create metaphoric visions that would rival and improve on Mailer's inventive, courageous, but finally self-defeating blast.

## CHAPTER 6

*To allow readers to appreciate the ironic depth of the research that went into preparing this essay, I might remind them that it was done long before the author had discovered current techniques for looking up terms—resources like Google or Yahoo. (You might ask yourself, as you read, "How on earth did this guy uncover all these examples?" And you might reflect, "Isn't it ironic that he offers not a single footnote, when most of his other essays here are overloaded with them?")*

*Ironically, the author was not aware, way back in 1983, of what would happen to ironic language after the 9/11 disaster. Essay after essay appeared declaring that, since the attack has made it clear that there is a real distinction between good and evil, IRONY was dead. Irony, taken as a synonym for radical skepticism about values, could not survive such a clear demonstration that values are real. Only slowly did a few defenders of other meanings fight back. And few of them even touched on the ways in which my final points about cosmic ironies relate to the awfulness of 9/11.*

This essay was originally published in *Georgia Review* 37, no. 4 (winter 1983): 719–37.

# The Empire of Irony

I begin with a strong temptation not to discuss the *empire* of irony but to conduct a requiem for the terms *irony, ironic,* and *ironically*. A couple of years ago I began to collect written and spoken claims that this or that event or statement was ironic, and the collection became so large, and the various meanings so diverse, that I soon suspected that anybody who used the words could not possibly have any precise meaning in mind.

Surely we should be suspicious of any terms that are used as frequently, as broadly, and with as little evidence of thought as is now true of the "ironic" family. Apparently no author can feel entirely respectable unless one or another of the clan appears at least once in every article or talk. Three years ago at the Modern Language Association meeting in Houston, I kept a tally of how many times the words occurred in the papers I heard. It came to an average of one and three quarters per paper. Since then I've been keeping a file of conversational snippets, newspaper clippings, and quotations from scholars and critics. It is a most amazing collection, ranging from street talk to the kinds of esoteric reference you will find in the titles of papers read at academic meetings and published in scholarly journals.

And the range of *meanings* is staggering. "I intend this overview of this situation of senior English professors to be sympathetic, not *ironic*." Here the word must mean something like "satirical," a usage that can claim a relatively long, respectable history. But what, then, of the following? "It is surely a bitter *irony* that the employment of excessively large numbers of teaching apprentices has resulted in punishing those apprentices who succeed in completing their graduate work." We might translate that one as "an unintended but embittering social disaster," or perhaps "a bitter twist of fate."

Flora Lewis writes in the *New York Times*: "It is *ironic* that the United States, proud of its flexible approach to problem-solving and economic growth, should be digging in its heels on the principle of private finance and damn the consequences." Here the word seems to mean something like "inconsistent," or perhaps—judging from what she goes onto say, "lamentably inconsistent"—"a regrettable betrayal of our past principles."

"An *ironic* reminder of the neighborhood's past," a feature writer says of a visit to the Bronx, "is the somewhat shabby 'House on Stilts.'" Here we learn, reading on, that the author means much more than any word can convey; the house was built on stilts in order to achieve a posh street address, and since the house is now decayed, what was once an effort to achieve status now looks shabby. Should that be "tragic"? Or perhaps "pathetic"? No, evidently it's ironic.

"*Ironically*, the UNHCR [U.N. High Commission for Refugees] received its accolade at a time when several donor countries were questioning its management." Here it may mean something like "embarrassingly" or "incongruously" or "paradoxically."

So far these examples seem to have at least a core of shared connotation: something like "contrary to what some people might expect." But what, then, do we make of the following? "Among the commonly held beliefs about the drug [cocaine] were that it was a performance enhancer; a mood elevator; a sexual stimulant; a nonaddictive drug. *Ironically*, medical science could not disprove these beliefs." We note here, as in other examples, the strange grammar of this strange adverb. Modifying nothing, dangling in solitude, the adverb resists our questions about whether medical science was unable to disprove these beliefs *un*ironically—that is, "just as we would expect."

Finally, an even clearer case of reversal of meaning: "One special *irony* is that some departments' public rhetoric denies the plaintive expressions of neglect we encountered in our surveys." Surely here the word means almost the direct opposite of what it often means. Instead of "unexpectedly" or "to our surprise," here it clearly means something like "*just as we would expect*, in a world full of nasty hypocrisy, the rhetoric of departments denies the suffering of job applicants." In short, the word now is simply a polite cover for a charge of expected hypocrisy.

So we see that *irony* and *ironic* have become little more than all-purpose, flexible slot-fillers, vogue words useful whenever one does not want to choose stronger, clearer terms. Or whenever one dares not do so because they will be too clear. Or whenever one simply has nothing to say and wants to sound educated. When *ironic* means simply "odd" or "interesting," uncritical minds can quite literally call anything under the sun ironic. They are like the lovely, knuckleheaded Harriet Smith in Jane Austen's *Emma*. Thinking about Farmer Martin, and unconsciously revealing her rising love for him, she says, "He was four-and-twenty the 8th of last June, and my birthday is the 23rd—just a fortnight and a day's difference! Which is very odd!" In 1983, Harriet, like President Reagan, would have not said "odd" but "ironic." (A colleague of mine once heard a radio announcer say that "the tornado struck out of an ironically blue sky.")

For those who would like to rescue the ironic terms for useful service, I provide here a little catalogue of useful synonyms. When in need, simply consult my little thesaurus, truncated as it is, and discover what you really want to say.

NOUNS (for substitution in such sentences as "He was using [or exhibiting] irony."):

| | | |
|---|---|---|
| banter | obscurity | sarcasm |
| buffoonery | opacity | satire |
| derision | overstatement | sly deception |
| equivocation | parody | teasing |
| jesting | persiflage | understatement |
| lying | raillery | wit |
| obliquity | ridicule | |

ADJECTIVES (for sentences like "She was ironic."):

| | | |
|---|---|---|
| ambiguous | furtive | pussyfooting |
| baffling | gnomic | puzzling |
| cabalistic | hoodwinking | sardonic |
| cryptic | hypocritically humble | self-abasing |
| deceptive | irresponsible | sneaky |
| duplicitous | noncommittal | sneering |
| equivocal | obscure | unforthcoming |
| equivocating | profound | unintelligible |
| evasive | puckish | vague |

OTHER ADJECTIVES (for sentences like "It was ironic."):

| | | |
|---|---|---|
| aberrant | enigmatic | peculiar |
| abnormal | extraordinary | perplexing |
| amorphous | idiosyncratic | preternatural |
| anachronistic | incongruous | singular |
| anomalous | irregular | surprising |
| confusing | monstrous | unnatural |
| contradictory | odd | unparalleled |
| disturbing | paradoxical | unprecedented |

ADVERBS (for sentences like "Ironically enough, the tornado struck while
I was sound asleep."):

| contrary to what | embarrassingly | shockingly |
| everyone expected | horrifyingly | to make matters worse |
| disappointingly | incongruously | |

Often, simple expressions like "instead" or "to everyone's surprise" will
work. Frequently the best revision, when you see an "ironically" threatening to blot your page, is simply to cut it, or to substitute a "but" or "yet" or
"nevertheless." "Ironically enough, she never did achieve her goal." Either
cut the phrase entirely or decide whether you mean "sadly" or "tragically"
or "appropriately"—or perhaps simply "as all who knew her hoped."

We should not be surprised that (please rephrase that as "ironically
enough") this chaotic range of practical uses is reflected in critics' talk
about irony. If one reads through the titles in bibliographies of works on
irony, one is forced to conclude that their authors are not talking about
a single phenomenon, unless that phenomenon is defined so generally as
to be beyond all study, all hope of understanding. Perhaps it would be
something like "Every phenomenon in the universe that does not appear
or behave exactly as I [the speaker] expected it to behave or wanted it to
behave."

My first suggestion, then, turning now to my true subject, is that we
face not a single creature, waiting to be defined or tamed, killed or revived, but rather *many* different creatures that share at best only a family
resemblance. In *theory*, this means that we have a problem in explaining
why the kinfolk hold these family reunions. *Practically*, this means that if
we want to talk with each other about the many matters that are loosely
called ironic, we should absolutely ban the words *irony, ironic,* and *ironically, except* when we are willing and able to add a qualifying word or
phrase and when—after doing so—we see that the "ironic" term really
adds something. No one can legislate for us what these or any other words
are to mean. But each of us can at least seek some degree of clarity about
what they are to mean in a given discussion, and that clarity can come, as
the terms now exist, only through using qualifying adjectives and explicit
definitions.

It is *deeply* ironic that the adjectives and definitions I suggested in my
book *A Rhetoric of Irony* have not taken the world by storm. That is to say,
I am disappointed, but not surprised. Nobody's adjectives are likely to suit
everybody. But for me it is impossible to talk sense about our indiscriminate
pile of stuff without some such distinctions as the following:

1. Some things we call ironies are not embodied in language, and some are. If tornadoes can be ironic or appear ironically, they do so in a different sense from that in which Jonathan Swift is ironic. We might call them natural ironies or ironies of natural events, though I would prefer other terms like *coincidences* or *acts of God*. Note that such ironies are in literally infinite supply, because every event is a coincidence from *some* point of view.

2. Of those ironies that are not embodied in language, some are the results of frustrated human intentions and some are not. Usage now says that whenever someone's intended result is frustrated, the result can be called ironic ("Ironically enough, it rained before . . ."). Again, note that such ironies, which might be better called surprises or frustrations, are infinite in number. "I intended to impress you with this speech. Ironically enough, you . . . " Currently the sentence could be completed with either "were impressed" or "were not impressed," so little does the expression mean by itself.

3. Similarly, of those ironies that are embodied in language, some are the result of human intentions and some are not. *Intended verbal ironies*, designed by human speakers who expect them to be seen as ironies, are now only a small branch of the huge family, though once they were the whole clan.

4. Of intended verbal ironies, some are intended to be seen as "stable," interpretable, with some stopping point in the act of interpretation, and some are intended to be essentially unstable, with the hermeneutical act inherently, deliberately endless.

Stable *intended* ironies go like this, *when they work*:

a. A *Doonesbury* cartoon shows a mother complaining about having to finish a legal brief by a deadline. "I've been reading the law for six years now," she says to her daughter, "and I'm still no good at it. I swear, sometimes I think I'd go back to being a homemaker if I weren't even more incompetent at that."

   "Sure you would, Mother," the daughter says.

   "You're right, I wouldn't," her mother replies.

b. My colleague Herman Sinaiko is reading a committee proposal for reforming the curriculum. He looks up from the document and says, "Most exciting!"

   "What's wrong with it?" another colleague asks.

c. A couple of years ago the dean of Grinnell College, Wally Walker, wrote a letter to the school paper attacking vandalism and pointing out how many good things could have been financed with the fourteen dollars per student that vandalism had cost Grinnell in the previous year. In the next issue of the paper there was an anonymous letter that read like this:

> After reading Wally Walker's ridiculous and half-baked letter to the editor in last week's *S&B*, I was exceedingly pleased that he is being replaced as Dean. Wally, I hope you do shut up and fade away for the next eleven years because your scurrilous and archaic attack on vandalism betrays an appalling ignorance and lack of sensitivity toward contemporary college students. . . . no administrator who fails to understand the phenomenon of vandalism (and even partakes of it a little) can ever hope to succeed at a progressive liberal arts college. Vandalism is more than just wanton, irrational destruction of other people's property. It is a life-affirming, consciousness-expanding experience which is an integral and essential part of the modern youth subculture, and it's time we brought it out in the open. Let me explain first that I only do vandalism occasionally— breaking windows and shooting out lights with pellet guns two or three times a week.

The author then moved to a solemn analysis of why vandalism is increasing in our time:

> Frantically searching for signposts on the road of life, we seek meaning and significance in our class. . . . we yearn to escape from the alienating straitjacketing constraints of the everyday world and seek refuge in one where the only laws are those of projectile motion.

After giving good reasons for vandalism—such as that it is better to break inanimate objects than to kill animate ones—the author concluded:

> Fourteen dollars per student is a very small price to pay for the peace of mind and mental health of the majority of the student body . . . vandalize something today.

Most readers—though as we shall see in a moment, by no means all— recognized early in the letter that they were dealing with an ironic spoof.

d.  I hear a waitress in a cafe, standing at the cash register, say to a male customer: "Don't give me an argument on Monday morning. Just shell out." She sounds angry indeed, and I expect a fight. But the man replies, smiling as he pays his bill, "Damn it, Belle, why'n hell don't you give yuself a good night's sleep before coming to work and takin' it out on us?" After overhearing a few more such friendly exchanges, I finally have to conclude that they are in fact flirting—just like Beatrice and Benedick.

But, of course, such intended stable ironies are not always stable. Our lives are full of failed intentions with ironic jokes, and some of our best ironists know how to exploit those failures. A couple of years ago Donald Barthelme published a clever and baffling piece in the *New Yorker*, called "Kierkegaard Unfair to Schlegel." He engaged in some preliminary sparring with the question of what irony is for—"I turn my irony against the others" for political purposes, the narrator says. Then an interviewer appears out of nowhere.

> Q. You are an ironist. (!)
> A. It's useful.
> Q. How is it useful?
> A. Well, let me tell you a story . . .

It's a long story concluding with the claim that irony is useful in simply wiping out "clutter." But then the narrator goes on to consider Kierkegaard's theory that irony is really an expression of the subjective freedom that would annihilate one reality without taking the responsibility of finding another; it "softens and mitigates that deep pain which would darken and obscure all things" and prevents our finding, in religion, a reconciliation with the world.

> Without discussing whether or not the true reconciliation [to things as they are] is religion . . . let me say that I believe that Kierkegaard is here unfair to Schlegel. I have reasons for this . . . but my reasons are not so interesting. What is interesting is my making the statement that I think Kierkegaard is unfair to Schlegel . . . Because that is not what I think at all. We have to do here with my own irony. Because of course Kierkegaard was "fair" to Schlegel. In making a statement to the contrary I am attempting to . . . [well] I might have several purposes—simply being provocative, for example. But mostly I am trying to annihilate Kierkegaard in order to deal with his disapproval.
> Q. Of Schlegel?
> A. Of me.

And the narrator trails off into other anecdotes.

Now it should be obvious that all intended stable ironies are potentially unstable for any reader who decides to reject the author's intentions as well as for any author who, like Barthelme, intends to undermine all guesses about his intentions. Any reader can, with a little imagination or carelessness or stupidity, double-cross any ironist simply by discovering readings that the author never dreamed of. Many an intended irony produces an irony of fate when sleepy readers take the ironies straight. The anonymous letter defending vandalism turned out to have been written by Dean Wally Walker and landed him in a peck of trouble when some students and many trustees, for reasons he might have predicted, took it straight and thought the dean had lost his marbles. [*In 2004, re-reading Harriet Beecher Stowe's* Uncle Tom's Cabin, *I'm impressed by how many of her ironic strokes deserve quotation here. Many readers have misread the ironies, attacking her for expressing contempt for Negroes by using the word* nigger *and for downgrading blacks in innumerable passages where she actually intends full stable ironies.*]

Every such misunderstanding of stable irony is itself ironic, according to other definitions, and when we consider all the daily misunderstandings in the world, we may at first find no wonder in the fact that members of the irony family have extended their empire to cover the whole cosmos. But I think we should go on wondering, and here I'd like to wonder in two directions.

## II

First, the simpler question: Why does almost everyone, in every culture, go on attempting stable ironies, when to do so gets ironists into so much trouble?

When Dean Wally Walker wrote a perfectly straight attack on vandalism, he got into no trouble at all. But when he wrote the ironic letter praising vandalism for what he thought were obviously absurd reasons, he got himself and Grinnell College into a mess of trouble. Why do so many of us take that kind of risk?

One standard answer is that we do it in self-protection. Whenever we use irony, we are disguising a truth, usually a hostile or embarrassing truth, one that we don't dare speak right out. The conversation between the waitress and the customer must really express a secret hostility: she really *didn't* want any back talk on a Monday morning. And Wally Walker perhaps secretly would like a bit more vandalism, or perhaps he believes (but dare not say) that we all need a little vandalism just to keep going.

It's not hard to find examples of irony used as self-protection.

> "You called me a stupid ass."
> "Yeah, but I was being ironic."

"How do I know you were being ironic?"

"Well, you know that I don't think you're stupid, don't you?"

But though some examples fit the theory, many—perhaps most—do not. When the popular song says, "I don't love you—no, not much!" (and when Sinaiko calls that dull report "most exciting"), there isn't the slightest possibility that the surface words express a forbidden or scary truth.

A second theory is that we use irony simply because it is pleasant. Straight talk is comparatively dull; irony makes things more interesting, more fun. A life with nothing but straight statement would be intolerably dull; we play with irony for the same reason we play other games. We are in fact all members of the species *Homo ludens*, the game-playing animal, and there are two supreme games, both akin to and indeed practiced in poetry: the play of irony and the play of metaphor. It is not hard to find examples that would seem to bear out *this* theory. Much of the ironic writing I love best seems quite detached from any purpose other than sheer fun. Here's the adolescent Jane Austen, writing a mock history of England for her family's amusement:

> Henry the 6th
>
> I cannot say much for this Monarch's sense. Nor would I if I could, for he was a Lancastrian. I suppose you know all about the wars between him and the Duke of York who was of the right side; if you do not, you had better read some other history, for I shall not be very diffuse in this, meaning by it only to vent my spleen *against*, and skew my hatred *to* all those people whose parties or principles do not suit with mine, and not to give information. This King married Margaret of Anjou, a Woman whose distresses and misfortunes were so great as almost to make me who hate her, pity her. It was in this reign that Joan of Arc lived and made such a row among the English. They should not have burnt her—but they did. There were several Battles between the Yorkists and Lancastrians, in which the former (as they ought) usually conquered. At length they were entirely overcome; the King was murdered—The Queen was sent home—and Edward the 4th ascended the Throne.

Little but pleasure here—the pleasure of a family sharing the fun with their child-genius as she reads aloud to them. But again we can object that the sheer pleasure theory applies to some ironies but not to all. There is no doubt that many a commonplace message can be enlivened by turning it into irony, or that irony, like metaphor, provides some of our most marvelous delights. But here we must face the uncomfortable fact that when ironies are piled on ironies—when ironic moments, each presumably de-lightful in itself, are multiplied—suddenly all readers discover that they are bored.

There have been critics who would deny this limit, and I see no way to prove that there is no reader in the world for whom my principle would not work. But I know from my experience with Art Buchwald and Russell Baker, on their bad days, and with most ironic essays by students, that though pleasure is sought, always, it is not a sufficient drive to explain the production of *all* this stuff. As the narrator of Barthelme's story goes on to say, at one point,

A.  But I love my irony.
Q.  Does it give you pleasure?
A.  A poor . . . an unsatisfactory. . . .

Thinking about all this led me a few years ago to a third explanation, one with two parts. In *A Rhetoric of Irony* I argued that behind all other reasons for intended ironies lie two deeper reasons: with irony, we communicate both more efficiently and more effectively than with straight talk. Irony is more efficient, I said, because it communicates more in less space. Sinaiko is able, with the word "exciting," to communicate not just the notion of dull, the opposite of exciting, but also his full sense of contempt for the report. The reader must share Sinaiko's values to some degree even to understand the real meaning of "exciting," and Sinaiko has thus said much more with the one word than he could have with the word "dull." Secondly, irony is more effective because the little intellectual dance we must perform to understand it brings us into a tight bonding with the ironist: the ironist has built an intricate structure and we have reconstructed it, following that lead; we are thus caught in the tight web of his or her mental processes, and what is communicated is much more than the mere message. Even if we say, when we are done, that we disagree with Sinaiko's conclusion, we have been forced to take part in his mental processes for the duration of our effort to understand irony, and we have thus been bonded to his way of thinking much more closely than if he had said simply, "How dull." Because our emotions, both sympathy and hostility, are inevitably bound up in any such aggressive activity of reconstructing meanings, the irony has thus engaged us in a way that no straight talk ever could.

Obviously much irony of this kind is by no means secret or self-protective but open and blatant. What makes it qualify for any such adjec-tive as "stable" is precisely that the ironist actually intends us to catch the irony, even if we do imagine someone who is so stupid as to miss it.

In my book I worked hard at a fourth explanation. Perhaps I even over-worked it in my zeal to undermine the half-truths about how irony is the mother of confusions and fragmentations. Whenever a piece of intended irony works, when a clever ironist manages to hook us, we come closer than at any other time to a full *identification of two minds*. The only figure that can rival irony in achieving this effect is metaphor, but I think that the bonding is even tighter with irony than with metaphor. The complex path of almost instantaneous inference that both minds must trace together constitutes a kind of proof that they are of the same stuff. In the moment of identification, the receiver loses his or her private identity in a way that is more dramatic than in our ordinary surrender to other people's meanings. The borderline between ironist and interpreter in fact disappears. The intri-cate steps that Jane Austen's and Barthelme's minds have taken, we have been required to take with them, and our minds thus become in part in-distinguishable from theirs. Thus whenever we dwell with a master ironist for a long time—for example, when we read *Don Quixote* for the several days or weeks or years that are required to read it well—the part of us that becomes identical with the author's mind can become so substantial that we come to feel made over, or at least inhabited, accompanied by the powerful voice of the invader.

For more than two thousand years, a standard way of talking about true friendship was to say that it consists of one soul in two bodies. Insofar as my friend and I both desire the same things, believe the same things, enjoy the same things, and insofar as I want his or her well-being as much as I want my own, we become ensouled with one soul, animated by the same principles or mental patterns. Well, in moments of effective ironic communication, when much remains unspoken and much is understood that is not said, the two minds engaged together come closer to identity than is ever likely with straight talk.

This is a very curious matter, considering how many people have talked about irony as the mother of confusion and how often irony goes awry. When I become sure that an author is being ironic, I am often surer of our true communion than when an author says things normally. When Ring Lardner writes "'Shut up,' she explained," I know with delicious certainty that he intended a joke and I know what joke it was. He and I live together in that moment far more intensely than would have been true if he had written "'Shut up,' she snapped, while trying to maintain a tone of superior calm." In short, though some of your ironies may baffle me, whenever they do not, when I know that you are being ironic, I know you.

When Jane Austen gives her ironic account, she leads us not only to infer far more facts and judgments about the Yorkists and Lancastrians and certain kinds of history than could have been said "straight" in the same space, but also to infer a great deal of warming knowledge about the kind of person she is—that kind that we ourselves have had to become in order to understand her. That author—whether merely playing a game, like Austen; or trying to induce thought about life and art, like Barthelme; or trying to reinforce argument, like Swift—that human being is my kind of human being, my friend. And does not friendship, genuine friendship, redeem the world?

You can no doubt imagine how pleased I felt, in pursuit of this theory, when I ran across Edith Wharton's comment on her friendship with the ironist Henry James:

> Perhaps it was our common sense of fun that first brought about our understanding. The real marriage of true minds is for any two people to possess a sense of humour or irony pitched in exactly the same key, so that their joint glances at any subject cross like interarching search-lights. I have had good friends between whom and myself that bond was lacking, but they were never really intimate friends; and in that sense Henry James was perhaps the most intimate friend I ever had, though in many ways we were so different.

## III

But this brings us to the second large question: Why do people use words like *ironic* for so many kinds of talk that are not at all like those we have examined, and for so many events that have no intending ironist back of them?

So long as we are thinking mainly about ironies intended to be read as stable, these explanations for its imperialism can account for things pretty well. In my book I spent perhaps three-quarters of my time on the finite, limited kind. The unintended—nay, no doubt "ironic"—result was that some people concluded I didn't care about or value or even believe in the possibility of unintended, unstable, unlimited ironies, what might even be called cosmic, metaphysical ironies. Well, I do, and I shall now prove that I do by taking the true ironologist's oath of office: I hereby affirm that I do, I really do, believe in all that stuff. But what, in fact, is it that we are talking about?

Could it be that the reason we are all so free with calling events ironic these days is that we are, as always, in need of ways to express our sense that there is, in the universe itself—in what used to be called "the whole of creation"—an ironic principle? I myself think so. We all know that in things as they are, in the universe as it is, in man's nature as *it* is, there is a principle that renders our every move, our every word, inadequate, undercuttable, subject to corrective crosslights at least some of which are beyond our vision. And we always need a language to express our sense of that principle. So: I believe, brothers and sisters; I not only believe in, I positively embrace that principle, the principle of cosmic irony. Indeed, I wish to celebrate that very elusive Supreme Being, the ironic universe, that glorious mocker of man's enterprise, the great *I am* who qualifies everything we say with a devastating "That's what *you* think!"

Many of you will recognize what I have just said as placing me in one branch of the romantic ironists: those who also celebrated, rather than deploring or lamenting or cursing, the ironic universe—that "infinite absolute negativity," as Kierkegaard called it, the ironic principle that always lurks ready to expose our finitude. To the romantic ironist that principle is real, and we are always in need of ways to express its reality. For some of these ironists, its negative and frustrating force in human lives has been so real that its negations have become the ultimate truth of life. The result has been nihilism and despair. We have in our time a spate of "principles" and slogans like Murphy's Law, words dramatizing, with wry comic force, just how universally the gremlins seem to operate. For others—I am joining this branch here—awareness of how beautifully and brilliantly the cosmos exhibits our limitations has been cause for awe and even celebration.

What the romantic ironists of this latter kind can be said to have discovered is not a new truth and not a truth that died when romanticism died (if it ever did). Rather, they have discovered a distinctive way of talking about a condition of our lives that predates and underlies all thinking about them. That condition had been expressed by the older philosophers and theologians something like this: We find ourselves in a universe that works in ways not dependent simply on our individual wills nor designed simply to fulfill our wishes: our world is contingent, a world of creatures. That world is not only full of accidents that violate our deepest desires; it is, even in its deepest regularities, even when it is *most* rational, radically indifferent to many—perhaps even to most—of our desires and expectations. And when the working of the universe—or as it was often put, when the will of God—conflicts with my will, it is up to me to change my will. That is to say, the burden of proof in conflicts between me and the ironic universe was formerly always seen, by those who saw deepest, as placed upon me. God moved in a mysterious (not to say ironic) way, *His* wonders to perform—not mine.

Now, so long as thoughtful people could believe in some kind of infinitely powerful and ultimately benign creator as the central explanation of how things worked, and also in a mysterious counterforce, the devil, who explained why and when they did *not* work, the mystery that things so often do not work out for our visible good could still be talked about as itself somehow accidental or temporary. Ideally things will work, or work out, if given time; the devil will be conquered, and those of us who have lived right will find in our final blessing that things have indeed served our deepest desires. No final irony!

What many people decided, as the eighteenth century wore into the nineteenth, was that things were in one sense more complicated, in another sense more simple than the traditional view. As faith in a supreme and supremely rational Lord waned, and as belief in a literal devil disappeared, the essential nature of the universe—the picture of how and why it works as it does—necessarily shifted. People who had believed that the universe promised to work out, somewhere, somehow, as triumphantly rational (that is, as just, intelligible, and benign)—such people came to see the universe as not keeping its promises; or, perhaps more accurately, they saw it as giving promises that by their nature did not mean what they seemed to say.

At first people could talk comfortably about God as the supreme ironist, seeming to make promises that He had not in fact made, and finally fulfilling the secret promise that He *had* made. But most intellectuals by our time have lost all sense that a supreme being made them any promises in the first place. Brought up as atheists, people could hardly talk of God, the supreme ironist. How could a nonbeing who says nothing be an ironist?

Instead, people in our time tend to say only that "things"—or "skies"—"are ironic," or that the universe as a whole betrays humankind's expectations by undermining every belief and every hope. "If *things* can possibly go wrong *they* will." And of course the burden of proof has shifted: now if the universe surprises me or disappoints me, it has betrayed *me*—let *me* down, not shown me *up*. But for most of the romantics, the memory of having been promised something was still strong; and they could thus say, with a powerful sense of wry, often bitter discovery, that *God* was an ironist. Some of them, of course, could still believe that the resulting ironies were glorious, not hateful, but others set the tone for modern nihilistic bitterness about a world that creates us only to destroy us.

It's obvious—to repeat—that God cannot be an ironist if there is no God. If God is really dead, so too is one kind of irony—*intended, stable, cosmic* irony. God's intentions must die with Him. If no promises have been made—if every human aspiration is equally a *human* invention and thus a human mistake, since it will finally be frustrated—then everything we say is equally illusory. To say that such a universe is ironic, as many moderns have chosen to, is quite different from saying that a God-ruled *universe* is ironic. It must be bitterly, dully, monotonously ironic; every affirmation is equally affirmable and deniable, all purposes equally defensible, equally illusory. Not only is every literary work by definition undermined by the ironic truth that to attempt it was to pursue an illusion; every artist should recognize that only silence makes the kind of nonsense that makes any sense, as Samuel Beckett has so beautifully failed to realize for us. Every statement can only lead to aporia, or rather to that kind of aporia upon aporia that we have labeled *mise en abîme*.

Living a coherent, intelligible life in such a universe is impossible—not even suicide is available as an enterprise worth undertaking. So it is hardly surprising that our century has been full of efforts to rediscover a universe that after all does make promises, promises of a kind that, from my perspective here, might make it possible to *celebrate* a universal cosmic irony. Escape routes from a positivism that itself led to complete skepticism have been offered us in great number. All of them—*all* of the new sociologies, anthropologies, structuralisms, rhetorical epistemologies, all of the new religions and revivals of old religion, even some of the new deconstructionisms—can be considered as efforts to find a "center" that can make promises, so that an honest observer of the promises, seeing that they have led to surprising outcomes, could *intelligibly* say, "It was ironic, given the center's promise X, that Y should have occurred."

The announcer who said that the tornado struck out of an ironically blue sky was talking nonsense—*unless* he believed that the center has somehow promised us that blue skies will not destroy us. But of course most of us, even the most serenely atheistic, even those who are most aggressive about unmasking all presences, still believe that somehow the universe *does* make promises, at least of the minimal kind that justifies our expecting certain things to act according to natural laws—things like transistors or viruses; even the weather; perhaps even human minds.

As you would expect, I find most inviting those new cosmologists who talk explicitly about irony and who use it themselves in great abundance. And I find it curious that when I make a list of these, they turn out to share another profound characteristic: they all find it necessary to develop a radical critique of traditional notions of the individual private self, the self that is bordered by the skin.

We might consider here Kenneth Burke's dramatism, a program that revels in systematic ironic undercuttings: whatever I *think* I say turns out to mean something else, because "I" am really an indeterminate "we," working in a drama that accommodates roles over which "we" have little control. Man is essentially the inventor of the negative, committed to constructing hierarchies of value but doomed to recognizing their inadequacy. Every human statement is, for Burke, necessarily "ironic," when viewed from any rival, incongruous perspective. Irony here becomes synonymous with "dialectic," which in turn is a synonym for "comedy," the comic drama in which we discover just how limited is everything we say.

Or we might pursue the work of Jacques Lacan in "deconstructing" the self, in a program surprisingly similar to the work of American social psychologists earlier in this century. Though I am not myself Lacanic, and am therefore not clear about how far Lacan would go in recognizing the analogies of his work to traditional theological enterprises, it is clear that he sees our human nature as "speaking illusory messages" from our childhood dream of private individuality—messages that must be undercut ironically by our adult discovery of what it must mean to any creature to learn that the private, all-powerful self simply does not exist.

Or we might look at the way in which the anthropologist Gregory Bateson deconstructs the self. He is another wild man who makes wonderful sense (so long as we don't follow him in his claims to originality). Like Burke and Lacan, Bateson discovered that there is no such thing as a privatized, independent self bounded by a skin. The self is radically and inescapably a *social psyche*, made of many selves, dependent on "the other" (not just other people, but everything not inside the skin). We are condemned to misery so long as we insist on behaving as if we could develop an independent, coequal relation with that "other." Or, finally, we might add to our list the recently fashionable Soviet thinkers Mikhail Bakhtin and Lev Vigotsky. In some ways their critique of the isolated "individual" is even more thoroughgoing than any found in the West.

All of these would-be renovators of man's enterprise would lead us eventually to expect cosmic irony whenever we open our mouths or put pen to paper, especially when we talk about ourselves. Born and reared to an illusory faith in our infinite powers and our centrality, we are charged by our universe to discover our mistake: not my private self but "the other" made me; not my self but the world of selves (perhaps it may even be true that some sort of supreme selfhood) controls my fate—or, in the language of some new theologians, provides my boundaries or my "limits." Indeed, my very self is not mine but ours.

Of course, one cannot resist "private" strivings, "private" efforts, like mine here to say something in "my own name." Short of silence or suicide, I cannot express with full humility what in fact I know about how puny and misguided my private world is, as compared to "the other" which made it and grounds it. Thus I cannot myself commit the supreme ironic act of annihilating the significance of my "self." Surely "I" do exist as something-or-other, inside *this* skin and inside no other!

Yet if I cling to that self—to my private, narcissistic, and in fact only half-existing separate identity—I inevitably suffer the kind of punishment that "the other" knows how to give with unique force: the ironic laughter of the wisdom that mocks whenever we puny ones make overweening fools of ourselves.

If I am right, it is not just carelessness but some half-sense of such truths that leads everyone these days to use "irony language" in increasing profusion. What is a writer to do, addressing a typical academic or intellectual audience, or even when writing a newspaper column, in a situation that in the past could be met by saying, "God intended otherwise," or "God punished him for his overweening pride," or "God mocked his boastful endeavors," or "It was an act of God"? Can you imagine a syndicated columnist saying, not "ironically enough," but rather "in the eyes of God the result must have appeared amusing"? The mystery of life, the frustrations it steadily offers to our lives, along with the wry sense we have that such frustrations have *some* kind of meaning, leave us with a desperate need for a language that does not simply say, "I was surprised," or "I thought it incongruous or paradoxical."

So: "*It*" was ironic. The *tornado* struck ironically. Irony is in things as they are, not simply in my view of them, and lacking the older vocabulary for dealing with our finitude, we do what we can.

I am suggesting, then, that we are all steadily addressed by a supremely ironic message, spoken by "all that is not me": "Whatever you say will be at best partial, and most likely plain false. The falsity will be especially true of whatever you *claim* has been spoken by supreme centrality. You are most subject to undercutting precisely at those moments like this one, when you aspire to statements about the essentially ironic nature of the cosmos. Just keep humble, my friend, because I who made you finite, made you *in society* with me and my creatures, made you dependent on me for any truth you utter. You may praise me, if you like; you may deny me along with most thinkers in your time; but don't think for a moment that the words you use in your praise poem or your denial tract will mean what *you* think they mean."

If the world we never made talks anything like that, then of course cosmic irony will be with us here in every word we speak or write about irony, laughing himself/herself silly, as we deliver our bits of wisdom.

Now, of course, I know better than to expect anyone to accept any theological implications in what I am saying. I really do not want to claim that I have discovered a new proof for the existence of God, the "ironological proof." All I would claim is that a serious look at how we use language ironically, and how we talk about irony, will lead us to recognize a striking parallel between traditional God-language and modern irony-language.

The strongest religious traditions have always celebrated the Being who by His very existence dramatizes our finitude, our insignificance. And their opponents have stressed, with increasingly dramatic force as modernism progressed, the absurdity of worshipping the inhumane force that frustrates our every wish and finally destroys us.

I submit that as we deal with the "it" that we say is "ironic," or with the even more impersonal force that leads us to say things like "ironically enough," we have a similar choice. As you would predict, my concluding hope is that we might acknowledge and delight in the cosmic irony that leads us to talk in those ways. In our quests for knowledge about irony, as in our ordinary language for dealing with inescapable anomalies and incongruities, we unwittingly rival "the other": that always elusive, sometimes even absconding center who alone knows what's what. And in doing so, we are always heading—as the fine old neglected myth puts it—for a fall.

*For most of the world, Richard McKeon is relatively unknown—whether as philosopher or rhetorician (or better, rhetorologist). To me, as this essay will reveal, his "architectonic" probing of how philosophies relate makes him the most important of twentieth-century thinkers. He should be read by everybody, but unfortunately "everybody" finds him difficult to read. I have sometimes made the ironic claim that nobody can understand any one of his essays, read for the first time, without having already read several others.*

For a fuller version of this essay, with much richer references to McKeon's work, see the version originally published in *Pluralism in Theory and Practice: Richard McKeon and American Philosophy*, ed. Eugene Garver and Richard Buchanan (Nashville, TN: Vanderbilt University Press, 2000), 213–30.

# Richard McKeon's Pluralism

## The Path between Dogmatism and Relativism

As I struggle one more time to probe a few of Richard McKeon's foundations, overt and covert, remembering how skillful he was in finding flaws in such efforts, I keep thinking of my first experience with him.[1] In a way it explains why many of his interpreters have thought of him as a dogmatist. It also pushes me inescapably into the two questions that will be my center here: Why did so many of his critics and even some of his disciples think of him as a relativist, and why were they wrong in ignoring his universals?

In 1943, I escaped for a few hours each week from my chores as a Mormon missionary by enrolling in a course on Plato's *Republic*. The chairman of the University of Chicago English department, Napier Wilt, had in effect ordered me to take the course, taught by a professor I'd never heard of before, one Richard McKeon. Since Wilt had provided my scholarship funds, I felt obliged to obey him, though I wondered whether a course in the *Republic*, a work I had already read on my own, would perhaps be a waste of time.

As it turned out, there was only one other student in the course—one we then must have called a "co-ed." Since she said hardly a word throughout the ten weeks, the greenhorn Mormon missionary found himself in every three-hour class forced into a kind of deep philosophical probing he'd never before even dreamed of.

McKeon's first assignment was to read the whole of *The Republic* and come back prepared to discuss it. I re-read it, and found it again fascinating but full of outlandishly obvious logical fallacies—absurd "proofs" that I wrote about scornfully to a friend back in Utah.[2] At the beginning of our first real session, McKeon asked us what we thought of the work. The conversation between the two of us—what the young woman was thinking through it all I'll never know—went something like this:

"Oh, I found it on the whole delightful, especially the section on the cave."

"Delightful? Only the story parts? What about the arguments?"

"Oh, they're interesting, but logically really messy."

"Mr. Booth, has it never occurred to you that reading a philosophical work is not like reading a novel? Here we'll not be looking for the 'exciting' parts. We're looking for the argument." (Of course I have no literal record of his statements, but I swear that my report comes pretty close to reality: his words seared themselves into my timid soul. I remember these words as precisely what he spoke; the rest of the conversation really occurred, but I couldn't swear to any one wording.)

"Well," I replied, disguising my terror, "as I said, the arguments are often just plain silly. For example ... "

And I pointed to one or two of Plato's "obviously absurd" analogies.

McKeon punched hard.[3] "Mr. Booth, you have not really read the book; you've only toyed with it." And from that moment on, he patiently and decisively wiped the floor with me, uncovering careless "literary" and "logistical" misreadings that I still remember. For every objection I raised, he had an answer that would stump me, always referring to the text as his authority: "Hasn't it occurred to you to compare how *this* analogy relates to what he says in book 10, or to the larger analogy between the soul and the state?"

In short, Plato, with McKeon's help, had an answer for every objection I could contrive. After a few weeks of this treatment, I happened on Professor Wilt in the quad. The conversation went something like this:

"How's the Plato going?"

"Oh, it's challenging. [I didn't want to say terrifying.] But I really don't think it's good to be such a dogmatic Platonist as Mr. McKeon is. He's got this absolute conviction that Plato's 'ideas' are real, and he even agrees with Plato that literature, and even music, should be judged by *real* moral standards. He even defends that crazy stuff about the moral effects of distinct musical modes. I'll stick it out, but I do find his dogmatic Platonism weird."

"Oh, is that so? Have you not heard that Richard McKeon is thought to be a dogmatic Aristotelian?"

I had not heard. Having never had a course in philosophy, I had not even the foggiest notion of what an "Aristotelian" might be, let alone a dogmatic one. McKeon had mentioned that Aristotle had spent a lifetime *unsuccessfully* trying to refute Plato. What kind of mind was I then dealing with?

Well, it was the same kind that I met in a later course with him after the war, that of an absolutely dogmatic Humeian, not just eager to defend

Hume from every conceivable attack but brilliant at exposing the stupidities of any of us who raised what seemed to us obvious objections to Hume. It was a mind that had earlier produced a "dogmatically Spinozist" book on Spinoza, that obviously heroic geometrist of ethics who cannot easily be fitted under the umbrella of either a Platonist or an Aristotelian or a Humeian. As any reader of McKeon might predict, I later met in him an equally persuasive dogmatic defender of Democritus, of Cicero, of Kant, of Dewey, and—somewhat peripherally from McKeon's point of view but highly important in my own thinking—of Anselm: reading McKeon's account of Anselm's ontological proof left me never again able to say flatly that "I don't believe in the existence of God." I had learned from McKeon's reconstruction of Anselm—and then from Anselm himself—that only a fool could say that.[4]

The question of where the real McKeon is to be found, beneath such a variety of radical defenses of seemingly contradictory systems, has plagued many of his serious students. The real McKeon traveled in his works over the whole range of life and of thought about life—a range that he himself classifies autobiographically under three extremely broad headings: the history and methods of philosophical inquiry; the aims and possibilities of education in all of its intricacies; and the hopes and practices of politics, especially on the international scene.[5] He does not himself deal with these three McKeons as in real conflict, but those of us who look at them closely have no easy task in drawing them together.

In his biography of McKeon, for example, George Plochmann works hard to decide just where the real McKeon would be placed on McKeon's own schema of philosophical possibilities (the incredibly complex full chart McKeon long withheld from publication; it appeared only after his death).[6] "Where does McKeon himself fit?" Plochmann asks, and finally places the master, cautiously but firmly, by interrelating four out of the sixteen key terms in one of McKeon's various schemata: he has "reflexive Principles, essentialist Interpretation, linguistic Selection, and operational Method: two Aristotelian and two stemming alternatively from the Sophists and the Operationalists."[7] While I do not see such precise placements as utterly pointless, I know from experience that they always end in controversy with other McKeonites who would place him elsewhere on his own various charts.[8] Still, in spite of this slipperiness, I want to argue that Plochmann is right in not reducing McKeon to any kind of relativist: he was "not a chameleon."[9] Though he cannot be accused of utter relativism, his multifaceted forms of inquiry are genuinely always pluralist and thus threatening to all monists who, as true believers, are sure that some one system will someday sew everything up.[10]

As my opening anecdote illustrates, McKeon really, genuinely, passionately, unfalteringly believed that *when properly pursued*, the diverse projects of Plato *and* Aristotle *and* Kant *and* Dewey and an indeterminate number of others were sound, true. Though true only in their own way: they revealed structures of genuine truths, and methods for pursuing truths, approaches that were and are ultimately, finally, irrefutable. They are not irrefutable in the sense pursued by one of his students, Richard Rorty, turning it all into a hodgepodge of pointless controversy.[11] Rorty's campaign to undermine the importance of systematic philosophizing would have distressed McKeon.

For McKeon, the major philosophies are irrefutable in the sense that they each reveal ONE true path to ONE vision of ONE genuine aspect of truth. Platonic inquiry will forever yield real truth, when pursued by full-fledged Platonists: not just a corner or slice or aspect of truth but a total vision that is so profound, so persuasive, that it can *seem*, to any true believer, to embody a refutation of all the others. (McKeon was not just playing a game in that Plato course I took.)[12] Yet the same can be said for Aristotle and a small list of others, only some of whom I have already named. The list of the fully *comprehensive* philosophies, in contrast to the fragmented ones, was never very long for him, but there was never a moment, after his twenties, when he offered the hope, either to himself or to any future philosopher, of developing a single philosophy that would genuinely refute or encompass all those others.[13]

Such a plural commitment means, among other things, that there can be no single right angle from which to photograph the center of this multifaceted figure. The quest for common values or universals that somehow unite or harmonize the many McKeons and his many heroes will work in different ways for different questers, depending on where they in turn come from—just which first principles, methods, purposes, and notions of commonality of subject matter they adhere to.

Leaving for others to detect where my own multiple selves can be located, I shall here simply consider three McKeons—not identical to but overlapping those he traces in his "Spiritual Autobiography": (1) *the historian of thought* who discovered how and why thought is always to some degree circumstance-bound, subject to shifts in political realities and intellectual fashions; (2) *the philosophic semanticist* who reconstructed the major philosophies with more genuine and penetrating "entry" than any other prober I've encountered;[14] and (3) the *philosopher* who, moving beyond or beneath history and circumstance and mere semantic interpretation, was all the while committed to a wide range of truths underlying philosophical diversities: (3a) the moralist, (3b) the committed educator, (3c) the political activist, and finally (3d) the metaphysician who postponed until quite late the unmasking of his ultimate fundamentals. (Some have chosen, as I've said, to harmonize these various selves under the general term *rhetorician* or *architectonic rhetorician*. I can understand that, but I fear that the term *rhetoric* has for most current readers seriously misleading connotations; besides, it implies a neglect of the sense in which he was a metaphysician or even a theologian: that's why we perhaps need a new term like *rhetorologist*.)

**The Historian of Thought**

The problem of discovering the true believer underlying all of McKeon's sympathetic reconstructions as an insider is complicated by many factors. Perhaps most important is his passionate and incredibly learned historical pursuit of what earlier philosophers had actually said—what might be called the historical "facts" in contrast to the caricatures constructed by other historians of philosophy. His "historical semantics," the effort not just to understand but to think the thoughts that other thinkers really thought, as they wrote in a variety of philosophical vocabularies, was practiced so diligently that his reconstructions always sound—as in my Plato class— almost like what a dogmatic disciple would have said, even when one can find evidence elsewhere that McKeon saw the author as sadly misguided or at least as so limited as to be finally of little use.

As Plochmann points out, he very rarely spends energy attacking other philosophers; when he dismisses them at all, it is usually for their having only a corner on some truth—not a single, grand ultimate truth but one of the truths that was treated more fully by one or another of the fully comprehensive philosophies he most respected. His criticisms were most often not claims that a given thinker was just plain wrong but that he (invariably he) had in effect stopped too soon, having started on one possible path.

In his article on G. E. Moore, for example, it is clear that McKeon has not in any sense tried to refute Moore but rather somehow to place him on the right platform—a platform that Moore rightly sensed as much lower, for McKeon, than McKeon's own. Re-reading Moore's three-sentence reply to McKeon's twenty-seven-page critique, it's not hard to see why Moore might have had trouble deciding just what he could reply to. McKeon has both understood and acceded to most of Moore's major points: he has thought Moore's thoughts, and has then simply insisted that Moore's lines have all been cut off too short and thus compartmentalized and trivialized. As

Moore said, "I can quite understand anyone [like McKeon] thinking that the things I have not dealt with are far more important than those I have dealt with."[15]

## The Historian of Ideas

When we take seriously this historical semanticist, the historian of ideas—the one who more than any other performed tracings of fully developed, comprehensive ideas, not of the fragments that Arthur Lovejoy made fashionable with his *The Great Chain of Being*—we discover a kind of identical twin: the *philosophic* semanticist who is not doing just history of what others believed but who is—to repeat—*thinking with* those others. He is thinking with them not just in order to do justice to them historically but to take in fully the truths they offer and relate them to other philosophies, doing full justice to radical ambiguities in key terms. This is the man who recognizes the full truth of diverse truths, and thus falls into a variety that is overwhelming both to him and to those of us who would like to discover the real McKeon. Again and again he makes it clear that the quest for a single, overarching, complete philosophy is absurd—the point that Rorty has picked up and inflated.

Is the quest for a coherent Richard McKeon, the man who embraced so many versions of the whole, equally absurd? It all depends on the meaning of the word *coherent*. What cannot be doubted is that when you probe his writings in a search for the final, ultimately correct, version of the range of philosophical possibilities, hoping for a single philosophy of everything, you are doomed; studied carefully, his final schema will yield far more than just $16 \times 16$ squares but thousands of legitimate possibilities.

In his later years, whenever anyone made some hard-and-fast claim about the supreme validity of any one of these possibilities, he would almost snarl, "You're entitizing!" That is to say, you are pinning things down that are inherently, essentially, forever *un*pindownable. He carried this habitual deconstructing so far that most of us who were strongly influenced by this fluid, evasive McKeon have been much less troubled by the deconstructionist revolution than disciples of other earlier schools have been; McKeon had already deconstructed us with his attack on entitizing.

Thus, it can be said that a fair share of the claims made by Jacques Derrida and others against literal fixations of truth through precise language had long since been made by McKeon, and indeed by many of his most admired forebears. Perhaps the most shocking of these, to traditionalists, was his repeated argument that facts are not as much found as made. They are constructed by the particular philosophical perspective of the constructor. A careless reader of some parts of his work could easily—and quite falsely—lump him with the more extreme positions mocked by Alan D. Sokal in his recent spoof that trapped the editors of *Social Text* into publishing his satire without recognizing it for what it was.[16] But McKeon's claim that facts are always in some sense made by us was never extended to the claim that Sokal's mock-speaker makes: a denial that "there exists an external world, whose properties are independent of any individual human being."[17]

It was this deconstructionist side that confirmed some critics in their accusation that he was a relativist: he had sold out all first principles, betraying his original commitment to Spinozist, or Aristotelian, or even Ciceronian/rhetorical/operationalist groundings; he was simply saying, "Anything goes, so long as you make it complicated." Even though he again and again declared that he was pursuing a path between dogmatism and relativism, his refusal to slide decisively and finally into any one philosopher's home plate inevitably led superficial readers to declare, in effect, "Since I can't find a fixed label for him, or even a short list of philosophical principles that he declares as primary, he can only be called a relativist." Such critics either did not know, or could not understand, his many statements like this one: "There is *doubtless a single inclusive truth*, but there are no grounds for supposing that it will ever receive full and exclusive expression in any human philosophy, science, religion, art, or social system" (emphasis added).[18] The word *doubtless* in that sentence is to me extremely important; McKeon never doubted the existence, at our center, of a central, though elusive, truth. He was an ontological monist, while laboring as a philosophical pluralist.

### The Philosopher-as-Man and His Universals

What did he see, or feel, or choose to live with, as that center? Dodging the larger philosophical issue of where he fits on any philosophical grid, especially his own, I shall now rephrase the search for *the* McKeon as the search for just what universal values can be discerned, if any, as underlying all of his quests. Did he find, as he sometimes suggested, that all of the philosophers for whom he shows greatest respect embraced certain shared universals, though in different vocabularies? Did they all in some sense end up with the same truth, though in different languages? A full treatment of this question, looking in detail at how his heroes could be reconciled, would require a book in itself, with a detailed look at two or more philosophies that seem to clash right down to the ground. And it would require a much fuller treatment than I can manage of a troublesome question that I come to later: How is his pluralism to deal with what look like flat contradictions in practical decisions that seem to stem from philosophical orientations?

My various questions can be brought down to earth quite simply: Can a McKeonite pluralist embrace, and even fight for, any one universal, any one standard, any one value, seen as valid in all cultures and historical periods and thus defensible in all defensible philosophies? Since the word *universal* is radically ambiguous, some redefining will be required along the way.

The questions can be divided into three parts, depending on which kind of universal one is seeking. (1) Does McKeon the man exhibit a consistent practice of character-virtues that none of "his" philosophers would question? (2) Are there discernible "intellectual virtues," universals about how to think, exhibited by all of his heroes, universal habits of thought that underlie the striking differences of methods and principles and purposes? (3) Would all true philosophies finally come to agreement on practical judgments of the toughest questions about right and wrong behavior: questions like the legitimacy of slavery, of torture, of totally free speech, and so on?

1. Did McKeon himself express and practice a strong adherence to any recognizable set of virtues, values that he himself never questioned—and that thus were universal in his own biography?

This one, unlike the others, can be answered simply and clearly: yes. His writings like the rest of his life reveal an intense commitment to a broad-ranging, relatively conventional code, most of it shared by most of us, and most of it, so far as I can discover, never questioned by him. The classical virtues, for example, most notably the four cardinal virtues, permeate every nook and cranny of his writings, as they do the writings of his philosophical heroes, and as they did most of his encounters with those of us who worked with him personally.[19] Such obvious virtues are of course widely shared, much more widely indeed, even among nonphilosophers, than many cynics in our time care to recognize. (On another occasion it would make an amusing project to probe the work of the great relativists and "nominalists" [Rorty's term for himself], uncovering the substantial list of universals that their actual codes abide by.) In a longer account, one might provide anecdote after anecdote and quotation after quotation to support the claim that McKeon lived at least the following virtues. Though listing them is inevitably banal—since they are so widely embraced—it underlines just how he differs from any true relativist.

*Wisdom?* All of his heroes honored it and pursued it vigorously, under one definition or another. It's a major end of all of their projects. It exists, somewhere; pursue it! McKeon pursued it day and night, in every classroom, in every article.

*Courage?* What serious thinker has ever claimed that cowardice is superior to courage? And what could take more courage than attempting, as all of them did, to encompass it all? And does it not require even more courage to undertake, as McKeon does, to understand the whole of philosophical history and produce a dialogue among the heroes? (I ignore for the moment the obvious fact that courage, like other virtues, is sometimes hard to distinguish from excesses like rashness, intemperance, blind indifference to fate, and so on.)

*Temperance?* None of his real heroes were intemperates of the Friedrich Nietzsche kind, say, or even René Descartes with his intemperate worship of certainty through the logistical method.[20] It may be unfair to claim that in McKeon's view Descartes was intemperate, but for the mature McKeon, the logistical method when combined with the existential interpretation was never fully inviting and indeed represented the intemperance that results from overconfidence in any hard-proof method. Intellectual intemperance was one of McKeon's *bêtes noires*: it's another term for dogmatism. The freedom he extolled was never a freedom from rational standards and pursuits.

*Justice?* Whether defined as political and social and economic justice or as responsibility to treat other philosophers fairly and honestly, justice is at least verbally honored by all major thinkers, and it would not simply be verbally honored but was recommended at length and *practiced* by McKeon. (For how the concept of responsibility relates for him to justice, see "The Development and the Significance of the Concept of Responsibility." Or have a look at the word *responsibility* in the index of Zahava McKeon's edition of *"Freedom and History."*)

Already here we have a rather impressive list of universal virtues, however conventional. McKeon was always aware that the banality of a concept does not diminish its importance, if its surface meanings are "deconstructed"—a word he did not use—and its full range of possible meanings explored. Stimulated by his way of approaching key terms, I have often asked beginning students, before they've even heard of the cardinal virtues, to list the qualities they most admire in their friends. The resulting list always includes something like "guts," for courage; "being fair," for justice; "being smart," for wisdom; and "being cool," for temperance (and perhaps also for wisdom). When they then read Plato, say, they usually recognize that they join him, in all their postmodernity, in embracing at least four universals. To embrace them as ideals, however, is a much different thing than practicing them, as McKeon seemed to, at every moment of every day.

Thus, pluralism of McKeon's kind fully eschews relativism: real values really exist and should be practiced by all of us on all occasions. Any thinker who seriously violated any one of the four—and one can find such thinkers throughout history—simply would not enter McKeon's pantheon. It is true that the four cardinal virtues often conflict with others—as justice can conflict with mercy, or courage with prudence. But even those who celebrate mercy or prudence do so with a full acknowledgment that justice and courage are real values, whether or not they conflict with others. I shall later look further at the question of "incommensurability" and the necessity of casuistry if and when we embrace McKeon's universals.

2. The second question—Are there more specifically intellectual universals?—overlaps with the first but leads to greater complexities. I find in McKeon's work an impressive list of never-questioned intellectual virtues and goals.

The most obvious of these, perhaps, is the one that reformulates justice as the McKeonesque passion for a kind of golden-rule-of-scholarship: Treat other thinkers' ideas with as much care as you would hope they would treat yours. Put universally: it is *always* wrong, regardless of your philosophical position, to attack ideas you have not tried honestly to understand. He reports often on his belated discovery of his youthful violations of such justice, as in his account of his most important philosophical discovery, when finally putting together the seemingly conflicting views of Plato and Cicero:

> I had read the great philosophers with something less than intellectual ingenuity or sensitive insight, as functions of *my own limited point of view* rather than as presentations of problems, to be considered in their own right before being dismantled to solve my problems. . . . [21]

In short, to raid a philosopher without really attempting to think his thoughts was for McKeon a blatant intellectual vice. Any of us who lived closely with him would testify to a grand difference between his actual practice of this form of justice and the practice of most people who claim to accept it.

Followed honestly, this virtue leads to a second one: the "commandment" from the nature of things (or from human nature, or—as he never puts it—from God's creative intent) that we ought, in all intellectual encounters, to pursue mutual understanding, not controversy but dialogue. Essay after essay concludes—especially in the period when he was working with UNESCO on the problem of universal rights—with statements like the following (in these quotations, the italics are mine: McKeon rarely used italics; indeed, he refused to employ most standard devices for heightening rhetorical effect):

> Analyses of arguments for communication, separated from analyses of arguments for demonstration, may provide not merely the method by which to advance dialogue in philosophy but also materials by which to lessen tensions and oppositions between cultures. . . . Mutual understanding in the sense of agreement concerning what the question is and what is required in a satisfactory solution is *necessary* if philosophers are to resume their dialogue, or even continue their efforts to convince each other of the truth of their respective positions, and it is *essential* also to the solution of social and political problems—to make possible agreement on common courses of action for different reasons, appreciation of alien values, and confidence based on understanding.[22]

Followed honestly, this virtue, the habitual pursuit of understanding, leads to a third sibling, concerning education. Every thinker should not just think but join other thinkers in working on how to educate thinkers who know how to understand: "Thou shalt be a teacher, and a teacher of teachers," working to educate people who themselves practice the intellectual virtues. In his own autobiographical account, something like a full one-third of his life was devoted to teaching and educational reform.[23] Though he does not state outright that in doing so he was following a universally valid commandment from God, or from human nature and its inherent, universal needs, he implies that commandment throughout. In the following he makes it explicit:

> I urged [as we tried to develop the University of Chicago College curriculum] three objectives: the development in the student of taste and broad acquaintance with the arts, literature, history, and philosophy, sufficient to direct his interests and afford guidance into the rich satisfactions and improvements which exploration in these fields might afford; the formation of abilities which are necessary to the recognition and appreciation of artistic, cultural, and intellectual values, as opposed to the random associated reflections which frequently accompany the attentive attitude and proper remarks that pass for appreciation; and, finally the analytical abilities needed to integrate taste and interest, on the one hand, and critical judgment and discrimination, on the other hand, into the context of the principles—philosophic and social, theoretic and practical—which are particularized in the character and attitudes of a man, and universalized in the philosophies and cultural communities men share.[24]

Followed honestly, this virtue of the passionate educator leads to a fourth: Every thinking educator should educate not just local students but citizens of the whole world. The world's hope for the future depends on educating everyone to share what he again and again calls "common values": to engage in the necessary politics, locally, nationally, internationally, that might ensure future generations of inquiring, dialogical world citizens. He became obsessed with multicultural issues that are now on everyone's mind: How can we produce dialogue across cultures, when both practical codes and seeming ultimate principles clash so obviously?[25] "World community consists in understanding *common values*, even when embodied or expressed in different ways, and in cooperative action for the furtherance or achievement of those values."[26]

This point deserves a full quotation from his long concluding paragraph about the "double commitment of philosophers," in "Philosophy and Freedom in the City of Man." That double commitment is

> the explication of the theoretic elements which have become imbedded in practical oppositions and are the tags and identifying marks of parties in the opposition, *and* the defense, in the course of that explication, of the freedoms which afford the *best means* for the peaceful resolution of such oppositions. . . . [A] world community is achievable in which *all citizens* are, in a degree, philosophers as they understand the problems of their communities and participate in their responsibilities of joint actions. . . . [T]he philosopher can assume a responsible role in practical issues and in so doing contribute something to saving philosophy from the two accusations which philosophers have in recent years vied most in applying to each other: the inconclusiveness of [those] philosophers who have dealt with important problems [such as the dialecticians in the European tradition] and the triviality of problems in which [other] philosophers [the ordinary-language crowd, for example] have achieved precision.[27]

When followed honestly, as he follows it, this passion for international education of a world citizenry of philosophically minded folk leads him inevitably to further universals, most notably freedom and responsibility (or one could say, these two lead him to the previous ones). Thus, in the paragraph from which I just quoted, he says,

> When oppositions of doctrines become doctrinal oppositions of parties, there is danger that the stronger will be found to be right, and the plea that force be placed in the hands of those who possess knowledge and love justice is easily converted into the assumption that those in power

are well informed and wise. Political freedom is *essential* to the resolution of international and national political problems precisely because political wisdom *must be shared by all* who are to benefit by it. . . . Justice in the interaction of competing and co-operating philosophies and cultures is the concrete form of the pursuit of inquiries *essential* to political freedom.

(Note that three of the four character-virtues reappear here as intellectual virtues; maybe even courage is implied.)

Followed honestly, these virtues lead to another universal, one that is openly celebrated in almost all of his writing and implicitly present in all: the drive for invention, creativity, discovery—for keeping the intellectual life fluid by what he sometimes calls "preserving perplexity," sometimes merely "openness." The art of rhetoric, in his elaborate, wide-ranging definition of that much-abused term, is largely the art of listening to conflicts in such a way as to keep honest perplexity alive, and thus to lead to new inventions/discoveries (he tended to favor the second of these terms, in my view because he really did believe that the truth, "the One," is really *there*, waiting to be discovered). This clearly depends on the universals of freedom and responsibility as necessities.

Again here I see him as a powerful postmodernist: if anyone has ever gone beyond preaching and actually practiced the golden rule of fully attending to "the other," not just with bland tolerance or benign empathy, but with understanding, a full entering into where the other resides, McKeon is the man.

3. We come now to the most difficult of the three questions about universals: Where do these universal character-virtues and intellectual-virtues lead in the contentious world of practical controversy?

What would the pluralist have to say, for example, about the much-contested universalist claims of Amnesty International that torture is always in all circumstances and cultures morally indefensible?[28] Or about the claim, which I would share with [*Eugene*] Garver, that slavery is universally indefensible? Or about the claim that infanticide is always wrong, regardless of any culture's specific needs for or uses of it? Or about the claim that love is, in all cultures and climes, superior to hate and should be cultivated by societies and pursued by all individuals? Or—to choose another value that at least seems implicit in what we've met already—the claim that the use of violence in resolving controversy is *always* not just inferior to the use of dialogue but in fact morally wrong?

Add your own list of universals (if you admit to having any) and thus make the question acute: Where does McKeon, the grand pluralist, stand—if anywhere—on universalist claims that have produced radical controversy not just in the political domain but among highly competent philosophers, including his own heroes?

To deal with this tough question, we must consider again how the three different McKeons would work together in answering it. The *historian of thought* dealt with conflict in the world of thought historically, as a historian should: What is the truest possible history of what has been thought and said in the past? *Do not cover up the conflict.* He constructed systematic accounts of how the cycle of fashions in philosophical subject matter had in effect duplicated itself at least four times: from those seeking truth about the Truth, ultimate substance, or nature; to those giving up on the search for such inaccessible substance and moving instead to the nature of thought, or epistemology; on to those who, becoming convinced that studying thought leads into hopeless controversy, turn instead to action, or pragmatics; and finally to those who, like most in our time except for the pragmatists, see philosophy as boiling down to inquiry about language: linguistics, semantics, ordinary language, deconstruction.[29]

This historian of thought seldom worried openly about whether the practical consequences of the systems jibed or clashed. Let's just get the history straight, and avoid dogmatism by embracing the truth of multiple perspectives embedded in this overwhelmingly complex history.

Meanwhile the *philosophic semanticist* was busily at work, pursuing the goal of discovering common ground (the pursuit that I've lately been labeling "rhetorology," in order to avoid the widespread pejorative sense of "mere rhetoric"). His goal was to uncover the full meaning of particular philosophies and then to resolve the conflicts and ambiguities of language that are revealed in any one philosophical controversy. This decipherer usually did not worry much about the determining, accidental effects of culture, of historical circumstance. The goal here was not historical valid-ity or placement but the recovery of multiple possibilities independent of historical fashion. Having, as philosophic historian, pursued Plato's claim that "what is on some grounds or in some circumstances true is at other times false and dangerous" (with the lurking threat of relativism), he was simultaneously pursuing Cicero's claim, equally true, that "despite the multiplicity of the forms of its (truth's) expression, 'truth is one.'"[30]

And meanwhile again, the philosopher eager to pursue and promulgate certain universal values in the practical world had to grapple with unlim-ited conflicts: his philosophical heroes often in practical affairs conflicted with his own views. It is one thing to reconstruct, as semanticist, what a major philosopher is really saying, and quite another to deal with major disagreements. What happens, to choose a prime example, when McKeon, philosophical celebrator of freedom and responsibility and universal dialogue, encounters a hero who, like Aristotle, defends slavery cogently, meticulously, in what can be claimed to be full harmony with his own principles about what is natural?[31] McKeon the philosopher knows that slavery always violates the universal value of freedom and that the slave owner violates the command to work with full responsibility for the education of anyone within his domain. McKeon the historical semanticist, however, knows that Aristotle makes a highly cogent case, one that was accepted— just like his arguments about women's natural inferiority—by myriads of readers over centuries.

Here I think one of McKeon's "selves" that I have not so far mentioned takes over: the philosophical progressivist who had a deep hope for and commitment to intellectual progress. Despite the many cycles of truth and error he had seen us go through in our quest for a better grasp of truth, he believed that since truth really exists, we can hope to obtain better handles on it. Indeed, his whole pluralistic project was designed in the hope that we could all be led to do philosophy better, and that hope included implicitly the acknowledgment that universals are not universally grasped, and that some universals, especially of the kind he was pursuing in UNESCO with its drive for universal human rights, were discovered by humankind later than others. Thus, though it has always in all cultures been wrong to violate with slavery the basic freedoms, it took Western cultures a long time to get relatively clear about it, and there are still cultures that have not yet made the discovery.

To take this move, siding in effect with Abraham Lincoln and Richard McKeon and Wayne Booth and Eugene Garver against McKeon's hero, Aristotle, leaves us still with the problem that even the firmest of universals may clash with some other universal: universals are not absolutes in the sense of precluding the necessity for thought about when and how they should be applied. If, for example, I happened to become president of a country practicing slavery, I might very well, like Lincoln, allow my respect for other virtues like prudence and tolerance to postpone my open declaration against it. Or if I happened to be prince of a kingdom so committed to and dependent on slavery that to ban it out of hand would lead to mass starvation and a destroyed kingdom, I might be justified in some sort of (temporary) compromise.

In other words, every universalist who believes in the full range of McKeon's universals, including hopes for the full education of all cultures into efforts at mutual understanding, must sooner or later become a casuist who refuses to treat any one universal as an absolute, beyond discussion. Cases usually land us in conflicts of universals that cannot be ultimately hierarchized into a fixed code. *Casuistry*, in the partly forgotten meaning of the term, is the art of looking closely at the particulars of a case, discovering how diverse values are embodied in the case, and then choosing—employing whatever wisdom one can muster—between those incommensurable values.[32]

McKeon does not talk much openly about the need for such casuistry, but I see built into his philosophic semantics a casuistry that is implicitly demanded by the historical semanticist. The twentieth-century philosopher has discovered these international universals—the drive for peace, the drive for unfettered inquiry (freedom), the drive for universal responsibility to all peoples—and he knows that many powerful earlier philosophers did not accommodate such views in their visions. In judging the importance of Aristotle, for example, one would not reject the potentialities of his principles, methods, and purposes just because they enabled him to prove both the justice of slavery and a lot of other matters, such as the inferiority of women to men. Aristotle's circumstances, his historical moment with its various forms of scientific ignorance, led his philosophy astray there, as it led his astronomy astray, and it took millennia before most of us could arrive at agreement on the proposition that all slavery is wrong, just as it took millennia before astronomers could correct his highly plausible beliefs about how stars travel.

But casuistry is not merely historical placement: it is placing one genuine universal value against another and facing the necessity to decide which of two values a given case requires us to violate. To torture someone for having spoken something objectionable is always a wrong, in all circumstances. But that does not settle the question of whether to torture someone to save the lives of others is, though a violation, a necessary violation at this moment: a wrong that is right. The most honorable and virtuous of agents might be forced to commit the wrong, to avoid committing a worse wrong.

If my family were threatened by a terrorist, and I had reason to think that in torturing that terrorist I could learn where the bomb was and when it would go off, I might have to commit the atrocity—but I should never tell myself that in doing so I did something that was just plain right; it was necessary, but still a violation of a universal value. It would be like the action of a priest I once heard telling of his "wrong" behavior when the Nazis came to his door and asked whether he was hiding Jews in his house. "I lied," I remember him saying. "I lied deliberately. I believe that *all* lying is wrong, but I *had* to lie. And that night in my prayers I asked forgiveness for lying—for having *had* to lie. And I'm pretty sure that the Lord forgave me."

Here we see the distinction I've already referred to between universals and absolutes. I do not find McKeon fully articulating it, though he must have lived with it constantly: There are probably no absolutes, in the sense of values unalterable by cases, circumstances.[33] There are, however, universals, in the sense of values that no one should ever violate without in effect praying to the One for the violation of its nature.

His life thus implies for me some such summary as this: We all should recognize that actually embraced values are often in utter conflict, because this or that culture has not yet discovered the values that underlie all human aspirations. The history of cultural discovery should not be confused with the goals of philosophical inquiry: history must always be in part a history of irresolvable conflict. Philosophy is a search for truth, but it is inescapably embedded both in historical circumstance and the complexities produced by the reciprocal priorities among modes of thought. Only a pluralistic embrace of the Many can do justice to the One.

How should an account of a project as complex and elusive as Richard McKeon's be concluded? He himself offers a fine (characteristically dense) summary of much that I have tried to say, as he concludes his "Spiritual Autobiography" (because of the density, I have added a few comments in brackets, and again a few italics):

> Philosophical universality is easy to achieve by reducing all other views to the requirements and limits of one preferred creed and system, but it distorts the doctrines it refutes; and a similar easy and violent victory in imposing uniformity in political practices, with its consequences in suppression and hostility, is the *only alternative to a political universality based on common understanding and on common values. True universality* in intellectual, as well as in practical relations, depends on insight into the diversities of cultures, philosophies, and religions, and on acquaintance with the methods and consequences of science.

After then looking briefly at how "integration" and "universality" are to be achieved in the three areas of his lifetime commitment—intellectual inquiry, educational improvement, and international understanding—he turns finally once again to universal values:

> Values are based on the peculiarities of cultures [through a long history], but they are understood and appreciated, even by those who share the culture in which they originated, because of their *universality,* and international understanding is based on the recognition of *common values* in the vast

diversity of their forms and idioms. Understanding has a practical bearing both on action (because education and knowledge can build a *foundation* for international cooperation and world institutions) and on theory (because understanding and the preservation of peace are *indispensable* conditions for the progress of science, the construction of values, and the cultivation of the good life). These three—the *understanding* of order in nature [the progress of science], in the relations of men [the progress in our grasp of practical universals], and in knowledge [philosophy and theology, etc.], the *education* of men [*and women!*] sensitive to the marks and uses of that order [the construction of communities that respect universal values], and the appreciation of differences in the modes in which peoples express that order and seek their fulfillment in accordance with it [the cultivation of cultures that practice his kind of pluralism!]—are the three related aspects [why, oh cautious McKeon, why that weasel word *aspects* when you clearly mean something like "universally valid commitments"?] of a problem which *we all* face in our individual lives, our communities, and in the world relations in which *all* communities have been placed.[34]

I am tempted to conclude, then, by labeling this great cautious inquirer into universals as a deeply religious man. His worship of the One, the inaccessible, incomprehensible, single truth, was in my experience always oblique, tacit, even a bit dodgy. Knowing how the very word *religion* sets off controversy that freezes dialogue and blocks understanding, he almost always kept silent about his own parallels with the great theologians. But anyone who pursues the works I have neglected here—his great edition of Abailard's *Sic et non*, or the unparalleled collection of medieval thinkers—will discover a man who respects the great believers far more than he respects the great doubters.[35] Though many of us have described him, finally, as an "operationalist" or "rhetorician," my current label has to be something like "rhetorical theologian" or even "rhetorological prophet." Few other thinkers in our time or any other have probed as deeply and constructively into the mysteries of a value-laden creation that permanently eludes our efforts to pin "It" down. He pursued that probing religiously, in both senses of the word. He was at it steadily and aggressively at every moment of every day, and he was all the while motivated spiritually: he felt driven by his connection to the *mysterium tremendum,* the One.

*This essay is a reduced version of the introduction that I was asked to write for Mikhail Bakhtin's* Problems of Dostoevsky's Poetics. *I cannot resist revealing that, because of Bakhtin's and Dostoevsky's continuing fame, I have received more royalties for this introduction than for any other article of mine—and more than I get for some of my books. From my present perspective, I delay for far too long any explicit reference to how my speculations relate to the work of Bakhtin. But if you read carefully, you will see that he is, from the beginning, a hero who transformed my (and innumerable others') thinking about fiction.*

This essay was originally published in *Problems of Dostoyevsky's Poetics,* by Mikhail Bakhtin, ed. and trans. Caryl Emerson (Minneapolis: University of Minnesota Press, 1984), xiii–xxvii.

# How Bakhtin Woke Me Up

To understand why Bakhtin's work fully justifies the recent explosion of Western interest in him, we must move back a bit in time. What were we in the West saying about the relations of ideology and form while Bakhtin was writing and rewriting, losing and finding again, his thousands of astonishingly various yet impressively harmonious pages?

Formal critics all begin with a truth that recent ideological critics too often neglect: Form is in itself interesting, even in the most abstract extreme. Shape, pattern, design carry their own interest—and hence meaning—for all human beings. What some critics have called *"human* meanings"—ideological or theoretical meanings—are not required. Nothing is more human than the love of forms. The relations discovered or invented in pure mathematics, like the forms we find, or think we find, in the physical world, are felt by all who pursue them to be more worthy of pursuit than sheer chaos would be, even if there were any sense in which a genuine chaos could be pursued, studied, "formulated."

Our "pure," "abstract," "disinterested" interest in forms has proved confusing to formal critics when they have turned to forms made by human beings. Works of art still obviously respond to our love of abstract, or "meaningless," form, but they often come laden with other interests. Abstract painting and sculpture, primitive and modern; nonprogrammatic music, whether by Bach or by recent mathematical explorers; complex word games; patchwork quilts; computer "art" based on elaborate equations—all testify to our capacity to enjoy patterns disconnected from any obvious meanings that seem attachable to ideologies. Yet the very act of making even the most dessicated work of art imports into it meanings that carry both maker and receiver into territory other than a pure contemplation of pattern. Sooner or later every formal critic must therefore struggle with the problem of how to deal with the scandal of what is often called "content."

One way is to follow some of the formalists and fight *meaning* openly, as a taint on pure form. In our century an astonishing number of critics have equated art with the purgation of meanings. Is it not obvious that the closer we can come to a simple, pure vision of form, uncontaminated by the practical interests that clutter our nonartistic lives, the closer we come to what is properly called art? Countless manifestos have declared for purity and against the philistines who naively import human interests into their responses: "It matters not what artists paint, so long as they paint beautiful forms." "The listening public is the enemy, insisting on sentiment and on melodies that can be sung." "Do not ask whether a given literary character or work is moral or immoral, only whether the design is right."

In the late nineteenth century Pater and others were already telling us that all art aspires to the condition of music, in which form and content are so subtly intertwined that no critic can draw a line between them. In our time many formalists have told us that even Pater's terms were not austere enough: art is not a question of beautiful intertwining of ideas, for there should be no "content" to intertwine. Music itself properly aspires to the condition of pure mathematics—or alternatively, to the undoctored, inartificial forms of natural sounds. Form is all—or, as the newest version has it, language is all.

Everyone who has pronounced thus boldly for a purified form has been confronted by the scandalous fact that all actual works of art are loaded with ideology. The scandal is most pressing when the "messages" are as blatantly obvious as the religious passion of *Paradise Lost* and the B-minor Mass and "The Waste Land," or the programmatic, existentialist urgency of most of the best twentieth-century fiction. But it is equally embarrassing when art works more fully disguise their ideology; discerning critics can easily show that if purification is the goal, the artist had better turn the whole business over to indifferent machines. And even that surrender can be probed for its ideology. A whole history of art in our century, not too badly distorted as such histories go, could be written as a grand competition for the position of chief purifier, artists and critics catching each other out for failing to expunge lingering "impurities."

Of all the arts, fiction has been most resistant to the drive for purification. It is so obviously built of impurities that some artists have simply repudiated it as a faulty enterprise from the beginning: poets in their credos often take swipes at mere storytellers who are stuck with the task of providing a "good read." And many a novelist has aspired to the condition of story-free poetry. Since to tell a *story* is in itself to confess a betrayal of *pure* form, the thing to do is to frustrate story in some way: by leaving the pages unbound, to be shuffled by the reader; by telling everything in alphabetical order; by imposing various word games and tricks with point of view, reminding everyone that structural intricacy is the only legitimate interest; by commenting explicitly to remind readers that your fictions are "generated" not by any interest in characters and how they relate but rather by number systems or stochastic devices like shuffled cards or computers. But the shameful fact is that as soon as you *name* a character and allow even one *event*, readers will, in truculent naïveté, treat them like people in human situations, and all the effort at totally pure form has gone down the drain. [*The diverse movements satirized in this paragraph have pretty much disappeared recently.*]

The obvious failure of pure formalism to deal adequately with even the simplest fictions has led to various attempts to treat ideology not as scandal but as mystery. Any engaging story presents us with a complex truth. While human events are not in themselves art, a fictional account, unlike double acrostics, is clearly an art that is somehow *made of* human events. If art is somehow concerned with form, if form is what distinguishes art from life, and if fictional forms are embedded in the materials of life, how can we talk about the *art* of fiction?

A second way of dealing with the scandal, then, is to embrace it: to downgrade formal interests and to identify a work's art with its ideology, judging works according to their surface truth or falsehood. In effect, one can thus simply delete the boundary between art and life and treat every art work as if it were direct, primary experience. Despite the discrediting of this "philistine" view by centuries of attack, it still persists: in censorship programs directed at our schools; in some political criticism, not only in totalitarian regimes; in some hasty attacks on sexist or racist works—attacks too often launched with inadequate attention to the targets; in the programs of certain moral and religious critics who, like John Gardner in *On Moral Fiction*, often forget their own claims to respect the distinctive values of art. And many a new sociological or "neo-Marxist" critic has embraced sophisticated forms of *anti*formalism. For them, all art and all criticism is "political." And it is easy for them to show that any work of art, when *probed* for ideology, will reveal ideology. Even the blank canvases, the $4\frac{1}{2}$-minute silences, the self-destroying machines, the pure circles and spheres and triangles of the most minimal art cannot escape their meanings: these seemingly innocuous games are offered by human beings to other human beings, and they thus carry the meanings of their situations and of the makers' acts in those situations. Thus even the purest form itself becomes ideology, and in a curious way left-wing and right-wing critics have been joining hands in judging art by ideological standards alone.

A third way is to move unsystematically back and forth, in an uneasy compromise between talk about form and talk about meanings, depending on what the work itself forces on our attention. Form in this eclectic view comes to seem like a kind of easily removable envelope, one that contains the content. This was one chief classical way of thinking, based on the *res/verba* distinction: "things," as content, offer all the "meaning," and "words," or language, as form, do the carrying job, like some delivery service that doesn't much care what is in the packages. The New Critics, at least when they turned to fiction, tended to treat its form this way.

A fourth way might be called "Aristotelian," or perhaps, to avoid the claim of really having understood Aristotle, "neo-Aristotelian." Here we reject the notion of a separable "content" altogether and rely instead on a form/*matter* pairing, in which neither form nor matter can be distinguished in separation from its twin. When torn from its form, any matter simply becomes inchoate, or is placed into another form that changes its fundamental nature. This kind of formal method sees both language and the ideologies that language inescapably embodies as shaped by some conception of a human action, or by an idea to be taught, or by some attitude to be promulgated in the world. Works of art are, like everything else that really *exists*, analyzable as both form and matter. As existing things they exhibit an identity of the two; what the matter has become *is* this shaped thing.

In this view, you cannot even describe the form, say, of *Oedipus Rex*, without describing with great precision the moral and intellectual qualities of the characters who act and suffer; their action is the form. A statement of the plot that did not include a precise appraisal of Oedipus's full character—in modern jargon, his "values," including his "ideology"—would have no formal validity at all, and a statement about "content" that extracted moral views from the shape they are given in the play would be almost as pointless. Similarly, in "Leda and the Swan" the intellectual convictions expressed are not a content formed by the words but a formed idea: a specific form imposed on words that in themselves could express a great many different ideas. *Form* in this view is thus shattered into innumerable *forms*—all of the "things" in this domain, the substances that have been made by artists. These substances, unlike those that occur in nature, are steeped in values; there is no such thing as a fictional form that is value-free, abstracted from the commitments of the characters and their author.

We can see why Aristotelians prefer to speak of many forms rather than of form when we observe how they deal with the notion of plot. In most of the attacks on plot made by those who were interested in a higher or purer fictional form, it became synonymous with intrigue, and intrigue became abstracted from the human value of characters involved in it. When E. M. Forster chose to summarize the structure of Anatole France's *Thaïs*, what occurred to him was—since the priest and the prostitute each ends where the other began—that the *plot* might be represented in the form of an hourglass, or, for even greater simplicity, as an *X*. Working at that level of abstraction, we could say that, since *Macbeth* is the story of how a regicide and his wife get caught, after initial successes, then the plot amounts to the shape of a circumflex, or perhaps, to dramatize the fall, an inverted check mark. Innumerable "structural" analyses of literature have worked at about that level of abstraction, a level which leads to the provocative claim, often made by Northrop Frye and his students, that all literary works have the same story: "the loss and regaining of identity."[1] If such a claim is true—and for all I know it may be—it is not very useful, from the point of view of anyone trying to talk about how ideology and form relate [*in dealing with the differences among individual works*].

The key word in this mode is *useful*. What can it mean to seek a *useful* language for talking about a story, about its plot, about its "essence" or "unity" or "soul"? Useful to whom? Well, why not useful to everyone? "Aristotelian" critics have always aspired to be useful not only to readers and spectators and other critics but useful to creative artists as well. The *Poetics* has often been called a "handbook" for *writing* tragedy; it tells us, in its detailed analysis of the ingredients of existing tragedies and its strongly evaluative account of the best ways of mixing those ingredients, just how we might go about making, or improving, other objects of the same kind.

It does not do so, however, by offering any simple rule book or algorithm. Its analyses are all steeped in value judgments, not of technical or formal beauty separable from moral qualities but of a shaped action, a "synthesis of incidents" or events that represent choices made by moral or immoral agents, and thus in consequence deserve, as "plot," to be called the "soul" of the work.

Thus what Bakhtin calls ideology is an essential part of the Aristotelian analysis; the forms Aristotle treats are made not of abstract shapes but of values: values sought, values lost, values mourned, values hailed. There is no more of a hint in Aristotle's formalism than in Bakhtin's dialogism of pursuing designs like hourglass shapes or spiraling curves or abstract symmetries or asymmetries of any kind. People in action cannot be reduced to mathematical figures or equations, and neither can "imitations of action."

The unity sought in every version of genuinely Aristotelian formal criticism is thus an *ideological* unity, a unity of action that is implicated in ideological matters, whether overtly, as in epithets conferring a good or bad quality on a character, or implicitly, in the ordering of values conferred by any plot sequence. The significant point, as we move toward a comparison with Bakhtin's version of "ideological formalism," is that here the unity *is* sought; it is a unity of effects pursued by an artist, an artist whose artistry is defined as a skill with architectonics. Effect (whether tragic, comic, satiric, horrific, mystifying, or celebrating—different Aristotelianisms produce different catalogues of the possible or admirable effects) is everywhere the end, and technical problems are discussed as means to given ends. Such functionalism comes to a point of caricature in Edgar Allen Poe's "The Philosophy of Composition," in which every choice by the artist is described as if calculated by a mathematician toward a single, named emotion. But even in the subtler functionalists, among whom I count my own mentors, Ronald Crane, Elder Olson, and their associates, there was never any question but that the key word was *unity* and that the unity we should seek is that of effect. The "perfected" work could thus be reconstructed and accounted for, by the acute critic, as an organic whole, with a kind of "soul," or essential informing principle, by reference to which one could explain, ideally, every choice the author had made.

The author, like the work itself, was implicated in ideology from the beginning. Since authors found themselves addressing audiences who shared some values and did not share others, they had to find effective ways to embody values in fiction and drama, values that would make the work *work*. Authors were thus in charge of created unities that consisted of choices exemplified and judged (though from quite another viewpoint they were not in charge, because their culture imposed norms upon author, work, and audience).

Any critic who begins to study fictional technique from such a base, as I did at mid-century, will of course attempt to see every artistic stroke according to its function in a whole. Even the norms that a novel embodies—its ideology—will be understood to serve the unity that, for any reader, is realized not in a conceptual scheme or "meaning" but in a given effect (however complex that effect may be). Thus when I turned, in the 1950s, to reconsider the "objectivity" that critics were touting at the time as a major achievement of all good fiction, it was natural for me to ask whether objectivity was in fact a supreme goal of all good fiction, whether an *air* of objectivity was in fact functional toward all important fictional ends, and whether any kind of genuine objectivity was in fact possible for an author, regardless of how much technical purification was achieved. Working as what might be called a "constructive formalist," I inevitably answered no to all three questions. Objectivity is not a supreme goal. It is unattainable, in itself, because the author's voice is always present, regardless of how thoroughly it is disguised. And even an *air* of objectivity is only on *some* fictional occasions helpful: many of our finest moments with novels are realized by illusions of quite "unobjective" kinds.

My opponents, as I saw it, were all those who had demanded a kind of "point-of-voyeurism" in all good fiction, inventing abstract and absolute rules about how this or that sign of the author's presence should be purged. I thought of myself in part as correcting, from within a rigorously formalist school, a gross but fashionable error of pursuing objectivity at all costs, an objectivity that was in most accounts reduced to surface matters of point of view. Critics had insisted that if an author violated certain rules against "telling," if an author failed to "show," to "dramatize," the result was not "objective" and was therefore somehow bad. About the furthest anyone at the time had gone beyond such useless rule-making was to make the claim, often referring to Keats on Shakespeare and the ideal of the "chameleon poet," that the novelist should take on the coloration of every character, without imposing heavy moral judgment. Some few critics had extended this notion to the very structure of the novel, claiming that "justice" to all characters was the supreme fictional goal. But most critics, and especially the practical critics, had reduced the question to one of technical purification: An author should create a *surface* that would be, or seem, objective.

As I see it now, my own replies to such arguments were often almost as superficial as were those of my targets. If I had not been ignorant, like almost everyone else, of the work of Bakhtin and his circle, I might have grappled with a much more sophisticated attack on the "author's voice" in fiction, one that would have forced me to reformulate, if not fundamentally to modify, my claim that "the author's judgment is always present, always evident to anyone who knows how to look for it.... The author cannot choose whether to use rhetorical heightening [*in the service of his authority and of the reader's effective retelling of the story*]. His only choice is of the kind of rhetoric he will use." So far as this argument goes, my debate with the critics I knew still seems to me sound. But the challenge presented in full force by Bakhtin requires an entirely different level of encounter.

That challenge has little to do with whether or not the author claims privileges of omniscience or exercises inside views. Indeed, it has nothing at all to do with the author's effort to produce a single, unified effect. Its subject is not the ordering of technical means toward certain effects so much as the quality of the author's imaginative gift—the ability or willingness to allow voices into the work that are not fundamentally under the "mono-logical" control of the novelist's own ideology.

> This problem lies deeper than the question of authorial discourse on the su-perficial level of composition, and deeper than a superficially compositional device for eliminating authorial discourse by means of the *Ich-Erzählung* form (first-person narration), or by the introduction of a narrator, or by constructing the novel in scenes and thus reducing authorial discourse to the status of a stage direction. All these compositional devices for elimi-nating or weakening authorial discourse at the level of composition do not in themselves tackle the essence of the problem; their underlying artistic meaning can be profoundly different, depending on the different artistic tasks they perform.[2]

This statement might at first sound like the "functionalism" I have ascribed to the neo-Aristotelians. For them, as for Bakhtin, the essence of the problem depends on "the different artistic tasks" performed by different works. And the different formal achievements that Bakhtin would account for are, again, like those addressed by Aristotle, "formed ideologies"—not value-free forms imposed on a "content" that alone contains the taint of value judgments or ideology, but rather formed values, formed ideologies. The form itself, in both views, is inherently ideological.

But for Bakhtin the notion of diverse *tasks* is quite different from a collection of literary effects, like tragedy or comedy, satire or eulogy. The artist's essential task is not simply to make the most effective work possible, as viewed *in* its kind. It is rather to achieve a view of the world superior to all other views; fiction of the right kind, pursuing the right tasks, is the best in-strument of understanding that has ever been devised. It is indeed the only conceptual device we have that can do justice, by achieving a kind of objec-tivity quite different from that hailed by most Western critics, to the essen-tial, irreducible multicenteredness, or "polyphony," of human life. In free-ing us from narrowly subjective views, the best novels achieve a universally desirable quality, regardless of the particular effects that in an Aristotelian view might be considered their ends [*the overall effect sought by the author*]. Like the universally desirable "sublime" pursued by Longinus, the quality pursued by Bakhtin is a kind of "sublimity of freed perspectives" that will always, on all [*admirable*] fictional occasions, be superior to every other.

His defense of Dostoevsky as the supreme master of such sublimity always depends on larger views that are more fully developed elsewhere.[3] Commentators dispute about just how large those views are—that is, about the degree to which Bakhtin's unsystematic system is religious or metaphysical. To me it seems clearly to rest on a vision of the world as essentially a collectivity of subjects who are themselves social in essence, not individuals in any usual sense of the word; to this degree it is definitely incompatible with all but the subtlest of materialisms. His "God-term"—though he does not rely on religious language—is something like "sympathetic understanding" or "comprehensive vision," and his way of talking about it is always in terms of the "multi-voicedness" or "multi-centeredness" of the world as we experience it.

We come into consciousness speaking a language already permeated with many voices—a social, not a private language. From the beginning, we are "polyglot," already involved in the process of mastering a variety of social dialects derived from parents, clan, class, religion, country. We grow in consciousness by taking in more voices as "authoritatively persuasive" and then by learning which to accept as "internally persuasive." Finally we achieve, if we are lucky, a kind of individuality, but it is never a private or autonomous individuality in the Western sense; except when we narrowly restrict ourselves arbitrarily to monologue, we always speak a chorus of languages. Anyone who has not been maimed by some imposed "ideology in the narrow sense," anyone who is not an "ideologue," respects the fact that each of us is a "we," not an "I." Polyphony, the miracle of our "dia-logical" lives together, is thus both a fact of life and, in its higher reaches, a value to be pursued endlessly.

It will be obvious to any literary historian that literary works have tended *not* to do justice to our dialogical natures in this sense. Just as in our individual lives we are tempted to close out voices prematurely, in order to keep things simple and to dominate the world, authors have generally experienced an irresistible temptation to impose monological unities upon their works. Many of the greatest achievements, great when viewed from the perspective of Aristotelian formalism, will thus appear seriously maimed when we ask whether their forms reflect dialogue or monologue.

Bakhtin puts the point another way. Human existence, created as it is *in* many languages, presents two opposing tendencies. There is a "centrifugal" force dispersing us outward into an ever greater variety of "voices," outward into a seeming chaos that presumably only a God could encompass. And there are various "centripetal" forces preserving us from overwhelming fluidity and variety. The drive to create art works that have some kind of coherence—that is, formal unity—is obviously a "centripetal" force; it provides us with the best experience we have of what Coleridge called "multeity in unity," unity that does justice to variety. But we are always tempted to follow that drive too far in the direction of imposing a monologic unity. Lyric poems, for example, marvelous as they can be, tend toward becoming monologues—the poet inventing a single voice, one that belies the actual polyphony of his own inner chorus. Even drama, which on its surface seems polyphonic, and which became for Western objectivists a kind of model to be emulated by fiction, is by nature monologic, because the dramatist is always imposing upon his characters what they must say, rather than allowing their *personalities* the freedom to say what they will, in their own way.

The one grand literary form that is for Bakhtin capable of a kind of justice to the inherent polyphonies of life is "the novel." If we think of novels not as some formalists would do, not as the actual works that we ordinarily *call* novels but rather as a tendency or possibility in literature, one that is best realized only in certain novels and is entirely lacking in others, we can begin to study with some precision the conditions for achieving the elusive quality we have in mind. What we seek is a representation, at whatever time or place and in whatever genre, of human "languages" or "voices" that are not reduced to, or suppressed by, a single authoritative voice: a representation of the inescapably dialogical quality of human life at its best. Only "the novel," with its supreme realization of the potentialities inherent in prose, offers the possibility of doing justice to voices other than the author's own, and only the novel invites us to do so. This is not a matter only of length; epics have all the space in the world, but they still tend to be monologic. It is more a matter of the technical resources of narrative in prose—the inherent capacity of narrative to incorporate languages other than the author's (or reader's) own. In various kinds of indirect discourse, novelists can maintain a kind of choral vitality, the very same words conveying two or more speaking voices.

They can, but of course many actual novelists do not. Turgenev, Tolstoy, indeed most who are called novelists, never release their characters from a dominating monologue conducted by the author; in their works, characters seldom escape to become full *subjects*, telling their own tales. Instead they generally remain as objects *used* by the author to fulfill preordained demands.

It is in Dostoevsky and in Dostoevsky alone that Bakhtin finds the polyphonic ideal realized. The greatest of all contrapuntalists genuinely surrenders to his characters and allows them to speak in ways other than his own. Heroes are no longer diminished to the dominating consciousness of the author; secondary characters are no longer encompassed by and diminished to their usefulness to heroes—or to the author. Characters are, in short, respected as full subjects, shown as "consciousnesses" that can never be fully defined or exhausted, rather than as objects fully known, once and for all, in their roles—and then discarded as expendable.

It is clear that any rhetoric of fiction becomes transformed, in this view, from what it will be if we begin with an Aristotelian interest in form and function. In the finest fiction, the author's technique will not be marshaled to harmonize everything into a single unified picture and to aid the reader to see that picture; the unity of the work will not be identified with the total choices of the implied author—the sum of James's choices, the ultimate impact of Austen's voice. The author will have "disappeared" from the work in a manner far different from what was meant by James Joyce when he described that poseur backstage, like God impassively viewing his handiwork and presenting his drama with pretended indifference, "silently paring his fingernails." Techniques will be viewed as performing their highest service by preserving the autonomy of the novel's characters. Raskolnikov in *Crime and Punishment* speaks for Raskolnikov as an inexhaustible personality; he does not speak either as a mouthpiece for Dostoevsky or as a negative example of how we should *not* speak. Svidrigailov, Ivan, Lisa, Sonya—all are treated not as objects serving the author's plans but as subjects, ends in themselves, defying any temptation the author may have to fit them into his superior plans.

Of course Dostoevsky did not carry out this impulse of his genius to the full; practical demands of publication, his readers' need for some sort of closure, the need for a plot, led him to cheat on occasion, as when he tries to give a clearly monological, conventional Christian epilogue to *Crime and Punishment* (92). But the reader has long since found that every main character pursues independently his or her "idea," that idea being not anything definable in propositions, overtly stated or covertly believed by the author; just as the author exhibits a kind of disinterestedness in allowing characters their freedom, so there is an unlimited openness of the characters to developments out of their "idea" into unpredictable futures.

It is not that the author's voice is entirely absent in "the novel's" highest manifestations.

> The consciousness of the creator of a polyphonic novel is constantly and everywhere present in the novel, and is active in it to the highest degree. But the function of this consciousness and the forms of its activity are different than in the monologic novel: the author's consciousness does not transform others' consciousnesses . . . into objects, and does not give them secondhand and finalizing definitions. (67–68)

The challenge of such views to my own about the author's voice is clear and deep. Again and again I have sought, like most of my Western colleagues, to put into propositional form my summaries of what an *author* is up to and of how a given character's role *contributes* to the author's overall plan. At times I have even allowed myself to talk as if characters could be reduced to pawns in a huge game of chess of which the author alone knows all the rules. I have in fact never until recently, goaded by Bakhtin (and earlier softened up by Burke), confronted fully the possibility he raises of an ideology that "knows neither the separate thought nor systemic unity" of any kind.

> For him [Dostoevsky] the ultimate indivisible unit is not the separate referentially bounded thought, not the proposition, not the assertion, but rather the integral point of view, the integral position of a personality. For him, referential meaning is indissolubly fused with the position of a personality. . . . Dostoevsky—to speak paradoxically—thought not in thoughts but in points of view, consciousnesses, voices. (93)

Thus any effort to deal with "objectivity" in the Western sense, like mine in *The Rhetoric of Fiction*, will not serve as a reply to Bakhtin's case. I argued, I still think rightly, that there is no such thing as objectivity in fiction, because the author's voice is always with us, whether open or disguised. And I used that argument to defend certain open forms of control as one legitimate expression of the author's voice. But the challenge of Bakhtin is quite different: Granted the legitimacy of a wider variety of technical ways of expressing beliefs and values (or "ideology," including direct commentary), must we not agree that "objectivity" in Bakhtin's quite different sense makes for an art superior in kind to the art of most novelists, regardless of whether their techniques are "objective" or not? Is it not true, as Bakhtin claims, that the techniques for freeing characters from the author's direct control are inherently superior to those that make it easy for the author to dominate?

It should be clear by now that what is at stake, in reading Bakhtin, is far more than the question of how we read a novel or even how we evaluate it. The effort to transcend the author's voice in this book is not a handbook treatment of the technical means to specific artistic effects; it is rather part of a lifetime inquiry into profound questions about the entire enterprise of thinking about what human life means. How are we to know and to say anything to each other about what our lives mean, without reduction to destructive or irrelevant simplicities? When novelists imagine characters, they imagine worlds that characters inhabit, worlds that are laden with values. Whenever they reduce those multiple worlds to one, the author's, they give a false report, an essentially egotistical distortion that tells lies about the way things are. Bakhtin's ultimate value—full acknowledgment of and participation in a Great Dialogue—is thus not to be addressed as just one more piece of "literary criticism"; even less is it a study of fictional technique or form (in our usual sense of form). It is a philosophical inquiry into our limited ways of mirroring—and improving—our lives. . . .

[*I here cut four long paragraphs initially very important to me, dealing with just which contemporary critical movements Bakhtin challenges most forcefully: (1) those who "think that the way to understand human behavior is to base literal propositions on studies of individuals" as isolated countable units; (2) those who, like myself, care too passionately about the literal formal construction of individual works; (3) those who see language as having no reference to any kind of reality other than itself; (4) those who, like me in much of my work, understate the role of history and culture in shaping artistic development. I also cut a paragraph describing what seem to me his weaknesses.*]

Every thinker must pay a price for every virtue, and I find that most of what look like Bakhtin's weaknesses are the inevitable consequences of his strengths. If he is "vague," so is every thinker who attempts to approach difficult and general concepts that stand for ultimate and thus ultimately elusive concerns. What is vague from a hostile point of view is wonderfully "suggestive" when we consider it from inside the enterprise. If he is repetitive, why should he not be, when what he is saying will surely not be understood the first, or third, or tenth time? When talking about truths like these, once said is not enough said, because no statement can ever come close enough and no amount of repetition can ever overstate the importance of elusive yet ultimate truth. . . . If he creates huge heaps of works and calls them "the novel," leaving out of the heap many works that you and I call novels, why, so does everyone who tries to think not literally but analogically or dialogically.

In any case, I can think of no critic of recent years—and of course he is recent only as translated for us—who more effectively performs that essential task of all criticism: prodding readers to think again about critical standards as applied to the various canons and anticanons those standards lead to. It is true that for most of us in the West, Dostoevsky himself needs no act of rehabilitation or defense of the kind that was needed in the Soviet Union during most of Bakhtin's lifetime. What requires defense, for us, is the very idea of superlative genius and of a criticism that claims to demonstrate, with reasoned discourse rather than mere assertion, the grounds for greatness. Even if he had written nothing else—and my brief account of this book does great injustice to his astonishingly broad enterprise—his passionately reasoned celebration of what the novel can do would place our crisis-ridden criticism in his debt.

*Eight years before completing* The Company We Keep, *I submitted this essay to* Kenyon Review *and was a bit surprised when they accepted it; ethical criticism was by no means at the forefront then.*

The essay appears here as what Kenneth Burke called a "representative anecdote" for *The Company We Keep*. It is a lucid and concise account of Booth's virtuous metaphorizing with friendship.

This essay was originally published in *Kenyon Review*, n.s., 2, no. 2 (spring 1980): 4–27.

# "The Way I Loved George Eliot"
## Friendship with Books as a Neglected Critical Metaphor

> I want to be loved. That is even the deep-lying reason why I elected to write. When I was eighteen, I read *The Mill on the Floss*, and I dreamed that one day I would be loved the way I loved George Eliot then....
>
> —Simone de Beauvoir

> What does every earnest man seek in the deep instinct of society, from his first fellowship ... but to find himself in another's mind: because such is the law of his being that only can he find out his own secret through the instrumentality of another mind. We hail with gladness this new acquisition of ourselves. That man I must follow, for he has a part of me; and I follow him that I may acquire myself. The great are our better selves, ourselves with advantages....
>
> —Ralph Waldo Emerson

## I

Most critics who have attempted any kind of ethical criticism have sought ways of judging the effects of literary works on the lives of their readers—what modern jargon would call aftereffects. Will this book work for good or ill in the life of the reader as lived after the last page is turned? A full ethics of fictions would of course attempt to talk about such effects, but it takes no trained statistician to tell us that empirical inquiry into the effects of art is extremely difficult to conduct, and its results almost impossible to interpret. We all know from our personal experience that some art works are good for us and our children, some bad; nobody in his heart of hearts can really doubt that a ten-hour daily dose of television is bad medicine for children. But even such an obvious matter is not—I am told—now "established beyond dispute" among those who seek hard proof.

How much more difficult it would be to prove to a skeptic that this or that book, or kind of book, was ethically damaging or improving. Even if we had ways of holding the reader's critical maturity as a constant, which we do not, the effort to prove change on this or that scale seems doomed by the number of variables involved and even more by those twin bugbears of all serious research into human character: the inherent inaccessibility of the subject's true condition of soul, and the inherently irresolvable disputes about what scale of "improvement" should be used.

Such difficulties did not, of course, prevent critics in the past from claiming that such-and-such works were ennobling or debasing. It is only in the last hundred years or so that critics have increasingly refused even to suggest that the value of art works is subject to a reasoned discrimination on ethical grounds. By mid-twentieth century most critics seemed to take one of two positions—either that all true art is inherently a boon for humanity, since by its very nature it performs some kind of "consciousness-raising" in those who attend to it, or that questions of good or ill effects are entirely inappropriate in discussions of art. According to the second position, not only are assertions about effects simply that, assertions, not subject to proof; but also questions about effects are essentially alien to the artistic or aesthetic domain—the domain that ignores consequences, the practical, the calculated, the moral. Non-art *does*; art simply *is*.

Such talk will be questioned, I am convinced, by anyone who thinks about his own experience with art works without reference to aesthetic theories. But anyone who reads much ethical criticism will be driven to understand why those who love art have often been offended by attempts to subject it to what Iris Murdoch has called "the sovereignty of the good." Ethical critics are not, on the whole, pleasant people. From Plato through Tolstoy and on to the Marxists and Babbitt, Leavis, Winters, and John Gardner, they have said nasty things about the works many of us love; they have been grossly dogmatic in their assertions; they have been—especially in modern times when they were put on the defensive—often shrill in what they have said about other critics and about works of art that failed to meet their standards. What is most striking is how often what they say can in no sense be called inquiry or study or scholarship; polemical, hortatory, "moralistic," it is too often a proper study only for the student of homiletics, not for the student who would like to learn about the qualities of literary works or of literary experience.

If empirical studies of effects on character are difficult or impossible, how, then, are we to talk about an *ethics* of fictions? One way, though by no means the only one worth pursuing, is to shift our attention from *consequences* to *the qualities of experience sought or achieved* by authors and readers *during the time* of reading or listening. Instead of asking whether this book or poem or play will make me a better person after I put it down, we might ask whether we can describe with any precision what sort of relation I have with it *before* I put it down.

We all carry about with us a large vocabulary of terms for our relations to things and people, terms of love and hate, pleasure and pain, interest and boredom, activity and passivity. If we could begin by thinking systematically about such terms, as applied to books, we might find at the end that we had discovered a vocabulary that would make it possible to talk together about the ethical quality of literary works—not in the sense of labeling them simply as noble or wicked, *imprimatur, nihil obstat,* or "to the Index," but in the sense of describing accurately, for public testing, the facts—loaded with value judgment—of our various encounters.

It is some such hope as this that has led me recently to think again about the unfashionable topic of friendship, and of discrimination among types of friends. The neglect of friendship as a serious subject of inquiry in modern thought is itself a strange and wondrous thing; after millennia during which it was one of the major philosophical topics, the subject of thousands of books and tens of thousands of essays, it has now dwindled to the point that our encyclopedias do not even mention it, and our publishing lists reveal only a forlorn sociological study here (*The Friendship Game*, by Andrew Greeley), a study of male or homosexual friendships there (*Friends and Lovers*, by Robert Brain).

Even more striking is the decline in talk about books as friends. [*Though many of my claims here are outdated, it is still amusing to find that if you Google "friendship" on the Internet, you get almost eight million references; but if you call up "friendship with books" you get 110.*] In the nineteenth century the personification was fashionable; in our time we have replaced the warm metaphor with cooler ones: the work as labyrinthine web, as one more cell-block in the prison house of language, as puzzle, as code, as *écriture* expressing itself, or—at the upper limits of human warmth—as a world to be entered, or an object made to be analyzed or even admired. No one would be caught dead today writing in the way that for William Ellery Channing, in 1838, was as natural as breathing. "It is chiefly," he says, "through books that we enjoy intercourse with superior minds. . . . In the best books, great men talk to us, give us their most precious thoughts, and pour their souls into ours. God be thanked for books. They are the voices of the distant and the dead, and make us heirs of the spiritual life of past ages. Books are true levelers. They give to all, who will faithfully use them, the society, the spiritual presence, of the best and greatest of our race."[1] Martin Tupper, at about the same time, wrote a sentiment similarly embalmed in Bartlett's *Familiar Quotations*: "A good book is the best of friends, the same today and forever." Sound sentiments, I would say, though they have an old-fashioned ring to our ears, and their authors give us little help of the kind we are seeking: they say little about how I might distinguish narrative friends from enemies.

Authors went on writing that way well into this century. Here's Helen Keller, speaking in 1902 of how books felt to her in her sense-deprived world: "In a word, literature is my Utopia. . . . No barrier of the senses shuts me out from the sweet, gracious discourse of my book-friends. They talk to me without embarrassment or awkwardness."

The point in reviving the metaphor of friendship would not be to revive this sort of extremely general talk about all "books," as if they were all equally our friends. Rather it would be to discover a vocabulary of discriminations among kinds of friendship, and for that we are forced, by the paucity of modern discussions, to look at the ancient tradition that saw friendship as one of the most valuable of all things in the world, and pursued talk about its degrees and kinds as one of the most important of human activities.

That tradition, which endured into the nineteenth century, never forgot that the quality of anyone's life is in large part identical to the quality of the company he keeps. As one modern commentator on Aquinas says, "Man's whole pursuit of happiness is in a sense a pursuit of friendship, a pursuit of something more than himself, since he feels and knows that he is not complete alone." As Aristotle had put it, "Without friends no one would choose to live, though he had all other goods." He makes clear that he is talking not only about what we would call affection among friends in the modern sense but all bonds of love between parents and children, kings and subjects, neighbors and citizens, husbands and wives, and so on.

Everyone in the tradition begins with the obvious point that I will feel friendly toward anyone who seems to offer me a benefit, any good thing of any kind. Such benefits can be of three kinds: either a pleasure, or some practical gain, or a quality of company that is not only pleasurable and profitable in some immediate sense but also good for me, or good for its own sake, since hours spent with that friend are seen as the way life should be. The three kinds are not of equal importance or stability. People who become friends only because they give each other pleasure—for example, sexual lovers or members of gourmet cooking clubs—stop being friends as soon as the pleasure-giving stops. Those whose friendship is based only on some immediate practical gain—partners in a business, say, each of whom possesses a necessary skill—fall apart as soon as the utility is no longer clear. The fullest friendship arises whenever two people not only offer each other pleasure or utilities but believe that they are equals in all their aspirations and thus are good for and with each other. These full friends love to be with each other because of the quality of life lived during the time of association. As Aristotle says, a true friendship is a relation of virtue with virtue, or as we might translate, of strength with strength and aspiration with aspiration. A full friend "is said to be one who wishes and does good things, or what appear to him to be good, for the sake of his friend," or "one who wishes his friend to be and to live for his own sake, as appears in mothers in regard to their children." In short, my true friend is one who "has the same relations with me that he has with himself." Such friendships will last as long as the reciprocal love of virtue lasts, quite possibly until death and even beyond.[2]

Not [*it's obvious to me now*] that the implied authors of *all* fictions purport to offer as gift one or another of these friendships.[3] To talk of *fictions* in our sense rules out the deliberate liars and tricksters and exploiters, all those enemies or put-on artists who exclude the reader from the author's truth. But even these almost always *claim* to address us with a friendly offer: "I would be your friend; join me, because if you do I'll give you something that no other story will give you in quite the same way—either some kind of pleasure, or something that is useful, or—best of all—a way of living together in friendship that will be, while both pleasant and useful, somehow too valuable to be reduced to either the *utile* or the *dulce*." All fictions, even the trickiest, come not as tricks but as gifts. They may turn out to be tricks, but when they do, we no longer call them fiction; we have other useful names for them.[4]

All stories, in short, claim to offer something to us that will add to our lives, and they are thus like the would-be friends we meet in real life. We never *accept* the offer unless we see ourselves as getting something from it: we seek the companionship only of those who give us a reason to, but all fictions implicitly claim to give us a reason to accept some level of friendship. This claim holds just as much for those works in which the dramatized characters are repugnant as for those that offer us characters who are overtly lovable.

This is no place to go into detailed distinctions among the kinds of friends. You will find them beautifully, even movingly, described in books 8 and 9 of Aristotle's *Ethics*, and again in Aquinas's two hundred pages of commentary on those books. You will also find them echoed in every discussion of friendship in the Renaissance, perhaps most marvelously developed in Montaigne's *Essays*. All we can do here is ask whether the basic distinctions among three kinds of friends can provide a useful start in talking about the people we join when we read: the pleasure givers, the useful, and those we love for what they are.

It is obvious that a value judgment is built into this hierarchy, but it is not a simple one. Though the *offer* of the disinterested friendship is by its nature a claim to be of the highest kind of the three, we never know in advance of close inquiry that the offer is genuine or that the implied author knows true friendship from a hole in the ground. And he may prove to be a snake in the grass. Or, to put it more politely, we do not know in advance whether what looks like a loving offer will on examination give us no grounds for that "reverence," or respect, that Kant, in his discussion of friendship, places in troublesome opposition to the love which insists on a sharing of intimate faults as well as virtues (*The Metaphysics of Ethics*, "Conclusion of the Elementology").

Similarly, to decide that a book offers me "a mere pleasure" or "a mere utility" does not yield an automatic rejection. Many an offer of pleasure proves superior in value to many a claim to full friendship. We cannot hope to find along this route easy judgments of good and bad. What we seek are fruitful ways of talking together about how books "deal with us"— ways of talking that themselves have ethical value. What we teachers of literature like to say to each other is true: many a "bad" book can be turned to profit by learning how to talk about it. The value of such talk is by no means confined to its power to correct our misreadings or to protect us from evil influences. Like other expressions of friendship, it is both immensely valuable as an educational force and finally self-justifying: friendly talk about literary friendship becomes, like that friendship itself, one of life's final goals.


## II

The challenge, then, in this kind of metaphorical criticism, will lie in our power to discriminate qualities of friendship which we ourselves, as readers, have in a sense created. We thus judge ourselves as we judge the would-be friends we have re-created. Here is circularity with a vengeance. But we need not fear it, so long as we do not pursue hard, final judgments of "wicked" or "blessed" but ways of sharing and testing our experience in public discourse.

Suppose we begin then with a rough classification of the minimal *pleasures* that authors promise and deliver. To every book that comes my way, I offer a tacit message: "All right, yes. Do come in for a moment. But either you please me in some way or I will admit you to my company no more." Rather than try to cover the infinite range of subjects that can meet that demand—sex, gossip, politics, instruction in flower arrangement, careful observation of architectural detail, and whatnot—it will be more helpful to think of the pleasurable *activities* that keep us visiting—regardless of the subject: keep us, that is, glued to the text.

Reading activity and the pleasure it gives can vary, first, in the sheer *quantity* of operations we are asked to perform; next, in the degree of responsibility given the reader, what we might call the *reciprocity* between author and reader; third, in the intensity of the *activity* required; and, finally, in the *kind*, or *range* of kinds, of activities. In real life we find these same variables. Some companions offer me a lot of whatever they are good at; others offer precious gems though few. Some companions, second, dominate the conversation, while some play an equal role, and some ask *me* to dominate. Third, some wake me up by the intensity or depth of their offering, while others are satisfied with a steady or slack pace, and others bore me. Finally, some offer me only one kind of pleasure, while others may range over many of life's values. It's exactly the same in reading fictions. Needless to say, I can by my own sluggishness or narrowness refuse even to acknowledge an offered gift in any of these dimensions.

On the scale of amount of activity required of me, we find many a book or story seeming to say, "Watch me, just watch me, passively, and you'll have fun, with absolutely no psychic labor or cost of any kind." Since even the simplest story requires some imaginative activity on the part of the reader, no story can imply as much sheer passivity as some other forms of entertainment: the Johnny Carson show, circus clowns, jugglers, golf matches on TV, or Marineland. But miscellaneous collections of stories or jokes can come close.

I've been reading in a little anthology, *The Oxford Book of Literary Anecdotes*. The anecdotes are usually about half a page or less, and I read one here, one there, as the days go by. I never read for longer than ten minutes at a time. Yet I shall go on reading in it, because though some of the anecdotes are pretty feeble, some are a lot of fun, and they all are quite good at filling the odd ten-minute periods with something I consider worth having: anecdotal pleasure. The implied author, in this case named as an editor, James Sutherland, has earned my respect as an entertainer and my passive engagement as a reader. Yet almost anything can distract me from that book, and it thus illustrates nearly a "zero-degree of activity" (to borrow a fashionable terminology): any less active, and I'd fall asleep.

Note that to reach that near-zero degree I have had to describe no connected narrative at all but a loose collection. As soon as even the simplest story is encountered, the reader is required to get moving on some constructive activity. Put another way, every story offers us the pleasure of imagining characters and events in some world not exactly our own, of wondering how those events will turn out, and of concluding that somehow they have hung together. We are so determined to have this pleasure that we will try to find it even where it is not being offered. Think of those interminable, formless story summaries that our children give us after the movie or TV program, somehow losing all dramatic focus but expecting us to be as breathless about their rambling as they were about the taut version they viewed. Or we might think of those accounts of dreams that demand our attention without expecting us to do anything but wonder that such a thing could be imagined at all: "And then this huge bird, with the absolutely fantastically long sharp beak, came flying down at me, and . . . "

Even when we shift to stories that do have a point to their structure, we all know that some author-friends pack in a great deal for us and others are slack. Authors who pack a tight suitcase require the reader to unpack a great deal too. At one extreme is *Finnegans Wake*, packed by the most garrulous companion in the history of travel, with nooks and crannies and secret compartments that thousands of readers are at this very moment no doubt working to open. On the other hand is your favorite detective puzzler, who keeps you focused on a very small number of pertinent facts, buried under a large number of impertinent ones, and requires you to concentrate on the task of sorting the two out in order to arrive at a clear, unambiguous clearing-up of every problem in the simplified world as imagined. The work that you are asked to do here is done with considerable intensity, but when you get through and ask yourself what this friend has asked of you, the answer is, "To work on one puzzle for several hours, a puzzle the solution to which does not any longer concern me." Only a special kind of reader is ever tempted to go on unpacking the secrets of a particular mystery after the first reading. And only an especially well-made mystery can support even for an hour such continued demands for more reward. Yet we all know that such undemanding gifts can lead us to return to their authors again and again, saying, "Tell me another."

We might at first think that in the quantity of work required we have found a first criterion of ethical excellence: surely the more I am asked to reconstruct from the innards of a work, the richer the gift and thus the better the friend. But we shall find later that our choices among friends are not that simple.

Our activity can vary, second, according to whether the work to be done is reciprocal or weighted toward author or reader. "Easy writing's curst hard reading"—Sheridan's *mot* is clearly a judgment against authors who don't do *their* fair share. But what is a fair share?

Whatever our final judgment on those friends who require more or less pleasurable work from us, we can discern here again a useful scale of description, ranging from those who, like Joyce, spent almost a lifetime laboring on a single work, and ask us to do the same, implying that we may never become their equals in energy, wit, and learning, through those who labor long to make things easy, implying that they are our servants in this one respect and that we are gentlemen and ladies of leisure, and on to those who either labor little or imply effortless creativity and yet require us to work hard reconstructing thought and organization that they have not quite expressed.

At both extremes of this scale many readers get off the boat. The author who expects me to work *too* hard because he too has worked hard, like the author who gives me no sense that he cares at all, simply falls off the chart of friendship: we stop reading. But for those who manage somehow to keep us going, there is a great difference between the classical notion of the writer as servant making things easy to entertain his master and the modern reversal in which the reader is asked to slave away at work that the author did not deign to do.

Turning, third, to the scale of intensity, which is in large part a product of quantity plus reciprocity, we begin, as we began on the scale of quantity, with the minimal level of catching the point of some anecdote, however mild the point may be, and move toward the moments we generally describe as powerful, transforming, radiant, overwhelming, or sublime.

We might take as the lowest level of intensity our involvement with simple stories like Aesop's fables. The listener simply follows a story line about a nondescript greedy farmer, or a goose that inexplicably lays golden eggs, and experiences a single, pure motive leading to a single, neat, but bland moral climax. Intensity can be added to any such tale by any device that draws the listener's imagination into active reconstruction. The more concentrated the reader's activity per word or line, the greater the intensity. A kind of ultimate on this scale can be illustrated with a piece of complex irony by Jonathan Swift, spoken by an unreliable narrator, the so-called projector who is often satirized as *A Tale of a Tub* progresses: "Last week I saw a woman flay'd, and you will hardly believe how much it altered her person for the worse."

The invitation to concentrated activity by this one-sentence story, this sly "friend," could not be more intense. If I accept my assignment as implied reader, I must perform at least the following activities while reading this one sentence.

1. I must decide whether the statement is outlandish as it stands.
2. To do so, I must consult my standards about flaying people live and about the proper tone for talking of such matters. *"This* tone is clearly 'impossible.'"
3. I must decide whether the implied author means it as it stands.
4. I conclude that he cannot do so.
5. I wonder about what, then, he may mean to say by it.
6. I decide that he is surely against live flaying, or the jest would not work, but that *that* can't be his point.
7. I must decide whether the implied author wants me to believe that he saw a live flaying last week or made up the fiction for his purposes.
8. I decide that he did not, but I must both accept and reject the fiction that the narrator, "the projector," unlike my friend, the implied author, saw that flay'd woman.
9. I then speculate about the relation between the projector and the implied Swift, making use of other ironies from the *Tale*, many of them equally condensed.
10. I then speculate about what the implied author really wants me to believe about how surface appearance relates to reality.

And so on. It would take more than these ten steps simply to describe minimally what our companion, the implied Swift, requires us to do if we are to join him in his incredibly intricate dance. We thus have a great quantity of activity, with an inferred total reciprocity, yielding maximum intensity.

There is only one other kind of invitation that can match such irony in the level of intensity invited, and that is of course metaphor. "Take physic, pomp," Lear cries, on the heath.

> Expose thyself to feel what wretches feel,
> That thou mayst shake the superflux to them,
> And show the heavens more just.

We obediently perform an amazing dance of interpretation, first recognizing that neither *physic* nor *pomp* can be read literally, then performing extraordinary feats of translation, trying our best to imagine what sort of shaking of what kind of superflux Lear and the "silent" Shakespeare have in mind. All the while we are adding to our picture of Lear's character and suffering soul. Looking more closely, I see that Lear must really be talking about laxatives and purgations: that superflux is not just the superfluities of wealth but the diseased flux produced by the right purgative, and my picture of the Lear who has shown himself increasingly obscene and scatological in his rising desperation is now intensified.

It is important to note that none of this reconstruction can be avoided by an act of will. Once I have read "Take physic, pomp," I can no more resist being shaped into the pattern of this metaphor, provided I know what the words mean and have been following the play, than a carpenter who knows how to do tongue-and-groove joints can resist seeing one when it is before his eyes. Even if I object to having my mind tamed to consider laxatives and fluxes, the command issued by the metaphor will have been obeyed: a part of my mind has been shaped into an intense, active discussion about the gross parallels between taking physic and curing pomp's indifference to poverty and suffering. We see here a breaking down of the sharp distinction, useful in other contexts, between implied readers and "real" readers. Any ironic or metaphoric shaping required of the implied reader will become "mine" whenever I encounter the text, regardless of any repudiation that "I" may later decide on. Whether the gift offered by this would-be friend is nourishing or poisonous, I have already imbibed.

Pleasurable activity, finally, can be of many different kinds. A cross-word puzzle can require as much reciprocal reconstructive activity as a fine poem. My engagement is as intense, as all-absorbing at some moments in an adventure movie as it could ever be in the reconstruction of the most beautiful metaphor of all time. Thus discrimination of kind and range are required. Crossword lovers learn to make discriminations among the characters who make different kinds of puzzles, praising those highly literate, subtle people implied by the puzzles that appear in the *New Statesman*, and sneering at what they call the merely verbal ones that most American papers carry. Similarly, we must distinguish kinds of activities, kinds of pleasures.

We might distinguish them according to the traditional triad: aesthetic, cognitive, and moral; beauty, truth, and goodness. If reading a story were simply a collection of moments, as it is not, we could say that some authors offer us mainly rich *imaginative* moments of reconstruction (say, Virginia Woolf), some engage us primarily in active *thought* about the truth of things (say, Thomas Mann), some emphasize practical questions and choices (say, John Bunyan), and some (Shakespeare, Dickens, Homer) cover the whole range.

But a vocabulary of friendship reveals a curious way in which distinctions break down. Though stories almost always engage all three of these dimensions of life in some degree, even the most purely "aesthetic" fictions never can avoid a practical twist: even the purest, most aggressively "poetic," least moral tale, even the many recent invitations to gambol irresponsibly among masterpieces of pure formlessness, will work *as* story only if they make the implied reader "want more of this friendship"—that is, want to *move* forward, rapidly or slowly, from here to there, from beginning to ending and then, sometimes, back again. And this means that the most powerful effect on my own ethos, at least during my reading, is to concentrate my desires and fears and expectations on some future fulfillment: I am made to want something that I do not have. As reader, my whole being is concentrated on "how it all turns out." My most powerful activity is that of desiring certain future rewards, both justice for characters in the story, the good and the wicked, and what we might call aesthetic justice—a satisfying completion of the form. We may not want to call this patterning of desire (by no means always in a narrowly "moral" domain) a practical effect, but it has one obvious and inescapable effect on my own practice: it determines *who I am to be* for the duration of the experience. I can't think of anything more practical than that.

The focusing of our desires is of course clearest in adventure stories that threaten—or promise—disaster. If I pick up the best seller *Jaws*, for example, I find this opening:

> The great fish moved silently through the night water, propelled by short sweeps of its crescent tail. The mouth was open just enough to permit a rush of water over the gills ... the eyes were sightless in the black, and the other senses transmitted nothing extraordinary to the small, primitive brain.

If I choose to go on, I do so because I want more of this threat described in this special style—or more of what is threatened, on page 2, as a man and woman "fumbled with each other's clothing, twined limbs around limbs, and thrashed with urgent ardor on the cold sand."

> "Now, how about that swim?" she said.
> "You go ahead," he said. "I'll wait for you here."

Already I can hardly wait for the promised bloody encounter between such a primitive brain and such a sexy thrasher. But if I move on to enjoy *that,* I do not do so in mere passive curiosity of the kind that keeps me browsing in those literary anecdotes. I am both fearing spectacular bloodshed and desiring it, learning to enjoy the prospect of bloody death for those who don't matter, hoping for final safety for the good guys (who don't matter very *much*) and learning—learning all the while both that happiness for these characters is defined as escape from danger and that happiness for me is watching people fall into danger and then—sometimes—escape from it.

We won't go into the other lessons I am learning—about what makes a good (that is, atrocious) literary style, about what makes a gripping narrative manner, and so on. Though the quantity of activity will be fairly low, the intensity will be high indeed, *if* my buddy Benchley has his way with me. But note that the reciprocity will be either nonexistent or immensely high, depending on whether I suspect Benchley of not himself savoring the effects that he hopes *Jaws* will have on me. The difference between my relations with a hack and what we call the "sincere artist" is immense, and it requires a study in itself. But for now the point is that by patterning my desires toward a given goal, bloody adventure, the story at each step molds me into *its* shapes, giving me practice, as it were, in wanting certain outcomes and qualities and ignoring certain others. I become, for the hours of reading, *that kind of desirer*, with precisely the kinds of strengths and weaknesses, whatever they are, that the author has built into the structure.

What is often forgotten is that exactly the same kind of "practical" patterning of desire will result if the story I am gripped by is on the other end of the scale of bloody adventuresomeness: say, *Finnegans Wake*:

> riverrun, past Eve and Adam's, from swerve of shore to bend of bay, brings us by a commodius vicus of recirculation back to Howth Castle and Environs.
>
> Sir Tristram, violer d'amores, fr'over the short sea, had passencore rearrived from North Armorica on this side the scraggy isthmus of Europe minor to wielderfight his penisolate war . . .

I may choose not to go on reading *Finnegans Wake*, of course, as in fact I have chosen not to go on reading *Jaws*. But if I do go on, it will be because I desire more of "this," whatever *this* kind of companionship is. I shall be shaping myself into the particular kind of shape recommended by this friend just as much as I would be in reading *Jaws*. In short, the shaping of desires will occur just as much when my reading is nonlinear and recursive, as in fact it has to be in *Wake*, as when the work I'm reading is, like *Jaws*, strictly sequential. We are not now judging what I want, only insisting that unless I want something, I stop reading. (We rule out, in all of this, what our course descriptions label so depressingly "*Required* Reading.")

Notice again that in this one kind of activity, the journey toward a desired reward, the distinction between what the implied reader does and what the flesh-and-blood reader does disappears, at least during the reading experience. The implied reader I become cannot desire fictional blood without *my* desiring blood. I cannot, as implied reader, fear Tess's doom or hope for Elizabeth's marriage to Darcy without *my* fearing and hoping for those things. The quality of the desire may be quite different, as my "real" self sits back and says, "The *real* me doesn't care a whit about Tess's chastity or about whether she finds a good husband; I don't even believe that Tess is real, so how could I *really* care about her fate?" But if I am engaged and all my desires are concentrated exactly on her fate, just as, in a movie, watching a psychopathic killer, my heart will go on pounding and my palms sweating, even as I lean to my equally anxious wife and say, "Remember, it's only a movie."

There is an immense difference between this kind of effect and the more usual and narrower question of ethical effects of particular examples set by characters explicitly shown within the work. Traditionally, moral criticism of fiction concentrated almost entirely on the latter: something like, "Does Tess of the D'Urbervilles provide a good model for our daughters?" or, "Would I want my daughter to marry one of Eugene O'Neill's or Steinbeck's heroes?" We are changing this question to two others that to some people will sound equally square. First, "Does what Thomas Hardy asks you to desire and fear and deplore and expect in the life of his story provide a good kind of life for you, or for your sons and daughters?" "Is that 'slice of life' critics used to talk about a good slice?" We leave aside, you remember, the question of whether it will prove carcinogenic in the long run. For now think just of the two to ten hours that will be spent desiring Tess's happiness, fearing and increasingly expecting her tragic doom, and deploring the forces in life that ensure the doom.

To desire her happiness, we must accept, of course, the implied picture Hardy presents of what happiness would be for Tess: discovery of a man who, unlike Angel Clare and Alec, but very much like the implied Thomas Hardy, would appreciate her true quality, protect her from too much thinking about what the Parliament of the Gods foredooms us to, and yet provide her with lots of reading experiences of the kind this novel provides, the kind that, be it said, judges life primarily by how our desires for the future turn out. The second question arises naturally from the first: Would you like your daughter to marry one, even for a few hours—not one of the characters but the implied Thomas Hardy, whose patterns of desires will have become hers while she reads?

A full ethics of fictions would look closely at various possible shapes of desire. Desire is, of course, one kind of activity, and you can see that some of our earlier terms would be of use again here. But we would need new terms now for the total shape of our experience, what Aristotle calls the plot, but what we have no good modern term for.

We now have a scale of questions about the activities that go to make up our total companionship with a given implied author: whether they are many or few, whether reciprocal or one-sided, whether intense or relaxed or sluggish, and whether broad or narrow in range. All of these help to form the strongest activity of all: the patterning of desires and gratification that the author takes us through. It is this pattern, far more than anything any seeming spokesman for the author may do or say at particular moments in the story, that most powerfully reveals the implied person who offers it all: "Here is my notion of good companionship," he cries, "Read me, read me! Spend your hours with me and I will show you what life can be at its best."

## III

The second kind of friend is one who explicitly subordinates pleasure to usefulness. The useful things authors offer us can range over every conceivable value. There are novels that would teach me how to get rich quick, how to behave socially as if I were rich, just which wines are the tastiest, which cars are slickest, which modes of stroking or stabbing of rivals are most useful on which occasions. Needless to say, this kind of offering is not confined to modern literature, as we can see if we ask how much of what the *Odyssey* or the *Aeneid* offers us purports to be useful information about our noble past and instruction about how to live.

Except for plain information, perhaps the most frequent offering—often dismissed out of hand as a sure sign that a literary work is subliterary—is of moral guidance. Many a critic has told us that didactic poetry is by definition inferior. But the truth is that most of the literary friends we praise offer us moral instruction in addition to, or as a basis of, whatever pleasurable activity they would share. Any judgments we may finally come to about any particular moral offering will thus depend on how it is offered, and our judgment of that will finally depend on our notion of who makes the offer—that is, it throws us back on our vocabulary of would-be friendships.[5]

Here is the beginning of a poem called "Don't Quit—Fight One More Round":

> When things go wrong, as they sometimes will,
> When the road you're trudging seems all uphill,
> When the funds are low and the debts are high
> And you want to smile, but you have to sigh,
> When care is pressing you down a bit,
> Rest! If you must—but never quit.
> (Author unknown)

It concludes, two stanzas later: "It's when things seem worst that *you mustn't quit.*" The trouble with such verse is not that the advice itself is trite, or that the diction is flat and the imagery either nonexistent or stale; no doubt all of these faults contribute. But the real trouble is that the speaker does not earn the right to offer his good advice. He clearly would like to be my friend: the offer of disinterested advice sounds genuine on the surface. But the troubles he expects me to wrestle with—low funds, being "a bit" care-ridden—are not the troubles that really get *me* down. The responses he warns against don't sound like *my* responses to real trouble (a sigh, a sense of trudging uphill). What is worse, they are not convincingly *his*: his poem does not in any sense either illustrate or conform to his message. The poet has mastered no troubles in writing it, and the activities it invites me to in no way illustrate the mastery of difficulty through courage and stamina. In short, the good thing it offers costs the giver very little—it is a cheap gift.

We can see the difference by looking at another "didactic" poem, one that most of us would not at first reading be likely to call didactic because it proclaims a *counter*-morality that most students of literature might embrace. It's by the youthful Yeats, the culminating poem in the volume of 1899, *The Wind among the Reeds*:

### The Fiddler of Dooney

When I play on my fiddle in Dooney,
Folk dance like a wave of the sea;
My cousin is priest in Kilvarnet,
My brother in Mocharabuiee.

I passed my brother and cousin:
They read in their books of prayer;
I read in my book of songs
I bought at the Sligo fair.

When we come at the end of time
To Peter sitting in state,
He will smile on the three old spirits,
But call me first through the gate;

For the good are always the merry,
Save by an evil chance,
And the merry love the fiddle,
And the merry love to dance:

And when the folk there spy me,
They will all come up to me,
With "Here is the fiddler of Dooney!"
And dance like a wave of the sea.

Whatever else this poem does, it speaks to me as a friend who would teach me to order my values in a certain way: fiddlers on top, priests next. If the implied poet and I are to meet in friendship, it must be as two members of a select group who understand, first, why priestly prayers are inferior to songs and, by implication, poems; next, why the implied poet is superior to his described brother and cousin; and then, why reading it is thus, in the ultimate scheme of things as judged by St. Peter, a moral act superior to conventional morality. So far the description is surprisingly similar to what we might give of the previous poem: it would teach me a moral lesson, one that is by 1980 as conventional as "you mustn't quit."

But note now the huge difference. In "The Fiddler," as re-created by the reader, my friend the poet asks me to do a poetic dance with him, not an especially intricate dance, not anywhere near as demanding as Swift required, not, be it said, full of original images or fresh diction or experimental verse forms. Rather, the invitation is to come dance to a quite conventional poetic music. Yet the "fiddling" is so masterful, so persuasively merry, so lilting, that one knows oneself to be in the hands of a master fiddler. Yeats thus asks us to imagine a mutual friend, the fiddler, who represents a kind of music that the poet himself has worked hard to illustrate. In consequence, all of our *activities* help make the message plausible. The resulting pattern of desires aroused by the poem clearly underlines its moral point: It makes us long for a world in which everyone, everyone would dance like a wave of the sea, instead of sitting around glumly reading prayer books.

We have found asked of us, then, an inversion of "ordinary" morality, an engagement in an easily accessible activity that exemplifies that superior morality, and an imaginative longing for a world in which everyone accepts it. Everything about the poem fixes a hierarchy of folks in which the fiddler, the poet, and the implied reader embrace as friends who are superior to the bulk of mankind. Everything, that is, except the ingratiating accessibility of every line; in its refusal to demand any special learning or skill in the reader, the poem implies that all readers can understand it easily and thus have a fair chance at accepting the good it offers.

A closer analysis would reveal further moral, intellectual, and aesthetic hierarchies implicit in the poem. Obviously the almost universal distinction between what is didactic and what is not is far too simple to account for many different shadings of openness or insistence and the many different axes of value that can be insinuated or preached openly. No fiction, how-ever purified it may seem on the surface, will be free of all didactic taint, if to recommend or reinforce this or that value judgment is to reveal didactic taint. But an astonishing number of the fictions we admire, fictions that are generally called nondidactic, are, like "The Fiddler," quite openly di-dactic precisely in this sense: When we consider their effects closely, with full attention both to what is stated and what activities are required of the implied reader, they insist on a precise ordering of values, one that is not shared by all readers in advance and that is thus recognizable as a "good" recommended by the friend implied in the fiction itself.

Despite the almost universally held dogma to the contrary, I can see no reason why it is a critical error to judge the quality of the goods such poems offer us. It is true that most critical attempts to discriminate among them are based either on offensively narrow moral creeds or on offensively superficial reading. But then, every critical mode is subject to corruption, and we should not let the special difficulties that threaten in this direction deter us, if we decide that the results may be important.

That there are special difficulties no one has ever denied. We have al-ready seen that we cannot judge the "goods" offered either by "Don't Quit" or "The Fiddler" simply by extracting a propositional statement and then judging *it*. The true differences in quality among the good things "didactic" poets offer us always depend on the quality of the implied author's total act, his way of holding and offering his gift. The quality of the gift as it might be summarized or stated separately from the poem is not irrelevant, but it can be qualified almost beyond recognition by accompanying goods and evils. A way of dramatizing this complexity that will lead us closer to our discussion of full literary friendship is to say that when I take the beliefs offered by these two poems in the abstract, I agree with the moral of "Don't Quit," and I disagree, or at least find grotesquely oversimplified, the notion that fiddling and poems are self-evidently more important activities than praying. Whether others agree or not—and I suspect that most readers will not—it is clear that Yeats's doctrine is curiously self-praising, while the other teaching is both generously offered and indubitable. It is a doctrine that all those youthful, lazy louts in the "me generation" ought to have drummed into their ears daily. And yet I also have no doubt about which implied author offers me the superior friendship. Though the *type* of moral good offered by "Don't Quit" is at least as important as Yeats's, and the con-clusion, flatly stated, is to me less subject to question, the author of "The Fiddler" wins hands down. But he does not win by achieving a simple extreme of any one of the four qualities I have described. He wins not by offering some absolute large quantity of psychic activity, or some extreme of intensity or reciprocity, or some perfect quality in the patterns of desire. He wins our friendship, as our "real" friends do, by a distinctive and admirable balance that in its totality overrides any minor faults in any one quality.

The still-youthful Yeats, that relatively callow, self-aggrandizing, arrogant fiddler putting down his priestly brothers, that young cultist of high art is, in spite of all, able to create a friend who offers me a good that he himself—the implied Yeats—takes with immense and lovely seriousness, and I come away sure that to go on discussing that good with him—that is, to go on reading more of his poems—will be one of the best things I could possibly do for myself.

We are now launched fully into a vocabulary that goes beyond, subsumes, but may very well contradict at some points the vocabularies of activity, of patterned desires, and of proffered goods. We are moving toward a way of describing total implied friendships ethically. Though I have in the last few pages inched toward open appraisal of one poem as superior to another, I hope that I have illustrated a way of talking about such matters that goes beyond the traditional moralistic judgment of works according to either the truth of the moral or the virtue of the characters presented. But it also avoids the equally simplistic modern claim that the entire morality of art lies in craft. The whole morality of art lies in an immense number of things that go into building a friendship between two characters, the implied author's and the implied reader's.

That such talk will not easily lead to flat judgments like "true" or "false" or "virtuous" or "wicked" can be illustrated even more clearly by looking at another covertly didactic poem.

*ygUDuh*

    ydoan
    yunnuhstan

    ydoan o
    yunnuhstan dem
    yguduh ged

    yunnuhstan dem doidee
    yguduh ged riduh
    ydoan o nudn
  LISN bud LISN

           dem
           gud
           am

           lidl yelluh bas
           tuds weer goin
     duhSIVILEYEzum
        (e. e. cummings)

Let's again ask our three kinds of questions about this companion. First, what kind or degree of pleasurable activity does he ask of me? In this respect the poem couldn't be more different from Yeats's. Initially opaque, it requires an immense amount of intense deciphering energy at the start, enough to put off most readers except the professionally committed or those who have already come to trust e. e. cummings. What's more, even after the typographical trickery has been mastered, there is no explicit spokesman here for the implied author: an intense activity is required in making moral inferences, inferences from oblique signs provided by speakers who could not themselves ever make them.

Second, what is the utility offered, implicitly or explicitly? Beyond the gift of an intriguing game, a game that includes moral deciphering, the poem claims to offer me a moral position superior to that of the bigot, or more probably two bigots, speaking in it. Moral instruction is obviously too stiff a term for what we feel in the offer, but moral instruction is there— or at least a reinforcement of the average liberal reader's conviction that people who talk like this have absurdly bigoted notions about the world. Looked at directly, the doctrine is of course tainted by its own bigotry; in capitalizing on one rejected act of stereotyping, it relies on another—unless we can find some way to assume that cummings intends some further irony that will save his bigots from the contempt the poem heaps on them.

If we then attempt to think about the total quality of the life lived with the poem, the full quality of friendship it extends to us, we find ourselves now able to compare it with the other two poems on various scales. First, as "Don't Quit" was easier than "The Fiddler," requiring less intense activity, so "The Fiddler" is easier, less intensely active, than "ygUDuh." This difference is most striking in the matter of moral inference: "Don't Quit" invites none; "The Fiddler" sort of allows some but puts it all out front; "ygUDuh" demands a lot and attempts to reward us for and with it.

As for reciprocity: "Don't Quit" is entirely one-way: *I* know something good for you and offer it to *you*, who *need* it: *I* offer, *you* receive. "The Fiddler" offers at least two goods, an aesthetic lesson downgrading conventional morality, and an exemplification of it in experience, a pattern of desires and fulfillments. The giver practices the good before our eyes and requires us to engage with it actively; he realizes its value in reciprocity with the fiddler and, by perhaps shaky implication, with the flesh-and-blood Yeats. "ygUDuh" similarly offers us two goods, a moral message, inviting us to join the implied author in a position superior to the bulk of bigoted mankind, and the story that embodies the message and requires us actively to figure it out.

But note that the kind of good offered, including the patterns of desire, is quite different in "ygUDuh": this would-be friend *does not simply celebrate a hierarchy, while allowing the inferior people to get into heaven.* Rather he *mocks* the bigot's moral and intellectual inferiority, and requires us to do the same, or we shall not enjoy that punch word "civilize" as applied to these bums claiming to save the Japanese whom America was fighting at the time. If we are to savor the wry irony entailed in imagining such bums claiming to civilize anybody, we must join not only an elitist who, like Yeats, looks down on those with an inferior morality, but one who, unlike Yeats, looks down mockingly. More important, the technique of the poem similarly looks down on those who cannot decipher it: in achieving a maximum intensity and reciprocity for both implied author and reader, it has implied a kind of friendship that is about as snobbish as a friendship can be. One cannot join the implied cummings just by opposing bigotry: one must also join a literary elite, one that values a sense of being very advanced indeed.

To put our description this way implies that I think more highly of the ethos of Yeats's poem than of cummings's, which I do. But note that my judgment does not necessarily follow from the description. One man's snobbish friendship is another man's saving remnant of the pure in heart. It would be easy to put our description in words that reverse the evaluation: cummings insists that we wake up, that we think about our morality and our use of language, and that we think even harder about the hidebound conventions of our literary tradition. Yeats lulls us into a complacent, sleepy acceptance of an inverted morality that was after all conventional among intellectuals already in his time, one that in our time is surely banal.

If our vocabulary of the ethos of friendships did not allow for such differences in evaluation of what we find, it would be useless as a vocabulary for fruitful discussion. There is thus no easy way to determine at what point we should take our stand and say that this or that fiction seems to us morally harmful, or aesthetically degrading, or full of false doctrine about life. But by talking about the quality of our meeting, during the time of meeting, we can hope to avoid freezing labels onto our judgments in destructive ways; instead of saying that cummings's poem is immoral, or "Don't Quit" a piece of contemptible trash, we can discover a release into profitable kinds of talk about each. Though we may finally conclude either that we want no more of that kind of company or that it would be probably harmful to this or that kind of immature reader, we are no longer dependent on the quality of the friendship *offered* to determine the full quality of the relation *achieved*.

Just as in real life we are not bound to deal with people only on the terms they would dictate—our own qualities can either raise or lower the quality of any meeting—so it is in our meetings with literary companions. Presumably the better we are at conducting ethical criticism, the more we will accomplish, not only for ourselves, in each encounter, but also in a curious way for the work itself. That poor implied author lies there trapped, in a sense, inert until we bring him alive and ask, "Now, then, what good things would you like to offer me?"

We must now add one further qualification to what we have said about "ygUDuh," and it is an important one. I have found that students who are troubled by cummings's asking them to be bigoted about bigots and condescending toward poor readers then try to rescue the author. Since they don't want to feel bigoted, or to think that cummings was bigoted, they will assume that we should really read the poem as expressing and asking for compassion for the bigot or bigots dramatized. If we think of cummings as trying to stimulate the kind of debate that resolving these two contrasting readings would require, he comes off as an entirely different and more defensible kind of friend than in my first reading: he is now self-consistent, compassionate toward all mankind, and much more likely to prove beneficial, in his companionship, to my own psychic growth.

The question then becomes, Does the poem in fact invite that kind of rich inquiry, or does such inquiry, springing from a generous determination in the critic not to think ill of a famous author, impose this ethical depth upon it? Regardless of where we come out on this question, cummings's ethos will remain unchanged in the *technical* dimension—what his enemies will perhaps call elitist avant-gardism.

## IV

These three poems illustrate much too briefly three kinds of moral reorderings or reinforcements that implied authors can offer us. Our analysis shows that such friendly offers cannot be flatly judged without reference to the ultimate ethos of the would-be giver. As is true in real life, I cannot know whether to accept a useful gift without appraising the character of the giver. When a would-be friend offers me a marvelous deal, I can often look into the facts behind the speaker, but in the literary friendships we care about, the deal is inseparable from the friends who offer it: their total ethical value to my life is what they offer.

Obviously these three friends—the platitudinous Dutch uncle, the care-free dancing partner, and the antibigotry crony—are a crude sampling from the immense range of relations offered by literary works. Our usual impoverished vocabulary, reducing ethical distinctions to "artistic" works (all good for you) and "didactic" works (some good for you and some bad, depending simply on what they would teach), is suddenly enriched into an unlimited range of possibilities: the implied author as clever, sardonic iconoclast, claiming to do me good by taking something from me I mistakenly value (Samuel Butler in *The Way of All Flesh* or *A Fair Haven*); the implied author as night watchman crying the alarm (*1984*); the implied author who will take infinite pains to bring me some saving mystery of infinite worth (Dante, Milton, Spenser, Bunyan). And so on.

When we consider the variety of friends we happily embrace, we can see why critics have so often made the mistake of saying that doctrines don't matter. Some of what such great souls would offer me I cannot accept, and my refusal to do so *does* attenuate to some degree my full friendship. But with such large-souled folk who offer so much so intensely, with such clear evidence that they are themselves in pursuit of the good and would rejoice if I joined them—with *such* folk, any specific lesser good offered becomes less important than that grand friendship itself. What is more, the gifts that I reject—let us say some details in Dante's Thomism—are usually of a kind a true friend might offer me; the very act of thinking about whether to accept them—of "discussing" the offer before rejecting it—is itself a fine gift of another kind. Such authors would teach us, and they do teach us, through the shapes of desire they offer as gifts more than by any specific doctrine we could accept or reject.

The key question in the ethics of fictions, then, so long as we pursue it under this friendship metaphor, becomes, "Is the offered friendship in fact what it claims to be?" Is the pattern of life this would-be friend offers in fact one that two friends will pursue together? Or is this the offer of a sadist to a presumed masochist? Or of a seducer to the seduced? Of a rapist to his victim? Of the exploiter to the exploited? Is this a friend, a lover, a parent, a prophet, a crony, a co-conspirator, an *agent provocateur*, a tyrant, a therapist, a sycophant, a suck-up? Or perhaps a sidekick, a lackey, a vandal, a bloodsucker, a blackmailer?

The possibilities are obviously as various as the vocabulary for praising and damning acquaintances in life. And just as in life we do not decide to associate with only one kind of person, even though we have terms that discriminate among kinds, so in literature: exploring this vocabulary will not necessarily lead to any particular decision about which literary works we shall dwell with—and in. But it should uncover ways of talking that help us determine who are our true friends.

The fullest friendships, the "friendships of virtue" that the tradition hails as best, are likely to be with the works the world calls classics. [*Classics might well be defined as those works that have proved successful over the years in building friendships.*] When I read *Persuasion*, *Middlemarch*, and *War and Peace*, when I "perform" (or see performed) *King Lear* and *The Misanthrope*, I meet, in their authors, friends who demonstrate their friendship not only in the range and kinds of pleasures they offer, not only in the promise they fulfill of proving useful to me, but finally in the irresistible invitation they offer to live a better life, during these moments, than I might otherwise live.

I say to them in reply that if I don't choose to live *with* you, I shall lose something more precious than any one point I can make *about* you: your company is superior to any company I can hope to discover among the ordinary folk with whom I live—including myself. After all, you are a select version, superior even to the flesh-and-blood author who created you. To dwell with you is to grow toward your quality. You lead me first to a level of activity in all ways higher and more intense and in a curious way more fully generous and reciprocal than I am likely to meet anywhere else in the world. And you mold that activity into patterns of longing and fulfillment that make my ordinary dreams seem petty and absurd. You finally thus show what life can be not just to a coterie, a saved remnant looking down on the fools, slobs, and knaves, but to *anyone* willing to work at earning the title of true friend.

*This essay, which may feel to some readers too self-centered, was commissioned by Salim Kemal and Ivan Gaskell for their book* Explanation and Value in the Arts, *for the series Studies in Philosophy and the Arts. They asked me to deal explicitly with diverse responses to* The Company We Keep: An Ethics of Fiction. *That's what I concentrated on, suggesting throughout that, since no one ethical theory will ever triumph, what we need is an embrace of the pluralism that other essays here, in this present collection, celebrate. The fact that ethical theories inevitably conflict does not mean that each of them can successfully refute all rivals: truths are multiple.*

The pluralism that Booth is referring to here is operative in all of his essays and books, but see chapter 7 in this volume, on the work of Richard McKeon, for a helpful introductory account of what he means by the term.

This essay was originally published in *Explanation and Value in the Arts*, ed. Salim Kemal and Ivan Gaskell (Cambridge: Cambridge University Press, 1993), 71–93 (copyright 1993 by Cambridge University Press; reprinted with permission).

# On Relocating Ethical Criticism

## I

Invited to "discuss ethical criticism in the light of responses to [my] book *The Company We Keep*," I was naturally tempted by the glorious opportunity to give the more careless among my readers a public lashing. Like most authors, I've been puzzled, and sometimes angered, by a fair number of grotesque misconstruals.[1] But it will be more profitable here to ignore the blind and the halt and turn, instead, to explore what it might mean that the great majority of reviewers have chosen to embrace the project, if not the details, of my effort to rehabilitate ethical criticism.

I had thought, as I began writing the book in the mid-1970s, that the critical world, busy with its attacks on authors, intentions, referentiality, and any form of closure, would be generally hostile to my project. Friends confirmed my expectation: "It's really courageous of you to take up such an unfashionable cause. You'll be crucified." Our predictions of hostile responses were based, at least in part, on two dogmas inherited from mid-century and seemingly still dominant then. On the one hand, most practicing critics had been graduate-schooled to believe that all practical questions—ideological, ethical, political—are irrelevant to our appraisals of *artistic* worth: the surest sign that a critic had been badly educated was any hint that judgments about "life" could intrude on aesthetic judgment. Though critics were everywhere beginning, once again, to ferret out the political origins and intents of literary works, everybody but Kenneth Burke and a few Marxists and feminists seemed still convinced that the domain of the "aesthetic" was immune to all practical questions. On the other hand, most critics seemed to share with philosophers and social scientists an even more basic dogma of modern thought, one that in a sense undergirded the first: It is the very mark of philosophical naïveté to think that you can derive an "ought" from an "is," a "value" from a "fact." In literary criticism this dogma reinforced the first: You cannot base an appraisal of ultimate literary value on a description and analysis of the literary "facts," especially if those facts are simply personal "value preferences" or commitments. Even when factual analysis reveals, as of course it always will, that the work is embedded in commitments, overt and covert, the critic's job is never to say, "This poem is good (or bad) because its ethical, moral, or political center is sound (or faulty), or because it is likely to produce good or bad effects in its readers."[2]

So I felt, as I began, that my enterprise was quite probably doomed to be attacked as just one final, forlorn, "post-Arnoldian" bleat of alarm: Let's get moral again and save the world from the relativists.[3] What happened, however, was quite different. During the decade of composition I began to discover that our critical climate is far different from what it was not so very long ago. Beneath or alongside or perhaps even subsuming more visible transformations traveling under labels like deconstruction, feminism, new historicism, and cultural critique was a transformation from "neutralist," or "formalist," or "aestheticist" stances to open conversation about "values," "virtues," "character," and "morality." The same critical hunger that led me to write the book had long been shared, more or less silently, by an astonishing number of readers in a wide variety of positions—professional critics, popular reviewers, and "common readers." (Of course many of the latter had always just taken for granted, often in quite indefensible ways, the close connection between art and "life.") To read through the reviews now, in a batch, is to hear a vast collective sigh of release: "Your book means that at long last we can talk about what we have always *cared* about, without being accused of naïveté."

The expressions of gratitude are usually followed, of course, with objections. For some I am too much inclined to say "Good ethical criticism depends heavily on the ethics of the reader," too careful about not pasting labels of "good" and "bad": earlier, gruffer moralists like Leavis did it all better.[4] For others I have the wrong ethical code—I'm either too pluralistic or not pluralistic enough, or too much or too little Aristotelian, or too much or too little infected by postmodern "fashions," or too little aware that though what I call ethical criticism is required, it should really be subordinate to political criticism: Every critical dispute boils down to a power struggle.[5] For several I am not systematic enough. They leave the book, they say, not knowing in advance what standards they should apply when judging the next novel: "After reading this book I am no closer to an ethics of fiction that is independent of taste, subjectivism, and political exigency than I was before."[6] But even such complainers have usually asserted that novels do educate, morally, and are thus subject to questions about whether they bless us or curse us.[7]

In short, if the book's half-hundred or so reviewers and the many who have written private responses are in any way representative, large numbers of readers are eager for serious engagement, once again, with the sort of question Plato asked aggressively at the beginning of our tradition. How, first, should we deal with—how can we even *talk* about—the inescapable fact that even the purest, most "literary," works produce actual, tangible, ethical and political changes in the lives of those who engage with them? And how must our appraisals of literary value be affected by our judgments about the value of those changes?

Further evidence of a major change of climate comes from sources entirely unconnected with my work. One sees everywhere new declarations of ethical criticism, new efforts to show just how we might talk responsibly about the ways in which art works work upon us, for good and ill. Some of these were being written, without my knowing about them, as I wrote mine, and some appeared before or along with it.[8] Many others, at what seems to me an increasing rate, have appeared since.[9]

Joining this new wave, no one needs to feel caught any longer in the intolerable conflict I had described almost two decades ago, in *Modern Dogma and the Rhetoric of Assent* (1974), between our objectivist theories that ruled out rational demonstration of value judgments and our inescapable need to assert and defend those judgments. Instead of feeling caught in that dilemma, as sensitive intellectuals like Bertrand Russell had felt through the century, we are now unapologetically embedding our literary appraisals in our moral, ethical, or political positions, often enough, unfortunately, with the kind of irresponsible passion that seemed to justify the objectivist purgings in the first place. But as we do, so we are increasingly aware that "everyone else"—everyone, that is, outside the circle of frontline philosophy and criticism—has been doing this all the while, even those who have most vehemently declared ethical and political judgments out of bounds. We have discovered that our choice, as I insist in the book, is not whether to practice ethical criticism. It is rather whether to do it well or badly—whether to acknowledge it in our theories and thus to lay the groundwork for a more effective and responsible ethical conversation.

Our plea, then, the plea of a mounting number of critics, is addressed to two camps. To those who profess "objectivity" or "neutrality" or adherence to the pure aesthetic object, we say, "Come clean: bring your true commitments into the light of day, so that they can be tested in reasonable discussion." To those who have too casually asserted their moral and ethical judgments—for example, the strident *New Criterion* crowd and other overconfident canonists and anticanonists who talk as if any strongly felt assertion made good ethical criticism—we say, "Come off your high horse: this kind of criticism is more difficult and complex than you have implied. Let's get our reasons out on the table, so that we can find ways of improving the ethics of our own behavior in appraising the company we keep in these fictions."

The problem faced by those who embrace ethical criticism is surprisingly similar to what it was for responsible critics like Samuel Johnson or Coleridge, before theorizing ruled evaluations out of the domain of rational discourse: to find ways of talking about our values that will escape the blinkers of the merely private preference, *without* moving to baseless assertions about the one right way of thinking and responding. Like many a professional philosopher since the challenges of Hume and Kant, we critics are driven to search for a path between a dogmatic monism, on the one hand, and a subjectivism or solipsism, or what Stephen Pepper calls "utter relativism," on the other.[10]

## II

No rehabilitation of ethical criticism is likely to last for long, unless we can relocate ourselves in ways that will avoid traditional distortions. I see four essential, and inescapably difficult, relocations:

1.  from blanket attacks on, or defenses of, large lumpings like "poetry" or "literature" or "the novel" or "the canon" or "popular culture," to detailed formal inquiry into the precise nature of our experience with particular works;
2.  from positivist or "scientistic" notions of proof that leave "rhetoric," and especially rhetoric about values, as inherently no more than a corrupt or decadent attempt to seduce or exploit or overpower, to rhetoric as "coduction," a *sharing* of wide ranges of good reasons for our judgments;
3.  from a worry about moral obligations or codes or lessons about them, and the resulting danger of immoral behavior, to appraisals of the ethical quality of human relations, especially the quality of relations between authors and readers; and
4.  from the search for a single hierarchy of goods to a radical pluralism of hierarchies.

*Relocation from Amorphous Lumping to the Powers of Particulars*

An astonishingly large proportion of current criticism, whether committed to ethical matters or neutral about them, attempts to cover domains so vast that no critic, however learned, can know much about the individuals that dwell there. Of course every individual literary form resembles, in unlimited ways, other forms, literary and unliterary (whatever *those* lumping terms might mean). Though ethical critics from Plato through Sidney, Johnson, Shelley, and Arnold to F. R. Leavis and Lionel Trilling have offered important and challenging judgments about huge heaps of works (some as large as "poetry" or "literature," some reduced in size slightly with adjectives like "pure" or "genuine"), in my view they were usually most useful when they settled down, as Johnson, for example, often does, to talk about the blessings and blights offered by particular works. What Johnson has to say about the novel in general is to me much less interesting, and considerably more difficult to defend, than what he has to say about *Tom Jones* and scores of other works. What Arnold has to say about the religious mission of poetry in general seems to me much less valuable than his penetratingly negative critique of his own "Empedocles on Etna." What Plato has to say about poetry in general is to me of less permanent value, and far more dangerous, than what he has to say when he settles down to the specifics of Homer's epics.

The reason is of course that every large artistic grouping—"poetry," "the novel," "literature," "the lyric," "satire," "tragedy," and so on—potentially includes particular works that for a given reader or culture may prove either beneficial or harmful. Though it may be true that "the rise of the novel," or in our own time "the rise of the visual media," will have large-scale ethical effects on the hordes who suddenly join that "rise," and though one would certainly not want to ban from criticism all speculation about such effects, there is a much greater chance of a meeting of minds, through a conversation that presents not just opinion but argument, when critics deal with their experience with *this* novel, *this* epic, *this* poem, *this* rock lyric.[11]

*Relocation of Standards of Argument: "Coduction" as Shared Rhetoric*

If our judgments are to include our sense of the human worth of our encounters with individual works, and not just our sense of the craftsman's skill,[12] we cannot hope to demonstrate the validity of those judgments according to any standard scientific or strictly logical paradigm. Nothing that has been written by logicians about deduction or induction will be adequate to the subtle, complex process through which we come to know artistic worth.[13]

To put the point another way, every moral judgment derived from standard models of proof can be undermined by an appeal to experience: "Yes, I know that anti-Semitic literary works are by definition bad, but in *this* work, *The Merchant of Venice*, which is admittedly anti-Semitic in many of its scenes, I find so much of this, that, or the other valued quality that I can't simply condemn it out of hand." "Yes, of course this classical work is sexist, even more so than its contemporaries. That fact reflects a genuine limitation in the imaginative power of the author. But just look at these other powers. . . . " The redeeming qualities can be of many different kinds, because—and this is the point we come to under the third relocation— literary goods themselves are of many different kinds.

Since no simple logical demonstration, conducted by a private investigator and then laid out in full cogency to the world, can do the job, the ethical critic is thrust into a community of inquirers—the community of all those who care enough about the work in hand and about engaging with it to enter into serious conversation about it. Most of us find that most of our appraisals of individual works, and even of entire genres, change over time, not only because we change with the years but *because discussion with other judges modifies our views*. We discover our plain misreadings: a passage that we deplored turns out to have been intended ironically. We see features in the work that our blinders had obscured. We reconsider the standards we've employed. Or we discover why some private association has temporarily deflected our full attention.

This week my wife and I saw a play performed splendidly by the Steppenwolf repertory company in Chicago: *Wrong Turn at Lungfish*, by Garry Marshall and Lowell Ganz. We were considerably moved by the moral and intellectual changes acted persuasively by the two leads, and we came away praising the play. Then we each happened to read, independently, a perceptive negative review of the play, by Anthony Adler,[14] and we found on comparing notes that we had both revised our appraisal downward—not as far downward as Adler claimed we should, but downward nevertheless. My wife said, "Well, we'll have to get hold of that play and *read* it, but I think Adler has a point."

Such malleability is sometimes mocked as a weakness; it can indeed be one, when we are swayed by whatever opinion happens to hit us last. But to me it is the very heart of defensible artistic appraisal: "I" don't do it, alone; "we" do it, together, arguing back and forth in a process that never comes to a permanent stop. Such coduction—the coinage I've fallen back on to distinguish the process from induction and deduction—can never yield an absolute judgment of absolute ranking. It is always comparative, and it is thus always dependent on the range of our previous experience. Even a Shakespeare or Homer must be subject to the shifts of coduction over time, as succeeding judgments are extended from culture to culture and age to age.

Such fluidity, which is rightly stressed by subjectivists, gives absolutely no support, however, to those who think that literary values are in no sense "in" the work, or that "everything is relative to the viewer." Some reviewers have been annoyed that I should spend so much of their time (most of chapter 4 of *The Company We Keep*) uncovering the absurdities in the arguments of utter subjectivists; to them it should go without proof that literary works have powers of their own, and that some of these powers are more valuable to the human spirit than others. Other reviewers, deeply committed to the freedoms of subjectivism, naturally find my "proofs" of the *potential* commands of the work's intentions unconvincing. It is in the nature of the case that this debate will continue.

What need *not* survive, I hope, are the twin notions that make ethical criticism pointless: that individual, private, isolated inquirers (if any such ever existed: see the section entitled "Relocation from Monism to Pluralism" below) could ever make meaningful judgments about literary worth; and that our mutual endeavors in refining and deepening our judgments never really get anywhere—that no ethical judgments, of literature or of anything else, are *in fact* superior to some other ethical judgments.

Some reviewers have lamented that the process I call coduction is what most readers will "discover they have been practicing all along."[15] But that is just the point. It is indeed what most critics practice, more or less well. My argument is that the rhetoric employed in their exchanges, written and oral, is inherently superior, for the purpose of appraising value, to any paradigms of more rigorous calculation or measurement. But of course that claim presupposes that practitioners work to increase their skill in coduction.

The reviewer who caught this point most acutely was Thomas M. Conley, in "Booth's *Company* and the Rhetoric We Keep," in *Rhetorica*.[16] Conley shows how the book both advocates and practices a rhetoric that the Stoics would have contrasted, as "ethical," to two other kinds of rhetoric, the one springing from a "physical" view of the world in which language strives for a reflection of things as they are, the other springing from a "logical" or linguistic view of the world, in which

> authors are wordsmiths who, consciously or not, manipulate syntactic
> or semantic permutations inherent in linguistic codes to reproduce old

> messages in new forms or produce potential new meanings. These "mean-
> ings" may or may not claim to bear on things [as in the "physical" orienta-
> tion] and actions [as in the "ethical"]. In the extreme, even someone who
> simply provides as the text a box full of pages qualifies as an "author";
> but since words have [in this "logical" orientation] absolutely no objective
> correlative referents, the number of "messages" that can be construed is in
> principle infinite—the "meaning" of the "text" is radically indeterminate,
> as some of them put it. The text, as an organized collection of words, is
> an embodiment of those codes; and so it is up to the reader to decode
> the message(s) and up to the critic to explore the limitations and possible
> extensions of the code embodied in a given text. (172)

Conley sees, more clearly than most reviewers, and in a historical context
deeper than I will ever command, just how sharply contrasted my theory
and practice are from each of these alternative rhetorics.

> In an ethical orientation, that is, one featuring human action, "rhetoric"
> is rather more comprehensive than it is in the two other orientations.
> ...Instead of accuracy [the aim of the "physicalists," who are the main
> targets of contemporary "linguistic" attacks], probability is the goal, for the
> issues in action are not verifiable in the way issues in knowledge are, in
> part because they involve "facts" that haven't yet happened.... Instead of
> arbitrary pleasure taken in the permutations of words [the professed goal
> of some "linguistic" programs—for example, Barthes's], the construction
> of communicative patterns of desire is the goal. Probability and emotion
> in such a rhetoric must be combined to establish the grounds for action or
> the avoidance of it.... The best texts are those which achieve ... more than
> mere utility, more than mere pleasure: occasions for the coduction of value,
> episodes in our continuing efforts to become "the best character possible,
> under the circumstances." (173)

Conley's grasp of this radical attempt at a "new" rhetoric, a rhetoric actually
as old as the hills, enables him to understand a part of the book that hardly
anyone else has even mentioned: my advocacy of a kind of "hypocrisy upward" that we are led to by the way in which our "patterns of desire" are
*in fact* improved by association with implied authors who (because their
flesh-and-blood authors have purged their quotidian vices and weaknesses)
are better than we are. The relocation of rhetoric from "proof" to ethical
conversation requires rethinking about what a self, or character, is, how a
character gets formed (in part by playing roles "assigned" by stories and
talk about them), and how the moral or ethical quality of a character is to

be judged [*see chapters 6 and 7 of* The Company We Keep]. This unfashionable claim requires a third relocation for its support.

## Relocation from Moral Obligation to Ethical Quality

The notion that art works ought to teach us the right moral code, and that when they don't they should be condemned or banned, no doubt long predates Plato's *Republic*, and it is still inevitably active in our world today. I say "inevitably," because art works do in fact "teach"—that is, either implant or reinforce notions of moral obligation. Those who deny such effects have simply not looked honestly at their own behavior and at the world around them—most dramatically but not exclusively the world of the impressionable young.[17] Thus it would be absurd to reject outright criticism that leads to judgments based on such effects: much of what we call progress in the arts stems from strong feelings that this or that code has been overplayed or undervalued, and that art that does such-and-such moral or political job must be honored.

Nevertheless, such criticism can never be reduced to the syllogistic form

> X notion of moral obligation is bad (or good).
> Artistic work Y touts X (and thus may change behavior).
> Therefore work Y is bad (or good).

Such arguments usually suffer from our inability to test them empirically, though they make an empirical claim. But they suffer even more from a deficiency that is embedded in the still-widespread modern way of thinking about our "selves" and how we should live. By its very structure, this way usually leads to an opposition between the "individual," or self, and the others to whom some sort of obligation is owed: some duty that requires the sacrifice of something that "I" would like to have. Moral behavior is what counters my selfish ends; selfish behavior is what immorally serves my ends. This notion—that morality is found in pursuing altruism at the expense of "self"-ishness—produces serious limitations when it enters critical discourse about literary value. Not only does it oversimplify the effects of any given literary work, since they depend more on the total pattern of desires stimulated than on any particular code mentioned or preached, but it deflects us into irresolvable disputes about hard scientific evidence— "*Prove* that watching TV or listening to this or that rock record led to this crime"—and thus bypasses the most important questions.

The best critique I know of the "moral obligations" theory of ethics appeared a year after *Company*, though I made some use of its author's earlier manuscripts and articles: Charles Taylor's *Sources of the Self: The Making of the Modern Identity* (the book might have had a longer subtitle, adding: "with some illustrations of ethical criticism"). Even though it does not mention *Company*, I think of it as one of my best confirmations, because it undertakes, in a more fully developed philosophical form, precisely the same relocation from moral obligation to ethical quality that undergirds my enterprise.

Taylor's chief target is those modern notions of the individual that see "self-development" as something that occurs in opposition or indifference to the "webs of interlocution" that we all in fact are constituted by and live in (36). Taylor argues that all theories about the world, including those that deny the objective reality of "the good," are implicated in qualitative judgments about what makes a good human life. Modern theories that try to bypass this inescapable implication have left us on the one hand fumbling with utilitarian calculations, and on the other spluttering passionate, unargued assertions of our privatized moral obligations.

It is this effort to shift from moral obligation to ethical relations that led me to a revival of the metaphor of books as friends. Though it has the disadvantage of leading at times to a kind of sentimentalized criticism that was badly overworked in the nineteenth century, it has the great advantage of reminding us that the main motive for practicing ethical criticism in the first place is to share with others our inescapable sense that some literary "company" is worth keeping, some simply a waste of life's precious hours, and some positively debasing. Though you and I will never come to full and final agreement about just which literary company is ennobling or degrading, usefully shocking or harmfully destabilizing, we should be able to say to each other, about a novel, poem, movie, or video, not just, "It's a 'good' (or poor) read," or "You'll like it (or detest it)," but something like, "You really ought (or ought not) to have this experience: it will be good (or bad) for you."

### Relocation from Monism to Pluralism

A further productive muddying of the critical waters results from the fourth essential relocation: from the search for the one right critical path, the one right ethical or moral code, the one right method for conducting our ethical lives, to an embrace of plurality on all fronts. This century has produced a flood of philosophical critiques of the "quest for certainty" or the search for the one, single, universal view of things.[18] Many who have become aware of the age-old problem of "reciprocal refutation"—that is, every major philosopher's claims to refute every other philosopher—have tended to turn to the one most plausible explanation: "None of them is true." Others have turned to an eclecticism that allows for a bit of truth in each of many philosophies, the whole salmagundi of odds and ends somehow constituting a stew of truth. Only in this century—perhaps as a result of increased semantic sophistication, perhaps as a result of our unprecedented anthropological awareness of the need for *cultural* pluralism—have we developed systematic critical pluralisms that go beneath the seeming reciprocal refutation among major philosophies to seek a reciprocal intertranslatability that would allow us to say: "Though many philosophical views may be in error, partially or in their entirety, it is in the nature of our effort at comprehensive knowledge, and in the nature of the universe itself, that we will both have and need a plurality of comprehensive visions." Our choice, facing the imposing totalizing visions of Aristotle, Plato, Augustine, Kant, Spinoza, Leibniz, Hume, and so on through Marx, Freud, Derrida, and the new feminists into the indefinite future, is *not* to make a flat choice from among them. Nor is it to struggle for some new and all-encompassing synthesis or some way to prove them all wrong. Rather it is to select, as I have just done in my listing, those few that seem irreducibly and persuasively comprehensive: Given their assumptions about fundamental subject matters, questions, and proper philosophical method, we find them able to "account," at least in principle, for everything. We can't know in advance how many alternative views will survive such a pluralistic critique, but we can look for those total perspectives that in their comprehensiveness take into account, though always in forms that will look reductive from alternative perspectives, the data and principles of the other views.[19]

## The Charge of Relativism

*[In my original essay I next moved to an eleven-page refutation of Martha Nussbaum's charge that, though she strongly admires the book, she feels it moving, as it embraces "pluralism," too close to what she calls relativism. I have cut these pages here chiefly because the issues are addressed elsewhere in this collection, especially in chapter 7 on Richard McKeon.]*

In short, some standards can be translated, though always with what will seem, to "native speakers," like significant loss. As ethical critics, we thus need not agree about just which ethical theory is supreme. On the contrary we ought to give up, at once, all hope of ever agreeing on any one supreme theory. All we need to agree on is the importance of addressing, as clearly and honestly as possible, the full quality, including the emotional effect, of our engagements with the works or lives we choose to discuss.

My claim, then, is that Aristotelians, Platonists, Kantians, utilitarians, pragmatists, existentialists—add your choice—will not and need not come to final agreement in their appraisals or their notions of how to conduct controversy. Disagreement will itself be ethically useful, provided that the critics have derived their disagreements not from imposing their systems crudely on individual literary works or large lumpings of literary kinds but have challenged their chosen systems with honest reports of their direct encounters and of their always-shifting thought about those encounters. The company we keep with philosophers and theologians, like the company we keep with literary works, is inherently interminable: not resolvable with either inductive or deductive reasoning but profitably continuable in the kind of conversation I have dubbed "coduction."

*This essay was commissioned by James Phelan and Peter Rabinowitz for their anthology* Understanding Narrative. *Some of the author's troubles with this assignment—by no means all—are reported in the first few paragraphs.*

Among the longest chapters in the present volume, this essay is a rich and challenging example of Booth's use of the metaphor of friendship to test the ethical depth and soundness of an author's literary offering of it.

The essay was originally published in *Understanding Narrative*, ed. James Phelan and Peter J. Rabinowitz (Columbus: Ohio State University Press, 1994), 99–135.

# The Ethics of Forms

Taking Flight with *The Wings of the Dove*

When I accepted the assignment to "do an essay for our volume, one that will combine theory with practical criticism," as the editors requested, I felt no compunctions about undertaking once again a task that thousands of us perform annually: raiding a book for critical purposes. I would simply do a careful "ethical" critique of some major novel. Then I thought over those I would like to read again, chose *The Wings of the Dove* (published in 1902), and began my first re-reading in about three decades of a novel that I remembered as impressive but more formidable than lovable.[1]

Long before the middle of the book, however, the reading had forced me to ask how my project would appear to that master of moral subtleties, Henry James. I had of course promised him that I would try to obey his commands—that I would do my best to surrender to whatever the book demanded of me before drawing back and becoming the professional critic: I would struggle to *under*stand before pursuing any *over*standing. But of course I was still driven by the assignment to look for my point of critical entry.

The story I found myself meeting, however, threatened to condemn that assignment. The touching account of Milly Theale's betrayal seemed to nag me about the fundamental difference between those like Kate Croy who comfortably *make use of* others, and those like Milly who learn how to find their life by *living with*, and even *for*, others.[2] Whatever I might finally say about this novel, I could be sure that it was not written to be *used*, to be reduced to a counter in some critical economy—even mine. It was written to *be*, or to *act*, or to *teach*, or to make us *see*—choose your own critical view of what novels are written for; but do not, if you want to enter Henry James's drawing room, say that his elaborate tales are written to be *used* a century later by this or that critic with an ax to grind.

195

I was being reminded, in short, that no other moral fault, in James's rich display of faults, is given more attention than the reduction of beauty or truth or goodness to market value.[3]

Yet in the way the story is told I seemed to find a confirmation of my project: James-the-old-intruder was inviting me to turn my attention away from the story of Milly and Kate and Merton to attend to his idiosyncratic way of telling it—a way not all that idiosyncratic by standards of our time but radically so in his. As I went on reading, more and more slowly, sometimes exasperated by James's subtlety, deflected from the "story" by his many reminders, explicit and implicit, of rhetorical manipulations, I soon realized that I was caught between two seemingly contradictory demands:

- "Don't use me, because like every other thing of beauty I am not to be turned into a commodity."
- "Do use me critically, just as my author 'uses' you by calling your attention to his blatantly manipulative way of telling his story."

Indeed that second demand at times seemed almost explicitly directed to Wayne Booth, the lifetime practitioner of point-of-voyeurism. The full strength of this demand will perhaps not be fully intelligible to those who have not read at least one of James's late novels. For any such who happen to have stumbled upon me here, and also for readers who, though they have read *The Wings of the Dove*, find that their memory of its details is as dim as mine was a few weeks ago, I offer here a summary of the plot: what I shall call "the raw chronology" (what Gérard Genette calls "story" and some narratologists have called the *fabula*,[4] what my mentors used to call the "material plot"). If you already know the story well, please skip forward.

Only when you try to summarize the real action of any one of the late James novels do you discover just how complex his plots are. When I look at the summaries provided in any of the reference books, what is most striking is how little evidence they provide about what really happens. The mere outline of how, say, a nondescript "Kate" lies to and seeks the fortune of an equally nondescript "Milly" cannot tell us whether the lie was noble or base, and it thus gives us no notion of what the story is really about—of how we are made to hope for, or fear, or in any way enjoy a given resolution. As Martha Nussbaum insists in her account of *The Golden Bowl*,[5] the moral meaning of any one choice—whether to lie, whether to seek a fortune—is found only within the full specificity of circumstances and characters, not in any one principle allowing or forbidding lying or pursuing a fortune.

The following summary is only slightly more useful than the kind I have just mocked. But at least it hints at what I think James was striving for in his elaborately ethical probing: How should one live one's life? What forms of perception and behavior can be justified, in the face of the ultimate fact of tragically early death?[6]

Kate Croy, beautiful and talented and morally sensitive daughter of an impoverished and unscrupulous English gentleman, is urged by her widowed sister, helplessly poor and burdened with four young children, to cultivate their rich aunt, in the hope that Kate might relieve their poverty both by marrying rich and by receiving some of the aunt's fortune. Kate at first resists, sensing all the ways in which truckling to her aunt will infringe on her freedom and violate her principles. But after falling in love with Merton Densher, a highly attractive, witty, intelligent London journalist with little income, and experiencing—in a trial period living at her aunt's—some of the genuine amenities of life that are made possible only by money, she realizes just how essential it is *to her* not to marry poor. Living with her aunt while Merton is in America on an assignment as a journalist, she meets her aunt's guests, two Americans, one an orphaned but rich young woman, the beautiful, innocent, generous-hearted Milly Theale, the other Milly's devoted and intelligent confidante, Susan Stringham, a former schoolmate of the aunt.

Kate and Milly become friends, and we learn that Merton and Milly have met and become friendly in America. Milly and Susan Stringham learn that Milly has an incurable illness, one the fatal effects of which can only be postponed by living life to the hilt—and especially by loving and being loved.

When Kate learns of the illness, she sees the chance both to obtain a fortune for herself and Merton and at the same time to do a favor to the dying Milly: she persuades the reluctant Merton to pay court to Milly, hoping that Milly will leave her fortune to him on her death. To make the scheme work—Merton only gradually realizes the full nastiness of it—they must of course continue to deceive everyone, especially Milly, about their own engagement: the world must believe that although Merton has indeed been in love with Kate, Kate now feels nothing for him, and he is thus perfectly free to shift his affections to Milly. The highly intelligent, courageous—indeed in most respects admirable—Kate proceeds on a course of openly lying to Milly, even while acting in every other respect as Milly's most intimate and loving friend. Merton himself, while attending regularly on Milly, assuages his confused conscience by scrupulously refusing ever to tell an actual lie; he simply exercises his natural charm on her and thus allows the deception to proceed.

For some time their plot seems to be working: Milly becomes radiantly happy as she lives her waning life fully in a Venetian palazzo, courted, as she has increasing reason to believe, by the most charming young man she has ever known. A far less charming suitor, Lord Mark, a bland, empty-hearted moral nonentity who has been one of the vulgar aunt's candidates for marriage to Kate, arrives in Venice to win her hand. He also has learned of the fatal illness and worked out his own plan to obtain Milly's fortune through a kind of "deathbed marriage"; he makes his crude proposal to Milly and she politely and firmly refuses him. Meanwhile Merton, who has been "courting" Milly daily, though with no formal statement of intentions, is becoming increasingly uneasy about the various moral issues in his situation: He is doing all this for Kate, assuming her love for him, but what proof does he have of her love? Does she really love him enough to justify the whole plot? He insists that to prove her love she must "come to him," in his apartments rented specifically for that purpose, and the ravishingly beautiful creature, who really does love him, comes, for one night. She then returns to London, leaving him to continue his false courtship until the girl's death.

Lord Mark, having learned that Kate and Merton are in fact engaged, gets his revenge for Milly's refusal by telling her, basely, of the whole base scheme, and Milly is devastated: she "turns her face to the wall," refuses ever to see Merton again, and prepares to die. Susan, her confidante, desperately trying to save her, attempts to persuade Merton to go to her and deny the engagement to Kate, but this is a lie he refuses to tell. ("We *are*," he later moans to Kate, when she wonders, back in London, why he didn't go ahead and tell Milly that they were *not* engaged, "We *are*, my dear child, I suppose, still engaged" [bk. 10, sec. 1, 358].) He simply waits, day after day, hoping—by now more fully caught up in Milly's beautiful spirit than he can acknowledge to himself without acknowledging that he has behaved like a "brute"—that he might see her again. She finally relents, for reasons we do not learn, and invites him back for one last meeting—which we are not privileged to witness.

The final events—all of book 10, considerably more than a tenth of the whole novel and, along with book 5, much the longest in the book—consist entirely of Kate's and Densher's wrestling with what all this is to mean for them—how they are to live with what they have done and with what it has meant for Milly. And it is all from Densher's point of view. For several weeks he does not even visit Kate—though he still assumes their engagement. When they do meet he has received a letter from Milly, intended to be received on Christmas Eve; he has chosen not to open it except in Kate's presence. But Kate throws it into the fire, and Merton resists the impulse to rescue it and discover what Milly would say to him at the end. They soon discover, from lawyers, that a part of what she would have said is that she is after all making him, in a splendidly magnanimous gesture (or perhaps an act of revenge against Kate? we are never to know for sure just how much Milly has inferred), her heir. Learning of this, Kate is exultant: their scheme has worked. They have the money they need to marry, and they have it with Milly's blessing. Merton, however, having been awakened to a fully moral perception of the whole experience, tells Kate point-blank (or as point-blank as anyone ever tells anyone anything in this novel) that he will marry her only if she'll join him in repudiating the money; on the other hand, she can have the money—without him. She says that she'll take him, without the money, if he can swear that he is "not in love with Milly's memory." Since he refuses to do that, they separate, aware that the whole experience has changed them both and—we are left to assume—made their marriage an impossibility. We are left to speculate: Will Kate take the money? Will she marry someone as awful as Lord Mark? Has she been morally destroyed or perhaps deeply enlightened by what has happened? Readers have—for reasons that should be obvious—shown much more curiosity about her fate than about Merton's.

(A bit later in this essay I offer two complications producing a strikingly different "plot," what we can call, adopting James Phelan's terminology,[7] "the actual progression"—or what Genette calls the "narrative" or "narrative discourse." James could have told that story straight out. What he offered instead was a story full of elaborate metaphors—some his, some attributed to the characters—and a story full of the most intricate shifts of point of view.)

My question thus became, as I carried through with my determination to face James down if he could not answer my questions well: Is your presentation of these potentially contradictory readings of any great value to me, one of your devotees? In the terms I raise in *The Company We Keep*,[8] are you really good company, in the sense of being my true friend, working for my weal? Or are you simply showing off?

## The Many Kinds of Reading

To address such questions properly, we must back up and underline the complications that make ethical questions about narrative methods extraordinarily difficult.

In the first place, the question as put won't do. It should not be, "Is this novel, is this implied Henry James, *my* true friend?" Who but Wayne Booth cares about that? The question should be, "Is this novel, when given its full due, a true friend potentially to *all* readers who read it with any care?" And that question thrusts us into the facts about diverse readers and readings. Are they not unlimitedly various? Can anyone these days deny that the effects of *The Wings of the Dove* will vary from reader to reader, and for each reader—as for me—from reading to reading? Do we not hear, as we pursue ethical questions, a strongly ethical demand from several critical camps that we celebrate diversity and deliberately ignore or violate the work's own demands?

Since the phrase "the work's own demands" is for many itself absurd, I can hear some critical friends saying: "The only ethical stance is to pursue freedom of spirit, or sharpness of perception, or political awakening, all in the name of the deepest of all truths: there is no fixed truth anywhere, and—even more certainly in an uncertain world—there are no single certain readings."

Yet if one wants to talk about the ethical value of a work *in general* and not just about what it has done to or for any one reader, one can hardly reject all concern for what it seems to ask every reader to do—not just "me" but "us"—regardless of how strongly we may want to emphasize what we can do to it.[9] In short, the serious ethical critic is always faced with two tasks, not just the one that earlier ethical critics performed in describing *the* moral health or disease of any one work. To talk about the ethical powers of a work as being actually in the work, regardless of readers' differences, is one thing. To talk about a work's actual ethical effects is quite another. Can the two tasks in any way be reconciled? I think they can be, if we distinguish three kinds of reading that we all practice.

### First, Reading-With

We all engage, at least at times, in readings that I shall call "reading-with": the reading we do when we simply accept what seem to us the obvious demands of the text. The title is, say, *Poirot Investigates*, and the author is Agatha Christie. The cover calls her "The Unsurpassed Mistress of Mystery," and the title page adds a picture that includes some pearls and some blood. We know that a murder will occur, that Poirot will encounter many suspects and some fools who are confused by them, and that the book will end with the murderer exposed. No problem here, unless we are determined *not* to read-with: we know we have a specific kind of whodunit, and we read for the mystery and for the mystery alone. Or let's say that the title is *The New Awakening*, described as "A Novel"; the publisher is Virago Press, a publisher noted for its feminist endeavors. In the opening pages a stupid, cruel husband is shown mistreating a mousy wife; at the end the wife is—in one way or another—no longer a mouse; she's awakened at last. Again no problem: we read *for* that moment of liberation. Or we pick up a book with the title *Merovingian Art from 500 to 751*, or *Plato's Epistemology*, or *Cognitive Science: A Synthesis*; the publisher is, say, Cambridge University Press, and we find, on reading, that the title's generic promises are roughly fulfilled. No problem: we read the book in the same spirit shown toward the others; we cooperate.

Of course each of these readings will be in one sense entirely different: we "hear" radically different questions and answers. But all such reading is the same in one crucial respect: we never question—if we go on reading at all—the terms of the contract clearly specified by the work's emphasis on its own genre. We rely—even the least sophisticated *and* the most critically up-to-date among us rely—on our past experience of genres, slotting in the new work until and unless we bump into powerful violations of generic expectations. We can even say that two readers who read the "same" text in entirely opposed ways, one as a tragedy, say, and the other as a comedy, are still reading it "in the same way," for our purposes here, so long as each of them thinks the reading is reading-with.

*Stories* that we read-with (putting aside for now scientific and scholarly and political discourse that is not overtly storied) come in three subtypes: (*a*) those that so clearly invite a probing of *meanings* that most or all readers agree that the invitations are "there on the page"; (*b*) those that so clearly seem to be "just story," just plain gripping event-after-event, that only highly motivated critics bother to find meanings in them; and (*c*) those that seem happily to respond both to readers looking for profound meanings and to those who hope for a gripping experience of story. Aesop's and George Orwell's tales are of the first kind: they demand, if we are to read-with them, that we think about (and then perhaps talk about) meanings, ideas—the relation of the story to "life." With or without moral tags attached, readers have to work hard to avoid seeing a moral point in an Aesopian fable. The second kind—"Puss in Boots" and most murder mysteries and thrillers like *Jaws*—in effect asks us *not* to worry about meanings: "Just keep moving, if you hope to enjoy me in my primary being."

If tales all fell clearly into these first two kinds, the life of the critic would be simpler. But most do not. A great deal of our critical energy has always gone into making sense of the third kind (surely the largest pile): those that allow readers to move in either direction while *believing* that they are reading-with. Nothing the story-centered reader encounters disrupts the story: it all seems to be just "what happened." Yet everything the meaning-centered reader encounters supports or invites a given interpretation of meanings.

Readers of popular fiction generally read-with; they just assume that they have the second kind of work (type *b*) in hand, and they suppress all concern for meanings. For them, as for me early in my reading life, that becomes the only kind of reading. They usually do not re-read, and even when they do, they are likely to make their second time through pretty much like the first; they—we critics in some of our moods—seek simply to renew the original pleasure. As Peter Rabinowitz and Janice Radway have both argued, this kind of reading has been either ignored or condemned by modern criticism, and the pleasures and profit derived from such rapid, "unreflective," but deeply engaged reading-with have been almost universally underrated by critics while being exploited by commercial authors.[10] For some recent critics it is as if the only way to make reading such works worthwhile is to go to the opposite extreme, "reading-against."

### Second, Reading-Against

The reader who reads-against sets out to find in the text whatever it does *not* promise or invite to, whatever its author presumably never intended but unconsciously either allowed in or specifically banned. There are several terms on our critical scene for this fashionable kind of reading: "strong," "resistant," "deconstructionist," "anti-intentional" and so on. For many critics, as I have already suggested, this could be called "the only intelligent" or "the only ethically defensible" type of reading. My central question here can be thus rephrased: As I impose my ethical question on *The Wings of the Dove*, am I reading-against or reading-with?

### Third, Re-Reading

The third type is not quite a blend of the other two, though it at first looks like that. It is what some of us do when, after having had a rewarding experience that we think of as reading-with (whether simply "for story" or for multiple meanings), we decide to go back and re-read, trying either to deepen or clarify the experience, or to discover how the author managed to achieve the results we love, or why he or she did not achieve such results. We might call this "critical reading," were it not that most readers-against see their kind of reading as the only really critical kind. For want of a better term, call it "critical re-reading."

Such reading again comes in different kinds, depending on our critical interests. For now, we need only distinguish re-reading that probes for deeper *meanings* and re-reading that probes for an *understanding of structure*—the principles that determined the author's act of composition.

Re-reading for meanings is often conducted as if the novel might just as well have been written backward; re-reading for structure, in contrast, cares deeply about every flashback, every foreshadowing, every expansion or contraction of the raw events, every shift of point of view.[11]

Sometimes critical re-reading, whether for meaning or for architecture, can lead us to deplore our having read-with on the first go: we've been had. Why did we not see these vile meanings that the author obscured or never suspected, or these structural flaws that the author concealed? But often such re-reading can lead instead to heightened admiration, especially when it is assisted by other readers who see qualities we had overlooked.

### Responding to Explicit Invitations

We now have three kinds of stories and three ways that they can be read—with two subclasses of critical re-reading. Whether we find this complexity annoying or not, I would claim that I did not invent it—that it is thrust upon us by the explicit and implicit invitations that various works offer to any attentive reader. Works "try" to tell us, in myriad ways (quite aside from their authors' statements outside the text) not only what genre to place them in when reading-with, but also whether they will be more rewarding when the reading-with leads us to re-read critically. Note that in this scheme it is in principle impossible for any work to invite us to read-against its full being, however chaotic or anti-intentionalist that being might be. At the most negative, all a work can do is invite us to read-against generic expectations that we *mistakenly* thought appropriate.

A. C. Bentley's *Trent's Last Case*, for example, starts out as if asking to be read entirely "with"—as a whodunit. But as Trent's solutions to the crime are successively undermined, and as he faces the issue of capital punishment, even the first-time reader is invited—or could one say "forced"?—to move to critical re-reading: "Just what is the genre here? What have I foolishly taken for granted in reading earlier detective fiction? What, indeed, does this surprise ending, with its explanation of the book's title, say about fiction, about detective fiction, about the relation of stories to life, about politics and justice, about truth . . . ?"[12]

Though it would be absurd to expect Bentley's novel to invite us to read-against its every stroke, it is not absurd of us to read-against it and ask questions not on its list, most notably questions that are raised in the second kind of critical re-reading, reading for architecture: "Just how did you put this together? What is your architecture here? Did you do the best possible job in ordering the parts, in handling point of view, in expanding or contracting scenes?" To ask those questions of *Trent's Last Case* is to read-against, even when, as I have discovered in this case, to do so increases one's admiration for the writer. The book responds to my questions about its architecture, but it does not itself raise them, just as it invites no questioning of its own ethical value. (Note that most "formal" critics in the past—including me—have assumed that to appraise structure and technique is to read-with. It has taken me decades to realize that to ask *Macbeth*, "Why did Shakespeare begin you just this way?" or "Why did he prolong the Porter's scene?" is to read-against *Macbeth* even though Shakespeare usually—not always—stands up brilliantly to such questions.)

### The Invitation to Attend to Architecture

When we ask of *The Wings of the Dove*, first, what kind of reading it "wants" and, second, whether that kind is ethically constructive, the answer to the first question is clear: anyone who has as much as dipped into this novel, *reading-with* it, will feel, as I did, a pressure to re-read critically—that is, to combine the first and third kinds of reading. What is more, that pressure will move us toward thinking not only about moral and philosophical meanings but about construction. Many a fine novel—for example, any one of Jane Austen's—resembles Bentley's in this respect, never even hinting at wanting to raise questions about structure; *Pride and Prejudice* invites critical re-reading, but only the kind that attends to a deepening of moral insight.[13] *The Wings of the Dove*, in contrast, openly demands that we attend precisely to its author's act of composing.

What it does not even hint at is the kind of question I am asking here: Is it really good for us—as readers, as creatures in the world—or even for the art of fiction, to spend hours, days, months, reading-with James's explicit invitations and finding ourselves practicing a highly intricate kind of critical reading, the kind that generations of critics since Percy Lubbock have now exhibited? He never for a moment questions—and he always implies—the superiority of the kind of experience he struggles to provide. In his commentary outside the novels, he does occasionally claim explicit ethical value to what he calls his "method." Yet within the novels themselves he only implies it, never states it.

But surely we have a right—more clearly in this decade than in any earlier time—to *read-against* and demand an answer: Have the hundreds of thousands of hours and millions of words spent on the *art* of fiction,

fiction as *poetry*, fiction as a well-wrought urn, exemplified a kind of life worth living? Many an exasperated reader has answered no, both with respect to such novels and to the criticism they inspire.

If the answer for me were not in some sense yes, I obviously would not waste my time by adding to those discussions here. But the details of the answer are not at all obvious. To put the matter as sharply as possible, shouldn't I be spending my time on some more self-evidently worthwhile form of life: working for aid to starving Africans, say, or tutoring deprived children, or—closer to home—becoming a media critic? Here I am, in my early seventies, as sure of my own coming death as Milly could be of hers—though not quite as sure about the timing—and I spend a large slice of my remaining time trying once again to appraise the gift James has offered to share with me. Does that make sense at the deepest levels of meaning to which we can probe? Why work at this rather than enjoying the latest Dick Francis or Sue Grafton romp?

## James's Plans in Prospect

In the planning stage of *The Wings of the Dove*, James not only ignored our present "reading-against" question; for a long time he did not even talk about the "how" of telling. We can never know what really went on in his mind and heart as he worked and reworked his plans in his notebook. But what he said he was up to was not the construction of meanings or antimeanings, whether metaphysical, psychological, political, religious, or ethical. Nor was it about clever play with chronology and point of view and proportions. Rather it was all about finding a powerful story, an action, a plot to be read-with *as story*. That task for him, as for all storytellers, involved first the discovery of what characters of a given kind would do to one another, and why.

In short, he began not with an "idea" at all but with a "situation"— what Aristotle called an "action" or "imitation." This was never for James a static picture, a mere "image," as some have suggested; the words I have put in italics in the following passage show just how much his mind is on the need for *action*, for narrative movement, rather than on doctrine or how to draw out the right tricks from his copious trick bag:

> the *situation* of some young creature . . . who, at 20, on the threshold of a life that has seemed boundless, is suddenly *condemned* to death . . . by the voice of the physician? She learns that she has *but a short time to live*, and *she rebels*, she is terrified, she cries out in her anguish, her tragic

young despair. . . . She is like a creature *dragged shrieking* to the guillotine—
to the shambles. The idea of a young man who *meets her,* who, knowing
her fate, is terribly touched by her, and who conceives the idea of *saving
her* . . . [perhaps by offering her] the chance to *love* and *to be loved.* . . . But
the young man is *entangled* with another woman . . . and *it is in that that
a little story seems to reside.* I see him as having somehow to *risk something* . . . to *sacrifice something* in order to *be kind* to her. . . . the anecdote,
which I don't, by the way, at all yet *see* [James's italics], is probably more
*dramatic* . . . on some basis of *marriage* . . . marriage with the other woman,
or even with both! The little *action* hovers before me as abiding, somehow,
in the particular *complication* that his attitude (to the girl) engenders for
the man, a *complication culminating in some sacrifice* . . . *or disaster.*[14]

And on he goes, through pages of planning, toward the discovery four days
later (November 7, 1894) that his "little action" requires

the man's *agreeing with his fiancée that he shall marry the poor girl in order
to come into her money and in the certitude that she will die and leave the
money to him* [James's emphasis]—on which basis . . . they themselves will
at last be able to marry.

James then tries out more and more possibilities for plot—well over twenty-
five hundred words with not one word about anything but "my story pure
and simple."

Three months later, when he re-reads his speculations, he finds them
good—but suddenly introduces for the first time an ethical note that relates
to my main point here. This story will do something *for him,* something
that "compensates" him for five years of "bitterness," "wasted passion
and squandered time," "unspeakable . . . tragic experience," "long apparent
barrenness," "suffering and sadness intolerable": the "story" is "strongly,
richly there; a thing, surely, of great potential interest and beauty and of
a strong, firm artistic *ossature.*" Note that what it will give to him—the
gift to his ethos, as we might put it, to stress the ethical note—is the
gift of discovering the right "ossature," the right bone structure for his
story: after years of barrenness, he can at last once again tell a story worth
telling.

It is hard to tell here whether James is thinking of the compensation
as granted by the story emerging—the "what," the raw chronology—or by
the "how," the lessons he has learned, through the painful years, about
the art of dramatic "showing" through scenes in order to create a beautiful
"actual progression." Just what the "ossature" of any story is can always be

hard to determine. But it is beyond question that the beauty he is probing is the beauty of a well-constructed story—one that will engage readers in an ossature that inextricably combines the "what" and the "how."

## James's Plans in Retrospect: The Preface

That is where his mind still dwells nearly fifteen years later when, fresh from re-reading and revising the work, he writes his long, detailed preface. He begins as before with the firm bone structure of the *action*. For several pages one finds, as in the notebooks, nothing whatever about meanings. It is again all about an action, the action of Milly's "struggle"—of the young woman's "disintegration"; of the "act of living"; of the "battle"; of how his heroine will be "dragged by a greater force than any she herself could exert"; "contesting every inch of the road"; of a "catastrophe determined in spite of oppositions"; of the "drama" of her wresting "from her shrinking hour . . . as much of the fruit of life as possible"; and of the drama of her opponents' "promoting her illusion . . . for reasons, for interests and advantages, from motives and points of view, of their own" (Norton, 3–5).

But he soon shifts to the topic not mentioned in the earlier notebooks: the "how" of the story's telling and the effects of the "how" on the reader. This topic, perhaps even less fashionable in 1994 than the topic of what makes for good raw chronology, he celebrates in loving and prolonged detail, as if to say, "Just think, dear reader, of the problems I faced, and of the hitherto unimagined solutions they led me to!"

Since my subject inescapably expands itself from the effects of reading "the novel itself" to the issue of reading and writing the kind of criticism it leads us to, I must dwell a bit on this material that a few critics may still want to call "extrinsic." The great point, he says, was

> that if in a *predicament* she [Milly] was to be . . . it would be of the essence to create the predicament promptly and *build it up* solidly, so that it *should have for us* as much as possible its *ominous air* of awaiting her. . . . [O]ne begins so, in such a business, by looking about for *one's compositional key*, unable as one can only be to move till one has found it. . . . [T]hough my regenerate young New Yorker [Milly] . . . should form my *centre*, my *circumference* [those who observe and exploit her] was every whit as *treatable*. Therefore I must trust myself to know *when to proceed from the one and when from the other*. (Norton, 7; emphasis added)

Then, following an account of how, by not using serialization, he set himself free to "begin as far back" and as far "behind" Milly's own story as he wished, James celebrates just what opportunities freedom from editorial constraints granted him. It yielded

> the pleasure of feeling my divisions, my proportions and general rhythm, rest all on permanent rather than in any degree on momentary proprieties. It was enough for my alternations, thus, [of point of view and locations in time and space] that they were good in themselves; it was in fact so much for them that I really think any further account of *the constitution of the book reduces itself to a just notation of the law they followed.*
>
> There was the "fun," to begin with, of *establishing one's successive centres [in order to] . . . make for construction,* that is, to conduce to effect and to provide for beauty. (Norton, 8; emphasis added)

There followed from this fun the anguish of not being able to carry out his plan as fully as hoped. He "mourns" at some length, viewing the "gaps and the lapses," the "intentions that, with the best will in the world, were not to fructify" (Norton, 9). He specifies the "gaps" (some of which seem very strange to me, since in my reading they were not felt as gaps at all). But then he recovers his confidence: each piece is, after all, "true to its pattern, and . . . while it pretends to make no simple statement it yet never lets go its scheme of clearness" (Norton, 11). After citing proof of his own clever strategies, particularly what he claims as consistency with point of view and his tact in withholding intimate scenes that other novelists would have provided, he turns to stronger self-praise, disguised as a criticism of the disproportionate length of the two "halves" of the work:

> For we have time, while this passage lasts ["the whole Venetian climax"], to turn round critically; . . . we have time to catch glimpses of an economy of composition . . . interesting in itself: all in spite of the author's scarce more than half-dissimulated despair at the inveterate displacement of his general centre. . . . The latter half, that is the false and deformed half, of "The Wings" would verily, I think, form a signal object-lesson for a literary critic bent on improving his occasion to the profit of the budding artist. (Norton, 12–13)

The invitation here to turn one's attention from Milly's sad/happy fate to James's botched proportions could not be more open. And he goes on, a bit boastfully, about the tricks he plays to divert the reader who accepts the invitation into his games.

> This whole corner of the picture bristles with "dodges"—such as he [the critic? myself, in 1994?] should feel himself all committed to recognise and

denounce—for disguising the reduced scale of the exhibition, for foreshort-
ening at any cost, for imparting to patches the value of presences, for
dressing objects in an *air* as of the dimensions they can't possibly have.
(Norton, 13)

Though James is probably sincere in his regret about the faulty proportions of the two "halves," he is also rightly proud of his skill with
"dodges," disguises, foreshortenings, and illusion producing. His strongest self-congratulation is reserved for the constructional inventions of
volume 1:

> I recognise meanwhile, throughout the long earlier reach of the book, not
> only no deformities but...a positively close and felicitous application of
> method, the preserved consistencies of which, often illusive, but never really
> lapsing, it would be of a certain diversion, and might be of some profit, to
> follow. (Norton, 13)

I quote at such length—perhaps about a twentieth of what James writes
about the story's architecture in the preface alone—in order to emphasize
not only his notion of the ideal author, the genius of form, but also his
picture of the ideal reader: a reader who, like the imagined critic who
could teach other authors how to do it, finds that to "read-with" requires
critical attention to the pleasures of compositional subtlety.

Asking whether a particular move is a fault, he says, "distinctly not"—
not for the careful reader:

> (Attention of perusal, I thus confess...is what I at every point, as well
> as here, absolutely invoke and take for granted; a truth I avail myself of
> this occasion to note once for all....The enjoyment of a work of art...is
> greatest, it is delightfully, divinely great, when we feel the surface [of the
> work], like the thick ice of the skater's pond, bear without cracking the
> strongest pressure we throw on it. The sound of the crack one may recognise,
> but never surely to call it a luxury.) (Norton, 14–15)

And then he goes back to a demonstration of what he wants his ideal
reader to do: place the strongest possible pressure on the "thick ice" to
discover just why his subtle way of "driving portents home" (Norton, 15),
by transforming raw chronology and point of view, will resist cracking
under the weight. And he concludes, after much more on similar points,
with a cheerful lament that space does not allow him to say as much as he
would like to say about the novel's *construction*!

The novel itself fulfills James's hopes for this kind of attention—does so, that is, for any reader who is willing to read-with its subtlest invitations. So we can now bring our ethical pursuit to a head by asking, bluntly, how we are to value all of what many from the beginning called mere artificiality, fussiness, and even elitist destruction of the true value of "story." Should we not after all join his brother William, a habitual reader-against, in calling it perverse?

> You've reversed every traditional canon of story-telling (especially the fundamental one of *telling* the story, which you carefully avoid) and have created a new *genre littéraire* which I can't help thinking perverse, but in which you nevertheless *succeed*, for I read with interest to the end (many pages, and innumerable sentences twice over to see what the dickens they could possibly mean). (Norton, 458)

Or do we allow the master to have his way with us—and then praise him for having offered an ethical gift in requiring us to attend not just to the *what* of the story but to the *how*?

## "The achieve of, the mastery of the thing"

So far as I can discover, our question has never been addressed except in a most perfunctory way—either in the form of brusque expressions of annoyance like William's or brief praise for the "poetry" of James's novels. What more can one say, other than "I like it" or "I detest it"?

The full effect is of course beyond summary; it can be known only to those who have succumbed to the master's demands and followed his steps as he takes them, with or without the assistance of his guidebooks. Indeed the *full* effect, for the serious critic, can come only for those willing to follow step-by-step a detailed comparison echoed inadequately by what I present in the section below entitled "The Story-as-Told." Only someone who has read with full attention to his point-of-view manipulations can then face the full force of the question: Was that experience a good way to live?

My own response to this late, late Henry James, in spite of some frustration along the path of this essay, can best be described as gratitude. I was myself surprised by just how powerfully this great implied author affected me, purged entirely of the daily pettinesses that we know the "real" James was capable of in his "declining" years. I had spent a lifetime arguing that implied authors are always not only different from but *to some degree superior to* their makers, purged of whatever those makers took to be their living faults. I was therefore not surprised to find myself engaged with a "James" who was the most "Jamesian" figure I had ever met—even compared with his other late novels. What was a bit surprising was the gratitude I felt for one more experience with what others considered his "fussiness."

"James" has invited me to re-create under his tutelage a beautiful structure—not just *any* abstract structure but a structure of beautifully realized human creatures highlighted miraculously by the artist. He offers me the chance to pretend, for the duration of my reading, that I too live "up there" with him, able not only to appreciate what he has done but to do it myself. Nobody, including James himself, has ever lived for very long in this empyrean: sharing not just the intensity and depth and wit and wisdom of other fine artists but the special precise attention to getting it all right—to creating it all better than anyone else could, even given the same "materials."

We can explain something of this power if we examine the more important steps he took that were by no means necessary, given the raw chronology he finally arrived at for the story of Milly, Kate, and Merton. Their *story* could be told in innumerable ways, without violating its factual and moral intricacy. It could, for example, be told as a simple chronological melodrama of two lovers plotting for the fortune of a dying woman and ending with the ambiguities and beauties of this novel's ending. Even if we decided to tell essentially the story that James tells, no longer just the story of Milly that he first planned but with as much emphasis on Kate and Merton as we now have, we still could make many un-Jamesian choices.

### Metaphoric Extravagance and Point of View

Turning now to what James actually wrote—not just the story but its full treatment—we come first to his "choice" (though by this time in his career he could hardly choose differently) to bestow on all of his main characters a metaphoric and imagistic gift that is totally beyond what any flesh-and-blood character could exercise. They all *think* in elaborate characteristic metaphor and imagery, and they needn't have done so. One could take this book and cut out every one of the passages that begins "It was for him *as if...*" and one would still have a readable story (in one sense a more readable one).

Of all the marvels that would be lost in such a cutting, the one most pertinent here is the effect on the reader of having to sort out just who is responsible for each metaphor or image. There is a "dialogue" of different imaginations here, producing a "polyglossia" that makes the effect that Bakhtin attributes to Dickens seem simple by comparison; indeed even

Bakhtin might see Dostoevsky as at least rivaled here, if not surpassed. It is a dialogue that requires us to attend to each stroke, alert to the distribution of responsibilities.

That James sees his own allocations of metaphor in something like this light is revealed in a marvelous passage where he plays with three imagists at once: Kate, Milly, and the narrator. It occurs in Venice (bk. 7, sec. 3) when the two women are reveling in their successes among the British socialites and at the same time relishing those moments when they can "put off their harness" and their social "masks," and relax together (I feel uneasy about what the ghost of James will want to say about my intrusive commentary below in brackets):

These puttings-off of the mask [There is no hint that this image would be used by either of them: it is the narrator's alone.] had finally become the form taken by their moments together . . . whenever, as she [Milly] herself expressed it, she got out of harness [an image all three might share]. They flourished their masks, the independent pair, as they might have flourished Spanish fans [Clearly this "as" belongs to the narrator alone.]; they smiled and sighed on removing them; but the gesture, the smiles, the sighs, strangely enough, might have been suspected the greatest reality in the business. ["Strangely enough" to whom? we have to ask by now. The narrator seems to hear our question and replies:] Strangely enough, we say [Aha! So "we" say it!], for the volume of effusion in general would have been found by either on measurement to be scarce proportional to the paraphernalia of relief. It was when they called each other's attention to their ceasing to pretend, it was then that what they were keeping back was most in the air. [In the air for them? Certainly not in this form, because neither knows all of what the other is keeping back.] There was a difference, no doubt, and mainly to Kate's advantage: Milly didn't quite see what her friend could keep back, was possessed of, in fine, that would be so subject to retention; whereas it was comparatively plain sailing for Kate [Is this metaphor Kate's? Probably not.] that poor Milly had a treasure [quite possibly Kate's way of thinking of Milly's secrets?] to hide. This was not the treasure of a shy, an abject affection . . . ; it was much rather a principle of pride relatively bold and hard, a principle that played up like a fine steel spring at the lightest pressure of too near a footfall. [At last one that is surely Kate's: her self-conscious picture of what will happen if she presses too close to the truth of Milly's illness: a steel trap will be sprung; the hunter will become the hunted.] Thus insuperably guarded was the truth about the girl's own conception of her validity; thus was a wondering pitying sister ["Sister" is obviously an ironic metaphor here, because Kate is much more than a "wondering pitying sister."] condemned wistfully to look at her from the far side of the moat she had dug round her tower. [Kate's image? Probably not, since Kate would not want quite to think of herself as laying siege to an enemy's castle; but like all the others, James's image has become ours, in our pity for the besieged Milly.] Certain aspects of the connexion of these young women show for us [Yes, for us: again the two central characters are shut out!], such is the twilight that gathers about them [James's and ours, not theirs], in the likeness of some dim scene in a Maeterlinck play; we [ah, yes: we, joining behind or far above both characters] have positively the image, in the delicate dusk, of the figures so associated and yet so opposed, so mutually watchful: that of the angular pale princess, ostrich-plumed, black-robed, hung about with amulets, reminders, relics, mainly seated, mainly still [all ours, though possibly joined by Kate], and that of the upright restless slow-circling lady of her court who exchanges with her, across the black water streaked with evening gleams, fitful questions and answers [ours and definitely not Milly's]. (bk. 7, sec. 3, 261–62)

And so "we" go on observing Kate circling Milly ("like a panther"), "with thick dark braids down her back, drawing over the grass a more embroidered train." Under James's tutelage we extend the Maeterlinck play to include Milly's confidante, Mrs. Stringham. "We" come to know more about both of these hearts than either knows, even about herself, and we thus read the relatively literal apologia for Kate that follows with an awareness totally different from what it would have been without the elaborate metaphor (Norton, 262–63).

Metaphors by their very nature require greater creative energy in the receiver than straight talk. They risk more; many a reader will just get off the metaphorical boat and condemn the clumsy author. But when they work, they bind us to the author—in this case not just James but his two characters—with no route for escape.

## Silences

Another requirement on our creative powers as readers is even more powerful—what might be considered the opposite of rhetorical amplification: suppression, silence, deliberate omission from the narration of crucial events in the raw chronology. The most revealing of these suppressions of what other novelists would have considered essential is James's silence about what happens when Densher is at long last invited back to the palazzo for a final interview with Milly. James's friends and critics objected to that omission, just as he himself had rebuked H. G. Wells, decades before, for failing to dramatize the crucial courtship scene between lovers in the novel *Marriage*.[15] But once one has been tuned to vibrate on James's inimitable wavelength, the effect can be an enormous stimulation of the imagination. I have found myself working over that omitted scene again and again, imagining the lovely frail girl who has dressed herself up, perhaps for the last time, in order to present to the man she loves a courageous and inoffensive front. I am helped in these reconstructions by the hints Merton later gives to Kate:

> "Did she receive you—in her condition—in her room?" [Kate asks].
>
> "Not she," said Merton Densher. "She received me just as usual: in that glorious great *salone*, in the dress she always wears, from her inveterate corner of her sofa." And his face for the moment conveyed the scene, just as hers equally embraced it. "Do you remember what you originally said to me of her?"
>
> "Ah I've said so many things."
>
> "That she wouldn't smell of drugs, that she wouldn't taste of medicine. Well, she didn't."
>
> "So that it was really almost happy?"
>
> It took him a long time to answer, occupied as he partly was in feeling how nobody but Kate could have invested such a question with the tone that was perfectly right. (bk. 10, sec. 1, 362)

We have no good critical vocabulary for the ethical effect of having one's mind preoccupied with all this "perversity" in the telling: piling up obtrusive metaphors, deliberate excision of "essential" parts, to say nothing of the obsessive transformations of point of view that we come to next. How can I express my conviction that it is good for me to be required to go through all this, and to know that if I return with similar attentiveness to the other late novels I'll be invited to similar—but always fresh—re-creations? I have no doubt about it myself—the "I" who is so much inclined to pre-occupations of far less defensible kinds. My ultimate defense, if I could ever fully work it out, would have something to do with what happens to the "back of my mind" during the waking hours before and after returning to the desk to wrestle with this recalcitrant work. Its scenes and languages and puzzles form a running accompaniment while I'm trimming my beard and showering, while paying bills, while driving. In other words, it has made me over—in James's direction.

Of course none of this kind of questioning could be considered significant if we once lost the belief that some ways of spending our lives are better than other ways: Why should it matter how I conduct my waking

THE ETHICS OF FORMS | 215
dreams, especially when they are only "at the back of my mind"? But if any value judgments about ways of living make sense, then those authors (and composers, painters, and so on) who subtly lead us to live moments of high creative intensity even when we are not directly engaged with their works are indeed among our truest friends.

As Milly says to the obtuse and bewildered Lord Mark, "One can't do more than live." "And you don't do anything?" he asks in his confusion. "I do everything," she replies. "'Everything's *this*,' she smiled; 'I'm doing it now. One can't do more than live.'" She is acting, she says, under the great surgeon's advice—

> "...the best advice in the world. I'm acting under it now. I act upon it in receiving you, in talking with you thus. One can't, as I tell you, do more than live."
>
> "Oh live!" Lord Mark ejaculated.
>
> "Well, it's immense for *me*." (bk. 7, sec. 4, 270–71)

It's immense for us too. Though we may not put quite as much emphasis on expensive rococo surroundings as James and Milly seem to do throughout the novel, we live in the greater richness James provides, both in taking in his moral probing of how Milly and Kate and Merton behave and in the discovery that we have been led to create and re-create all that, both while reading and long afterward.

The part of this new life that explicitly wrestles with James's self-chosen constructional task would be described in conventional terms as "formal" and hence "aesthetic." But obviously here the aesthetic task has become deeply ethical. To *get the craft of it right*, to keep the ideal of the highest excellence constantly before one as a demand to *do it better* than what at first seemed merely good, so that those who travel with us—our readers— will get it right too: that is the ethics of craft. It required of James courage, persistence, and a willingness to risk hearing once again from his brother a gentle mocking of his results. It required, in sum, a kind of conscientiousness that fuses morality and the love of beautiful form. And it requires of us an echo of those virtues.

The beautiful thing is that—in contrast with Milly's luxurious purchases—ours are in unlimited supply: there is no zero-sum game here. Our "possession" of these gems never diminishes the supply; indeed, the more lovers such works find for themselves, the better, since talking with other lovers about the treasures "appreciates" their value.

Are not the hours we spend sharing with James and his readers—at least when we are at our best—hours that James might well have had the surgeon add to the remedy he offers Milly? If she was to *live*, why did the doctor fail to order her to spend some time reading the novels of Jane Austen or George Eliot, perhaps, or even, in a postmodernist, reflexive ploy, *The Wings of the Dove*?

## The Story-as-Told (the Actual Narrative, the Discourse, the Handling of Point of View)

[*In the earlier published essay, I offered a five-page, single-spaced appendix tracing every point-of-view shift throughout the book. I now reduce it to a brief dramatizing of James's brilliance. It might be taken as a small step toward the critical act that James hoped some "literary critic" would undertake, "bent on improving his occasion to the profit of the budding artist." Or perhaps it is only a failed try at demonstrating the "attention of perusal" that he claims he wants, at every point, absolutely "to invoke and take for granted."*]

What is most striking about point of view throughout the novel is the shift from Kate's interior, through much of the first half, to Densher's, dominating much of the last half. We are in effect entirely inside Kate, age twenty-five, for all of book 1. Then we have hints of moral problems in dialogue between Kate and Merton—their "inside views" strikingly different. (Kate confesses: "I do see my danger of doing something base," but "I shall sacrifice nobody and nothing" [Norton, 60].)

Note that this concludes one seventh of the book with what, from one point of view, is "only" background! Of these pages, about half are "inside" Kate, but much of book 2 is also about her, as seen through Merton. Such expansiveness obviously explains James's lament about his "misplaced middle"; but he understates the effect the misplacement will have in centering our emotions on Kate. So we do not see inside Milly until book 4!

Book 4, section 1: We are at last inside Milly, talking with Lord Mark at a dinner party, which actually took place a short time after book 3, section 2. Milly is baffled by all the changes. She thinks of Kate as a "wonderful creature." She speculates about Lord Mark and Kate—it's clear that she herself cannot consider him as a possible mate (Norton, 107). She accepts herself as a "quantity"—someone whose life has real importance (Norton, 109), as it does for us through much of the book.

By the beginning of book 5 we are for awhile mostly inside Milly as she deals with Lord Mark and others. Scenes dramatize her "felicity" but also her puzzled speculation about Kate and Lord Mark. "She was somehow at this hour a very happy woman, and a part of her happiness might precisely have been that her affections and her views were moving as never before in concert" (Norton, 134). We have meanwhile been "told," in various ways, that the "concert" is misguided, the felicity doomed. In book 5, section 2 (Norton, 141–42), Kate probes Milly about her health, with Milly meanwhile reaching out to Kate for friendship: She tells her, "I absolutely trust you."

After Milly learns from the doctor, Sir Luke Strett, that she has a "great rare chance" to *live*, while he implies, quite clearly, that she will soon die, we are given (in bk. 5, sec. 4) five pages of Milly's interior monologue about her plight. Kate rushes to her in the evening to find what the doctor has said; to Milly, Kate looks suddenly the way she must look when she is look-ing at Merton, and she infers—correctly, of course—that the two of them must have a "connexion" (Norton, 157–58). She dissembles her illness to Kate, saying mainly, "I'm now to go in for pleasure." Kate makes heavy assertions of her loving desire to help—while we know of her hopes about Merton. . . .

Book 5, section 6: Again inside Milly. Kate instructs her about the ways of the world, claiming that she is "giving away" everything, including herself. But of course she is not: readers know what she is really thinking. Largely because of the use of inside views, we are led increasingly to see Milly as the "dove," with the others as predators (Norton, 171ff.). So by the end of volume 1, our attention is entirely on Milly, a total contrast from the earlier parts, where we were entirely interested in and concerned for Kate.

Moving along, we become more and more aware of Merton's problems. Sexually attracted to Kate, yet puzzled by her admitting that her cleverness has grown "infernal," he is still ignorant of her plans to capture him.

Book 6, section 2: Inside Merton Densher. Kate still is not telling him her full plan; he is still frustrated about their physical separation. Two long, intense embraces, partial physical satisfaction. Kate hints at her plan: he should "lead Milly on," because Kate has a "beautiful plan," which she does not reveal. He wonders why she will not "come" to him. The chapter is all about her plan.

After twelve pages on Lord Mark's proposal to Milly and her rejection—she loves Merton, as he actually loves her—we have an amazing shift of point of view: It is all about Merton's moral dilemma, all of it por-trayed from his perspective and most of it with inside views. Almost all of book 9 and all of book 10 are "inside Merton." The novel has become, in James's final intention, about his moral conflicts. He finally realizes he is to marry Kate and get the money Milly has offered—but only if she'll "come." He is aware that "something has broken in me," but what can he do?

At the end Kate burns Milly's letter granting the cash, Kate and Merton resist the *internal* temptation to rescue it. He will marry Kate, "as we were," but "We shall never be again as we were!"

## Conclusion

Such a summary, even in the fuller form, provides only a beginning to the kind of appreciative analysis that would do justice to the full achievement of James's creation. But I can confidently offer the following prediction.

If a hundred years from now there is any sensitive historian of ideas still practicing, nothing about us will seem more absurd than our repeated undervaluing, with our reading-against, of what great novelists do as they create their works. Here we have James working away month after month, at the height of his imaginative powers, making thousands of subtle, highly "personal" choices each day during the hours when he is most alive, most of those choices quite consciously directed to fulfill highly articulated and conscious intentions. And here on the other hand we find a fair number of half-baked critics, schooled in critical dogmas and unschooled in how to reconstruct the vast created edifices built by the great, pronouncing their ostensibly egalitarian dogmas about there being "no such thing as intrinsic merit." Every lover of the high achievements of any art—of classical music or jazz, of mystery writing or sci-fi, of painting or satirical cartooning—should rise up in anger about the debasement of the world that occurs when people pretend that it's all one great heap of equivalent stuff.

*Written six years after my retirement in 1991, this essay could be described as a summary of my lifetime teaching vocation. It does overlap somewhat with what I said in* The Vocation of a Teacher, *but I still wish that book had included even more ethical exhortations of the sort given here.*

*Readers of* Vocation *may be struck by the shift in my views about the deconstruction movement. When it first emerged, I was shocked by it and felt inclined to attack. Gerald Graff and I even contemplated doing an aggressive spoof, taking as our target those we saw as denying all facts and values. It took me quite a while—and a lot of closer reading—to recognize that I had viewed the founders of the movement all wrong, even though I was right about some of their more careless disciples. In another essay not included in the present volume, I finally went so far as to see "Deconstruction as a Religious Revival"; see* Christianity and Culture in the Crossfire, *ed. David Hoekema and Bobby Fong (Grand Rapids, MI: William B. Eerdmans, 1997), 131–54.*

This essay was originally published in *College English* 61, no. 1 (September 1998): 33–47 (copyright 1998 by the National Council of Teachers of English; reprinted with permission).

# The Ethics of Teaching Literature

Many teachers these days mistrust words like *ethical* and *literature*, because they suggest a naive return to old-fashioned questions and methods that they consider by now utterly refuted. The mistrust is understandable when we consider some of the extremer defenses of "traditional values," with their narrow definitions of literature: the many polarizing D'Souza-ist and Himmelfarbian sermons attacking all postmodernist movements in the name of narrow traditional values and this or that canon.[1]

Because of my persistent efforts, continuing here, to get all sides in current disputes to listen to the enemy, I have been accused by some of being a postmodernist (a "Pomo"), by others of being a traditionalist (a "Trad"), and by some of being merely a cowardly fence-straddler. Such easy labels fit hardly anyone. And what both defenders and enemies of postmodernism too often ignore is a reassuring fact underlying the differences of vocabulary. Most of those now labeled Pomos turn out, when you look at their work closely, to care as much about the ethical or moral effects of literature and the teaching of literature as do the Trads. When we follow their lead in expanding the domain of literature to include the whole world of "story," ranging from the ancient classics to yesterday's soap opera, and when we then do a bit of deconstructing of our other vocabulary differences, we find assertions about ethics and character, justice, responsibility, faith, hope, and charity all over the Pomo scene. In Jacques Derrida's recent work, for example, we find impressive moral exhortation at almost every point: about justice, about responsibility, about "Teaching and Learning to Give" (see, for example, his *The Gift of Death*).[2]

Many teachers of literature and composition at colleges and universities have shown that they care intensely about ethical issues, although they express themselves in the language of postmodernism rather than that of traditional ethics. In last December's *College English*, for instance, there is Lee Ann Carroll's "Pomo Blues: Stories from First-Year Composition."[3] The essay that will serve as my central example is by Elizabeth Anne Leonard, in the May 1997 issue of *CCC* [*College Composition and Communication*].[4] A Ph.D. candidate, author, and teacher of writing, Leonard avoids traditional ethical language, even as she explores the ethical problem of how a responsible teacher can construct a self for herself that will in turn help students construct selves of the kind she hopes for:

> How can I teach [my students] to see themselves as constructed and yet not let the construction get in the way when the Muse knocks? How ... can I encourage them to interrogate the academy and its power structures and simultaneously enjoy the experience of becoming a creator, a thinker? ... [I]f I'm changing students, how do I change them in ways that I feel are most useful to them? (222)

Though some definitions of the word *useful* might raise problems here, is it not obvious that Leonard's project shares everything except vocabulary with many a Trad ethicist who wants teachers to build character? I might even call hers a moral project, if that word had not been corrupted to the point of suggesting some moral*istic* project in the service of fixed rules.

The word *ethical* can perhaps shift us from judgments about specific commandments or codes toward joining Leonard's concern for the construction of a certain kind of person. Ethical thinking at its best has always pursued not literal "thou shalt nots" but a range of "virtues": characteristic habits of behavior considered admirable. (On the term *habits*, see Aristotle's *Nichomachean Ethics*.)[5] Traditionally the virtues included every capacity or strength or competency or habit of mind and heart that the practicer, the self, the character (or his or her critic), could admire—or at least could bear to live with. A virtue was any excellence (*areté*) that could be praised, whether the successful navigation of a ship or throwing of a discus or raising of a family. (For the most influential work reviving the traditional sense of virtue as personal excellence, see Alasdair MacIntyre's *After Virtue*. The most challenging revival of ethical inquiry into the whole domain of "the self" is Charles Taylor's *Sources of the Self*.)[6] Virtues in that broad sense obviously do include many of William Bennett's Sunday school list,[7] but neat lists like his would never include the striking virtue Leonard practices in constructing a challenging essay or in thinking about how to create better "selves."

Throughout the history of thought about the virtues there has of course been controversy about whether this or that *virtù* is really a vice, or even—as in some Renaissance texts—merely an expression of taste. But what has not changed is that most ethical debaters, even among aggressive Pomos, have shared Leonard's implicit assumption that some people practicing one set of virtues are genuinely superior to some other people who may practice certain other virtues but lack some of the essentials. I cannot think of a single postmodernist who does not condemn, as ethically debased, all those who treat the "other" as enemy or as beneath contempt.

Through most of this history, debaters have recognized that no one Sunday school list of the essentials will work when applied without relying on what came to be called *casuistry*—a much-maligned term for the necessity of weighing virtues against each other and making choices among them.[8] Ethical thought about truth-telling, for example, leads not to an absolute rule, "Thou shalt never under any circumstances lie, no matter how much harm the truth might produce," but rather to "Try to become a person who can think through why lying is generally bad but sometimes required in the service of higher causes."

My first claim, then, is that the traditional ethical goal of building *character* can be harmonized with Leonard's effort to build *selves*—persons with a genuinely admirable, or "useful," ethical center. Although she avoids the words *ethics*, *ethos*, *morality*, and *character*, and although she never uses the word *literature*, she obviously teaches literature, in my broad definition—the world of story—and in doing so she hopes to produce results of the kind we all *ought* to hope for. (Note that as an ethicist, I have a right to italicize that word *ought*, one that is used by an astonishing number of writers who overtly claim that there are no firm moral or ethical principles.) This claim obviously depends on a strong subclaim, one that in itself is an ethical proclamation: The gaps and battles between premodern and modern and post-postmodern are themselves the kinds of social constructs that can prove unethical, producing fake battles that we all *ought* to avoid.

## Ethical Teaching and Its Opponents

What worries me far more than the ever-shifting misunderstandings over the terms for ethical criticism is the widespread neglect of the concern at the heart of Leonard's essay: how to *teach* ethical reading and writing— how "English," whatever we call it, can "change students in ways that are most useful to them." In the early decades of this century many books and articles, often influenced by John Dewey, talked openly about the goal of teaching as the building of character (see especially Dewey's *Democracy and Education*).[9] But Dewey's complex case for ethical teaching quickly became caricatured with the slogan "Teach the child, not the subject," as if working for the desired kind of child meant ignoring the value of learning skills and content.

For reasons that I suspect nobody will ever fully explain, the words *moral* and *character* were banned from much of the academic scene in the 1950s and 1960s—as they are mostly ignored by Leonard. Though they inevitably survived in religious writing, particularly that of right-wingers, in "English" and other humanities departments they were pretty much abandoned. Only now do they seem to be coming back, and the return is still hotly contested by many. (See, for example, the "symposium" published in *Philosophy and Literature* on the teaching of morality in college courses, in which seven of us "ethicists" try to persuade a professor of political science that all colleges should, and the better colleges actually do, teach ethics.)[10]

As readers here will have long since inferred, my main hope is to strengthen that rebirth. It is not just that I'd like to see words like *ethical, character*, and *virtue* rescued from the dominance of the right-wingers who identify every Pomo movement with evil and decay. Much more important is the hope for a deeper kind of thinking about what any ethical teacher should work for in the classroom, regardless of whether the language is Trad or Pomo. We should seek Selves for ourselves as teachers that, in Leonard's words, will change students' Selves in ways that we are sure are most useful to *them*.[11]

I find it distressing that even the Pomos I admire join too many of the Trads in failing to talk about how to teach literature ethically. Recently I was invited to attend a conference in Wales entitled "Literature and Ethics" (Aberystwyth, July 4–7, 1996; organized by Dominic Rainsford, with Andrew Hadfield and Tim Woods). I couldn't attend, but I received abstracts of seventy-two papers. Many of them did address my first problem directly: they actually were working to harmonize the traditional language of ethics and the language of postmodernism, thus underlining my sense that ethical language is undergoing revival. But only one of the abstracts, only *one* paper out of seventy-two, even mentioned teaching or pedagogy or any of the problems connected with getting students to think about such matters.

Now I have no doubt that many of those three-score-and-twelve literary critics actually care a lot about teaching and about the ethical effects of teaching this or that kind of story in this or that way. They just didn't bother to mention it, at least not in their abstracts. . . .

As I labored to complete that last paragraph, I suddenly wondered, "How often did I myself mention teaching in my own major ethical effort, *The Company We Keep?*"[12] So I checked, and found less than a page, out of five hundred pages! While it's true that the whole book implies opinions about how we should teach, the least I could have done would have been to provide a full chapter explicitly developing the points I make on that one page.

That lone pedagogical anecdote went like this:

> Twenty-five years ago at the University of Chicago, a minor scandal shocked the members of the humanities teaching staff as they discussed the texts to be assigned to the next batch of entering students. *Huckleberry Finn* had been on the list for many years, and the general assumption was that it would be on the list once again. But suddenly the one black member of our staff, Paul Moses, an assistant professor of art, committed what in that context seemed an outrage: an overt, serious, uncompromising act of ethical criticism. As his story was reported in corridors and over coffee in the lounges, it went something like this:
>
> > It's hard for me to say this, but I have to say it anyway. I simply can't teach *Huckleberry Finn* again. The way Mark Twain portrays Jim is so offensive to me that I get angry in class, and I can't get all those liberal white kids to understand why I am angry. What's more, I don't think it's right to subject students, black or white, to the many distorted views of race on which that book is based. No, it's not the word *nigger* I'm objecting to, it's the whole range of assumptions about slavery and its consequences, and about how whites should deal with liberated slaves, and how liberated slaves should behave or will behave toward whites, good ones and bad ones. That book is just bad education, and the fact that it's so cleverly written makes it even more troublesome to me.
>
> All of his colleagues were offended: obviously Moses was violating academic norms of objectivity. For many of us, this was the first experience with anyone inside the academy who considered a literary work so dangerous that it should not be assigned to students. We had assumed that only "outsiders"—those enemies of culture, the censors—talked that way about art. I can remember lamenting the shoddy education that had left poor Paul Moses unable to recognize a great classic when he met one. Had he not even noticed that Jim is of all the characters closest to the moral center? Moses obviously could neither read properly nor think properly about what questions might be relevant to judging a novel's worth. . . .
>
> Our lengthy, heated, and confused debates with [him] never . . . honored his claim that teachers should concern themselves with what a novel might *do* to a student. . . . We had been trained to treat a "poem *as* poem and not another thing" and to believe that the value of a great work of fiction was something much subtler than any idea or proposition derived from it or used

to paraphrase its "meaning." We knew that sophisticated critics never judge a fiction by any effect it might have on readers. And sophisticated teachers do not ask whether the works that they teach might harm students. "Poetry makes nothing happen" [Auden's famous line], we were fond of quoting to each other. . . . To have attended to Paul Moses's complaint would have been to commit—in the jargon of the time—the "affective fallacy."

Paradoxically, none of this interfered with our shared conviction that *good literature in general* was somehow as vital to the lives of our students as it was to us. To turn them into "readers," and to get them to read the good stuff, was our mission. (3–4)

I would want to word that mission slightly differently now, stressing more strongly—as in fact the book later does—better and worse ways of reading and of teaching others to read. And of course the book later defends *Huckleberry Finn* as not guilty of Moses's charge. But the point here is that we were tacitly ethical critics, while openly repudiating that role.

What I hope we *all* hope for is that more teachers will devote themselves to the pursuit of some version of the ethical aims of education. Whether we think of ourselves as Trads or Pomos, whatever our official specialty is called (English, composition, writing, reading, speech, textual analysis, creativity, linguistics, gender studies, racial issues, cultural critique, new historicism, rhetoric), let's join Leonard and *think* about the ethical aims of education: *What kind of person pursuing what kind of ideas and practices and social improvements do we hope to see emerging from our labors?* To paraphrase Leonard once more, What ethical improvements *in ourselves* should we seek, in or out of the world of story, that will help our students create selves most useful to them—useful not just in the narrow utilitarian sense but in the sense of yielding an ultimately rewarding life, working for an ultimately rewarding and defensible society?

When we think of the aims of education in that broad sense, we're faced with many opponents besides those I've already hinted at; some of them use vocabulary that makes them sound as if they might be on our side. Perhaps most prominent these days is what we might call the "content and commandments crowd": those who think that the way to improve English education is to force teachers and students to work toward specific, predetermined examination results on a statewide or national scale. When President Clinton [*and much later President Bush*] touts national standards, he talks as if he is the most virtuous, most ethical pursuer of educational excellence in the world. Yet he never really addresses the question of what kind of person or character or self will be produced by the imposition of such rote standards.

Not long ago I heard a lively speech by the director of Chicago's school reform/renovation/revival/resurrection project, Paul Vallas. It was absolutely confined to how to raise scores on tests. In the question period a woman asked him what kind of *person* his revolutionary efforts are designed to produce; his answer was unhesitating, almost shouted: "The kind who can score higher on those tests." *My* thought was, "That means the kind who, the moment they find out that I am a teacher of English, grimace and say, 'Oh, I gotta watch my grammar!'"

Now it's true that in Chicago, in this new program that puts low-scoring schools and teachers on probation, some scores have gone up a bit—but only in science and math. They've actually gone on falling in reading and writing and grammar and spelling. Is that surprising? Is it surprising that if teachers are driven to drill in vocabulary and grammar the scores in vocabulary and grammar continue to go down? What kind of student really scores high in vocabulary? Obviously it's someone who has learned to love reading and writing and has thus learned hundreds of new words each week rather than reluctantly memorizing a short list imposed by a teacher obeying a principal, who is obeying some external committee that is obeying the governor, who is obeying President Clinton, who is, of course, obeying God.

Who are the students who score high in grammar? Well, that depends on whether what you test is mere terminology for grammar, or actual usage. The ones who learn to use *effective* grammar are the ones who have learned to love reading and writing and speaking, at more and more complex levels. It's true that somewhere down the line, once students have become genuinely motivated, serious study of grammatical history and terminology can become not just interesting but fun. But if like me you were taught rote grammar mainly by teachers who were bored by it, you know just how deadly that can be. In my junior year in high school, a fine first-year teacher who stressed engaged reading and writing left me determined to become an English teacher; I wanted to become someone like her. Then in my senior year I fell under a pious drillmaster in English-as-names-and-dates-and-grammatical-rules, and quickly changed my career to chemistry, where things could at least be interesting. Only in college, where my English teachers taught English as inquiry, and my science teachers taught science as rote, did I quickly change back.

Does the content-and-commandments crowd really think that our dropout rate is caused by students not being taught this or that content? Students drop out mainly because they have learned that the classroom is not for them: boring, dull, empty of personal relevance, alien, "somebody else's idea of how to live, not mine."

What is especially troublesome about the overemphasis on content or mechanical skills is that the "idea of how to live" that it conveys is utterly futuristic: "The point of learning today is to prepare for something tomorrow." Fourth-graders must learn what they'll need in the fifth grade, whether they hate it or not; high school sophomores must memorize details about such-and-such a deadened classic, whether the teacher loves it or not, to prepare them for the junior year. The goal of the senior year is not to have a glorious, exciting year but to prepare for college admission or to ensure that when some firm hires a graduate, she will be a good speller, or will never say "between him and I," or will never, like Leonard in her title, use "which" when the rule books and grammar checks would require "that."

## A Paradox Underlying the Case for Ethical Teaching

Obviously it's misleading to say that we want students who simply love us English teachers and our interpretations of a subject or text, though for many such emulation will be a useful first step. As Leonard's article implies, to seek emulation lands us in a paradox: We hope to produce a kind of person, and we don't want to be authoritarian about it, and yet we often realize, with some uneasiness about our arrogance, that the kind of person we want them to become is the same kind that we want to become—and we want them to see us as already having achieved. Intentionally or not, every successful teacher is likely to impose an image of what an admirable person is, and that person then gets imitated. I remember how some of my fellow graduate students took up pipe smoking after they'd fallen under the influence of Ronald Crane at the University of Chicago—holding their pipes with precisely his gestures. Far more of us took up his intellectual and pedagogical habits (virtues), many of them admirable but some now to me questionable.

That paradox and the controversies it generates are too often ignored by morally committed teachers. On the one side of the ethical crowd, too many moralists attempt to impose a mechanical code, like the Ten Commandments, or the twelve virtues of the Boy Scout oath I once chanted, or Stephen Covey's *Seven Habits of Highly Effective People*.[13] It all comes down to "commands": Our schools should produce students who don't cheat or steal or kill, students who honor their fathers and mothers, who stay off drugs and handle their sexual desires responsibly. Why? Too often the implied answer is, "So they can succeed in the marketplace." Some virtue-touters never worry about whether students are motivated toward further learning: we should be training them to be "good citizens," which too often means those who will stay off welfare and passively accept low-paying jobs.

At the opposite extreme, a fair number of anticonservatives, traveling under various names, put their commandments in equally routine, unthought-through terms: *liberation, creativity, empowerment*, even *rebellion*. Always fight back, resist all institutional demands, wear a beard or earring like mine. Some on the left implicitly lead students to drop out by spreading the notion that schools always and inevitably implant conventional or reactionary values that are not at all cool.

So while the "content" buffs moan about ignorance of grammar or violation of codes, the conservative ethical crowd too often wastes time moaning about lack of courtesy or civility, or failure to implant work incentives. And meanwhile some of the self-and-social-construction crowd moan about our failure to produce revolutionaries.

It is not surprising that such differences and paradoxes produce the kind of controversy that might make us want to retreat into mere talk about verbal skills and vocabulary lists. Any one picture of ethical norms advocated aggressively by any one faction will seem offensive to other factions—a fact that leads some neutralists to extend the separation of church and state to separating moral and ethical talk from public schools. Do I want my child taught by someone who aggressively teaches that *all* abortion is wrong, or that *no* abortion is wrong? Do I want my child taught by someone who aggressively teaches that all ethical norms are merely socially constructed, and the goal of education is to show that they have no ultimate validity, or on the other hand that nobody who talks about our being socially constructed should be listened to? Of course I do not, so let's just keep all such stuff out of the classroom.

## Why English Teachers, If They Teach Stories Ethically, Are More Important to Society Than Even the Best Teachers of Latin or Calculus or History

Where does all this leave us, back in the classroom, suspicious of code teaching, aware of ethical ambiguities, but committed to the ethical goal of producing students who are themselves committed to pursuing defensible values? Fortunately, there is one really effective answer to that tough question—an old answer, even a clichéd answer, a tired answer, but still the right answer: Get them engaged with the world of story (including "literature" in the old sense) and teach them to deal critically with that engagement. Entice them not only into loving this or that book or fixed list but into loving both the seductions of story and the fun of criticizing those seductions.

To teach reading (or viewing or listening) that is both engaged and actively critical is central because it is through stories, in narratives large and small rather than in coded commandments, that students absorb lessons in how to confront ethical complexity. It is in dealing with narrative conflicts that they imbibe the skills required when our real values, values that are not merely social constructs, clash. To put the point again in jargon that I would never use with any but the most advanced students, literature teaches effective casuistry: the counterbalancing of "cases." It is in stories that we learn to think about the "virtual" cases that echo the cases we will meet when we return to the more disorderly, "actual" world.

Obviously no one story or list of stories will produce good ethical effects on every student. Many of our finest stories—Genesis; *Middlemarch*; *Absalom, Absalom!* (name your favorite)—can have destructive effects when read uncritically; on the other hand, stories that the teacher detests, for whatever reason, can be taught in ways that hook students into the complex enterprise I'm pressing for here. The whole business boils down to teaching students how to read ethically—not just feeding them powerful narratives that have some chance of getting through to them at a given level but finding ways to teach them what might be called ethical or responsible reading (or listening).

That never totally successful process can be simplified as the quest for a kind of triple vision. First, students must learn how to engage fully and in a sense naively, practicing what Coleridge calls "willing suspension of disbelief" and what Peter Rabinowitz calls "becoming the narrative audience":[14] what might be called "genuine listening." They must learn the fun of being "taken into the narrative world"—often even in a sense taken in, experiencing the fun of total escape from the everyday world. Second, they must learn how to join simultaneously what Rabinowitz calls the "authorial audience"—the kind of critical audience that implied authors invite them to join as they distance themselves from the credulities of the story they are telling. The authorial audience knows, for example, that geese do not lay golden eggs, and it enjoys the fabulist's construction of a narrative audience that believes they do. And yet it also joins the implied author in the metaphorical interpretation: When "geese" are laying "golden eggs," it's probably stupid to cut them open looking for more gold. Third, students must learn how to become fully critical, skeptical readers and listeners, questioning both the "taking in" of the narrative "world" and the implied author's opinions about it: "Is it really always wrong when some situation (goose) is paying off, to reach for even greater payoff by exploring the situation's (goose's) innards?"

In short, students can learn the rich, complex experience of combining full listening with critical analysis of what is "heard"—what I have elsewhere referred to as *under*standing and *over*standing. They need to learn how to *think* about, and possibly reject, the values of the story-world they first "took in."

We all know from both personal experience and observation of our students that when stories really work, when we are fully taken in by a story-world and feel ourselves loving and admiring or hating and detesting portrayed characters, our own aspirations and habits of thought are changed. The changes are inevitably less frequent and usually less dramatic for any highly trained teacher than they are for youngsters. But even for us, they are far more dramatic than is usually recognized. I have an elderly colleague who told me that reading Martin Amis's *The Information* recently changed his mind about assisted suicide: he's now seriously considering it. Another elderly friend reported recently that reading Kawabata's *Sound of the Mountain* had somehow inspired him, removing his depression over being so old.

When writing *The Company We Keep*, I interviewed many people, from professors on up to kindergartners, asking them what stories had changed their lives. Almost everyone gave an immediate response. "When I read *Les Misérables* I swore I would always try to rescue lost souls like Jean Valjean, even if they steal my candlesticks." "Reading Sinclair Lewis's *Arrowsmith* was what persuaded me to become a scientist; idealized, pure inquiry, untainted by any motive but truth became my highest goal; only later did I realize how complicated that goal could become." "Reading *Pride and Prejudice* was what saved me from running off with the first boy I fell in love with: I recognized that he was really Wickham." "When I saw the movie *Philadelphia Story* I decided that it was time to give up being a teetotaler, and maybe even get drunk for the first time." "Reading *Tom Sawyer* led me for a while to be much more deceptive with my parents, imitating Tom's treatment of his aunt." "At fourteen I stumbled on *The Story of O* in my father's den, read it, and as I see it now, it tainted my life for more than a decade." "In my teens I read Kerouac's *On the Road*, and I quit school and for a year went on the road, retracing the hero's journey. I regret that now, though of course I learned some good things from the experience."

I was recently chatting with a twelve-year-old who had seen the movie *Liar Liar*. "How did it make you feel?" "Well," that prepubescent cool girl said, "it made me want to try not to lie as much as I've been doing."

(All these quotations are from memory, not from tapes—therefore they should be read critically, "resistantly.") Every reader could add to my list.

The broad range of these experiences, from good to bad, further dramatizes the ambiguities of the word *ethical*. The move toward the belief that lying to adults is cool or cruel is an ethical change, bad or good; the ethos has been either harmed or improved, depending on where it was before the change. An inferior or improved self has been constructed.

## Practical Suggestions

I have six overlapping suggestions about how we might teach ethics.

> One: Always include at least one work you consider extravagantly flawed
> when viewed ethically, one that you suspect many students will
> themselves find repugnant: works like *The Postman Always Rings Twice*,
> or Mickey Spillane's *I, the Jury*, or the novel that intellectuals all over the
> world have overpraised, Céline's *Journey to the End of the Night* (the
> choice must always depend on your own best hunch about where the
> students already "are"). Too many of our lists are so biased toward values
> we ourselves embrace that students either get uncritically hooked or
> become bored and resistant.
> Two: Be sure to include some rival story that reveals that first story's dangers
> or stupidities. Provide at least one story that relies on values that
> contradict those relied on by the vile book. Seek out a story providing
> narrative proof of the risks involved in being "taken in" by the first
> choice.

These two suggestions, when fused, will ensure that our reading lists, indeed our entire curricula, provide internal clashes among the values we worry about: stories celebrating *these* virtues that in themselves criticize stories celebrating *those* virtues, inculcating the right kinds of hard thought about casuistry. What students really should "take in" is the excitement of dealing with value-conflict, of practicing "casuistry" in the good sense of the word.

> Three: Include some story in which the implied author, subtly calling for close
> reading, rejects the values espoused by the portrayed appealing characters
> or by especially sympathetic narrators: Students must learn how to join
> the authorial, not just the narrative, audience. . . . Even professional critics
> often show that they don't think enough about that kind of distinction.
> One reviewer of John Updike's recent novel, *The End of Time*, portrays

it as a totally evil celebration of vicious moral flaws in the hero. She just didn't catch the perhaps too subtle ethical clues that Updike thought would be self-evident.

Four: Teach the fun of locating within a given story signs of its implied author's unintentional incoherence or inadvertent revelation of flaws. Though some Pomos have carried this resistant quest so far as to kill all genuine listening, it is important for students to learn what too many teachers in my generation, emphasizing the quest for unity, failed to teach us: that many implied authors, even among the most perceptive, are ethically self-contradictory—just as we the readers are likely to be. Such internal conflicts can be, as Bakhtin stressed, evidence of wonderfully profound authorial probing, but they can also reveal sheer carelessness or commercial deceit.[15]

I knew last summer that my grandson had loved the movie *Independence Day*, and after I'd later watched the massacre-packed thing on a plane flight, I e-mailed him a question about it. "Why is it that the only people who come out alive are the ones the makers have made us like most from the beginning?" He wrote back: "I hadn't thought of that trick. But it makes me wonder about the new Jurassic movie. How did they decide who gets hurt and who doesn't—and why does nobody get eaten?"

These first four suggestions dramatize the inherent conflict between any teacher's deepest critical interests and her sense of what conflicting narrative realities *these* students most need at *this* cultural moment. This conflict is dramatized in one of Lionel Trilling's most interesting essays, "On the Teaching of Modern Literature."[16] He reports his experience at Columbia teaching a course in modern literature to freshmen. He chose the best modern works he could think of, judging them as a "literary critic." Since this was in the 1950s, the works he chose as "best" all sharply criticized or undermined what he considered bourgeois clichés. His only *pedagogical* thought was that since the works were powerful, they would wake his students up: an ethical goal.

What he discovered was that his students were in effect already indoctrinated in antibourgeois convictions, and if they were to be challenged in their current values they needed some nonmodern works. The list he constructed as best for students, when he thought as a literary critic, had to be changed when he asked himself, "What do *these* students most need?"

The point then is this: Never forget Trilling's confession about his error—his failure to think hard enough about pedagogy versus lit crit. Be sure to include at least one powerful story that challenges current hot clichés: Ishiguro's *Remains of the Day*, perhaps, or one of Austen's or George Eliot's works, or Gail Godwin's *The Good Husband*, or—well, why not?—the *Odyssey*.

We all know that none of these four suggestions will work in all teaching situations. If you are faced with a class of nonreaders who can't even handle works as complex as those I have mentioned, you'll have to translate all of my advice into more accessible works.

> Five: Turning from course lists to methods, we might fuse the four course-list suggestions by saying, "Make sure that you, along with the works you assign, are inculcating methods both of fully engaged reading—of *under*standing what the story itself is up to—and of critical oversight, of the *over*standing that results when we apply to a story values alien to it."

If you ask what is the best guide to combining understanding with over-standing the ethical effects of narrative, naturally I have a single absolute answer—my own book (that I've already mentioned twice, violating my firm principle never to load my work with self-citations): *The Company We Keep*. Another work, one that is a bit more pertinent to the current scene, is *Authorizing Readers: Resistance and Respect*, by Peter Rabinowitz and Michael Smith.[17] The book is precisely on this point: teaching students, high school or college, both how to respect a story's true intellectual and ethical demands and how to resist those demands responsibly.

> Six: Perhaps the most important methodological problem is how to build habits of genuine conversation, thoughtful talk by students who have learned how to practice penetrating criticism of one another's readings—and of the teacher's own biases. The most important single product—to use that commercial term increasingly popular with administrators these days—is the kind of person who can criticize others not just negatively but productively, and that requires daily practice in genuine critical conversation. If I had time, I would preach a bit about the difference between good and poor classroom discussion, dialogue and bullshitting, but instead I'll end with one institutional solution. Though it may appear too mechanical, it really works, regardless of what any teacher does in class. It is often hard to institute, especially in larger colleges, but I've experienced its blessings at three different colleges, small and large.
>
> I suggest the installation of at least one campus-wide, general-education requirement, one that, instead of providing totally unrelated sections traveling under some general pious title, will guarantee at least *some*

shared reading experience by all students. We never arrive at really good judgments of a story by ourselves; we need the opinions, the company, of other readers, and not just of readers who have been indoctrinated in some one course. Every college should ensure shared encounters outside of class among readers of the same stories: the same novel, the same history, the same movie, the same autobiography.

No one reader's, no one teacher's, reading is ever complete, final, perfect. What we want to perfect is the kind of spontaneous conversation that both mitigates the harmful effects of bad stories or bad readings and strengthens the effects of good stories and good readings. If everyone on a given campus has wrestled with the same story, or even better the same list of stories, regardless of whether those stories are judged as ethically good or bad, spontaneous conversation will erupt, and shallow readings will be deepened, mistaken readings corrected, vicious stories exposed. Instead of deduction from fixed codes, or induction from some straw poll, a form of critical dialogue emerges that I like to call *co*duction.

## Conclusion

None of this will ever prove to be easy. Teaching stories ethically is not only more important than any other teaching—as Leonard and I preach. It is more difficult than any other teaching. Teaching students how both to take in and not to be taken in by texts, how to unite ethical resistance and ethical respect, makes teaching the laws of thermodynamics look like child's play. This is not, however, a claim that only "English" is at the center. Stories dominate every field, even the hardest of sciences. Students can be harmfully "taken in," or genuinely liberated, by the explicit and implicit narratives that dominate every field. What could be more important than responding critically to the following story, "told" in many a textbook and popular account of science's triumphal march through history?

> Once upon a time ignorant people believed in gods of various kinds. Gradually, battle by battle, science, the only valid way of thinking, managed to knock down their superstitions. In this century we are at last moving toward complete mastery of the whole truth about the universe, as we pursue the final, total theory just over our horizon.

What could be more important than learning to respond critically to the naive, anti-Darwinian "creationist" histories, with the world created a few thousand years ago?

I could cite here scores of books, published through the past two centuries, telling versions of both stories. Some portray religion as totally annihilated in the war; some show it as fully and finally harmonized with science. My point is not to downgrade scientific or religious storytellers but to invite them to recognize how often they enter into our "English" territory. Is it absurd to hope that, since we all live in the world of story, we English teachers can find ways of joining with teachers from all fields in pursuit of a common goal, ethical education? Whether we consider ourselves radical, liberal, or conservative, Trad or Pomo, scientists or humanists or antihumanists, we surely must all aim to produce, using the world of story, not flunkies who can only pass tests—though they can do that—but self-motivated learners. They should be living in their time with us in ways that make the path to further learning irresistible.

The future of American education depends on teachers who vigorously pursue Elizabeth Leonard's question: "If I'm changing students, how do I change them in ways that I feel are most useful to them?"

*This essay was commissioned by the Woodrow Wilson Center for Scholars, designed for an anthology entitled* Moral Inquiry in American Scholarship. *All of us met several times to discuss our drafts, sometimes with considerable debate about them. It was an extremely profitable experience. As all readers here have discovered by now, my style contrasts sharply, depending on the expected audience. For this one, the hoped-for audience might be called . . . well, how about "scholars"?*

This essay provides, among other things, a helpful overview of most of the preceding essays. It was originally published in *In Face of the Facts: Moral Inquiry in American Scholarship*, ed. Richard Wightman Fox and Robert B. Westbrook (Cambridge: Cambridge University Press, 1998), 149–80 (copyright 1998 by Cambridge University Press; reprinted with permission).

# "Of the Standard of Moral Taste"

Literary Criticism as Moral Inquiry

The very phrase "moral inquiry" is for some literary critics an oxymoron. Moral indictment? Of course you can have that. Moral celebration? Perhaps. But inquiry? The word implies the chance of arriving at established, unquestioned conclusions. About morality, some still claim, there can be no such conclusions—and thus no inquiry about them.

Meanwhile, moral indictments seem increasingly fashionable. The accusers show no doubt whatever that certain works of art are corrupting public morality. The National Endowment for the Arts is attacked for sponsoring "immoral" artists like Robert Mapplethorpe. Schools are attacked for assigning "wicked" works like *Huckleberry Finn*, *The Catcher in the Rye*, and *To Kill a Mockingbird*. TV and movie producers are attacked for celebrating violence that may be imitated. Authors and publishers are attacked for producing books ranging from the violence of Bret Easton Ellis's *American Psycho* to the obscenities of Philip Roth's *Sabbath's Theater*. Record companies are attacked for producing gangsta rap and hard rock. Legislators, national and local, work on laws to protect us from being harmed by bad art.

These attacks naturally produce a flood of defenses. Some say that to fuss about the moral effects of art risks slashing the First Amendment.[1] Some argue—especially those who hope to profit from violent exploitation—that there is no scientific evidence for the harmful effects of their product.[2] Others make the more challenging case that to attack artistic works on moral grounds is to destroy our most precious possession: the "aesthetic" domain, which is not just different from everyday morality but in effect higher. As Wendy Steiner says in the conclusion to her recent *The Scandal of Pleasure*: "Art occupies a different moral space from that presented in identity politics." For her, since art is obviously "virtual," not "real," it should not be subjected to the kind of moral criticism we offer when everyday events offend us.[3]

Throughout this controversy, nearly everyone concedes, and all imply, that no matter what we do about the moral powers of art, those powers are real. Even the most ardent opponents of censorship do not deny that many art works can harm some who "take them in." And even the most ardent would-be censors imply by their every gesture that certain other works, in contrast, are not just morally defensible, not just beneficial, but essential to any full human life. This claim is clearest when we narrow our attention as I do here from all art to stories, then broaden it to include not just the highbrow stuff we call literature (novels, plays, poems, operas), and not just serious biographies and autobiographies, but gossip, talk shows, soap operas, TV and movie documentaries, and on to the stories and narrative songs we heard in childhood.

Whenever I ask adults who have been ardent readers whether they can think of any one work that changed their lives in a significant way, not just in childhood, almost all of them offer at least one clear example. They agree that when we really engage with the characters we meet and the moral choices those characters face, moral changes occur in us, for good or ill. No one who has thought about it for five minutes can deny that we are at least partially constructed, in our most fundamental moral character, by the stories we have heard, or read, or viewed, or acted out in amateur theatricals: the stories we have really *listened* to.[4] (From here on I'll use the language of "listening" to include all "taking in" of stories in any medium.)

Most of the world's successful moral teachers have also taken this generalization for granted, resorting in their homilies to story rather than straight prose exhortation. The authors of the Bible chose mainly to be storytellers, *narrators* rather than mere exhorters. They did not just lay down bare codes, like a list of ten flat commandments. No, they told stories, like the one about a troubled abandoned-child-hero who, as leader of his liberated people, almost botches the job of obtaining some divine rules printed on a tablet, and about a people who largely botch the job of receiving and abiding by them. They did not just print out the sermons of a savior; they placed the sermons into a story, and they surrounded them with other stories, especially the one about how He himself grappled with questions about His status as savior, and about how He told scores of radically ambiguous parables that force His listeners into moral thought. They did not *say* that for God to be incarnated as a man entails irresolvable paradoxes; they *told a story* about how the God/man at the moment of supreme moral testing is ridden with doubt and cries out, as any of us would have done, "My God, my God, why hast thou forsaken me?" Those authors "knew," perhaps without knowing what they knew, that serious stories *educate morally*—and they do so more powerfully than do story-free sermons.

In sum, the great tellers and most of us listeners have known in our bones that stories, whether fictional or historical, in prose or in verse, whether told by mothers to infants or by rabbis and priests to the elderly and dying, whether labeled as sacred or profane or as teaching good morality or bad—*stories* are our major moral teachers. Some stories teach only a particular moral perspective, one that can be captured with a moral tag, as in some of Aesop's fables and the simpler biblical tales. Many of them teach a morality that you and I would reject. But all of them teach, and thus in a sense are open to moral inquiry, even when they do not seem to invite it.

I could spend the rest of this essay summarizing a long history of arguments for this generalization—arguments a bit "soft," judged by some research standards, but to me convincing. Instead I must simply take it as assumed and move to more controversial issues. Even if "everyone" is right in assuming that stories teach morality, good or bad, can literary criticism inquire responsibly into the differences between the good and bad of that teaching without corrupting or destroying the domain defended by Steiner: the world of purified artistic pleasure, the genuinely "artistic," the "aesthetic"? Most of us believe that if we are to have criticism of the "right kind," it should reinforce the "right kinds" of moral effects and protect listeners from the "wrong kinds," without denigrating the glories of *art*. But to say that raises, in threatening form, the two questions central here: Who are the judges who earn the right to determine which are the right kinds? And just how should such judges practice their inquiry before passing judgment?

Few modern critics or philosophers have faced these twin questions with full attention. Even those who aggressively assert their moral judgments rarely discuss how we decide that one critic—for the fun of it, let's call him Booth—is more credible than some opponent. Yet obviously if I proclaim, "That work is morally disgusting," or "That work is morally inspiriting," I imply that I am more qualified to pass such judgments than is my opponent, because I know how to inquire about them. My claim here is that if we paid more attention to the two key questions, battles over opposing judgments might end in impasse less often.

### Controversy about Moral Criticism: A Potted History

Is genuine moral inquiry possible, or even pertinent, in appraising literary quality? The history of answers to this question in Western culture could be reductively summarized as a pendulum swing from yes to no to yes again.

#### Epoch I (About Two and a Half Millennia)

Before modernism of various kinds broke into our scene, almost every critic agreed that the moral worth of stories must be addressed with rational inquiry and that some inquirers do the job better than others. If one had asked Plato or Sir Philip Sidney or Samuel Johnson or Samuel Taylor Coleridge or Matthew Arnold whether the critic's job included questions about literature's moral worth, they would have scorned the questioner, even if they disagreed in their particular judgments. Every responsible critic, they assumed, must ask about the moral value of any work addressed. Such critics conflated, as I do here, narrow notions of "moral codes" with broad questions of total ethical effect: transformations of character, of self, of soul, of ethos. Is this work good for its listeners? Does experiencing it build their character in the right way? Is it morally educational or *mis*educational? Is this author using artistic power to heal or harm? Is this story potentially a true friend?

The more theoretically minded critics went further and faced an even more troublesome question: Is this work's moral quality an essential element in our judgment, not just of its moral value, but of its artistic worth? And again they answered with a firm yes. As one cliché put it from classical times on, the goal of *good* art is to "delight *and* instruct"; it should be useful as well as pleasing (*utile et dulce*). The subtler critics went further to show just how all art instructs *as* it pleases; it instructs *through* its pleasures— for good *or* ill. The highly "human" moral seductions that make us love art works are the powers that demand our critical appraisal. Rhetorically minded critics like Horace were aware that different audiences respond to different qualities, and they put the pairing of instruction and pleasure in either/or terms: good literature must *either* teach *or* delight: *Aut prodesse aut delectare*. But Horace made it clear in the *Ars Poetica* that he preferred the kind of poetry that does both simultaneously.

#### Epoch II (Not Much More Than Half a Century)

From the last years of the nineteenth century to the 1960s, more and more critics reversed the field to answer no: Moral rightness or wrongness has little or nothing to do with literary or aesthetic worth, and debate about the moral worth of any artistic work consequently leads nowhere. In *The Company We Keep*, arguing for a return to yes, I traced briefly this swing from yes to no and suggested possible causes for the widespread rejection of morally centered artistic criticism: the immense difficulties the moral critic faces in the seemingly irresolvable contradictions among critics; the philosophical fashion, starting in the eighteenth century, of assuming an unbridgeable chasm between the world of fact and the world of value, the world of "is" and the world of "ought";[5] the obvious incoherence and carelessness and dogmatism that too many moral critics exhibited; the decline of confidence in the demonstrative powers of any rhetoric that offered—as is always true of moral criticism—no scientific proof; the decline of religious faith, "religion" having been seen as the best or only source of moral standards; and so on.

Possibly the most powerful cause for the rejection of moral criticism of art was the new passion (growing out of the eighteenth-century invention of "the aesthetic") for placing art or poetry in the special domain celebrated by Steiner, the higher world of pure or artistic pleasure: a world exempt from the chaotic problems of a lower world. To impose moral judgments on what we meet in this utterly different world, as we embrace art for the sake of the embrace, was said to be not just difficult, nor just dangerous: it was irrelevant to true quality, and it should be ruled out of all serious criticism. Indeed, genuine literary art, often given the elevating label "poetry," is in this view somehow above all ordinary beliefs and practices. As Archibald MacLeish's much-quoted poem "Ars Poetica" put it, "A poem should not mean / But be." W. H. Auden's aphorism "Poetry makes nothing happen" became a slogan for many.[6]

Thus art, craft, beauty, skill, or fine style were put on one side of a great divide, and all practical intentions and effect on "life" relegated to the other side. When appraising even the most morally questionable works—Louis-Ferdinand Céline's *Journey to the End of the Night*, say—one should attend only to the question of whether the style was beautiful, or at least brilliant or original.[7]

### Epoch III (Still Far Short of Half a Century)

Then, starting in the late 1960s, critics of various shapes and shades began to say yes again. Indeed, the past three decades have produced an avalanche of moral arguments, one that has felt depressing or overwhelming to many traditionalists. It has been astonishing even to me, a critic who had thought he was fighting a losing battle in defense of moral concerns.

Following the lead of the few holdouts through Epoch II—for example, the Marxists, F. R. Leavis, Lionel Trilling, R. P. Blackmur—critics began once again to insist that stories provide, in Kenneth Burke's phrase, both good and bad "equipment for living."[8] Often these post-New-Critic newer critics aggressively attacked the "aestheticizing" or "formalizing" or "objectivizing" that had come to dominate Epoch II. Not only in literary criticism but in every artistic field, critics reopened questions about how stories change listeners and cultures. They thus began to reunite themselves—consciously or unconsciously—with the grand tradition of Plato and Sidney and Arnold.

It is not surprising that this reopening of ultimate "value" questions has felt threatening, not only to those who still rely on the hard-and fast fact-value distinction, but also to those who fear an influx of the wrong values, or at least of values that cannot be debated in rational inquiry. It has seemed to many not an opening at all but a *closing*: a destructive avalanche of irrationality that threatens to close off rational discourse and turn everything into "politics."

This opening, which can hardly be called a single movement because there is so much disagreement among its partisans, is by no means confined to those who emphasize, as I do, words like *moral* or *ethical*. Anyone who looks closely at the work of various "postmodern" critics will discover that many are pursuing questions about the ultimate effects that stories have upon our lives. Whether their overt label is feminism, Marxism, new historicism, deconstruction, cultural critique, gay studies, race studies, or postcolonial discourse, they astonishingly agree—though often so far beneath the surface that careless readers miss it—that stories have moral importance. Discussing that importance matters, not just because stories are beautiful, or fun, or good time-killers, but because they make a difference to our ethos—who we are, how we behave to others, and what our culture becomes. The new critics are asking, in short, precisely the same kind of questions that the would-be censors of media violence are asking— or at least should be asking. That many in this multiple movement fail to proceed with a scholarly care that deserves the word *inquiry* is lamentable, but it does not affect the plain historical fact of the opening, the return to yes.[9]

Nevertheless, though I personally embrace many of the questions producing this avalanche, I find that too many of the answers, like too many of the moral judgments offered by critics in Epoch I and almost all of the recent indictments of popular sex and violence, are arrived at with too little attention to my two central questions: How does one distinguish competent from incompetent judges, and how can even the most competent listener exercise *inquiry* about moral distinctions, not just between individual stories but among *kinds* of stories? These distinctions are acceptable and useful to others—"replicable," if you will—but clearly not in the scientific sense. Perhaps "followable" or "rationally discussable" should be our term for the standards we are pursuing.

### A Competent Critic or a Bumbler or a Fraud? How Do You Distinguish?

Even those who say no to our earlier questions assume in their daily practice a real difference between those critics whom they should listen to and those who don't deserve their attention. Each critic implies that "I, the judge, am obviously more competent than those I disagree with." But few critics, ancient or modern, postmodernist or anti-postmodernist, have risked pursuing openly the personal defects that can handicap the critic, as David Hume does in the essay I shall borrow from here, his classic defense of literary judgment, "Of the Standard of Taste."[10]

Hume's main point is implicit in all that I have said so far: Our need is not for rival lists of stories—books, movies, videos—to be condemned or celebrated, regardless of context, or for statistical counts of this or that kind of sex or violence, but for *listeners* who are qualified to converse effectively about moral qualities. We need a critical culture: a nation of experienced listeners who practice moral inquiry with at least as much competence as is exercised by a devoted football fan when judging a coach or quarterback. We have many such critical cultures supporting the most popular sports. We have versions of such cultures in those music lovers and amateurs who judge classical music performances or the originality of the latest hard rock disk. But we do not have a comparable culture pursuing *informed* moral inquiry about our heavily storied lives.[11] What we have instead is blind warfare among defenders of this or that canon or anticanon, or this or that new opening or return to old values. Too many warriors claim that conflicts about such matters cannot be rationally debated or that "the enemy" is hopelessly irrational and should not be allowed into the conversation. Too often the appraisers have not even tested their claims by listening to the stories they judge, let alone the rival critical approaches.[12]

As I move to Hume's standards, I must stress that to argue that some judgments are better than others is not to argue that my judgments are better than *yours*, or that any one group—a collection of professional literary or movie critics, say—is ipso facto more entitled to a hearing than any other group. What is important is to recognize that inquiry about moral quality is quite different from mere reporting of personal experience or emotional response. Moral judgments for or against a story are finally claims about qualities *in the judged works*, and they are thus always implicated in a potentially arrogant claim by the one who acts as the judge: "I have the qualities required for discerning such and such qualities in a work, and therefore what may look like my merely personal reaction is more than that, even though it includes my feelings and convictions. Though not objective in the sense of 'independent of all human preferences,' it is not merely subjective either. Even though not 'replicable' by every conceivable listener, it is sufficiently 'followable' to command attention from any listener who will attend to the work as closely and responsibly as I have done." The very possibility of such a claim has been attacked by one group of participants in the avalanche, extremists in the so-called reader-response movement. Though I share the view that all serious responses, however contradictory, should be taken into account, the claim of some that all judgments are equally valid is absurd. It is true that in some teaching situations something like this egalitarianism can make sense; a good teacher will be careful not to knock down an outlandish reading if doing so will cause the student to lose the love of story. But when we are appraising a response, we obviously must determine whether the appraiser has "taken in" what is there to be taken in. Has she really listened, or instead been taken in by only a fragment, perhaps even a misinterpreted one? There is nothing elitist in this point; just as inexperienced listeners can extract a scene from its context, often reversing the implied author's intended moral judgments, so "sophisticated literary critics" can fail to take in a story because their critical biases blind them. While their attention is on their quest for conceptual confirmations, the proffered story simply floats past them unheard. In short, a justified ethical judgment depends, as Hume well knew, on a transaction between the ethical quality of the work and the ethical powers and attention of the listener.[13]

The maiming of critical judgment comes in many shapes and shades. No listener, not even Hume or the proud critic you encounter here, is totally unmaimed, alert to all possible misreadings and the resulting misjudgments. We all discover, on later readings, just how much we have missed or distorted earlier—whether last year or decades ago. That is one reason for attending to alien criticism—it teaches us about our oversights. Some listeners, even among the "literate," are in effect incompetent—though it will always sound arrogant for any critic to say so. The most obvious examples are misinterpreters of irony. Every teacher of ironic works discovers highly intelligent students who miss the cues. My own favorite was a reading of Jonathan Swift's "A Modest Proposal" by a brilliant, fourth-year economics major: totally missing the ironies, he attacked Swift for his faulty statistics about the likely profit from selling children as food![14]

You may or may not rule out such nonlisteners from your conversations, depending on your patience and the time of day. Indeed, as in all other moral matters, the question of just which contestants deserve most attention will always be answered diversely—and seldom openly. David Hume's characteristically bold and risky essay is thus of great importance to us as we face the avalanche of controversial moral claims. Hume's subject is not exactly ours. The "taste" in judges for which he seeks a standard is not "moral taste" but the capacity to discern genuine beauty: artistic or aesthetic worth. His quest is, however, precisely to the point here. The qualities essential to the critic of beauty are indispensable in any appraiser of narrative morality.

Hume first faces the powerful arguments against the very possibility of his quest: the claims that judgments of artistic worth are necessarily no more than subjective opinions and that in consequence all aesthetic judgments can be considered relative only to the judge's subjectivity or culture.[15] As I quote his summary, I shall insert moral terms to achieve my "translation."

> There is a species of philosophy, which ... represents the impossibility of ever attaining any standard of taste [or moral judgment]. The difference, it is said, is very wide between judgment and sentiment [merely personal moral revulsion or celebration]. All sentiment is right; because sentiment has a reference to nothing beyond itself, and is always real, wherever a man is conscious of it. But all determinations of the understanding are not right; because they have a reference to something beyond themselves, to wit, real matter of fact, and are not always conformable to that standard. Among a thousand different opinions which different men may entertain of the same [scientific or factual] subject, there is one, and but one, that is just and true; and the only difficulty is to fix and ascertain it. On the contrary, a thousand different sentiments [or moral responses], excited by the same object, are all right: Because no sentiment [or moral response] represents what is really in the object. It only marks a certain conformity or relation between the object and the organs or faculties of the [individual judge's] mind.... One person may even perceive deformity [or vicious immorality], where another is sensible of beauty [or moral enlightenment]; and every individual ought to acquiesce in his own sentiment, without pretending to regulate those of others. (para. 7, pp. 136–37)

Hume's way of refuting such taste relativism is to turn to what he calls the "common sense" observation that some judgments simply carry, for all of us, more weight than others; nobody actually *practices* aesthetic or moral relativism. We all assume that the experience of qualified judges, over time, leads to conclusions that should be honored even by those whose initial responses differ.

> The same Homer, who pleased at Athens and Rome two thousand years ago, is still admired at Paris and at London [and, as this modern critic happens to know, still admired after another two hundred and fifty years in some quarters of Peoria, Illinois, and Phoenix, Arizona, and Richmond, Indiana, and Moscow, and Flavigny, France]. All the changes of climate, government, religion, and language, have not been able to obscure his glory. Authority or prejudice may give a temporary vogue to a bad poet or orator; but his reputation will never be durable or general. (para. 11, p. 139)

To face this argument with full honesty, I must admit that one of Hume's examples of "durable" quality, the "obvious" superiority of Joseph Addison to John Bunyan, has led some to reject his case; after all, far more people since his time have read and loved *Pilgrim's Progress* than all of Addison's works put together. Has not Bunyan stood the test of experience over time better than Addison? And doesn't that contradiction of Hume's judgment further demonstrate the case that all literary values are "contingent," relative?

Without giving up his attack on complete relativism, Hume might well have joined me by answering with one version of critical pluralism. His downgrading of Bunyan sprang from his own limited experience and lack of sympathy for a given kind of religious allegory. Within its kind, Bunyan's work has proved its excellence to all readers who like that given kind and are experienced in it. That in itself does not deny Addison's greatness, if not superiority, according to Hume's standards. As a reader and admirer of both authors, I would surely choose Addison over Bunyan if I were given the "desert island" test: Which author would you choose to take with you if you knew you would have nothing else to read? On the other hand, if I were choosing which author should be read to me on my deathbed, would not Bunyan win? He would certainly win over a lot of other allegorists *of his kind*—thus demonstrating Hume's case, from another angle, that differences of quality are real, however elusive.

If we rephrase Hume's question not as "Which judges are indisputably right?" but as "Which judges have earned at least a modicum of right to join in inquiry about the moral quality of a given story?" we can conduct a direct translation of the five criteria he next offers as his answer to the aesthetic relativists. In borrowing his discriminations, I shall again add moral language where needed.

As we consider Hume's list, it will be useful to conduct a thought experiment, one based on actual critical debates I have witnessed lately. Imagine that you and a friend have just seen the much praised and debated movie *Pulp Fiction* or just read the almost as much praised and debated novel *The Information*, by Martin Amis, and you find yourselves in radical disagreement. One is shouting "A bad work, however clever, because it's immoral! It celebrates violence, and discounts its consequences." The other is shouting back, "It's a wonderful work; it raises moral questions brilliantly and irresistibly." What questions would you want to put to each other, if you could be totally frank, about your different levels of qualification for judgment? What precise kinds of expertise or training would either of you want to claim in order not to feel at least partially disqualified? (Obviously, we should add after each of the five following requirements the qualifier "other things being equal." None of Hume's standards can operate in isolation from all the others.)

First, Hume turns to "*delicacy* of [moral] imagination, which is requisite to convey a sensibility of . . . finer emotions" (para. 14, p. 140). Some people simply lack either the genetic structure or the kind of cultural experience that allows for sensitive response to moral issues. For example, is a serial killer fully qualified to enter a discussion of the moral quality of *Dr. Jekyll and Mr. Hyde* or *In Cold Blood*? We have the right to ask—though perhaps under our breath, "Are you the kind of person who can attend to the moral nuances of *any* tale? Is it in your very nature to care about moral qualities and distinctions of any kind? Are you able to conceive of a real difference between a moral and an immoral act?" In other words, if you happen to know that your companion is a sadist who has loved to engage in violent torture from childhood on, you know that he is not qualified to judge whether the killings in *Pulp Fiction* or the series of vicious attempted maimings by the "hero" of *The Information* call for moral indictment.

It is not enough just to be someone who *feels* revulsion when a revolting act is portrayed. "Delicacy" of "sensibility" requires attention to the subtle and innumerable clues that every story offers about its actual moral quality. Clever narrators often plan quite subtle acts of indelicacy, early in a tale, as foreshadowing more brutal offenses to come; they assume listeners who catch the tellers' judgments. They may even praise a villain ironically, expecting the listener to catch the irony.

The second quality is more obvious, or at least easier to defend: what Hume calls "practice." If either disputant has never seen any movie before, or read any novel, or has never seen or read movies or novels of these generic kinds, the burden of proof lies heavily on him or her. To paraphrase an example used by Samuel Johnson, if someone calls a building "lofty," and I learn that he has never before seen any building taller than two stories, I have every reason to question the value judgment.

Under "practice" Hume also rightly includes the requirement of repeated encounters with the same work (para. 18, p. 143). If one disputant has seen the movie or read the novel three times, and perhaps even taught it to a class, and the other has seen or read it once quickly, obviously the "practicer" is the one who deserves more attention; there can still be dialogue, but the novice should acknowledge the status of novice. I happen to want to indict both *Pulp Fiction* and *The Information* as morally questionable. (Are you surprised?) But I have not even seen the movie (I now confess)—I have only heard descriptions of its violence and of audience's giggles when the blood spatters. What's more, I have many experienced young friends who have seen it several times and claim that I am wrong in avoiding it. How could I ever possibly claim equal authority in any discussion? On the other hand, I have read *The Information* with some care, and I can thus face any champion of the work and claim something like equal rights in the conversation.[16]

Most of us, especially if we have lived more than a couple of decades, know the shocking reversals of judgments produced by "practice." Novels that in our early years we thought elevating and noble now seem callow and even morally destructive. Operas we were bored or repulsed by when we were eighteen now inspire us. And we all find many occasions on which we are the novices and someone else is the real practitioner.

For Hume, "practice," if it is to qualify anyone fully, includes a closely related third qualification, "comparison." A critic "accustomed to see, and examine, and weigh the several performances, admired in different ages and nations, can alone rate the [moral] merits of a work...and assign its proper rank among the productions of genius" (para. 20, p. 145). If my friend has seen a variety of contemporary movies that include (and perhaps condemn) violence, and I have not, my friend's opinion deserves closer attention than my own.

Hume's fourth criterion is perhaps the most crucial: "prejudice." A listener must "preserve his mind from *all* prejudice," allowing "*nothing* to enter into his consideration but the very object, which is submitted to his examination" (emphasis added). Important as this point is, Hume obviously carries it too far with words like "all" and "nothing." As Louise Rosenblatt and other reader-response critics have insisted, no one manages that degree of freedom from prejudgments: without preconceptions,

prejudices—without the frame of mind produced by earlier experience—
we could not engage fully with any story (see note 16). At the same
time, Hume is surely right in saying that "prejudice is most destructive of
sound judgment, and perverts all operations of the intellectual faculties"
(para. 22, p. 146). If my friend reads *The Information* and says, "You know,
I detest all British authors, and it's lovely to see them brutalized by Amis's
British-novelist-hero," I must question his judgment of the book. But this
is where comparison of the standards themselves enters. If another friend
has read the novel thrice and says, "Look, dummy, the author with his gift
for comedy constantly criticizes the brutalizing," I must listen to her.

Hume concludes with "good sense," which amounts to sound reasoning
capacity: Critics who are unable to reason clearly will obviously be unable
to appraise the reasonings that fill all powerful narrative. (And—a point
only slightly less important—their arguments for and against other critics
will be faulty.) Hume writes, "The persons, introduced in tragedy and epic
poetry, must be represented as reasoning and thinking, and concluding, and
acting, suitably to their character and circumstances; and without judgment
[sound reasoning] a poet [and thus the moral critic] can never hope to
succeed" (para. 22, pp. 146–47).

In other words, if you are to judge the moral choices made by reasoning
characters—and the main characters in both works I am using as examples
do a lot of reasoning—how can you claim competence unless you can
think at least as clearly as the clearest of the portrayed characters or (more
important) as the implied author who has created those characters?

For Hume to bring the capacity for sound reasoning into his case is
significant not just to our quest for trustworthy moral inquirers but to the
history of all reasoning about values. Hume is often thought of as one of
the founders of the sharp and unbridgeable fact-value, is-ought distinction:
you can reason to hard, genuine conclusions only about fact, never about
values (see note 5). But in practice, whenever Hume turns to writing history
or to considering real-life problems like "Is there a standard of taste?" he
becomes a brilliant exemplar of sound practical reasoning about values.[17]
Radically skeptical about all hard and certain proof, even in so-called scientific matters, and especially skeptical about decisive demonstration of moral
and religious conclusions, he nevertheless always distinguishes those who
make their practical or rhetorical claims carelessly from those who use a
rational discourse to pursue common ground.

Implicit in at least the last three of Hume's five standards is one that all
five depend on, if critics are not to sit proudly alone, stroking their egos.
I refer not just to delicacy, not just to comparison of works, not just to
practice, not just to the struggle to cast aside prejudices, not just to sound

reasoning, but also to conversation with other critics. Any lone individual, however brilliant, can never arrive at trustworthy moral judgments about stories through a private investigation. Such judgments simply cannot be demonstrated by any form of rigorous deductive or inductive reasoning pursuable in private. Too many efforts at moral judgment imply syllogistic deduction from absolute premises: "Any work with the word *fuck* in it is immoral; *The Catcher in the Rye* uses the word. Therefore it is immoral." Instead, effective moral critics always employ a form of "-duction" that is not "in-" or "de-" but *coduction*: they *listen* not only to stories but to their friends' responses to stories, and they change their minds steadily as they listen. As Hume talks about the authority of the traditional judgments that we inherit from centuries of "friends" who have praised Homer and the other greats, he is implying, without ever stating, that coduction is essential to good criticism.

Considering all these requirements in any critic deserving full attention,[18] Hume is forced, as I am, to conclude that "few are qualified to give judgment on any work of art, or establish their own sentiment as the standard of beauty [or morality]." Indeed I would go beyond the word "few"; no one person, not even myself on the rare morning when I'm feeling in charge, is qualified. Only communicating coductors are. With that bit of tightening, I expand Hume's own summary:

1. The organs of internal sensation [and moral discernment] are seldom so perfect as to allow . . . full play [to moral principles], and to produce a feeling correspondent to those principles. They either labour under some defect, or are vitiated by some disorder. . . .

2. Where he [the critic] is not aided by practice, his verdict is attended with confusion and hesitation.

3. Where no comparison has been employed, the most frivolous beauties [moral virtues], such as rather merit the name of defects, are the objects of his admiration.

4. Where he lies under the influence of prejudice, all his natural [moral] sentiments are perverted.

5. Where good sense is wanting, he is not qualified to discern the beauties [or moral issues] of design and reasoning, which are the highest and most excellent.

[6. When no coduction has occurred, the critic risks absurdly private, prejudicial judgments.]

Under some one or other of these imperfections, the generality of men labour; and hence a true judge is observed, even during the most advanced [and morally sensitive] ages, to be so rare a character: Strong [moral] sense united to delicate [moral] feelings, improved by practice, perfected by comparison, and cleared of all prejudice [through coduction pursued with other critics], can alone entitle critics to this valuable character; and the *joint* verdict of such, wherever they are to be found, is the true standard of taste and beauty [and moral quality]. (para. 23, p. 147; emphasis added)

Hume rightly goes on to concede once more that differences of cultural background and differences of personal experience will affect all of these criteria. "At twenty, Ovid may be the favourite author; Horace at forty; and perhaps Tacitus at fifty.... We chuse our favourite author as we do our friend, from a conformity of humours and dispositions" (para. 29, p. 150). As we today might put it, "where we come from" makes a great difference. "It is plainly an error in a critic, to confine his approbation to one species or style of writing, and condemn all the rest. But it is almost impossible not to feel a predilection for that which suits our particular turn and disposition. Such preferences are innocent and unavoidable...." (para. 30, p. 150).

But these differences, he concludes, do not undermine his standards. Nor do they lead to the claim that there is only one right moral reading of any story. Though there can be many wrong judgments, we must always make room for different perspectives.[19] Dangerous as it may be in our own time to make this claim, we should not make *much* room for critics who do not meet Hume's standards. And whether you who have kept with Hume and me this far are inclined to celebrate or condemn the avalanche of moral criticism in Epoch III, I hope you will join me in a lament: too many who hail it, like too many who curse it, exhibit the faults Hume describes. Opening almost any literary journal these days, left, right, or center, one finds at most a smattering of the critical virtues Hume celebrates.

### Good Kinds, Bad Kinds: What's the Difference?

Hume concludes his essay with a few judgments that he considers self-evident. Since he simply asserts them without argument, he offers no help to the moral inquirer who decides to go beyond particular evaluations, asking not just, "Is work X more praiseworthy than work Y?"—that is difficult enough—but "Are there good reasons to grant moral superiority to some kinds of stories?" The question is not, Are some kinds of stories more beneficial for all readers in all circumstances? Obviously, no story will be either harmful or beneficial to every conceivable listener—a point that was forgotten by my ninth-grade English teacher, who almost destroyed my budding passion for reading by imposing *Silas Marner* on us and teaching it as if it were little more than a moral tract. What may heal one listener may drive another to suicide. Our question here is, Are some kinds of story more *likely* to be harmful or beneficial to listeners?

We are dealing at best, then, in probabilities that are beyond strictly scientific study. Even the rare critic who might meet Hume's high standards (if there is such a person) must depend on rhetorical resources that will not carry "hard" proof.

As a first step, we should reject the widespread notion that to prove immoral quality you must be able to prove harmful effects on behavior. It may well be impossible to prove scientifically that any story or kind of story has been the cause of any specific action. *Post hoc* never establishes *propter hoc*, especially when the connections between the listening world and the action world are as tenuous as they usually are. The presumed fact that the suicide rate in Europe went up after young men read Goethe's *The Sorrows of Young Werther* proves nothing, even though to most of us it may seem likely that Goethe's sympathetic portrayal of his hero would produce imitators.

Those who oppose laws against violent drama often talk as if we must wait for statistical studies of how many murders are caused by the violence before we have any right to exert public critical pressure. Sometimes they cite a statistical decline in the number of portrayed murders as evidence that things are getting better. That's nonsense. No matter how strong our conviction that stories get imitated, we should not let our inability to offer proof for that conviction silence our criticism. Our questions should not be in the form, "Was Johnnie led by this story to commit misdeed Y?" but rather, "Was the life Johnnie spent while 'taking it in' enhanced or corrupted or just plain wasted?" "What kind of life was he living, during the two or eight or twenty hours spent listening?" Put another way, "What kind of person was implied as the ideal listener to this story, whether or not it included portrayals of viciousness or violence?"

I can now deal with only two of the many differences of kind that could be explored in answering such questions, still using gratuitous violence as my most obvious test case. First, there is a crucial contrast between stories that in themselves engage in overt or strongly implied moral judgment or inquiry about the acts they portray and those that leave the inquiry entirely up to the listener. If we are concerned about the quality of the life lived during the listening, then we must attend to the ways in which what Hume calls our "delicacy," our moral sensitivity, is heightened or lowered by the author's strokes.

From this perspective, no story can be judged bad or good just because it does or does not portray a given violent act or expression. It all depends on where and how the detail is placed within the whole story. Everyone agrees, for example, that to beat or kill the innocent or to commit rape are evil acts, and almost everyone agrees that evil is likely to be furthered by any story that celebrates such acts. Yet we all know that many of the stories we admire most, including the classical epics and dramas and the Bible, are full of such acts. Modern moviemakers and authors of pulp fiction did not invent the joys of witnessing the rape of the Sabine women, or the slaughter of untold numbers of Philistines, or the delicious horror of seeing an enemy's severed head brought in on a platter, or the gruesome vision of a totally innocent God/man nailed to a cross, sweating blood as a bystander pokes a spear in his ribs. Go read again your favorite fairy tale in the Grimm or pre-Grimm version and prepare for a bloodbath. Most of us not only enjoy but admire many stories old and new that dwell on scenes of horrifying cruelty. Most of us have also reveled in bloody denouements and then, on reflection, felt some shame. Either the tellers exploited us by failing to provide any helpful moral placement, any set of clues about where to stand as we listen, or we missed the clues and simply wallowed in the blood and guts.

The best tellers make such mistakes unlikely for any fully engaged listener. Franz Kafka's story "The Penal Colony," for example, is one of the most physically sickening of "modernist" stories, yet in my view it is one of the most admirable. Should it be condemned because the anonymous victim is tortured to death, slowly, brutally, as it were before our eyes? Or—perhaps the most striking example of all—should the New Testament be bowdlerized to protect our children from learning the sadistic pleasures of contemplating a crucifixion?

When we look behind the general attacks on violent portrayals, we find that hardly anyone is naive enough to object to all violent stories. Rather, most of us give at least tacit approval to violence against those we think deserve it.[20] Consequently, criticism should pay more attention to the difference between those stories that provide reasons or explanations or moral clues and those that simply exploit our natural pleasure—I'm afraid that it is natural—in witnessing pain.

The stories we rightly celebrate by listening to them again and again, generation after generation, *place* and *judge* their violent portrayals: the best of the fairy tales, "The Penal Colony," the story of Cain and Abel, Christ's passion, the *Iliad*, *War and Peace*. . . . The stories we rightly question are those that present the evil in a way that leaves listeners utterly unaided in their judgment. They provide nothing like a moral *placement*— a street address in the moral world, a location within the intricate and often contradictory range of human virtues and vices in which we all live.

Authorial placement can come in many forms, only one of them—often the weakest—in direct moral tags. The conviction of modernists that the best authors maintain distance or "objectivity," that they "show" rather than "tell," led some critics to reject all direct commentary, especially if it had a moral tone. It is true that much of the traditional moral guidance that they objected to had been puerile. But when we ask for moral placement, we do not say that all moral placements are of equal value: "Sunday schoolish" sentimental placements of good guys triumphing over the wicked won't make for a good story.[21]

I could explore examples of many a modern novel or movie that admirably and unobjectionably judge their vividly portrayed violence.[22] But since premodern works are usually a bit clearer in their placements, I choose as my prime example *King Lear*, a play that offers some undebatable moral judgments while at the same time leading us into one of the most complex moral experiences in the history of drama. Putting the complexities to one side for the moment, consider the play's long list of unambiguous moral judgments that no serious critic could ever question.

One of the most obvious of these is the gruesome scene when Cornwall grinds out Gloucester's eyes with his boot. He does this on stage and *one at a time*, with Cornwall pronouncing, after he kills a servant for saying that Gloucester still has one eye left to witness the viciousness, "Lest it see more, prevent it. Out, vile jelly! Where is thy lustre now?" (act 3, scene 7, line 84). Shakespeare could have told the same story much more briefly: both eyes at once, with Cornwall saying something like, "This'll show you," or "Take that, and that." But he chose to stretch out the violence as far as possible.

Few modern spectacular effects are more gruesome than that. We can be sure that any production in our time will exploit the physical grindings, including blood and "jelly" visibly dripping. Would that make it immoral? Those critics of the media who simply tot up the number of violent acts per week would have to say that this scene should either be cut entirely or sent to the wings to be told less vividly, as the Greek tragedians would have done. Yet to cut such a scene would be to deprive us of a crucial moment in the moral experience of the play. As handled by Shakespeare, the scene is implacably judged, *placed* as unforgivable, monstrous, an act that no viewer should ever condone (regardless of visceral, or even pathological, thrills). Those critics who have followed Keats in praising Shakespeare as a chameleon poet—neutral, impersonal, objective, shifting from morality to morality—have ignored how hard he often works, as he does here, to ensure that we not only condemn vicious acts but feel in our guts just why we should. He could not be less neutral than he is here.

His moves throughout the play are worth tracing, if only because such moves are so often missing from modern works whose authors claim, when criticized, that they strongly condemn the violence they portray. First, in the scene itself Cornwall's courageous servant sees the outrage coming and protests: "Hold your hand, my lord!...better service have I never done you / Than now to bid you hold" (act 3, scene 7, line 75). In effect that is Shakespeare speaking, the implied author as moralist. Cornwall slays him for interrupting the cruelty. Second, we are forced, by the structure of events before the scene, to be on Gloucester's side in the encounter. Third, the play punishes Cornwall with defeat and death: Shakespeare does not let him get away with it. Fourth, and perhaps most important emotionally, we are taken vividly and distressfully through scenes dwelling on the miserable consequences of the cruelty, as the sympathetic Gloucester suffers from the blinding, driven to an attempted suicide.

Thus the moral judgment is not simply tacked on, like the last-minute deaths or imprisonments in those crime thrillers that used to conclude with a voice intoning, "Crime does not pay." In *King Lear*, it is not only that crime does not pay, though that is something; this crime is fiercely condemned, not with moral platitudes but with wrenching dramatic rendering. Even if it "paid"—even if, say, Cornwall became king—we would still know that it was, in Shakespeare's eyes, an unforgivable act.[23]

We have in this scene, then, a revolting act that in its very portrayal insists on our revulsion and on the terrible consequences of evil actions. How different this is from much of the violence that fills many of our books and screens. Too many of them portray no internal protests; no morally credited "servant" comes forward to say, in effect, "I'd rather die than allow you to perpetrate that act." What's more, we are not led to care for the victims; we experience no emotional consequences of the violence except perhaps physical nausea—and even that is diminished decade by decade as we see more and more vivid awfulness. Indeed, we are often led, by technical maneuver, to sympathize most strongly with the perpetrator.

Thus too many tellers imply, even when they feel quite moral as they tell their tales, that there are no real values according to which any act could be considered really immoral. The overt values are reduced to something like what the narrator says to the reader at the end of *The Information*, with no hint of distance between the authoritative voice and Amis's own:

> Your watch knows exactly what time is doing to you: *tsk, tsk*, it says, every second of every day....Beware the aged critic with his hair of winebar sawdust. Beware the nun and the witchy buckles of her shoes. Beware the man at the callbox, with the suitcase: this man is you. The planesaw whines,

whining for its planesaw mummy. And then there is the information, which is nothing, and comes at night.[24]

This brings us to the second distinction, between stories that provide flat, unquestioning placement and stories that take us beyond strengthened moral convictions to moral inquiry. After all, a story by Aesop, with its little moral tag at the end, does place the action in the moral world. But all motive for inquiry about such a tale must come from the listener, not the tale. Inquiry results only from questioning, and questioning results not from comfortable reassurance about previous placements but from conflicts among rival placements. It is true that clear placement that shocks listeners can in itself lead to inquiry of a kind: any listener whose values conflict with the placement is forced into debate with the values of the story. Even Amis forces me to think, once again, about nihilism, about the ways in which current mores encourage nihilistic thought and about how nihilism might be responded to, either in narrative or plain argument. Indeed, many writers and critics in our time have proclaimed that to shatter moral complacency in this way is the supreme task of literature.[25] To provide what I am calling placement would for them be to undermine the moral effectiveness of the negative challenge.

But wherever we come out on that issue, it seems clear that neither flat moral placement nor plain negative challenge is sufficient to produce lasting and productive moral inquiry. Flat placement, with labels like "wicked" and "virtuous," though they may assist naive readers, can easily kill all serious thought about moral questions. What would be the effect on us if every action in *King Lear* were as clearly placed in the moral spectrum as is the blinding of Gloucester? Well, it is true that we would have to call the play "moral," in the sense of reinforcing our abhorrence of gratuitous brutality. But we could hardly claim that Shakespeare had educated us in the demands and skills of moral inquiry.

On the one hand, then, we have short "moral" folktales with or without overt tags, or the scene with Gloucester's eyes, with its internal unequivocal judgments, or a fiction that shocks us with decisive implied negatives. On the other, we have stories that engage us in moral inquiry. A full treatment of the difference would require another long essay. But one inescapable point is this: a great moral educator like *King Lear* not only places many acts as clearly, undeniably wrong, and others, such as Edgar's self-denying loyalty to Gloucester, as unquestionably admirable; it also places such clarities into contexts that force listeners into conflicts that provoke inquiry. No one can really listen to the whole story and rest in simple comfortable clarity about how the portrayed world joins or violates the world that the

listener inhabits. Immensely troubling moral issues face the attentive listener at almost every moment. Just how should a foolish (and foolishly
mean) old father be treated? What is the meaning of an action that ends
with so much grief and so many equivocations? (As is well known, performances in the eighteenth century revised the ending so that Cordelia
and Lear do not die: they are happily united.) How much should we blame
Lear for his disaster? Just how immoral is his treatment of Cordelia? Is
there a difference in the level of wickedness of Goneril, Regan, Cornwall,
and Edmund? Just how much deception is justified, as the "good" minor
characters try to aid the sufferers?

Turning to even larger questions, How should one respond to the preva-
lence of violence in the world of the play? *Are* we "like flies to the Gods,"
who "kill us for their sport"? Just how *should* a king, sane or mad, deal
with the fact of widespread poverty and suffering? We may leave a fine
performance of this play feeling in some sense purged, as Aristotle says
great tragedy leaves us, but we are not purged of all moral confusion or
questioning. Rather, we are steeped in the task of interrelating, comparing,
contrasting rival moral judgments: we are caught up in moral inquiry.

When stories neither place values nor throw placements into productive conflict, they throw the would-be moral critic back upon Hume's first
chancy criterion: the claim to "delicacy," a preexisting capacity to make
the right judgments. She is left saying, "Though this work gives me little
help in figuring out where the author stands, that doesn't matter because
I am one of those rare creatures who can distinguish moral and immoral
acts."

### Conclusion: Authors as "Purified" Friends

Throughout I have been implying that one key question should always be,
"What kind of person, what kind of critical listener am I asked to be while
I dwell 'here'—while I join, in my listening, the world offered by this tale?"
Nothing could be more crucial for us or our children than the quality of
our lives as we listen to stories: that is, who we *are* during the hours of
listening, regardless of what happens next hour or next day.

But to repeat that point underlines the tricky task that is implied in
all of my questions: determining just what are the moral qualities of any
specific storyteller, as implied in all of the details of his or her seemingly
friendly gesture. To tell a story, and especially to publish one, is to offer a
gift that the giver presumably admires. Whoever the flesh-and-blood teller
(or, in the case of performed plays and movies, tellers) may be, the creator
I listen to here has chosen to offer me these actions, these qualities, these

placements or lack of placements, these stylistic nuances, these images, this implicit or explicit ethical "code" or "world of values," this "ordering of loves."[26]

We meet here at the end, then, a final sharp difference of kinds among the creators themselves implied in the stories they offer. In one pile, I suspect larger than in any previous era, we listen to tellers who think only or primarily of what will capture us as listeners—of what will sell the "product." The creators are not asking, "Is this story an act of friendship?" or "Is this implied portrait of my own character one I really admire?" The only question for too many is, "What will the audience buy?"

In a much smaller pile we still meet, thank God, creators who, while not pretending to be above the desire to capture as many listeners as possible, care mainly about telling the best story they can tell. And the word *best* for them goes beyond the mere craft of "grabbing" readers to include moral questions of the kind I have been raising. Some few even testify to asking explicitly, "Will this do any good in the world?" As James Baldwin once put it, "You write in order to change the world, knowing perfectly well that you probably can't, but also knowing that literature is indispensable to the world. . . . The world changes according to the way people see it, and if you alter, even by a millimeter, the way . . . people look at reality, then you can change it."[27] Others seem to ask not so much whether the work will improve the world as whether it will present the listener with an experience worth having. Or they may ask, "Would I want to listen to this one if it were told by someone else?" The creators we consider great are usually those who have worked hard, often through extensive revisions, to improve or purify the self-portrait implicit in any creative act. They thus create an implied self superior to the everyday creature whose frequently abominable or stupid actions we learn about in later biographies.

The cheering truth is that we still have a small but impressive chorus of fine creators, inquirers who labor passionately to become, during the act of creation, more morally perceptive than they could ever manage to be after they leave the desk. Although some in the first heap simply cook up a false implied portrait—whatever current culture demands—those of the second kind perform, in the very act of telling a story, an act of moral inquiry. Winnowing out day by day everything that violates their own best insights, they finally present an imagined persona far superior to what their spouses or lovers usually meet at the breakfast table. Consequently, those "selves" are often much more morally perceptive than you and I can ever hope to be—except in the hours we spend with them.

The effort to appraise the value of such heightened offerings resembles closely our choices (in our nonliterary lives) of friends and enemies. The final ethical judgment of any narrative offering is perhaps best thought of as employing the metaphor of friendship—friendship with friends superior to any we ever meet in the "real" world. Does this gift seem to me, I ask, now that I have lived with it intimately, like the gift of a friend? Or is it more like that of a con artist, or even a recruiter for gang membership? Perhaps this seeming gift is, in fact, a packet of poisons—the "gift" of an enemy?

You and I will always reveal some differences about which of these friends are worth recommending to our everyday friends. But if we work at freeing ourselves of the critical handicaps Hume describes, and engage in coduction rather than individual pontification, the astonishing revival of moral inquiry of the past three decades may prove to be not a destructive avalanche, but rather—

Alas, there is no adequate metaphor for my dream of a critical world full of tellers and listeners engaged in genuine moral inquiry.


## Appendix: A Selection of Moral and Ethical Criticism since 1970

Needless to say, I know many books that are higher in quality than some listed here but that do not quite belong on such a list. Moral (or ethical) criticism is not the only legitimate game in town. (I provide a few handy—and perhaps partly misleading—labels for some titles, the presence or theoretical location of which may seem puzzling.) If anyone listed feels offended, I know not what to do. To the many who will rightly be surprised to find themselves missing, I can only say, "Write to me and complain."

Altieri, Charles. *Act and Quality: A Theory of Literary Meaning and Humanistic Understanding.* Amherst: University of Massachusetts Press, 1981.

Barbour, John D. *Tragedy as a Critique of Virtue: The Novel and Ethical Reflection.* Chico, CA: Scholars Press, 1984.

Berthoff, Warner. *Literature and the Continuances of Virtue.* Princeton, NJ: Princeton University Press, 1986.

Bettelheim, Bruno. *The Uses of Enchantment.* New York: Random House, 1976. (Fairy tales; children's literature.)

Booth, Alison, ed. *Famous Last Words: Changes in Gender and Narrative Closure.* Charlottesville: University Press of Virginia, 1993. (Feminism with a structural formal emphasis.)

Booth, Wayne C. *The Company We Keep: An Ethics of Fiction.* Berkeley and Los Angeles: University of California Press, 1988.

Cairns, Douglas L. *Aidos: The Psychology and Ethics of Honour and Shame in Ancient Greek Literature.* Oxford: Clarendon Press, 1993.

Cavell, Stanley. The Claim of Reason. Oxford: Oxford University Press, 1979.

_____. *Pursuits of Happiness: The Hollywood Comedy of Remarriage*. Cambridge, MA: Harvard University Press, 1981. (Cinematic transformations—and exploitations—of cultural roots.)

Clausen, Christopher. *The Moral Imagination: Essays on Literature and Ethics*. Iowa City: University of Iowa Press, 1986.

Coles, Robert. *The Call of Stories: Teaching and the Moral Imagination*. Boston: Houghton Mifflin, 1989. (Therapeutic uses of story.)

Davis, Walter A. *Get the Guests: Psychoanalysis, Modern American Drama, and the Audience*. Madison: University of Wisconsin Press, 1994. (Psychoanalysis and philosophy.)

Eagleton, Terry. *Criticism and Ideology: A Study in Marxist Literary Theory*. New York: Schocken Books, 1985.

Gardner, John. *On Moral Fiction*. New York: Basic Books, 1978.

Gates, Henry Louis, Jr., ed. *Loose Canons: Notes on the Culture Wars*. New York: Oxford University Press, 1992. (The problems of racism placed in a larger context.)

Greenblatt, Stephen. *Renaissance Self-Fashioning: From More to Shakespeare*. Chicago: University of Chicago Press, 1980. (Labeled a "new historicist," the author might better be labeled a "moralist of cultures.")

Harpham, Geoffrey Galt. *Getting It Right: Language, Literature, and Ethics*. Chicago: University of Chicago Press, 1992.

Henberg, Marvin. *Retribution: Evil for Evil in Ethics, Law, and Literature*. Philadelphia: Temple University Press, 1990.

Johannesen, Richard L. *Ethics in Human Communication*. 2nd ed. Prospect Heights, IL: Waveland Press, 1983. (Public rhetoric, advertising, "everyday" communication.)

Johnson, Barbara. *The Critical Difference: Essays in the Contemporary Rhetoric of Reading*. Baltimore: Johns Hopkins University Press, 1981. (Deconstructionist, with strong ethical commitments.)

Kane, Sean. *Spenser's Moral Allegory*. Toronto: University of Toronto Press, 1989.

Kort, Wesley A. *Moral Fiber: Character and Belief in Recent American Fiction*. Philadelphia: Fortress Press, 1982.

Lanser, Sniader Susan. *The Narrative Act: Point of View in Prose Fiction*. Princeton, NJ: Princeton University Press, 1981. (Feminism matched with structural interests.)

Marshall, David. *The Surprising Effects of Sympathy: Marivaux, Diderot, Rousseau, and Mary Shelley*. Chicago: University of Chicago Press, 1988.

Massey, Irving. *Find You the Virtue: Ethics, Image, and Desire in Literature*. Fairfax, VA: George Mason University Press, 1987.

McGann, Jerome J. *Social Values and Poetic Acts: The Historical Judgment of Literary Work*. Cambridge, MA: Harvard University Press, 1988. (Poems as social acts.)

Miller, J. Hillis. *The Ethics of Reading: Kant, de Man, Eliot, Trollope, James, and Benjamin*. Oxford: Blackwell, 1991. (Deconstructionist, celebrating the ethical importance of all careful reading.)

Morson, Saul. *Narrative and Freedom: The Shadows of Time*. New Haven, CT: Yale University Press, 1994.

*New Literary History*. Special issue, "Literature and/as Moral Philosophy" 15 (autumn 1983).

Newton, Adam Zachary. *Narrative Ethics*. Cambridge, MA: Harvard University Press, 1995.

Nouvet, Claire, ed. "Literature and the Ethical Question." Special issue, *Yale French Studies* 79 (1991).

Nussbaum, Martha. *Love's Knowledge: Essays on Philosophy and Literature*. Berkeley and Los Angeles: University of California Press, 1991. (Moral readings of individual works, especially Henry James's *The Golden Bowl*.)

Packard, Vance. *The People Shapers*. Boston: Little, Brown, 1977. (Popular culture.)

Palmer, Frank. *Literature and Moral Understanding: A Philosophical Essay on Ethics, Aesthetics, Education, and Culture*. Oxford: Clarendon Press, 1992.

Parker, David. *Ethics, Theory, and the Novel*. New York: Cambridge University Press, 1994.

Phelan, James. *Reading People, Reading Plots: Character, Progression, and the Interpretation of Narrative*. Chicago: University of Chicago Press, 1989.

Rabinowitz, Peter J. *Before Reading: Narrative Conventions and the Politics of Interpretation*. Ithaca, NY: Cornell University Press, 1987.

Rosenblatt, Louise M. *The Reader, the Text, the Poem: The Transactional Theory of the Literary Work*. Carbondale: Southern Illinois University Press, 1978.

Schwarz, Daniel R. *The Humanistic Heritage: Critical Theories of the English Novel from James to Hillis Miller*. Philadelphia: University of Pennsylvania Press, 1986.

Scott, Nathan. *The Poetry of Civic Virtue*. Minneapolis: Augsburg/Fortress Press, 1976. (Broadly "religious" criticism.)

Sharp, Ronald A. *Friendship and Literature: Spirit and Form*. Durham, NC: Duke University Press, 1986.

Siebers, Tobin. *The Ethics of Criticism*. Ithaca, NY: Cornell University Press, 1988.

Springer, Mary Doyle. *A Rhetoric of Literary Character: Some Women of Henry James*. Chicago: University of Chicago Press, 1978.

Trotter, David. *The Making of the Reader: Language and Subjectivity in Modern American, English, and Irish Poetry*. London: Macmillan, 1984. (Poetry as "story.")

Warner, Marina. *From the Beast to the Blonde: On Fairy Tales and Their Tellers*. New York: Farrar, Straus and Giroux, 1995.

White, James Boyd. *"This Book of Starres": Learning to Read George Herbert*. Ann Arbor: University of Michigan Press, 1994. (Ethical effects of religious poetry.)

Williams, Raymond. *Marxism and Literature*. Oxford: Oxford University Press, 1977.

Yamagata, Naoko. *Homeric Morality*. Leiden, the Netherlands, and New York: E. J. Brill, 1993.

*This essay is one of several I have written on rhetoric and religion and the relations among these and other disciplines. It is to date my most succinct account of matters that have always been central to me but unfortunately neglected, as an ensemble of interrelated arguments, by the culture at large. My hope is that it will spur similar inquiries, particularly now, when the very possibility of religious faith is increasingly perceived by scholars as no longer self-evidently out of the range of serious consideration.*

This essay was originally published as "Can Rhetorology Yield More Than a Mere Truce, in Any of Our 'Wars'?" in *The Rhetoric of Rhetoric: The Quest for Effective Communication* (Oxford: Blackwell, 2004), 153–70.

# Rhetoric, Science, Religion

> The main reason religion needs to be privatized is that, in political discussion with those outside the relevant religious community, it is a conversation-stopper.
>
> —Richard Rorty

> Although scientists may officially eschew metaphysics, they love it dearly and practice it in popularized books whenever they get the chance.
>
> —Jeffrey Wicken

> Science without religion is lame; religion without science is blind.
>
> —Albert Einstein

> Science is constituted through interactions that are essentially rhetorical.
>
> —Alan G. Gross

As in most controversies, those who attack either religion or science usually make their case without showing any serious evidence that they have listened to their opponents: religion is superstition, utterly fake; science is the cruel enemy of human values. Fanatical nonlisteners thus waste book after book, article after article, attacking selected extremes, while dogmatically preaching some version of their own side.[1]

Even those who argue for some degree of genuine overlapping are often carelessly biased. One example is a recent article that attempts to show not only that the overconfidence of some scientists resembles religious dogmatism, but that *all* scientists are "gnostics" in the sense that they are certain that they are the only ones who have the truth, or at least the right road to truth.[2] For this author the only common ground shared by scientists and religionists is dogmatic excess!

Before attempting to exhibit science and religion as half-siblings, we must first look at how each of them has related to, or quarreled with, rhetoric. The relations have been quite different. That rhetoric and religion are inescapably akin has been obvious to everyone who has thought about it; even theologians who separate rhetoric from truth would concede that religions depend for survival on *preaching*, on being *evangelical*. No pastor can do well without a mastery of religious rhetoric. In contrast, rhetoric and science are most often seen as in no way related; they are as strongly divorced as are science and religion. As I said in chapter 2 [*of* The Rhetoric of Rhetoric], it wasn't until the late twentieth century that scholarly works began appearing about the rhetoric of science, and I have found that none of them strive, as I do here, to relate the *rhetorics* of science and religion.

## Religion and Rhetoric

Some classicists saw rhetorical probing as the proper route to the right kinds of religious thought. Others, like St. Augustine, felt deep conflict between their training in rhetoric and their religious certainties, while still acknowledging their inescapable reliance on rhetoric. In modern times most religionists have seen rhetoric as at best the mere altar boy to the priest.[3] While serious religious method, whether theology or prayer, can yield truths, rhetoric is what you use to spread them to the world.

This ambiguous relation between religion and rhetoric is curious, especially when viewed in the light of how opponents of religion have tended to regard the two as almost identical. For many, since religion is mere irrational faith, its language can be nothing *but* rhetoric, often mere "rhetrickery." Aggressive prophets of a positivistic worldview have used the same tactics against both rhetoric and religion. Religion and rhetoric, those twin dark burdens of ignorance inherited from the prescientific past, can both be simply dismissed. Neither of the two ways of tying rhetoric to religion—as dutiful altar boy or as forlorn doomed twin—can tempt anyone to inquire seriously into their deeper relations. But when rhetorical studies are seen as an indispensable and universal path to escape misunderstanding, and when religions are seen not as benighted, superstitious inheritances from the Dark Ages but expressions of a universal human need for explaining the world and escaping its horrors—the pursuit of deeper understanding of what is to be worshipped, and how—we already see a new reason for claiming their inseparability. This may explain why one finds these days so many discussions of "rhetoric and religion" or "the rhetoric of religions."

Especially since Kenneth Burke's *Rhetoric of Religion*, such studies have flooded the academic world. Anyone who pursues our topic behind the contrasting and often deceptive labels, playing with synonyms, probing the theological and scientific "rhetoricians" who avoid the language, will find thousands of discussions of how rhetoric, under somebody's definition, either serves or leads to somebody's definition of religion.

## Science and Rhetoric

When we turn to science, we find a much more rigorous divorce from rhetoric. Most scientists still think of it as having nothing to do with their serious inquiry; again it is often nothing but rhetrickery. The recent appearance of many books and articles on "the rhetoric of science" has produced many angry responses from those who fear that the very phrase undermines the claims of science.[4] Even scientists who feel some attachment to religion think of rhetoric as somehow irrelevant.

## Do the Diverse Rhetorics Overlap?

Because of these contrasting relations with rhetoric, many on both sides will consider the following two claims a bit peculiar, if not plain silly:

- Science (or pure reason, rationality, hard thought) is not really more completely divorced from rhetoric than is religion.
- The warfare between science and religion, between reason and faith, between rationalists and religionists, has been seriously reinforced by the neglect of genuine rhetorical inquiry.

My hope is to move at least some ardent defenders of religious commitment, and some scientists who think they will soon have the ultimate "Theory of Everything,"[5] to acknowledge that they have been mistaken in dismissing their opponent. It's not that they are wrong to defend religion or to pursue scientific thinking to the hilt but that they are wrong to see such thinking as the only legitimate kind. To put the thesis of this chapter in the most forceful rhetorical terms, then, I'll just ask all you readers who think of yourselves as scientifically minded: "Are you sure that your arguments and convictions are in opposition to religion?" Then, to all of you who think of yourselves as deeply religious, I ask: "Are you sure that your deepest beliefs contrast sharply with those held by scientists?"[6]

I will not be making the extreme assertion that rhetorology can totally unite any one particular religious denomination with the full scientific endeavor. While I admire Cardinal Newman's *An Essay in Aid of a Grammar of Assent* (1870) for its probing of rhetorical matters, I don't follow him in the claim that honest rhetorical thought will actually lead to one triumphant denomination—his brand of Catholicism. Instead, I claim only that a full rhetorology can lead us to recognize at least seven fundamental similarities between the rhetorics of science and religion. If "half-siblings" seems too strong, at least they belong to the same clan.

On both sides, many will think such a quest absurd. Some who are passionately religious might say,

> Your quest really is silly. It's all right, of course, for you to have your fun pursuing your coinage, rhetorology. It's a good thing to have serious study of inescapable conflict among fallen creatures as they pursue, ever since Babel, their always multiple, limited, and conflicting ends in history. But we have religion and theology providing the right kind of worship and valid study of a perfect Being who is beyond conflict, the Author of our being who is not dependent on our contingencies and not—except in rather peculiar ways—dependent on history. That God has indeed taught us certain rhetorical forms—the rhetoric of prayer, for example, or of the homily—and He may teach us how not to talk ("Thou shalt not bear false witness"). But is it not absurd to hope that the study of how we do talk will lead us to a Divinity who will not just forgive but embrace atheistic scientific inquiry?

Meanwhile the passionately scientific critic will be making almost the same points in different language:

> Your quest here is not just silly, it's dangerous. We've always believed that shoddy rhetoric and naive religious belief are tied together. What's new about that? You're just working in a closed circle of self-validating nonsense. And in so doing you undercut drastically the unique value of genuine scientific inquiry: the only human endeavor that escapes the corruptions of human bias.

Every effort to relate science and religion, whether rhetorically or metaphysically, can be accused of being overly ambitious. There has been an astonishing flood of books and articles in recent decades attempting to find some meeting ground. I have a shelf more than eight feet long containing books and articles on the subject, most of them published since Fritjof Capra's *The Tao of Physics*, in 1975.[7] The Templeton Foundation is now giving huge cash awards for the best books relating science and religion, and I am told that the foundation is flooded with applicants and recommendations.

No matter how we label the oppositions—reason versus superstition, dogmatic rationalism versus genuine human values, secular humanism versus religious fundamentalism, atheism versus theism—the conflict between hard thought about natural laws and hard thought about the source and grounds of nature and value will almost certainly outlive you and me and our grandchildren. Even those analysts who attempt to produce at least an armistice cannot promise that the threat of further warfare will ever disappear. And we may even see further examples of open violence, as when a pious believer concludes that it's a holy act to murder a doctor who is committing evil abortions.

## Rival Approaches

Battles among various versions of science and religion are overwhelmingly diverse. Some books still echo earlier portrayals of a flat-out war, with science the proud victor over religion; the superstitious enemy of truth just dies. Michio Kaku's *Visions: How Science Will Revolutionize the Twenty-First Century* (1997) predicts science's solution to every "why" question and every religious need; Kaku even includes the zany idea that science will develop genuine immortality, by downloading your brain and reinstalling it in some other body later. But many authors recently have sought some truce or accommodation or even full conciliation. Not long before he died, Stephen Jay Gould, perhaps the most popular of all biological rhetoricians, published a book, *Rocks of Ages: Science and Religion in the Fullness of Life* (1999). Gould claims total validity for both religion and science, but his major claim is that there is absolutely no overlap, because their rhetorics— a term he doesn't use—are totally distinct. He even invents the acronym NOMA, for NonOverlapping MAgisteria. The reason there is no overlap is that rational inquiry is for him on the science side; rhetoric is on the religion side, *unprovable* faith.

A surprising number of the new books, in contrast to those extremes, echo Cardinal Newman by reconciling science with one particular religion. John Polkinghorne, a brilliant particle physicist and priest, claims no conflict whatever between his version of hard science and his version of Christianity.[8] Some, like Ian Barbour, avoid such difficulties by digging more deeply into scientific method and theological arguments, claiming to find, in the tradition of Whitehead and Hartshorne, a meeting ground (process theology, leading to "pantheism").[9] And of course many studies are more superficial than Barbour's, pursuing one or the other of the three most tempting approaches: diplomacy, tolerance, or utter relativism— "There's no such thing as truth, so why bother?"[10]

For some sociologists the differences, not just between science and all religion but among diverse religions, are finally irreconcilable. In "Is There a Place for 'Scientific' Studies in Religion?" Robert Wuthnow argues that "the role of scientific studies should not be . . . to discover what is common among the various religious traditions, but to understand what is different and to gauge reactions to those differences. . . . To their credit, social scientists who study religion today are much more likely to insist on in-depth analysis of specific traditions than to settle for superficial generalizations." He claims to be probing "in depth"—but his quest is only for the differences.[11]

Putting aside the obvious differences, what are the shared unquestionable convictions of the combatants: the assumptions, commonplaces, topoi, firm platforms, or "places" on which they stand? (For simplicity, I'll follow Stephen Toulmin and call them the "warrants" taken for granted on all sides.) If disputants really probed for shared warrants—if they really listened—would they find far fewer real differences? Would they find what John Dewey pursued in his book *A Common Faith* (1934)?

As is obvious by now, any such quest is based on a prejudice: the assumption that, after all, there *must be some warrants that are shared*. I have been a passionate lifetime believer in science—of different kinds at different stages of my life. I have been also a lifetime pursuer of religious truth—again of radically different versions: from beginning as a devout orthodox Mormon, through increasing doubt to professed atheism, to a recovery of religious belief that some might call mere pantheism, or perhaps Deism. I still call myself genuinely religious, though I have often had to use metaphorical, symbolic, or mythological dodges when arguing with a fundamentalist Christian about whether the earth was created in six days, or whether Jesus was really dead for three days and then resurrected, violating everything we think we know about biology.

Can I really call myself fully religious, while being fully committed to whatever natural truth is thoroughly demonstrated? The answer depends a lot on definitions of terms.

## Why Mere Verbal Definitions Give Little Help

It is hard to think of any terms more slippery, more polymorphous, even perverse, than *religion, religious,* and *religiously,* let alone *spiritual* or *devout* or *belief.* (As chapter 1 [*of* The Rhetoric of Rhetoric] revealed, *rhetoric* is a good rival; even *science* has no single definition.) For some, religious terms refer simply to passionate commitment, to anything: "I watch *60 Minutes* religiously." For others religion is synonymous with what their enemies call superstition: belief in a superpower who can be appealed to for rescue from the human mess.

William James struggled with this diversity when preparing his Gifford Lectures, *The Varieties of Religious Experience* (1902—and many later editions). At times he almost gave up on the project, but he finally settled on a psychological definition: Religion is "the feelings, acts, and experiences of individual men [and women] in their solitude, so far as they apprehend themselves to stand in relation to whatever they may consider the divine." Abandoning all such attempts at full verbal summary, I move here beyond "feelings and experiences in solitude" to a list of seven *shared* warrants— the stable platforms that most who call themselves religious and most scientists consciously or unconsciously stand on as they present arguments.

That the search for shared warrants is not easy is dramatized by the experience of my friend, divinity professor David Tracy. As a Catholic theologian, he met annually for several years with leaders of other "great religions" who were hoping to find common ground. Returning each time from the discussion with Buddhists, Muslims, Jews, Catholics, and Hindus, Tracy would seem a bit discouraged: "We found little or nothing we could all agree on this year." But one year not long ago he came back looking positively optimistic. When I asked what they had *all* agreed on, he said, as I remember it, "We all agreed that something is radically wrong with creation."[12] Would they have needed even longer to come to agreement if scientists had been there? Well, if I'm right in what follows, they might have come to an agreement even sooner.

*Warrant One: The world as we experience it is somehow flawed.*

Something is wrong, deficient, broken, inadequate, lacking. Something is rotten not only in the state of Denmark, but everywhere. As the popular bumper sticker puts it, "Shit Happens." This or that corner of the world is falling apart as I write this sentence. Millions are suffering intolerably.

In one form or another everybody in the world believes in, and actually relies on, this warrant. We ignore it mainly in our moments of ecstatic happiness, when everything *feels* wonderful. But a moment or day or week later, we quickly fall back into acknowledging what David Tracy's group conceded: *something* is wrong, or something *went* wrong, with creation. For the purest of scientists what is *explicitly* wrong is our ignorance of a truth we should be seeking.[13] But even they live, day by day, in a world that exhibits multiple flaws, such as the failure of Congress to grant the money needed to finish this or that billion-dollar project, or the misbehavior of a lab assistant, or the cheating of a colleague. And more and more scientists these days face the threat that there is possibly an inescapable conflict in the whole of things: for example, the contrast between what the theory of gravity tells us and what quantum physics reveals. But even if that scientific "flaw" is finally removed, there will still be, for everyone, a range of flaws in the world as now experienced.

Implicit in the notion of wrongness is an inescapable value judgment: To judge anything as "wrong," one has to embrace some notion of something righter, which leads us (following Kenneth Burke's accounts of perfectionism) to . . .

*Warrant Two: The flaws are seen in the light of the Unflawed, some truth, some notion of justice, or "goodness," or of some possible purging of ugliness or ignorance; standards of judgment of the brokenness exist somewhere.*

Though some scientists may already be bridling here, wouldn't most embrace this warrant? They have standards of scientific truth and personal integrity in the pursuit of knowledge that will repair our ignorance. As many of them have fulminated against various postmodernist questionings of "truth," they are implicitly confessing that they embrace this warrant. As they attack scientists who cheat, they express the faith that scientific cheating is genuinely, universally, morally wrong—a faith that they could never demonstrate with hard research. Their standard of honest research was not just invented by them; it is in a sense "eternal," awaiting human discovery. Which leads us to . . .

*Warrant Three: There is some supreme order or cosmos or reality, something about the whole of things that provides the standards according to which I make the judgments of Warrants One and Two.*

Almost all who call themselves religious, and most scientists, even the most ardent atheists, believe in Warrant Three: there is a cosmos, often thought of in terms that resemble astonishingly what many theologians have called Supreme Being. Scores of books have reported the quest for *a final theory* that will explain *everything*. Why? Because "everything" is really *there*, waiting to be explained—and it is also *here*, supporting our pursuit of it. As Matthew Arnold's definition puts it, religion is belief in some power "greater than ourselves, making for righteousness."[14] His word "righteous," connoting something like dogmatic or arrogant, will put some people off these days. But what Arnold meant was "something righter than wrongness," and every scientist has to believe in that; otherwise the quest for truth is pointless. There is a larger "truth" awaiting discovery, a Totality of Truths that includes and judges the particular truths found in this or that research project.

These three warrants, intertwined, are nicely revealed by the David Tracy anecdote: something is radically deficient in the world as we see it—because we all agree that "Things could and should be better." His report of the discovery was not just that "Something is wrong with the world I live in" or "There's a lot of stuff around me that I personally disapprove of or grieve over." Everybody believes that "Something could and should be better about my world"—even if it is only that "I ought to have more drugs available," or "I don't have enough corpses yet buried in my cellar," or "Why can't I get every day the feelings I get in that new entertainment church on Sunday morning?" That is why M. Scott Peck made the mistake of taking my case too far. In his best-selling book *The Road Less Traveled* (1978), he argued that *everybody* in the world is religious, whether they know it or not. To me he corrupts the notion of religion by reducing it to the one warrant: passionate caring about *something*. (For a small minority of those who think of themselves as religious, ecstasy is the only warrant; for some ecstasy-pursuers, religion is all just personal feeling. I'm tempted to call such people "me-ligionists"—what Jacques Derrida called "irresponsible orgiasts.") But Peck was right about the universality. Even in moments when we are feeling total bliss about this or that reward of life, if someone interrupts and asks, "Is *everything* fine in the world?" we have to confess that millions are starving, hundreds of innocents are at this moment being killed, somewhere, hundreds will die today in a car crash or plane crash or suicide bombing or a new war. Even the most blissful me-ligionsts may concede, when questioned, that something is after all wrong: Too many in the world don't accept their celebration of this or that liberating feeling.

Thus almost all of us on all sides embrace the relation of the first warrant to the second and third. Warrant One implies a value judgment: "Something went wrong with creation," or "Something *ought* to have been righter," or at least, "I can see what would have been better." It's not just, "I don't like some things about it," but rather, "Some things are wrong when judged by what would be right, by what a full rightness would demand, by what the whole of creation as I see it—my cosmos, my God, my view of nature— implies as the way things should be but are not."

In the language of Christianity and Judaism this point is put as "the Fall," a temporal decline from what had been perfection. Some religions, even some branches of Christianity, deny that: "It" has been flawed eternally. But the three warrants do not need to be taken temporally. As Kenneth Burke makes clear in *The Rhetoric of Religion*, stories about temporal rising and falling can always be translated into nontemporal, vertical ladders: *temporally*, we were up there, fell down, and now we're down here trying to climb back up; *nontemporally*, we've always been a long way down the ladder, trying to climb up a bit with no hope of ever fully comprehending what is "at the top."

Thus lamentation about the universality of brokenness moves toward religion (and the implicit religion of scientists) only when it is linked with the second and third warrants—only when the lamenter realizes not just that shit happens but that shit's happening, and its definition in relation to what is not awful but good is somehow built into the very structure of things: some cosmos, a Something without which there would be Nothing. Disaster has always happened, from the beginning (or, as Bible literalists claim, *almost* from the beginning), but there was/is a place from which the Fall can be judged as a fall. It is defined by an elusive notion of its opposite, an order or cosmos which in some sense judges the happening as faulty and imposes "oughts" upon us. "Your laboratory research was tragically flawed; *you ought* to have known better." "Your colleague has violated scientific standards, and *you ought* to have warned her about it, or reported her lying to the authorities."

*Warrant Four, emerging from the first three: All who are genuinely religious (not just complaining) will somehow see themselves as in some inescapable sense a part of the brokenness.*

It's not just other people—those terrorists out there, say—who are out of joint. I am. I'm not as good, kind, effective, smart, learned, organized, courteous, alert, or wise as I ought to be. Even the best of us, even the strongest, the purest, the humblest, are inherently lacking, deficient, in need of further repair, or, as religionists put it, we are sinful or guilty. I am an inseparable part of a cosmos that includes this flawed fraction of itself, me, thus including in that fraction a sense of regret about my flaws.

In all honest scientists, this warrant is revealed as lamentation about personal ignorance: what I don't know and *ought* to know![15] And my guess is that many exhibit it as they curse themselves daily for their scientific deficiencies and failures.

*Warrant Five, following inescapably from the first four: The cosmos I believe in, the cosmos I may or may not feel gratitude toward for its gift of my very existence, the cosmos that is in its manifestations in my world in some degree broken—my cosmos calls upon me to do something about the brokenness.*

I must do what I can in the repair job, working to heal both my own deficiencies and to aid my fellow creatures in healing theirs. For many scientists, this can mean no more than "I have a duty to work at removing my own ignorance." But more often, even for "atheistic" scientists, it becomes a moral command to remove *the world's* ignorance. For some official religions, as in versions of Judaism and in the version of Mormonism still naggingly active in my soul, it produces floods of daily self-reproach: That which I have done I should not have done, and that which I have not done I should have done. In many denominations it produces missionary work; for many scientists it produces a lifetime vocation to teaching: the widespread ignorance of scientific truth is as appalling as "sin" is to devout religionists.

A major example of earlier scientific "fixing" was the alchemists' efforts to repair, with their science (or artistry), a universe not created by a perfect or imperfect God but by a perfect or imperfect Demiurgos. Modern scientific "cures" range from environmentalists' projects to some hopes for genetic engineering: obviously our bodies ain't what they ought to be, and maybe we can remove the flaws. Beneath all the varieties of cure, we see this one indisputable meaning of life: a purpose that transcends—and influences—our particular feelings of the moment. Has anyone here ever met a genuine scientist who does not share this sense of a passionate purpose for improvement—of *something*?[16]

*Warrant Six, an inevitable moral corollary of the other five: Whenever my notion of what my cosmos requires of me conflicts with my immediate wishes or impulses, I ought to surrender to that higher value.*

Rather than pursuing what is easiest or most pleasant or most reassuring to my present sensations or wishes, I obey or pursue *It*. Our impulses, our immediate wishes, *ought* to be overridden whenever they conflict with responsibility to cosmic commandments. We have obligations not just to others but to the Other. Religious talk dwells on this, while for scientists it is usually only implicit. But next time you meet a scientist who is furious about a colleague who has cheated, ask him or her why cheating is *really* wrong. If I am a genuine scientist, and I am tempted to make a reputation or fortune by falsifying my results, I have an absolute command, not just from my conscience but from my cosmos, to combat that temptation. If I feel that my culture is condoning such selling out, I must combat that cultural drive. (That more and more researchers are becoming "sinful," according to this standard, by selling out to pharmacy companies is relevant here but not crucial.)

None of us escapes the conflicts among three cosmic demands: "Pursue Truth!" "Pursue Goodness—the welfare of others!" "Pursue Beauty!" Many physicists engaged in the Manhattan Project (by no means all) have reported that their work on the bomb almost tore them apart, not just because of the conflict between the "command" to pursue scientific truth and the fear of human disaster, but because of the conflict between two versions of "goodness": ending the war versus refusing to kill hundreds of thousands of innocents. Nobody escapes the "choose the lesser evil" problem, but "choose the better Good" is even tougher. Nobody escapes the hard fact that something larger than our personal comfort or preference issues "commandments."

*Warrant Seven, a warrant that everyone, not only William James, would make essential to all religions: The psychological or emotional feelings connected with all of this.*

All genuine religions either openly or subtly offer spiritual "highs," moments of deep spiritual feeling—not just the excitement provided by some me-ligions but the deeper bliss that results from contact with the ultimate: the cosmos, the whole of things, God, Being, Nature, the source of all of our "commandments." I could fill the rest of this chapter with quotations from scientists about how thrilled they are when they make full contact with what they consider reality or scientific truth or the challenge of the ultimate mysteries of beauty: both words, *mystery* and *beauty*, fill Steven Weinberg's book, *Dreams of a Final Theory* (1992). Scientists feel in such moments that they have joined a "power bigger than themselves that makes for rightness—truth." (I have to admit that many scientists I've chatted with about this feeling admit that they share it, but flatly deny that it has anything to do with religion.)

Most religions offer in their myths explicit acknowledgment of finally irresolvable mystery: what some medieval theologians called Incomprehensibility. The Wholeness of the invisible cosmos is beyond rational demonstration. The Order is always some kind of numinous *mysterium tremendum*.[17] Many scientists get off the boat here: "We'll finally master it all." But others have captured something of this mystifying wonder, admitting that no human being will ever grasp the "incomprehensible" whole. But even those who aggressively claim that "in principle" science is the only faith that can capture it all usually reveal a spiritual sense of awe or glory or gratitude for that "all."

## The Neglected Blessings

Many religionists will feel impatient because these seven warrants leave out so many rewards that feel important to them: this or that blessing that "my religion considers essential and that scientists question." And many scientists may cringe at my attributing the warrants to them. On other occasions I have discussed those diverse blessings, the diverse psychological or emotional rewards in addition to the spiritual highs of Warrant Seven: the bliss of joining a community, of consuming the blood and flesh of Christ, of proudly obeying commandments about how to dress, of dutifully reading scriptures, of finding reinforcement for courage or humility or other virtues, of the escape from despair about the disaster-laden world through hope for eternal life.

The so far unmentioned blessing that for many religionists would be at the top, perhaps most challenging to my rhetorological project, is reliance on intervention by a providential God: the hope, comfort, and sense of loving protection provided by a God willing and able, with miracle, to violate the natural laws "worshipped" by scientists. For many on both sides this is not only one of the warrants of religion but absolutely the number one definition of religious belief: If you believe in a Great Meddler, you are religious; if you do not, you're an atheist. And for many scientists even a hint of such providential intervention violates the very notion of genuine science.

Fortunately, this belief is not essential to many of the most serious theologians, even within the Christian Judaic tradition. They have condemned praying for providential, meddling gifts as a reduction to a kind of cheap bargaining or bribery: our reason for obedience to our God becomes, many have lamented, merely an attempt to get paid back at the end.[18] Which leads me to . . .

But SPACE again suddenly shouts at me, "You're about to make this chapter so long that you'll have to cancel other chapters!" So I must end with three rough questions:

- Are not even atheistic scientists "religious" as they exhibit, explicitly or implicitly, the seven warrants? As they passionately pursue Truth, driven by a conviction about or faith in a cosmos that includes truth and the moral command to pursue it, do they not join "believers" who believe without "scientific" proof? Can any committed scientist give up the notion that "some power, greater than ourselves," some Cosmos, Being Itself, *provided* the conditions of his or her research, and still provides, daily, the whole range of possibilities that life itself yields? Of course that Supreme Being also provided the conditions that led to all of our disasters—which lands us in the messy waters of theodicy—how to pardon Supreme Being for creating the conditions that led my test tube to break just when its contents were most needed. Perhaps agreement that this is a deep problem in all religious belief provides another *warrant* on which we all join. But it's not a proper subject for this book.

- Should not even the most devout religionists concede that whatever truth science fully demonstrates is a part of what their God grants us?
- Finally—and most important—a version of the question underlying this whole book: Can we hope that by practicing rhetorology of some kind—Listening Rhetoric in its most committed form—we might diminish some of the pointless demonizing that diverse quarrelers commit? Can we not diminish the widespread effort to destroy enemies that don't even exist? Cannot serious rhetorical study, even if you reject my coinage for it, diminish the damage that too many of us inflict on too many victims too much of the time? As rival rhetorics create and defend rival "realities," cannot they concede that some rivals may be revealed as superior, if really listened to?

In short, even if you reject my "joining" of science and religion, I hope that you will at least be tempted to experiment with rhetorology on some other conflict that plagues your life.

*For many years the University of Chicago has sponsored a lecture by a faculty member assigned the task of explaining his or her field to the "general" audience—all academics of course. When I received the assignment, I was both thrilled and terrified. The task of explaining—one could call it "touting"—a field like rhetoric to scientists, philosophers, historians, art historians, lawyers—proved daunting. I can honestly say that I spent more time on more revisions for this talk than for any other before or since—not to mention how much revision I did for the publication after the talk. The good news is that the essay seems to get more attention than do most of the others collected here.*

This essay first appeared as *The 1987 Ryerson Lecture, University of Chicago* (Chicago: University of Chicago Press, 1987). It was reprinted in *The Vocation of a Teacher: Rhetorical Occasions, 1967–1988* (Chicago: University of Chicago Press, 1988), 309–34.

# The Idea of a University—as Seen by a Rhetorician

It is not often that a student of rhetoric faces an occasion that falls as neatly into his professional domain as this one falls into mine. The Ryerson Lectures were designed as occasions for what the founders did *not* call "ecumenical rhetoric"—discourse designed to bring together a community that is always tempted by modern forces to fall apart. I think I can claim, though with considerable anxiety, to be the first for whom this moment is a kind of personally profitable setup: I am in effect invited to talk with you, a predetermined audience, about what the very existence of such a rhetorical occasion might mean. That is scarcely a comforting thought: it puts me on the spot in ways even more threatening than were faced by my threatened predecessors. As classical rhetoricians taught, the easiest way to guarantee failure with any perceptive audience is to be seen in advance as an expert in rhetoric. More is properly demanded where more is professed, and you can understand why I see troubles ahead.

My first problem lies of course in the very word *rhetoric*. I was tempted, as I have often been in the past, to define that slippery term once and for all, but I have resisted, even though to grapple with its ambiguities would illustrate beautifully why Ryerson lecturers are notoriously nervous nellies. Just how much time should a lecturer spend claiming that, like Humpty Dumpty, he is to be the boss of definitions? Should I say, "Rhetoric on this occasion will *not* mean merely the art of winning, right or wrong, *nor* will it mean the clever use of bombast and trickery"? Should I insist that it will not even be the faculty, as Aristotle puts it, of "finding the available means of persuasion on any occasion"? Ted Schultz has recently advised me to abandon the sleazy term altogether and substitute something like "philosophy of discourse," or "theory of communication." But to abandon the term *rhetoric*, with its long, honorable history, just because it often suggests shoddy practices, would be like abandoning the term *philosophy*, just because people talk about "the philosophy of tennis coaching," or abandoning the word *science* just because Mary Baker Eddy and the scientologists have each borrowed it for their purposes. Rather than defining it or abandoning it, suppose we just put a big question mark by whatever your own definition would now be. You may or may not, by the end, want to apply the term *rhetorical study* to what we will have been doing.

I begin with a question that the very existence of these lectures forces upon us, no matter what our field: How is it that we can gather hopefully here, year after year, to listen to one another tell about our special work, when we know in advance that most of us, most of the time, have no real hope of understanding the special work of most of the rest of us? The trustees established the Ryerson series, with the special help of the Ranneys, on the assumption that it would be a good thing if specialists lectured "to an audience from the entire university on a significant aspect" of their research. They did not say, "Please talk down to that audience," or "Kindly choose some peripheral and general question of social, political, or ethical importance." No, we are asked to speak as specialists—and to make ourselves understood.

The trustees obviously assumed that we professors ought to be able to talk with our colleagues about what we do and why we do it. They must have assumed that everyone who *professes* a subject, any subject, no matter how esoteric, ought to be able to say something intelligible about it, or through it, or with it, to the nonspecialist. Clearly they hoped for something more than a series of merely ceremonial occasions, pious gatherings of hypocrites only pretending to listen. They assumed that we could follow John Simpson, say, talking of extending "space science and exploration to the third dimension—that is, to travel out of the ecliptic plane"; or Karl Weintraub talking about an "empathetic and sympathetic understanding of the past," an understanding that "gives us the burden of relative and relativized knowledge"; or Stephen Toulmin talking about "the inwardness of mental life"; or Saunders Mac Lane talking about how a mathematician deals with "fuzzy sets"; or George Stigler talking about the disharmony between sound economic principles and unsound economic practice; or—but I need not go on. You already know that the list is threateningly diverse. If we face its diversity honestly, we must wonder just how much understanding can occur across our disciplinary borderlines. Our hosts assumed that we are, in *some* sense, at *some* level, a *univer*sity, a community of inquirers who have managed to maintain *some* kind of message center or telephone exchange.

I must now risk shocking those of you who do *not* know the academy from the inside, and risk boring those of you who do, by dwelling for a bit on some of the more obvious reasons for doubting these assumptions. I ask you who are professors whether we do not have overwhelming daily proof that no one of us can understand more than a fraction of the frontline work of the rest. We are all simply shut out of almost all front parlors but our own, permitted only to do a little polite begging at the back door: "Please, sir, please give a poor beggar just a slice of nuclear physics to keep me warm, just a tiny portion of paleontology to keep up my illusion of keeping up, just a touch of cosmology—the new anthropic principle, say—to help me survive the next cocktail party." We don't like to talk about it, but we know that even Ryerson lecturers fail, at least partially, with most of their auditors. One Ryerson lecturer who has come to all of these lectures told me that he has understood only about half of what has been said: "I grasped almost nothing in a couple of the lectures," he said, "about a third in half of them, two-thirds in a few of them, and all in only one—my own."

Shocking as such a fact might seem from some perspectives, no serious scholar is likely to be at all surprised by it. Centuries have passed since that fabled moment—was it in the eighteenth century or the late seventeenth?—when the last of the Leonardo da Vincis could hope to cover the cognitive map. Since that fatal moment, whenever it was, everyone, even that polymath down the hall who is said to "know everything," has been reduced to knowing only one or two countries on the intellectual globe, granting all the other countries only the most superficial of Cook's tours.

Perhaps some of you here once shared the naive ambition that my wife and I pursued, long before we met each other. As youngsters who wanted to know everything, we once set out to read every book in the closest available library. Though both of the libraries were fortunately very small, neither of us made it even to the *M*'s, let alone the *Z*'s. And our fate is an emblem for the condition we all live in. It isn't that we don't try. The academy attracts those who aspire to omniscience. We are the kind who would like others to say of us what young Christopher Tietjens's friend says of him, in Ford Madox Ford's *Parade's End*: "Confound you, Chrissie. You know everything!" Tietjens is at the time making a list, *from memory*, of errors in the new edition of the *Encyclopaedia Britannica*. But not long afterward part of Tietjens's brain, and all of his hubris, are shattered by a bomb blast in the Great War, and he is reduced, in utter humiliation, to a pathetic attempt to memorize the very *Encyclopaedia* he had once scorned. Arriving at the *K*'s, he finds, under "Koran," the saying, "The strong man when smitten is smitten in his pride."[1] It is precisely in our pride that we are smitten when, for one reason or another, we discover just what a pitifully small corner of the cognitive world we live in. Though we can sympathize with Tietjens's impulse, we all know that even his original sense of universal mastery, as a young genius, was illusory. Not only can no one fully understand what any good encyclopedia contains, the encyclopedias themselves are almost uniformly inadequate and misleading; ask any expert in a given field whether a reading of the encyclopedia entries in that field can educate even the cleverest of readers to genuine competence. And if this is true of our collective enterprises like encyclopedias, how much truer it is of each of us as we try individually to figure out what on earth goes on in neighboring subjects, across the hall or on the other side of the quad.

In short, the painful truth we voracious students discover, at twenty, or forty, or sixty, is that what we sometimes call the "knowledge explosion" has left us all ignorant of vast fields of knowledge that every educated man and woman *ought* to have mastered. Is it any wonder that we tend to be defensive in debate, sure that our next class or public lecture will reveal the fatal truth: We are ignoramuses, and since we call ourselves professors, scholars, even doctors, we risk exposure as frauds?

Perhaps I exaggerate. There may be in this room a few polyphilomathematico wizards who can carry on a plausible conversation with experts in as many as—shall we say, ten fields?—ten fields out of the hundreds listed in the faculty directory. (I started counting them, but soon realized that I didn't know enough in many areas even to tell what would constitute a field. Take a look sometime at the listings under "Argonne National Laboratories," or the "Department of Behavioral Sciences.") It is no doubt true that many of us can give journalistic accounts of black holes, marginal utility, polymorphous perversities, ekphrastic poetry, and the oft-repeated rise, over about twenty centuries, of the bourgeoisie. But for even the most learned among us, the circle of what we might call *participatory* understanding does not extend very far.

During the past few months, preparing for this moment, I've been asking colleagues in various disciplines about just how much they understand of other people's work, using the following test: Could you, given a week's warning, read an article or book in a given field and then enter into a serious dialogue with the author, at a level of understanding that the author would take as roughly comparable to his or her own? The answers varied widely in ambition and persuasiveness, not to say chutzpah, but you won't be surprised to learn that no one claimed to be able to understand more than a fraction of what our colleagues publish. Some were embarrassed by their confessions; most were not. Some confidently blamed the bad writing in other fields. But all confessed.

We would expect such confessions (or disguised accusations) when the fields are obviously far apart: humanists don't usually claim to meet mathematicians where they live; botanists freely confess to bafflement about particle physics. But I was a bit surprised to find that hardly anyone claims to understand all the work even within the home department. One philosopher told me that there is simply no one at this university, inside his department or out of it, who can understand his work; he is the lone inhabitant of his tiny cognitive land. His circle of fellow-understanders consists of a tiny band of similarly trained folk scattered around what we might call the known world. Another philosopher tells me that he could understand, given a week's lead time, perhaps 80 percent of what his fellow philosophers publish. He believes that perhaps even more than 80 percent of them could talk with him about his work—"Not," he adds, "that they would have *really* understood it, but at least we might be in the same ballpark." A world-famous mathematician tells me that he cannot follow the proofs offered by most mathematicians; each subgroup of mathematicians has become so specialized that the other subgroups are unable to understand them, if by "understanding" we mean being able to appraise, with full personal confidence, the validity of the proofs and thus the soundness of the conclusions. The editor of a journal in biology says that he expects to understand about 50 percent of the articles he publishes, and he adds, "I work harder at that task than most of my colleagues." The editor of a chemistry journal says he understands 50 percent to 80 percent of the articles he chooses to publish, but he "gets" hardly anything in most of the neighboring chemistry journals.

Obviously, what my respondents have said depends on a relatively rigorous definition of "understanding." We surely ask more of ourselves than simply being able to respond, after taking in the opinions of others, with a plausible summary and an offer of our own plausible opinions. If we are to do justice to the question I am raising, we should at least for a while adhere to a more rigorous definition of "true understanding," something like this: I have understood you if and only if I can say to you, "Yes, *but*," and say it in a form that will lead you in turn to accept both my "yes" and my objections; not just my claim to have "got" your point, but my claim to have got it so well that I can raise an objection to it that you in turn must take into account. It is not enough for me to say to Professor Chandrasekhar, for example: "Oh, yes, I understand the theory of black holes. Black holes are inconceivably dense concentrations of matter; they are so dense that their gravitational force sucks in everything within range, including any photons that happen to be around, so that no light, and indeed no particles or waves of any kind, can ever emerge and therefore no information can come to us. That's why they're called *black* holes. . . . " You and I could go on like that, without even having to look anything up; that kind of understanding of black holes, or cost-benefit analysis, or ethnomethodology, or thick descriptions, or the double helix, is in the air, like a lot of other half-baked opinions we might pick up from reading the *New York Times* or *Scientific American*. I might even think I had understood black holes well enough to look the professor boldly in the eye and add a clever reservation, like this: "*But what* I think you've got wrong, professor, is that according to *my* notion of how scientific constructs work, black holes must be considered to be no more than plausible pictures, with no necessary connection with anything we might call the reality behind the pictures. . . . " And so on. Even if my earlier description, my "yes," were roughly on the right lines, which is unlikely, Professor Chandrasekhar cannot possibly respond either to my "yes," my report, or my reservations, with anything warmer than a friendly smile as a reward for trying. I could not possibly challenge him to the point of his saying, "Yes, you've taken the point of my most recent article; you have convinced me that you are a good judge of its quality, and I therefore must take your reservations into account. Let's inquire into your objection further."

But if I cannot claim that kind of understanding, in what sense do I live in the same university that honors Professor Chandrasekhar's achievements?

Lest you think I am indicting others on my behalf, I here present myself as an extreme but by no means unrepresentative example of the ignorant professor. I now serve as third reader on a dissertation being written by a young man in South Asian Studies. He is writing about a group of Indian poets, translating their poems and doing a critical poetics of their kind of poetry. Of course I cannot read the poems in the original, and I have not yet read all of his translations. What's worse, I have never read a single critical work by the non-Western critics he deals with. What on earth, then, am I doing on that committee?

Is it any wonder that when one eavesdrops on a group of experts in a given field, talking about experts in other fields, one hears a lot of contemptuous dismissal? Just listen to the chemists talking about the biologists, the biologists talking about the clinical M.D.'s, the surgeons and internists complaining about one another, the humanists talking about the social scientists, and the economists talking about everybody.

Roger Hildebrand provides what is for me the climax to my survey as he talks about his switch a few years ago from particle physics to astrophysics. To us outsiders, that might look like a small leap, really a shift within the same general field, as compared with the distance, say, between art history and chemistry. But Roger says that he had to spend the equivalent of about three full years "becoming a graduate student again" before he could feel some confidence in dialogue with frontliners in his new field—before he could judge the importance of a new article in that field. Just think how much work would be required if he decided once again to shift to microbiology, say, or constitutional law.

It is no doubt true that as we move across campus to the "softer" social sciences, through history, and on to the even floppier software occupying the brainpans of us humanists, we find a somewhat enlarged circle of those who at least claim to understand one another. The nonquantitative historians have told me that they can understand *all* of the *good* work of other nonquantitative historians. Most computer-armed prosopographers claim to understand the work of other cliometricians, and of course they claim to understand all the "easy" work of narrative historians—at least well enough to be suspicious of their inherently soft results. Lawyers all tell me that they can understand the legal arguments of all *good* lawyers. The cultural anthropologists say that they can understand everything worth reading in the social sciences. But when I press these various representatives, asking the lawyers whether they really understand the so-called critical realists, asking the cultural anthropologists whether they understand the quantitative sociologists, and so on, they often fall back on invective: "Those people are not doing true law or true anthropology"; or, "That gang has been badly trained."

Perhaps the largest circle of those who claim to understand one another would be found in English and other modern language studies. Hundreds of thousands of us profess to understand just about anything that falls into our hands. But when we look more closely at humanists' claims to membership in large circles of understanding, they appear pretty feeble. After all, in the quantitative and mathematical sciences, people tend to recognize when they have not understood one another. But we students of the human tend to think we have understood when we have not.

Here, for example, is the opening of a chapter by Jacques Derrida, the philosopher perhaps now most influential on literary studies:

> What about the voice within the logic of the supplement? within that which should perhaps be called the "graphic" of the supplement?
>
> Within the chain of supplements, it was difficult to separate writing from onanism. Those two supplements have in common at least the fact that they are dangerous. They transgress a prohibition and are experienced

within culpability. But, by the economy of differance [deliberately spelled with an *a*, as a special term], they confirm the interdict they transgress, get around a danger, and reserve an expenditure.[2]

Now I have worked for about a decade to become comfortable with the recondite language in which that passage is written, and I think I sort of understand it. Unlike some of my more traditional colleagues, I am utterly convinced that it is *not* nonsense, though it is opaque somewhat— more so than in the original French. Still, if I were to study the chapter that follows it carefully and then write a summary, the chances are about ninety-nine to one that Derrida would *not* say of it, "Bravo: you have understood." Just ask yourself how you have felt about the typical review or reader's report on your own carefully wrought opus. My own response to reviews is often, "How could anyone but a moron misunderstand me so badly?"

Let me offer now a true story that summarizes our plight. Each year a committee is appointed in the Social Sciences Division to decide on the award of the annual Galler Prize for the best dissertation done during that year. A couple of years ago an economist on the committee, after reading the submissions from other fields, announced that a dissertation from economics that he would now submit was superior to all the others, and should get the prize. The other committee members insisted that before granting his case they should have a chance to read it and compare it with the others. "No," he said, "that's impossible. You could not possibly understand it." "But how can we judge," they insisted, "if we are not allowed even to see the work?" He remained adamant, and when they refused to award the prize to a dissertation that they were not even allowed to see, he withdrew himself, and the dissertation, from the competition. He tells me now that the Department of Economics no longer even considers submitting dissertations for the prize, because they are sure that the non-quantitative "literary" types—the historians and anthropologists—simply could not recognize high quality in economics if they saw it.

Though that is clearly an extreme case, it helps make the point that even if we could create a university inhabited solely by geniuses—geniuses who, unlike most actual geniuses, were full of an infinite good will toward, and determination to understand, one another's disciplines; geniuses who would accept the assignment to work on our problem—we would find that under modern conditions of inquiry, conditions that we have no hope of changing fundamentally, none of them could come to an understanding of more than a fraction of what the others would take to be real knowledge.

Must we not admit, then, in all honesty, that we are indeed a pack of ignoramuses, inhabitants of some ancient, unmapped archipelago, each of us an island—let John Donne preach as he will—living at a time before anyone had invented boats or any other form of interisland communication?

## II

I assume that many of you have long since wanted to protest against my picture. We all know that the islands are not in fact totally isolated, that somehow we have managed to invent communication systems. Though it may be true that on each island we speak a language not fully intelligible on any other, and though it may be true that some of the islands conduct active warfare against some of the others, and though some islands are in a state of civil war, the fact is that somehow we do manage to talk with one another and come to judgments that we are convinced are not *entirely* capricious. We write interdepartmental and even interdivisional memos; we indite letters of recommendation at breakneck speed and in appalling numbers, purporting to appraise the quality of colleagues whose work we don't know beans about. We appraise other scholars according to what we take to be high standards, even when we ourselves cannot state literally what the standards are. We pass judgment upon students in "related fields" and on one another whenever promotion is at stake, and we seem not to suffer intolerable anxiety about our decisions. Even more shocking, in view of the plight I have described, we ask our deans and provosts and presidents to approve our judgments, and even grant the right to reverse them, implying that somehow *somebody* can be competent to judge work in *all* fields. Finally, we busy ourselves with a great deal of what we call "interdisciplinary work": degree-granting committees like Ideas and Methods and Social Thought; imperialistic fields like geography, anthropology, English, and rhetoric; conferences and workshops galore. None of us really thinks that *all* of these operations are totally fraudulent. We act *as if* our discussions and conferences and tenure decisions make *real* sense. Do they?

How do we actually work, as we run those of our affairs that depend on some kind of understanding different from the one I have applied so far? Do we work, as some say, only according to blind trust of friends and mistrust of enemies? Do we work according to guesses only? Are we, as some would claim, simply servants of money and power? In what sense, if any, do we employ a kind of reasoning and proof—knowledge and genuine understanding under any definition—that we might point to without shame?

After my informants of the past months have confessed their ignorance, I have asked them to tell me how they in fact operate when judging colleagues whose work they do not understand. All of them have said something like this—though never in this precise language: "We are by no means fraudulent, because we have available certain rational resources that your definition of understanding leaves out. We have learned to make use of our knowledge [one professor even called it "wisdom"] about character and how to appraise character witnesses; we have learned how to read the signs of quality even in the fields where we cannot follow the proofs. We have learned how to determine whether a referee is trustworthy, and we have learned something about how to judge the quality of a candidate's thinking, just by the way he or she writes and speaks." They have not gone on to say, though I wish we could have shared this language: "You see, what all this means is that we are experienced both as practitioners and students of—rhetoric."

When I press them further with the question, "Do you make mistakes with this kind of thinking?" the answer is always "Yes, sometimes." But nobody I've talked with has claimed that the process depends on a trust that is utterly blind, totally a matter of nonrational power-grabs or log-rolling or back-scratching or money-grubbing. Everyone, absolutely everyone, has played into this rhetorician's hands by claiming to employ a kind of thought that is not identical with what we do when proving conclusions in our frontline inquiry—and yet a kind that is still genuine thought.

Of course nobody has claimed that we offer our rhetorical proofs to each other and test them as well as we ought. Indeed my main point today is that we could all employ them better, and thus improve our quality as a university, *if* we all studied how such peculiar yet rational persuasion works. But even in our fallen condition, even as we in our imperfection now operate, we do not perform our personal and administrative judgments on indefensible, nonscholarly grounds; we perform those judgments on grounds that are considered nonscholarly only by those who think that all knowledge is of the kind yielded by frontline specialties, only by those who embrace uncritically the criterion for understanding, and thus of knowledge, with which I began. If knowledge is confined to what experts discover at the front line, and if understanding is confined to participation in full dialogue at the front line, then we operate ourselves without knowing what we do and without *understanding* each other. If we know and understand only what we can *prove*—with empirical observation, or with statistics, or with rigorous logical deduction—we will never *know* whether a colleague is worth listening to or promoting, unless we ourselves can follow his or her proofs, in detail, and then replicate them. All else is dubious, all else is guesswork, all else is blind faith. Without some form of shared rhetoric, the university would collapse.

One thing we all know is that we know more than that criterion implies. Though unable to tell for ourselves whether the new mathematical proof is indeed new and indeed a proof, we learn how to consider, with the eye of nonspecialists, both the rhetoric of scholarship that we cannot hope fully to understand, and the rhetoric offered us *about* the scholar, the arguments offered by those who give us some reason to trust or mistrust their judgment as specialists.

We all thus implicitly aspire to mastery in three kinds of rhetoric, leading to three kinds of understanding, not just one. There are, first, the many and diverse rhetorics peculiar to each of our various front lines. Here each small group of experts relies on what Aristotle calls *special topics* of persuasion, the often tacit convictions that are shared by all within a discipline and that are therefore available in constructing arguments within the field: the assumption, say, that photographs of bubble chambers and their interpretations can somehow be relied on; or the conventional agreements about how to deal with normal curves and chi-squares, about the proper use of graphs, about what makes a sound equation, or about how to do a sensitive report of poetic scansion or a convincing analysis of sonata form in a symphony. Though these assumptions shift over time, we can at any given moment rely on them without argument in their support as we construct our arguments to our peers. I'll risk offending some of you by dubbing this frontline stuff and its workings "rhetoric-1." If calling it "hard proof" will make you happier, feel free, but I know that few specialists will want to claim that they or their successors will find themselves, fifty years from now, relying on the same tacit assumptions, leading to the same conclusions, that they share today.[3]

A second kind—I'll label it "general rhetoric," or "rhetoric-2"—is what we share with members of every functioning organization or society—businesses, governments, clubs, families: the whole range of plausible or probable beliefs and modes of proof that make the world go round. Think of it as the self-evident warrants that even the most rigorous scientists must rely on when testifying before a government committee. Here we rely on the *common*, or general topics: "More of any good thing is better than less of it—usually"; "It's wrong to cheat in a scientific report"; "Actions that usually produce bad consequences should be avoided." Obviously, many of these are included in everyone's notion of "common sense": beliefs we rely on when trying to *make* sense in any argument.

Though these common topics are indispensable in every domain, they are especially prominent in our running of the university whenever we must appraise character. We all have a little storehouse of beliefs about character that we have to rely on, more or less efficiently, whenever we read a letter of recommendation or predict the future behavior of a colleague in order to grant or deny tenure. Such common topics, "commonplaces," crop up in all public debate. "It is probable that someone who failed to carry through on her previous research plan will fail in this one; turn her down." "Ah, yes, but she was deep in the anguish of a divorce then, and she's changed a lot. I say give her the grant." "Well, but her strongest supporter is Professor Smiler, who has usually been wrong in his predictions that young colleagues are late bloomers. Why should we believe him in this case?" Or, "The truth is that Louise and Harry used to live together, and they had an angry breakup. I think—though we must say nothing of it in public—that we cannot trust his negative judgment on her scholarly ability."

Rhetoric-2 is thus the set of resources available in the functioning of all organizations, not just of universities. Arbitrageurs and government officers function or fail to function depending on whether the trust they yield to their CEOs and Marine sergeants and colonels is justified. We in the university similarly succeed to the degree that our trust is granted when it should be, withheld when it should not be. The ease with which rhetoric-2 can be abused accounts largely for why rhetoric has always had, and probably always *will* have, a bad press. Philosophers and moralists have often wished that it would just go away—but of course they express the wish for a purer world in the only language available to any of us when we press our wishes on the world: rhetorical argument.

There is, third, a kind of rhetoric that is neither as special as the first nor as general as the second, a rhetoric relying on shared warrants that are proper or special only to those within a university, but to all within that university, not to any one special group. We have no name for this peculiar stuff that we all to some degree share, but call it "the rhetoric of inquiry," or of "intellectual engagement": "academy-rhetoric," or "rhetoric-3." We learn how to judge whether the arguments in fields beyond our full competence *somehow* track, whether the style of presentation *somehow* accords with standards we recognize. We learn to sense whether a colleague, even in a quite remote field, *seems* to have mastered the tricks of the trade—not just the trade of this or that kind of economist or philosopher, but the tricks of this whole trade, the trade of learning and teaching for the sake of learning and teaching. One often hears, in the Quadrangle Club, not just the contemptuous comments I have mentioned about fools and knaves but comments like this: "What a mind that man has." "What a pleasure to argue with that woman—she never misses a stroke." "He always seems to have just the right analogy to make his point." "Have you noticed how you always come away from a conversation with him having to think through the problem in a different way?"

All three of these rhetorics are of course highly fallible. Even our many versions of rhetoric-1, in our special fields, are notoriously unstable, as I have already implied, shifting in threatening ways from decade to decade and field to field. But the second and third rhetorics are much more obviously fallible—indeed, staggeringly so. Tough-minded appraisal of characters and witnesses through close reading of letters of recommendation and reader's reports, close listening during telephone calls and hallway conversations, careful appraisal of past records of performance—these are all dangerously unreliable, partly because charlatans can so easily mimic the proper use of the topics. If this were not so, we would not have so many successful frauds in every field. The Piltdown hoaxers, the Cyril Burts, the Darseys, the unqualified practicing surgeons, the undiploma-ed lawyers—all the hoaxers of our world succeed as they do because they have mastered the surface conventions of all three rhetorics and through that mastery have collected or forged references testifying to high quality. We read about so many successes in this burgeoning field of pseudoscientific conning that we are in danger of forgetting our reliance on the indispensable base of merely probable inferences—that base on which all of the conning depends. The breakdowns in the system result from, and depend on, a process—the practice of producing sound conclusions from rhetorical proofs—that by its very necessities opens the door to frauds. But this is not to say that we, their dupes, could not protect ourselves better if we would study rhetoric as hard as we study lab techniques, say, or formal logic.

Again and again I have been told by my informants that "it's not really very hard to tell competent work from incompetent, even if you know nothing about the details and cannot replicate the argument or experiment." And when I then ask, "How do you *do* that?" I am told—never in this language—that "I do it using rhetorics-2 and -3"—not the appraisal of frontline proofs but the careful judgment of both "general rhetoric" and "academy rhetoric." One editor told me, "Even when I know little or nothing about a special field, I can tell just by the opening paragraphs whether a would-be contributor is at least competent." What does that mean, if not that he claims to judge the author's skill in rhetorical conventions shared with other fields: skill in saying what needs saying and in not saying what should not be said; skill in implying a scholarly ethos appropriate to the subject; skill in avoiding moves that give away the novice; and so on.

Though the practice and appraisal of such skills is chancy, if we ruled them out we could not operate for a day without disaster. Most of our journals would have to be scrapped, most of our grants and awards would have to be eliminated, and the university would have to surrender to total balkanization or even tribal warfare, becoming not a *uni*versity at all but a multiversity, a mere collection of research institutes warring for funds.

We can see how rhetorics-2 and -3 work, in a genuine university, by probing the grounds for our belief about the quality of any one of our more distinguished colleagues. I believe, for example, that George Stigler is really a very good economist. I would bet my next month's salary on my belief that when Stigler does economics, he is working at the highest levels of competence in his field (at least on his good days), and that in doing so he is not simply playing an esoteric power game but is actually pursuing one genuine kind of knowledge.

But what's my evidence? Every bit of it, when taken by itself, is extremely chancy rhetorical inference, some of it of the second kind, some of the third, none of the first. I cannot really understand his frontline work, but when I dip into it I find enough similarities with work I do understand to give me some slight confidence. Still, my views of it are scandalously shallow. But then I start adding other bits. I've had some private conversations with George about the assumptions of economics as a field—highly general conversations, of course, with me trying to put him on the defensive but always ending on the ropes, and thus increasingly impressed. Similarly, our talks about literature and about campus politics have impressed me considerably with the general quality of his reasoning, even though in themselves they tell me nothing directly about his work as an economist. I find myself admiring his more popular stuff, as in *The Economist as Preacher*;[4] not only is he a master of English style, but he offers dozens of signs that he belongs to a community of economists who respect him.

Still, such reading in itself cannot tell me very much about his work as an economist. I could fill this gap by referring to his Nobel Prize, but the fact is that it doesn't impress me much more than it probably impresses him; we all know that Nobel committees can make grotesque mistakes. The seemingly uniform esteem of his local colleagues counts most for me, but it could not in itself settle the issue; obviously whole departments and whole fields can misjudge quality. Finally, the fact of his election by his colleagues to various important university committees can again carry only slight weight, in itself.

But note that all of these *weak* clues point in the same direction, and they all come to a head when I hear other economists who are said to be good—note well that phrase—say that George Stigler is good and *is said to be good*. Each reason for trust is in itself slight. My confidence could be shaken quite easily by countertestimony from someone I trust as much as I trust these witnesses, if I could find someone. It could be shaken if I discovered some obviously incompetent logic in his Ryerson Lecture—his foray into the nonspecialized academic rhetoric I am calling rhetoric-3. But after I have added together all the weak-but-still-pertinent reasons, it would take a good deal of contrary evidence to make me doubt his competence. What may be even more important, the half-comprehension that I gain by all of this peripheral activity adds to my own intellectual life. I take part, at a great distance, in Stigler's reasoning about economics, and I even dare from time to time to quarrel with him, ineffectually, about that weird first principle of his, the belief that people's behavior can be fully explained as the rational calculation of individual costs and benefits.

The relative weight of the three rhetorics thus varies from field to field, committee to committee, occasion to occasion. I once served on the Board of University Publications, and in the early spring we faced that annual ordeal, the decision about which of our colleagues should receive the Laing Prize for a distinguished book. We had all read the major reviews of each eligible book, and we had all been urged to read all of the books, though I doubt that anyone had done so. Then, after preliminary balloting (based mainly, you see, on the rhetoric-3 of the reviews we had read), we were asked to read with special care those books that seemed prime contenders. In the preliminary balloting that followed, several books came out ahead of Sewall Wright's collected essays. I can remember that I had read at— I think that's the right expression—*read at* several of the essays in that monumental collection, working away dutifully because the reviews had uniformly described Wright and his book as of major importance. The essays seemed authoritative to me—that fairly small portion of them that I could understand at all. The logic, where I could follow it, made sense. The language carried authority. I found, after *reading at* four or five of the essays, that I was admiring the character who emerged from the various projects; to me it seemed obvious that this man was a serious, responsible, highly intelligent scientist. But I simply had no way of detecting for myself whether his results were original or sound or worthy to be influential, let alone worthy of the Laing Prize. So, like most of the members of that board, I did not on the first round vote for Wright as number one, though he was among the highest. Rather, I voted for authors about whom I felt much more sure, because I could follow their frontline arguments.

Then, in our final meeting, a curious thing happened. Our late colleague Arnold Ravin spoke at some length about the true importance of Wright's work. As I remember his eloquent appeal, it went like this: "You must believe me when I tell you that this is a major collection by a major figure, a genius who has transformed his field again and again. Believe me, though you yourselves cannot be expected to see the quality in these essays, this book is head-and-shoulders above the others on our list." Now here is where this anecdote diverges from my story of the economist and the Galler Prize. *We argued back*, and Ravin *attempted to meet our arguments*. He gave another speech, longer and with different examples, with more testimonial quoted from other biologists, and with a repeated claim that since none of the rest of us were biologists, we were just not qualified to grasp the full, cumulative importance of this record of a life's work. Finally, after an hour or so of debate, we voted decisively to give the prize to Sewall Wright, an author whose work only one person in the room could fully understand. And we had no positive evidence even of that. We had only Ravin's words as evidence that he himself had understood Wright.

We voted, you see—and I think we were right—mainly on the basis of powerful rhetoric of kinds two and three. We trusted the rhetorician because his arguments made sense to us, because they harmonized with what the other experts had told us, because they were not contradicted by what little we could infer from our own efforts at reading the essays themselves, and because we had reason to trust the judgment and integrity of Arnold Ravin.[5] Some of his arguments would have worked equally well in an insurance company's boardroom (rhetoric-2). His passion, for example, was not mere passion: it became hard evidence, because we felt that Ravin was not the kind of man who would fake passion like that, and passion like that could not be aroused except by an exceptional case. (So much, by the way, for the still-fashionable inclination to contrast reason and emotion; a powerful emotion, carefully appraised, can often be the hardest of evidence in this kind of reasoning.) But some of his arguments were special to this special kind of place. For example, he argued that Wright had been mainly responsible for the creation of a new discipline—a claim that would seem out of place in a business context, say, or in a psychotherapist's office. And I remember his saying that if someone a hundred years from now wanted to know both the state of that discipline and the special problems and methods it encountered at the time the book was written, the book would still live. So we all came to a choice that in retrospect still seems to me eminently sound, though I would not be shattered if some other work, neglected by us in those final moments, turned out later to be more important than Wright's.

Would we have done better to tell Arnold Ravin, "All that is *mere* rhetoric. We must vote only on and for those books that we ourselves can understand?" To say no to that route requires us to believe that there is a real difference between sound and unsound rhetorical appeals, that there is a whole domain of knowledge—uncertain, chancy, elusive knowledge but knowledge nonetheless—that is important not only in the awarding of prizes and promotions but in the day-by-day intellectual life of the university. Not only does every hiring and firing, every promotion, every establishment of a new department or elimination of an old one, every choice of a dean or president, depend on such topical reasoning; our very survival depends on our control of that kind of knowledge—that is to say, on our repertory of rhetorical practices and norms. We depend on appraising the testimony and authority and general ethos of other people, as they appraise the testimony and authority of still others, who in turn depend on others . . . and no one can say where these circles of mutual trust end, except of course when societies and universities destroy themselves by losing the arts of determining when trust is justified.

Philosophers of science like Michael Polanyi and Rom Harré have argued that even the "hardest" sciences, even physics and chemistry and mathematics, do *not* depend mainly on the application by each individual of so-called scientific method to all beliefs, doubting every proposition until it has been shown to be falsifiable and yet not falsified.[6] Instead, they say, each individual scientist survives as scientist by virtue of indeterminately large networks of critical trust, based largely on assumptions shared by many or most disciplines (rhetoric-3). Each of them must rely, as you and I do, on broad ranges of belief that no one of us could ever hope to demonstrate independently. As Polanyi puts it, we are all inherently "convivial," dependent for our intellectual bases, as we are in our physical lives, on living *together*. Even as specialists, he says, we live in "fiduciary" structures that we have not constructed and could never construct on our own.[7]

## III

What we have arrived at here is a picture radically different from that of the archipelago of islands forced to remain incommunicado. We need another picture of how we relate as specialists. Those who worry about those lonely islands too often take as an ideal the impossible notion of getting more people to add more and more specialties, as if there were some hope of making each island self-sufficient. Attacking this "Leonardo-esque aspiration," psychologist Donald T. Campbell, in a splendid essay precisely on our subject today, suggested that the best way to combat the "ethnocentrism of disciplines," the "tribalism" and "nationalism" of specialties, would be to pursue the "fish-scale model of omniscience."[8] Picture each group of specialists as one scale in a total fish-scale pattern, both overlapping and overlapped by the interests and competencies of adjacent specialties. The total network, or fish-scale pattern, "knows" whatever is in fact known; though no one unit knows very much, each unit is connected to all the others, through the unbroken overlappings.[9]

Campbell hoped with this model both to relieve each of us from the anxiety to know more than anyone can possibly know and to encourage more productive specialization in the areas where the scales overlap. The new specialties thus developed would be in one sense as narrow as the others; like everyone else in the university, the new specialists would still be ignoramuses when addressing most fields. But by concentrating on hitherto-neglected connections, they would improve the efficiency of the entire network. The *university* of his model would in a sense know itself and know what it knows, while no one individual would have to feel guilty about not pursuing the impossible project of learning what the network as a whole had learned.

Campbell's model takes us in the right direction, but it may still be misleading, both as a picture of how we work at our best and as a practice to aspire to. Unfortunately, I can't find quite as neat a metaphor for my own notion of how we work. But suppose we imagine a fish-scale network in which each separate scale is not a scale at all but some kind of organism, perhaps like an octopus, with many tentacles, some of them reaching only to one or two adjacent scales, some leaping across to the opposite sides of the whole fish, as it were. The tentacles often intertwine, and they are somehow able to send half-intelligible, scrambled, but still not worthless messages to scales in unpredictable parts of the whole—well, by now the image becomes visually absurd. But the inadequacy of such images shouldn't surprise us, since the university is not really *much* like anything else in the universe. In my garbled image, a given physicist will not only occupy a given scale of expertise, as it overlaps adjacent fields, say mathematics and chemistry, but will also project "tentacles" across the entire network to the poets or musicians or art historians, as Professor Chandrasekhar did in his Ryerson Lecture. Occupants of a given scale, a given specialty, do not hope to earn full occupancy of more than two or three additional scales in a lifetime, but they not only hope for, but can achieve, a partial understanding of many. Remember that I am not yet pursuing an ideal university, only the best notion of how we ignoramuses actually work at our best. You might want to think here of professors who both occupy a single scale with high competence and extend themselves effectively into the larger network. (In one draft I began to list my heroes by name, but the list not only risked offending by its omissions but also quickly grew too long. I wonder whether any other university can offer as many professors of the kind I have in mind.)

## IV

What I have shown—or so I hope—is that we are by no means as full of fraudulence—really bad rhetoric—as my first picture suggested. You will have noticed, however, that my description, like all descriptions of human activity, is not what the social scientists call "value-free." Even the most neutral description of any human endeavor will reveal, to the careful listener, implied judgments and exhortations, and mine is no exception. Most obviously, I have implied throughout that for people to understand one another is not only a good thing in itself, it is the *sine qua non* of a genuine university. It follows from that, I think, that one of our main tasks is to improve our chances for genuine understanding—understanding, of course, of all three kinds. We need to expand the size, as it were, of each fish-scale and the area of overlap among the scales. We need to encourage ourselves in the growth of tentacles reaching from scale to scale. But, even more pressingly, we need to increase our understanding of how it is that we do in fact communicate by means of those tentacles, and how we might do it better.

The lines among the three kinds of improvement will always be blurred. Mastering the special topics of most fields will lead simultaneously to some improvement in the handling of the topics common to all rational discourse. Many fields, like my own, are built largely out of the topics and warrants that are shared by all scholarly and scientific fields. But though the lines are indistinct, we are all in effect custodians of all three kinds. The ideal university that is implied by all this would obviously be one in which we all worked even more steadily, aggressively, and effectively than we do now to increase the number of moments each day when genuine understanding takes place—with a consequent improvement both in the quality of learners and in the quality of judgments passed on the learners.

What I've said leaves me as uneasy about our future as I felt at the beginning. I am not at all clear where I might personally come out, if judged by the standards implicit throughout this essay: "The *true uni*versity exhibits throughout a form of vigorous intellectual curiosity *across* all disciplines." But I must also confess that I do dream of living in a university even more committed to interdisciplinarity. I love the life in this university as it is; I see it as the most committed to cross-disciplinary discourse of all universities. But I also see us as increasingly engaged in the futile pursuit of top prize as a *multi*versity. Surely it is not unrealistic, not the least bit utopian, to hope that we might resist the various temptations thrust on us by international competition, and instead set our own course, as we have often—quite miraculously, when you come to think about it—set our own course in the past.

## CHAPTER 16

*This talk, which was delivered to both high school and college students and published by Roanoke College in 1998, sprang out of the thinking that produced* For the Love of It: Amateuring and Its Rivals. *Like most of my public talks from childhood on, it will seem to some readers excessively sermonic: once again Booth has the truth, and he is determined to put it across. Can I preach a countertruth here? This talk is not a sermon but is intended, at least, as a stimulus to serious thinking.*

My own take on this essay offers its own counter-counter-truth: for all its sermonizing, it can provide a genuine stimulus to think about its abiding mysteries.

The essay was originally published in *The Jordan Lectures, 1998–1999* (Salem, VA: Roanoke College, 1999).

# For the Love of It
Spending, Wasting, and Redeeming Time

I should begin by warning you that in taking up your time here with this talk I'll be preaching at you about good and bad ways to *spend* your time. But as I look at my watch—an action we all spend a lot of time at—hoping to keep the talk under thirty minutes, I'm aware of an acute paradox: you and I are spending—perhaps wasting—our time right now. For one reason or another, we have chosen to be here, at this moment, with our allocated amount of time slipping past us, being spent, for good or ill: maybe wasted, maybe not.

That means I'd better make this talk pretty good, right? If I bore you, you've wasted your time. If I lead you into serious errors, I will have *harmed* your time. If I lead you to some serious thinking about other hours you spend, I will have been—in my own partial view—well, at least I may have been, *useful* to you. But will I have *redeemed* your time in the way that I felt time redeemed last week, when my wife and I and two other amateur musicians played Beethoven's A-minor Quartet together? While we were doing that, I forgot about time, was totally unaware of the so-called real minutes going by: my life was being lived entirely in the music time, and even if it had gone on not just for forty-five minutes but for four hours, I would never have looked at my watch.

I assume that everyone of you here has had that experience of being transported out of ordinary time, one way or another—what I'll call the time-escape. It can happen playing a tennis game or golf match; or watching a skillfully made horror movie; or attending a football match by our favorite team; or reading a gripping novel, worthwhile or trashy; or attending a really affecting church service; or getting blindly hooked into the Internet; or quarreling or fighting with an enemy; or getting drunk; or taking drugs. Time-escape and the desire for more of it, whether defensible or indefensible, is thus known to all of us, so I must ask,

> How many of you have experienced at least once this week one or another time-escape—being totally transported out of real time, into a different world?

Most in the room raised their hands.

My question *now*, then, is this: When have those escapes been of a kind you would be willing to defend, if appearing before some grand moral jury, or before St. Peter, say, as you ask to be admitted into heaven? My negative answers to such questions—and I often receive them from myself—too often come in something like this form: "Well, I felt that the time I spent was just sort of wasted; I felt worse about myself or about the world afterward than I did before." My more favorable answers go like this: "Well, I felt better about myself and about the world when I returned. It felt sort of like a blessing."

> How many of you who have escaped time this week in one way or another felt better about yourself or the world you live in after returning to ordinary time from your escape than you felt before?

Perhaps a fourth in the room raised their hands.

> How many have felt after at least one time-escape in the past that you had wasted or soiled your time?

Almost all hands went up.

Well, that kind of question forces us to recognize that one of the toughest questions we ever face in life is this: How *should* I spend my time? How do I choose among all the possibilities that life offers?

For hundreds of millions of sufferers throughout world history, that question would never even occur: they were forced to spend most or all of *their* time struggling to survive. Slaves and the starving usually had no choice. It was only when various versions of civilization arose that real possibilities of choice entered the human scene, at least for a fraction of those in each population. At first it was only those at the top who, by ordering the slaves to do the survival work, in the world of ordinary time, were free to decide whether to hunt or fish or play with concubines or play the flute or whatever. Gradually over the centuries, as religions and philosophies developed, and as notions of freedom and equality emerged, more and more people faced real choices about their time. A few of the upper classes could now make their own choices about all of their time; and more and more even of the laboring classes found themselves with *some* free time. By now, in most nations, most people have, like you here, at least some free choice about what sociologists call "leisure-time recreations." In short, as we face the twenty-first century, more of us probably have more free choices about time than most human beings have ever had before.

It may not feel that way to you students and faculty, with your papers to write and papers to grade and exams to prepare for; much of that doesn't feel much like free choice, does it? But actually it is. Unlike slaves or the starving, you could just drop it all and survive somewhere else. Every teacher here could survive somehow if she quit teaching and chose some other career; every one of you students could survive if you quit right now and went out looking for some kind of job or nonacademic training. We are all free, once we think hard enough about it, to choose how to spend, waste, or redeem our time.

What, then, to do with it—with *time*?

Thousands of answers have been offered, by philosophers, priests, rabbis, ticket vendors, salesmen of toys, touters of exercise machines and recreational vehicles. For many, the obvious answer has been religious, or at least bordering on religious. Very early the answer became "Spend your free time worshiping your God." The answer I'm playing with here is something like that, if you'll allow me to imply some deconstruction of that tricky word *religion*.

From ancient times to today, commandments have flooded us: Thou shalt not labor on the Sabbath; Sabbath time should be spent with God, no matter how hungry you may be. Bored with that, many have gone in the opposite direction: Eat, drink, and be merry, for tomorrow you not only *may* die but sooner or later *you will die*: so get all the pleasure you can, while you can.

It does seem to me that too many sermons I hear dwell boringly only on how to behave on Sunday, or on narrow conduct codes for the week. How often do they emphasize as I would that the choice of a career—in other words, of how to spend most of one's time from day to day—is itself a more important religious choice than whether to plagiarize a part of your next term paper: It will lead you either to spend or waste or redeem your time.

But today I'm not going to preach at you much about how to choose a good career—though I'm tempted to right now: Be sure to choose a career in which you'll be paid for doing something you love to do. When I decided, in my sophomore year, that I wanted to be an English teacher, my mother, an elementary school teacher, was horrified—she was sure that I'd be poor all my life and would never, as she put it, "amount to anything." My answer was always, "Why not get paid, even if it's only peanuts, for what you love to do?" And it still seems to me, fifty-eight years later, exactly the way to think about it.

Robert Frost dramatized his choice of being a poet like this:

> But yield who will to their separation,
> My object in living is to unite
> My avocation and my vocation
> As my two eyes make one in sight.
> Only where love and need are one,
> And the work is play for mortal stakes,
> Is the deed ever really done
> For Heaven and the future's sakes.
> ("Two Tramps in Mud Time")

Of course I'm not suggesting, any more than Frost is, that you should plan to make a living as a poet, but rather that, in choosing a career, love and need should and often can "be one."

But in any case, today, instead of talking about choosing a "vocation"—a full-time, money-earning, family-supporting career, a choice we all have to make—I want to think about how we spend our extra hours, our so-called free time, our "leisure time." As that time increases, more and more of us seem to be choosing to commit that free time to a second job or to overtime work: to further success or money derived from the main job. Some lawyers, like three I happen to know, are pressured by their bosses to spend *all* of their time, except when sleeping, on making more money for the firm. One of them works sixty hours a week, but his bosses complain because he doesn't come in on weekends.

On the other side, many who earn enough by working only six or eight hours a day choose to spend the remaining eight or ten hours, when they're not sleeping, on mere passive entertainment, by which I mean watching other people who are doing something interesting. Studies claim to show, for example, that the average American spends four hours a day watching TV. Doing so, he or she must often experience a time-escape, the pleasure of escaping from the world of ordinary time; and of course there's nothing *inherently* wrong with that form of escape. We all need the kind of relief from pressure that such passive enjoyment yields.

But my point here, as you've long since figured out, is this: To make our lives really worth living, we all need to find a radically different kind of time-escape, one that doesn't squander but rather redeems time for at least an hour or so each day. Find a loved pursuit—what I call an *amateur* pursuit, because the Latin root of "amateur" involves those "love" words: *amo, amas, amat*. Find a pursuit in which you are the one doing the doing, you are the producer, the engager; you are an active part of the production, not simply an excited viewer or listener.

As I've already suggested, my own ideal among such escapes is playing or singing music with other players or singers. I had been brought up loving to sing and listen to music, and I had played a bit of piano (just solos), and clarinet in a marching band. But by the time I got into graduate school, I became so obsessed with my scholarly work (which I only some of the time performed with love) that I just felt I had no leisure time. Actually, as I look back on it, I realize that I did waste a lot of time, reading crummy murder mysteries, for example, when I could have been learning to swim better or trying to write better poems. What I gave up, though, was any serious application to an avocation, what some call a hobby, or a recreation, but that I still prefer to call an amateur pursuit. The true amateur practices some difficult, awesome skill, for the sheer love of it.

Now I don't regret those four graduate years of scholarly labor, because I did love much of what I was required to do, as I obeyed my professors in my reading and writing. It was only two years after getting the Ph.D. that I began to suspect what I had been missing and made one of the best decisions of my life. Instead of just listening to music, too often only half heard in the background as I concentrated on a bit of Aristotle or *Tristram Shandy*, I began to think of making music myself. And since my wife, Phyllis, was a fine violinist playing in chamber music groups, why not take up the cello and earn the right to join those groups?

What I did not anticipate was a vast range of problems and questions that are raised by active *doing* as compared with passive *receiving*. I loved to listen to music, and I assumed arrogantly that I could learn the cello quickly. What I found instead was that learning to play an instrument, learning to make real music rather than mere squawks and squeals, was not just difficult: in effect it was hopeless, if I defined hope as reaching some kind of top approaching the professionals. I soon learned that I would never be as good on the cello as my wife was and is on the violin, because she started in elementary school.

I've recently written a sort of chaotic book on the joys and comic disasters that my amateur choice yielded: what I think of as my hopeless cello-reach. The book was an attempt to expand on my topic here today. When you decide to spend your leisure hour or two a day attempting to climb a peak that is absolutely, unquestionably beyond you, you land in totally different territory from where your life is when you sit comfortably and listen or watch other people struggle. You don't just escape from time in the hours you spend practicing and playing with friends; you enter into the country where your life is being created, not just received—received as it would be if, for example, you'd just got high on some drug. It is a new country where you and your friends don't just escape ordinary time, you discover or create a new kind of time entirely.

Because music itself makes such a good case for the escape from drab ordinary time, my book concentrates on the ways in which chamber music yields that escape, that discovery. But throughout I do try to remind everyone, as I'm trying to remind you this morning, of the vast and wonderful range of potential loves that you can choose from, once you've decided not to squander your time but to redeem it with love: active sports, serious reading, caring for a child, gardening, painting, working with a telescope, and so on.

Though we amateurs are often driven, and even plagued, by the desire to do it better, the real drive is the sheer love of the playing itself—not just the music but the playing of, with, through, *in* the music. It is our conviction that if anything is worth doing at all, it is worth doing badly. We usually manage to rise above the distractions and play for the sake of the playing. While the world is negotiating costs and benefits of a different kind, we are negotiating spirited interpretations. When everything goes well, the payoff is . . . But as my book demonstrates again and again, the rewards—joyful friendship, spiritual ecstasy, gratitude for life's mysterious, unearned gifts—are as impossible to portray in words as is music itself.

Once I got started thinking about all that, I was of course, as we are here, beset by overwhelming questions about the whole of life. Why ever attempt the impossible? Why bother at any stage of life to work for some new skill or know-how instead of dwelling comfortably with skills already mastered? If you happen already to be among the top ranks at tennis or rollerblade acrobatics, why attempt anything else, if you can be certain that you'll never even come close to professional competence? Isn't anything worth doing worth doing really well—better than you'll ever paint or photograph or golf or play chess or perform the role of King Lear in an amateur production or play the cello part in a relatively easy Haydn quartet? For that matter, why downgrade joyful, loving though passive moments—what I'm tempted to call couch-potato or ice-cream pleasures, just because they impose no requirements on the receiver? Aren't you, Professor Booth, simply expressing a moralistic, elitist bias?

Well, the answer is yes, if you'll drop the pejorative sense in those words *moral* and *elite*. Some time-escapes are in an inferior class, mere passings of time, the pleasures received rather than in any sense produced. (Some recreations are even more questionable, being harmful to others; but I won't discuss them much.) Some deserve the playful mockery that Laurence Sterne applies, in *Tristram Shandy*, to many a "Hobby Horse." Like him, I see some steeds as offering a worse ride than others, and some of you here may very well feel that I have downgraded your hobby horse to an ass. In contrast, real amateuring not only entails practice, even what might be called laboring: it lands us in aspirations that can produce many a moment of failure.

The twin notions of love and failure lead us inevitably to think about how all this relates to human loves, love of persons. All of us now have, or long for, a loving relation with a genuinely loving person who loves us in return. That for me is the one kind of love that clearly surpasses my loving pursuit of musical performance, or any other amateur pursuit. If some god told me I must choose whether to give up my cello or my wife, Phyllis, the choice wouldn't take a split second—though I might also decide to toss such a foolish god into the garbage. So don't assume that I think choosing the right amateur pursuit is more important than choosing the right person to live with through life. But I *am* suggesting that, as you make this more important choice, the choice of another person, perhaps then later discovering the supreme love that comes with having a child, you should think very hard about what that person really loves. Of course your loves will include sex. But if that possible permanent partner seems to love only sex, or a collection of passive time-killers, think again—and start looking for some other person, one who knows what it means to pursue the world of true love.

Well, such a sermonic tone finally forces me to face some of the problems that those of us who are committed students and teachers live with. How does my way of talking about amateur loves relate to a teacher's professional love of teaching or a student's love of studying and writing? Is not learning to improve teaching, to improve studying, to improve writing more important than learning to play the cello? Do we need all this preaching about finding an additional *amateur* pursuit when we already feel overwhelmed by the challenge of these other loving pursuits, doing our best not to remain amateur-*ish* in our pursuit?

I must confess that if and when you can honestly claim, "My passion, my deepest love, today, is getting this paper written better, or really digging deeper into Plato, or teaching my class better tomorrow"; if and when you can honestly say that working on an academic project is a genuine escape from the world of ordinary time into the world of love; if and when you find that, after you have sunk into the desk, as it were, you lose track of time and come out a few hours later surprised at how the time has flown, and feeling better about yourself and about the quality of the life you led during those "lost hours," *then* you should definitely not break it off in order to practice the guitar for an hour. I do experience such professional moments—moments when I would maybe call myself a pro-amateur, or am-professional. But for me they are relatively rare. Far more often I find myself, even in my beloved professional work, doing some of it not for love but because it is just plain required of me. And as a student I often felt, "God, how I hate writing this paper! But I'll flunk if I don't hand it in tomorrow." Those are the times when picking up the guitar, or the cello, or the golf club, or the gardening tools, or the chess set, or working hard at some worthy charity, can save you, redeeming your time.

Let me close with an example of what I mean. Four years ago, already beginning to struggle with writing the book about amateuring, I wrote the following journal entry:

> Early this morning was feeling overwhelmed. In-box full of correspondence and manuscripts requiring response "yesterday"; a 700-page book manuscript I'm reading for a press; Ph.D. students' dissertation chapters; requests for speeches at this and that conference; promises, promises. The bills have not been paid for two weeks. Have sworn that I'll spend at least four hours a day writing on the book [*For the Love of It*], until a draft is completed. But I have a cello lesson coming up Saturday. *But* I can't expect to practice after dinner tonight [my usual time] because we're going to a performance of *Measure for Measure*. *But* then I must . . .

In short, there was literally no time today when I could practice.
So what did I do?
Well, shortly after breakfast, feeling terribly pressurized, heart actually pounding a bit, I decided to behave like a grownup after all and settle down for an hour with the cello. Forcing my "self" to obey that decision, I felt better and better as the notes began to flow. The hour turned into ninety minutes, few of them troubled by any thoughts about what I was neglecting. All those other matters, undeniably "more important," judged in practical terms, were just forgotten while I worked away: first on Popper's Etude no. 22, and some arpeggios, then the fourth movement of the Beethoven A-minor, hoping that the Popper would pay off in the thumb stuff in the gloriously demanding climax. And glory be to the great God of Thumb Position, it did! I could feel myself able to play that stuff better than ever before—better than I did when playing it in London two years ago, better than I could have done eighty minutes before . . .

The result? I went back to my desk at eleven feeling more on top of all those pressures than I had for days; I worked on my book for two hours, then went home and faced the cruddy in-box for awhile, thinking as I worked, "A good day; at least I got the music in."

Now that might sound as if I were saying, "Take up a loving pursuit in order to relax your brain so that you can do your academic work better." But that's not, absolutely not, the main point. It's true that amateuring does, as my anecdote illustrates, enable the brain to return to other tasks more happily and flexibly. But is that the reason for amateuring?

Winston Churchill seems to answer with a yes in his lively little book *Painting as a Pastime*, as he dwells almost entirely on the practical benefits of amateuring. Like me, he made his amateur choice in his middle years— at forty. Churchill for a while talks as if he took up painting for the love of it, but quickly he turns to the question of utility, talking as if the real reason was to give his brain a rest.

As his choice of the word *pastime* suggests, and as his text later makes clear, Churchill thus has decided to talk of his newfound love as primarily useful in providing his overworked brain with a distraction from his more important political work: The painter serves the statesman. Though I suspect that in the hours of actual painting he often became a genuine amateur, he talks about it as in the service of something more important: It gives a holiday to the really useful part of the statesman's brain. G. K. Chesterton provides my refutation of that utilitarian view, responding to those who reduce the value of music to its service to healthy digestion: "They do not see that digestion exists for health, and health exists for life, and life exists for the love of music or other beautiful things."

Well, how can I conclude? We all know that no one summary of what life is for is ever completely satisfying for longer than a minute. But I do think that certain negative statements about what it is *not* for do not fade quite so fast. The gift of life is not for the possibility of eating, drinking, and being merry until we die. The gift of life is *not* for the chance to sit around watching other people make something out of it. The gift of life is the chance it gives to make something of it yourself. As students and teachers, many of you, I hope most of you, have already in effect chosen to act in accordance with that principle.

No matter how we feel about our present vocational directions, whatever our successes and failures, the good news is that vast numbers of wonderful amateur pursuits are available to most of us. Though millions of sufferers in every age still must struggle from day to day merely to survive, with little freedom to choose anything other than survival techniques or an occasional mournful song, the history of cultures shows that the lives of all but the literally starving can be at least partly redeemed by the song of the amateur. The song sung by the hungry peasant, like the song lived by every genuine amateur, by every gardener or painter or dancer or stargazer who is dwelling in the practice itself—that song should not be thought of as mere argument that life is worthwhile: the loving act sings the very gift of life itself.

CHAPTER 17

I have chosen to place this essay last for personal but I think also publicly arguable reasons: for me, and I hope for others, it best exemplifies Booth at his best—engaged, eloquent, focused on the student in all of us, that is, on ones who seek to learn and know and do, whatever our age. Certainly other essays might have been put in its place; this particular piece does not feature character ethics, for example. There is, it seems to me, something very "Chicago" about it—in part, no doubt, its preoccupation with method. But for me it is also essentially "Boothian," I mean an implied Booth (just one of many faces of the flesh-and-blood author) who is so committed to critical inquiry and argument. Call it once more, as I did in my introduction, the Rhetoric of Booth.

This essay was commissioned by the Carnegie Foundation for the Advancement of Teaching and was originally published in *Common Learning: A Carnegie Colloquium on General Education* (Washington, DC: Carnegie Foundation, 1981), 22–55 (copyright 1981 by the Carnegie Foundation for the Advancement of Teaching; reprinted with permisson). It was reprinted in *The Vocation of a Teacher: Rhetorical Occasions, 1967–1988* (Chicago: University of Chicago Press, 1988), 105–28.

# Coda

## Mere Rhetoric, Rhetorology, and the Search for a Common Learning

### I

One of my earliest experiences with curricular reform took place at Haverford College in the early 1950s. After some months of careful thought about what was wrong with an absurd accretion of requirements that had apparently never been thought through by anyone before, we on the curriculum committee had the instructive experience of seeing the faculty spend all of ten minutes on our report. The coup de grâce—only a pretentious cliché can do justice to it—the coup de grâce was administered by kindly old Ned Snyder: "Gentlemen"—and we were all gentlemen in those days— "gentlemen, we are already the best men's college in the country. Why on earth we should change is more than I can see!"

The Haverford faculty, in its wisdom, assumed that it had debated the subject adequately and dropped the report without a vote. The document disappeared without a trace.

I do not know that it was a good report; I never had a chance to find out by testing it in serious discussion. What I know for sure is that our failure to debate its merits exhibited our bad rhetorical education—"highly educated" and well-intentioned though we were. Skilled specialists, most of us, in the arts of reasoning in our specialties, we were totally unskilled— as many another faculty meeting of the time further revealed—in the art of reasoning together about shared concerns.

I must confess that having observed similar nondiscussions in many a meeting through almost thirty-five years of curricular discussion, I find failure haunting us here as we renew deliberation about general education.[1]

I may as well also confess that whenever I see a list of the essential ingredients of general education, I invariably feel that my own subjects have been radically underplayed. How could the Carnegie essayist be so blind as to list "The Shared Language and Symbols that Connect Us" as only one of six coequal subjects, on a par with those other interesting but far less important subjects, history, natural science, mathematics, ethics, and political science? Have they not realized that the study of all the rest depends on the quality of the shared languages we use in that study? Have they not recognized that the study of how to improve our capacity to share symbols—what many of us call *rhetoric*—is thus the queen of the sciences?

I know very well that to succumb like that to the temptations of disciplinary imperialism is to destroy from the beginning any chance of building a general education curriculum. So I feel guilty about such thoughts. But I would feel guiltier if I did not suspect that others secretly respond in the same way. The historians will wonder why history, which is obviously the most important and most neglected of studies, should be degraded to one-half of one slot out of six, and labeled only as a "concern with a common heritage"—as if we did not live and have our being in that heritage! The natural scientists, the social scientists, and the philosophers similarly must each squirm a bit to see that what is for them central has been pinned wriggling to the wall-chart—and what is more, labeled with an alien name. And this is to say nothing about those other scholars and teachers who cannot find themselves on the chart at all. . . .

Such imperialisms aside, at least for the moment, I assume that we could all agree on something like the sixfold list in the Carnegie essay. We know that when students graduate from our colleges radically ignorant and unskilled in these shared connections, the result is shocking. It is a scandal that so few of our graduates are even minimally proficient in more than one of the six fields. It is a scandal that even students who major in any one of the conventional fields that profess to deal with "connections"—I mention only English and philosophy—are often blind to the issues raised by words such as *shared* and *connections*. They have been systematically incapacitated for sharing anything except expertise with other experts in some subdivision of current inquiry. If you think I exaggerate, ask the next economics B.A. you meet what her study has taught her that would be useful in dealing with our rising mass illiteracy. Or try to have a good conversation about politics or literature with your university's M.B.A.'s or "behavioral psych" majors.

So far we might all agree that sharing the six sharings will minimally mark a person as "generally educated," as someone deserving a *Bachelor of Arts* diploma. Presumably our next move is to discuss what particular consequences for educational planning might follow from such agreement.

But experience teaches that trouble begins whenever we move from general goals to particular means.

Just think of the jealous responses we are likely to meet, within any one of the six general subjects. The sociologists, anthropologists, economists, legal theorists, and political scientists will quarrel, for example, about which of them deals best with our "shared institutions" or "shared activities"; the various schools of philosophy, anthropology, psychology, and literary theory will quarrel about which deals best with our "shared values." And so on.

Or think of the academic rivals who might claim that they should provide the substance studied under the first category, "competence in symbol-sharing." Agreeing that students must become competent in "the shared language and symbols that connect us"—that they must learn to read, write, speak, and listen effectively—many different experts can make quite plausible cases for the centrality of what they do. Most obviously, teachers of composition and of elementary foreign languages will make their case for a basic literacy. But a basic literacy taught according to what paradigms? Offhand, one can think of at least a dozen disciplines claiming to provide the central theory both for elementary instruction in how to read, think, speak, and write, and for advanced training toward degrees in linguistics, semiotics, logic, analytical philosophy, hermeneutics, communications theory, cognitive science, various kinds of structuralism and deconstructionism—not to mention the many versions of my own field, rhetoric. And what about the fields that the report does mention but does not include explicitly in the summarizing chart—the languages of mathematics, music, and the visual arts? Where are the symbolic sharings through the languages of film, photography, and TV?

We all know that the same kinds of rivalry can be found under each of the other five categories, even in the natural sciences. What, then, are we to do, when we turn from our general lists and try to design a general curriculum?

That question leads me nicely back to my own empire, rhetoric, just as it has led the Carnegie Foundation to place its money on the rhetoric of conferences and collections of essays, in the hope of making changes in the world. Whenever we are faced with a multiplicity of seemingly conflicting spoken or written claims, we turn to the art of rhetoric, the art of pursuing the understandings that lurk behind our surface symbolic disagreements, and the disagreements that lurk behind our superficial agreements. We think about how our discourse in these areas works and about how it might be improved. We analyze our terms and look beneath our verbal surfaces, searching for common grounds, from which we can then begin discoursing at a new and improved level.

In the ancient terminology of rhetoricians, we seek to discover the topics, the topoi, the places or locations on which, or *in* which, a shared inquiry can take place. Whatever conclusions we come to as we confer, we shall be practicing, well or badly, the arts of rhetoric. Whether we practice them well will depend only in part on the quality of the formal education we received in them, because our education—or miseducation—in rhetoric continues willy-nilly after formal schooling.

In using the much abused term *rhetoric* to cover everything any of us says at this conference, I know I take some risks. Rhetoric has always had a mixed press. When the International Society for the History of Rhetoric met in Madison, Wisconsin, in April 1981, one entire afternoon was scheduled for papers on the long history of *attacks* on rhetoric. But we do not have to go to history to discover that the term is suspect. At least nine out of ten references to it in the press today are unfavorable. In popular usage it generally refers to the sleazier branches of the arts of persuasion, often synonymous with bombast or verbal trickery or deliberate obfuscation. It is what we substitute for substantive action or genuine thought, what we fall back on when serious arguments are lacking. "Although the president's deeper purpose was concealed in the rhetoric, [he] sent a red hot message . . . in his speech last Wednesday." "But Miss Caruso dismissed Healey's statement as 'rhetoric' and vowed to bring in the second round of her proposed cuts." This is surely the standard usage.

You might then well say, "If *rhetoric* is such a bad word, why not just get rid of it and use the words stressed in the Carnegie essay, *symbol sharing*?" But it is not just the word that is debunked; it is what it stands for. "Reaction [to Mayor Byrne's announcement that she will move into the Cabrini-Green housing project] was mixed Saturday night, with many calling the move courageous but symbolic." Courageous—that's good. Symbolic, introduced with a *but*—that is obviously somehow bad, or at least inferior. "Alderman Danny Davis . . . said the move might be more symbolic than substantive." Obviously anything merely symbolic is not substantive, and if rhetoric is anything, it is an employment of symbols.

What people usually mean when they dismiss other people's efforts as "rhetoric" or, more often, "mere rhetoric" is that words or other symbols are being used to deceive or to obscure issues or to evade action. Animals cannot tell elaborate lies, only simple ones. Animals cannot use symbols as evasion. Only a rhetoric-endowed species can produce an elaborate chain of lies to achieve a cover-up; or a multimillion-dollar advertising campaign for products known to be either useless or harmful; or a diplomatic and political vocabulary for making the worse seem the better cause. Rhetoricians have often tried to wash their hands of such stuff, preserving the term *rhetoric* for cleaner efforts. But as educators, we cannot accept that dodge. If we confer symbolic powers upon our students, we take on all of the risks of symbolic power. If we train our students in the arts of reading, writing, listening, and speaking, we inevitably empower them to do great harm in the world—to use rhetoric for private, antisocial ends, to break rather than build connections. I must return to this problem in a few moments, but for now perhaps we can simply label the whole domain of the deceitful rhetoric we deplore as "subrhetoric." Different people will probably have somewhat different examples in mind; hardly a day goes by without my adding to a list that exhibits, as one of its supreme moments, Richard Nixon's Checkers speech, when his family, and then his dog, won the hearts of a nation.

One step up from subrhetoric, we find the word *rhetoric* used to refer to the whole art of sincere selling of any cause, not just the trickery part or the disguise, but the genuinely persuasive parts too, including the logical arguments. In this sense, President Carter's rhetoric was said to be poor and President Reagan's is generally said to be good, meaning that, on average, people come away from their encounters with President Reagan having moved more or less in his direction. Almost every day we read that the United States must "improve its rhetoric throughout the world," obviously meaning "we must sell our case more effectively."

Though it is hard to distinguish this level of rhetoric, which I will call "mere rhetoric," from subrhetoric, obviously its uses can range from the most noble to the most dangerous, from Churchill's wartime speeches to the typical piece of campaign oratory. In some ways, mere rhetoric is more dangerous than subrhetoric, because those who employ it are sincere; they have a position that they hope will prevail, and they themselves respect the rhetorical devices that they employ. Presidents Reagan and Carter both seem to believe in their hearts that they are good medicine for the country. More important to our analysis than their sincerity, however, is that they always give the impression of having used their rhetoric to put across a position that was known in advance, before the work on the rhetoric began. The case is already known: "OK, Sam, let's whomp us up some mere rhetoric to put it over. Let's see, who's our best ghostwriter on this subject? George? OK, George, you know what we want, now get cracking on the rhetoric." The fact is that most freshman composition texts, even those that have taken up with the renewed fashion of using the word *rhetoric* in the title, imply that one's case is found by some other art or science, and then one puts it over with mere rhetoric.

Even if that were our final definition of the art, rhetoric would still obviously be indispensable in all general education, since its uses are shared by all who engage in any kind of practical endeavor. But it is hardly the art that I could bring myself to defend as what we should use in debating general education. Presumably, as we discuss our various proposals, we do not think of ourselves as coming out of the discussion precisely as we came into it. We want to *discover* something through our rhetorical exchange.

Aristotle's *Rhetoric* goes one large step further toward the definition we are seeking. Instead of referring to an art of persuasion about a case that is entirely known beforehand, rhetoric for Aristotle is the *faculty* or *capacity*, found of course *in the rhetorician*, of *discovering* or *inventing* "the possible means of persuasion in reference to any subject whatever." Unlike the arts of medicine, geometry, arithmetic (and presumably politics, too, though Aristotle does not mention politics in this context), the art of rhetoric "appears to be able to *discover* the means of persuasion in reference to any given subject." It is thus used by all disciplines, except insofar as those disciplines have available apodeictic proofs, what we call "demonstrative" or "scientific" proofs. Rhetoric in this view is not a dressing added to the case to make it persuasive; the rhetorician discovers the case itself, using the art of rhetoric as an art of discovery. When the search is successful, the case is persuasive, though the conclusions it leads to may not be true for all time and are certainly not demonstrated in any absolute [scientific] sense.

This art, which I will call "rhetoric-B," is a marvel and a wonder. A scholar-teacher might honorably spend a whole career mastering its subtleties and passing the mastery along to students. Obviously, it is a much more important subject than what most people call rhetoric. It will of course include the study of the inferior rhetorics—how otherwise could one distinguish the "bombast" and "empty verbal ornamentation" of one's enemies from the "true eloquence" and "sensitive verbal enrichments" of one's friends? But its true home will be what we call "value disputes": in the political arena at its best, when a Pericles or a Lincoln or a Churchill reminds a nation of its deepest commitments; or in literary criticism; or in quarrels about the law or about constitutions. It comes into its own in every part of life where simple appeals to obvious facts or unquestioned logical proofs are not available—and that surely means most of what we do, even as scholars. Clearly, such a subject is immensely important, well worth the hundreds of pages of close study that Aristotle and Cicero gave it, and the many thousands that later students have added. There is nothing "mere" about it. It is the very lifeblood of our daily lives together.

But is it finally what we seek, if we are looking for the art not just of discovering, but also of appraising the values we share? One obvious problem is that it seems to lack any limits on its power. It can be taught to villains as well as to saints, and it can be employed either for or against the good of a society. It is, of course, an immensely seductive art, because its mastery is the road to worldly success. Rhetoric-B is the art of knowing what you want and finding the really good arguments to win others to your side. It is the art of the good lawyer, of the effective business leader, of the successful fund-raiser, and it is not to be scoffed at or ignored. But it does not itself teach us what ends it should serve; it is still an art without essential restraints, other than those provided by the counterrhetoric created by other warriors or competitors. The world it builds, left on its own, is a world of a free market of atomized persons and ideas, each privately seeking victory and hoping that in the melee a public good will be produced by some invisible hand. Thus all thinkers, from Plato and Aristotle on, have felt the need to subordinate it to some higher discipline capable of revealing proper ends or goods.

We see what happens when such higher controls are lacking, as various spokesmen for this or that new rhetorical theory—"communication skills," "propaganda analysis," "advertising techniques," "information science"— show themselves to be, in effect, available to the highest bidder: they fail to provide, from within themselves, any hint about limits to how and when their techniques are to be used.

But to what discipline or art now on the scene might we turn for the controls that each of our three kinds of rhetoric so clearly require? It takes no great skill in rhetoric to recognize that in our society at this time, there is open warfare about whether any superior "good" exists, or, if it does, what in fact it is and how it should be pursued. We seem to share no single notion of the good, or of the proper methods of argument to be used in its pursuit.

If we did have such agreement, we might of course deduce from it the proper uses of rhetoric: something like, "Service of the one true Lord requires, as Augustine teaches, that rhetoric should . . . " or "To restore our position as the world's greatest power, it is obvious that our rhetoric should . . . " or "By studying the right list of classical philosophers, we can learn those truths that we can then sell with our rhetoric." But we in America have agreed on something else instead—that we are to be a pluralistic society in which many different possible first principles will coexist. Some of them, like some scientists' and mathematicians' notions of what can be known, would rule out as trivial or noncognitive most of the proposals we offer each other about general education. Some of them would suggest a list of coordinate values. And some, like mine, would lead to a more aggressive kind of hierarchical ordering, with certain threatened educational deficiencies seen as much more important than others.

When first principles conflict, how do we proceed? One possible way is to use rhetoric-B to persuade other people to change their minds and accept the predetermined *true* first principles. Marshaling all of the possible means of persuasion in our situation, we would, in that view, try to win as many converts as possible.

But did the Carnegie Foundation's authors know, before they began to draft their report, not only how the report was to come out, but how those who read and discuss it were supposed to respond? Did I know, as I began to write, what general education program we all should fight for on our campuses, using the best rhetoric we can muster?

Clearly, we all admire most still another form of rhetoric entirely, one implied by my hierarchical progression from subrhetoric through mere rhetoric and on to rhetoric-B, namely, (surprise!) a "rhetoric-A." When we are working together at our best, we repudiate both the autocratic imposition of a program by some benign dictator and the warfare of fixed positions; instead, we try out our reasons on each other, to see where we might come out. We practice a rhetoric of inquiry that is to some degree similar to what I label, in "The Idea of a University" [*chapter 15 in this volume*], as "rhetoric-3." But rhetoric-A could be employed in all the three rhetorics of that piece.

To invent a label does not mean, of course, that the art we seek actually exists, and it certainly does not say that we will attain to it if it does exist. But if there were an art that promised to aid us in going beneath the surface of our verbal disputes, in order to discover the common values that underlie them and to build practical programs on them, would not mastery of that art be, for any pluralistic society, a noble art indeed?

Is there a rhetoric-A? Is there a supreme art of inquiry through symbols that is designed, not to win by cheating, as in subrhetoric; not merely to win sincerely, as in mere rhetoric; not just to marshal all of the good reasons there might be for accepting what one knows already, as in rhetoric-B; but rather to discover and refine, in critical exchange, our ends, our purposes, our values?

Let me stress again the curious point that we have intuitively elected to practice that unnamed art whenever we engage in conferences that permit open exchange of ideas. What is more, I suspect that, despite all our rhetorical faults as a nation, it remains true that no other society has ever committed itself so passionately to the search for rhetoric-A. Often this commitment is mocked, as people get impatient with committee work, with the cumbersomeness of representative government, with the absurdities of our thousands of national conventions, colloquiums, conferences, workshops, and commissions. "Just think of all the time, energy, and money that is being wasted at this moment by hardworking, intelligent people, who travel thousands of miles to confer together in muddleheaded fashion, using dubious arguments about unformulated questions, appealing to unclear principles and leading to ambiguous conclusions!"

Well, that's rhetoric-A for you. We seem to be stuck with it, not only when we confer in person but whenever we seriously take other people's views into account. So let us try for a somewhat clearer definition of this rhetoric that we seek to practice together when we are at our best.

Is it not *the art of appraising the warrants for assent in any symbolic exchange*? The definition may seem anticlimactic until we think about the ground covered by its four key terms:

> *Appraising*—the judging of the real validity or force, the power or weakness of something.
>
> *Warrants*—the reasons or motives given by one human being to another as support for some belief or action or change of mind (assuming that every thoughtful person will share the warrant. Such ostensibly hard stuff becomes only a subset of all the more or less good grounds we can give each other for changing our minds and hearts).
>
> *Assent*—rather than dissent, because, though the two notions of saying yes and saying no are indissolubly linked in all human exchange, assent is really prior. Of the many reasons one might mention, the most obvious is that "thinking together about warrants" cannot even be undertaken without a primal act of assent: "I" must assent to "your" equal right to a hearing in our mutual endeavors; note again the contrast with traditional notions of hard proof, sought usually in private inquiry by disproving other people's views, the results then imposed upon a reluctant world. What is more, the "I" who assents or dissents was long since constituted in a series of incorporations of other selves. Hence:
>
> *Symbolic exchange*—like the other, inferior rhetorics, this one is indissolubly bound with the notion that it takes at least two to tango. But unlike the other definitions, this one rejects the very notion of the private individual "self" thinking by "itself." We move, instead, to a kind of thought possible only for a radically social self: the dichotomy between the individual and his past and present "context" is unreal. Good thinking in this view will not be quite like the "clear thinking" touted in so many

handbooks of logic, something performed by the "individual" in opposition to all those sloppy thinkers "out there." Instead it will be "social thought" even when it is in some sense private; good thinking will be only that kind of thinking that takes into account what others have said or can say against it. And it will be, from first to last, richer than what could be said, or even thought, by any one party in the exchange.

It is clear that if there is such an art, it must include the skills of appraising arguments offered in the inferior kinds of rhetoric, and it must no doubt include the appraisal and placement of the various kinds themselves. In that sense, I have been trying to practice rhetoric-A throughout this essay. But rhetoric-A can be practiced in the simplest of exchanges—the argument with your neighbor over the smell of his gingko tree, the discussion with a student about a low grade, the debate in committee about whether to require competence in a foreign language. In fact, I want now to suggest that rhetoric-A is in fact the most general of all general arts, and that to neglect it in our general requirements, as indeed we too often do, is fatal. I know that I can trust you to discount the outrageous arrogance in such a claim. I fully expect other disciplines to make similar moves—and I ask only that, when they do, we insist on real argument in their support, not just the claim that freshman courses are needed to attract majors. The best curricula will emerge, I am suggesting, when each of our imperialistic claims is forced into the courts of communal discourse, where our various rationalizations are transmuted, under critical scrutiny, into that special kind of reasoning that I am calling rhetoric-A.

## II

To make my case, I must practice a bit of rhetoric-A on the notion of general education itself.

The trouble with all highly general terms like *general*, *shared*, and *connections*, is that, like *rhetoric*, they cover and sometimes even obscure essential distinctions. Some forms of generality are harmful—I offer the easy examples of totalitarian imposition of general aims and practices on a whole populace, and the soppy generalities offered by some "interdisciplinary" programs. Some sharings are dangerous—I cite only the exhilarated sharings that lead to mob action or national witch hunts. Some connections are intellectually inhibiting—I cite only the ancient lumping of matter into the four elements, and the highly up-to-date and fashionable lumping of all narrative, including history, as "fictional" and therefore a form of lying. If we try to build our programs simply on what is shared or what is general, we shall be vulnerable to the first sophist who comes along and insists that we teach lying, just because all human beings lie; and prideful self-serving, just because all men and women are self-serving; and the arts of vandalism, just because scientific studies show that all of us share a capacity to take pleasure in destruction. In short, implicit in the Carnegie essay's emphasis on what is shared is a demand for distinctions of quality and kinds of generality. Once we limit ourselves to what we might call "generalities *worth having*," how many kinds do we find appealed to in the search for a general education?[2]

Education can be general, first, in the sense of being generally shared by all students in a given setting. Many curricular planners have found themselves giving up on the hope for a reasoned selection of the knowledge most worth having. "Who can say that everybody must know a given Dickens novel rather than the great Chinese novel *Monkey*, or Platonic thought rather than Zen Buddhism, or the second law of thermodynamics rather than how to do a regression analysis in statistics? Nobody. But we can say that it is good for students to share a culture, locally, so we'll make up a list of more or less arbitrary general requirements ensuring that they'll at least have something to talk about together." Rather minimal thinking, this, but no doubt better than nothing.

Education can be general, second, in the sense of covering the general needs of all citizens in a given time and place. That it should fill this function was the standard argument used by the defenders of the great Hutchins program of fourteen required year-long courses at the University of Chicago. Usually their talk was explicitly about preparation for citizenship, as if to say, "We seek an education that all Americans should have, because it would be folly to expect anyone to exercise the choices presented by our society without having the fourteen competencies our comprehensive examinations cover. All citizens will have to exercise these competencies, regardless of what the future brings; therefore they should share a standard preparation in them."

A rather different curriculum emerges if we emphasize a third kind of general sharing: the methods and subject matters that all the genuine modes of inquiry share. Proponents of "*the* scientific method" have argued that all genuine thought depends on certain paradigms of proof, and that general education should build habits of thought that will be generally useful, in all fields, though such habits are obviously unshared by most citizens. Programs with emphasis on training in logic, semantics, linguistics, laboratory techniques, computer technology, and mathematics have emerged from such paradigms. They tend to show little concern about whether any two students have both read Shakespeare, or studied the

Constitution, or thought about the role of law in public affairs, or developed skill in communicating their "scientific" results, or learned the same computer language.

Entirely different curricula have been suggested by proponents of a fourth notion of generality, based on what is common to all people in all cultures, as if to say, "Our deepest connections are with humankind as a whole, and nothing is worse, educationally, than our chauvinistic concentration on Western culture. What all students should learn are the experiences that join them to the rest of the world, not the narrow and elitist canons of Western taste. What could be more absurd, in the modern world, than the Western provincial who knows all about Beethoven and is ignorant of the Javanese gamelan?"

Finally, education can seek the general in the form of conceptual generalizations that serve as comprehensive overarching principles, under which each discipline performs its work—whatever generalizes all particulars in a field or in all fields. Surely if there is some "general field theory," it should be our center. Many mathematicians and physical scientists have pursued a truly general truth that could provide a capstone for all knowledge. As Morris Kline has recently said, mathematics offers all the values offered by any field, and, in addition, is "the paradigm for the best knowledge available."[3] For certain religious planners, on the other hand, it has seemed obvious that an education without a knowledge of God as a capstone is not education at all but a misapprehension of fragments. They seem to say, "Surely an education that does not lead the student to try to put it all together, to see not just connections but the ultimate connectedness, can hardly be considered really general and is not worthy of being required."

## III

At first consideration, this list of rival sharings may seem daunting. Regardless of where we would place our own planning, we are all aware that there are these rival views—that the shambles the report rightly deplores comes in part from the failure of educators to think through which of these notions of the general they are pursuing and why. All five build on a rejection of trivial or base kinds of sharing. But are all versions of each of them equally important?

I am almost sorry to report my daunting discovery that I am unwilling to give up any of the five. Though it is easy to see how special versions of each can be in direct competition with the others, it is obvious that each is radically desirable, in the precise sense that we began with: there is a kind of scandal in giving the B.A. to any student who has *no* common intellectual bonds (1) with all other students, (2) with all other citizens, (3) with all genuine disciplines, (4) with all human cultures, and (5) with all who seek to discover truths that are truly general.

If all five kinds are desirable, then we can begin to play an interesting game. Which of the many sharings on the Carnegie report's list, all of them good things to have, can make the best case for itself as indispensable, according to one or more of the notions of generality?

Again I shall, of course, leave it to others to make their cases for disciplines other than rhetoric. But I would not be doing my duty by an ancient and honorable discipline if I did not claim that rhetoric-A, the development of the appraisal (and hence the skillful use) of shared warrants for assent in human exchange, is an art unrivaled in its service to all five kinds of general education. I hasten to add that it is an art that need not be taught under the title of "rhetoric." I cannot think of any course in which some contribution to its mastery could not be made, if a teacher really tried. But it is too easily neglected when it is not given a clear and distinctive place in the curriculum. And when it is neglected, all the other disciplines suffer.

Turning then to the first kind of general education: If students on a given campus are to share educational experience, whether achieved through requirements or simply by living together, they will do so largely in their use of rhetoric, good or bad. Only to the degree that they learn to practice rhetoric-A, appraising together the warrants for assent that they and their teachers and texts offer, will they learn what to share and what not to share, what positions to buy and what to reject. In short, rhetoric is the very medium in which students share most of their genuine education, including most of their classroom experiences, even in the hardest of the sciences. The rhetoric may very well be of inferior kinds; even the best teachers may find occasional uses for hamming, tear-jerking, blood-letting, and swinging from the chandeliers. But surely our ideal of education is the sharing of *good* reasons for changes of mind, and since for most subjects that we care about we lack rigorous mathematical or experimental proofs even for the simplest processes and conclusions, our hope must lie in rhetoric-A.

It seems equally obvious, second, that the primary need of all citizens, before, during, and after college, is a mastery of rhetoric. The business of American life is, after all, conducted—perhaps more than was true of any previous society—in rhetoric. Unlike people in traditional societies, we get our jobs, keep them, or lose them, and actually conduct them, with rhetoric. *The Chronicle of Higher Education* has recently made the claim that more than 50 percent of all Americans make their living at what the *Chronicle* elegantly calls "symbol pushing." You would think, then, that every college in this practical land would have at least one entire degree program in how to symbol push better than other symbol pushers. But if you have such a program on your campus, one that goes beyond the mere rhetoric of advertising skills, I shall be surprised, and I hope to learn about it.

Rhetoric as vocational training is obviously far more important than we have recognized. But I would stress even more strongly its value in serving our universal need for *political* savvy. All our political life, except what is done through bribery and violence, is conducted in one or another form of rhetoric. Working together in symbolic exchange is in fact our only alternative to tyranny; either someone will impose forms of life upon us, or we must learn to embrace forms of life by trying them out on each other. And if we cannot manage to do the trying out effectively, if we cannot rise above sub- and mere and B-rhetorics to an effective appraisal of our reasonings, we are doomed to some form of chaos, inevitably followed by some tyrant's takeover.

Our founding fathers did the trying out at a wonderfully high level. My students and I have been discovering just how high as we work over the rhetoric-A of Madison's *Notes* and the rhetoric-B of *The Federalist Papers*. (The founders were highly skilled in the use and analysis of the lower rhetorical forms, too; what we might call our founding uncles, like Tom Paine, owed their astonishing popular success to a rhetorical range [covering all of the types] that any of us might envy.) What is more, every generation since theirs has offered its demonstration that, unless effective rhetoric governs politics, money and violence will. The Constitution in this view is a marvelously shrewd effort to guarantee that rhetoric will have a chance, an effort to open up public spaces that will require, not just allow, that our many different would-be leaders listen to each other and listen to the governed. The fact that we survive at all as a democracy is a triumph of that great piece of rhetoric-A—and of our willingness to talk and listen according to its rules.

Third, rhetoric is general to all disciplines, in the sense of their depending on it in daily practice. Though many disciplines are described as if rhetoric were beneath their high-minded endeavors, one has only to look at the rhetoric used in each field, both in its publications and its teaching practice, to see the absurdity of the claim. The fact is that every field depends, often to a surprising degree, on the skills I am talking about.

I'll not insist, as some rhetoricians have done, on the claim that even the hardest proofs in the hardest sciences are conducted *in* rhetoric: "the rhetoric of the laboratory," "the rhetoric of the equation," "the rhetoric of the graph." But even if we grant the name of pure science to the processes of decisive and final demonstration, we know that most of the business of scientists, even when they are writing in their frontline journals, depends on obviously rhetorical arguments, like exploration of hidden or overt analogies, colorful metaphor, appeals to the character of the speaker and of supporting institutions, and direct or subtle manipulation of readers' emotions. We should not have needed *The Double Helix*, or *Lucy* (the book purporting to reveal how anthropologists work), to teach us how small a portion of every scientist's scientific life is decided by scientific evidence.[4]

The infusion of rhetoric, of our kinds of reasons, good and bad, is usually not noticed, especially when it comes in the form of appeals to certain root metaphors that everyone in a field simply takes for granted. When it is noticed, it is usually treated as a kind of impurity that could be washed away if only scientists were more scientific. But rhetoric is inescapable, even in mathematics and physics. Leaving aside the obvious rhetoric of the grant proposal and the seminar room, a very large part of what every inquirer in every field says in "scientific" debate with colleagues is not backed with certain proof. As Michael Polanyi has shown, in his great book *Personal Knowledge*, no scientist could ever prove scientifically most of the scientific beliefs he or she accepts.[5] In every science, scientists believe most of what they believe about it—all except their own very tiny specialist's domain—without even being able to follow, in detail, the proofs that other specialists would offer. This does not mean that they believe their colleagues on what is called "blind faith." They believe their colleagues because they share more or less reliable warrants for assent of the kind that rhetoricians have always studied. For example, nobody could absolutely disprove any of the wild popular assertions of pseudoscience, the theories of Velikovsky or van Daniken, the experiments of hordes of parapsychologists, the reports of UFO-ologists, and whatnot. Yet all scientists of repute reject these schemes by the dozen, annually, without investigation; life would be intolerable for them if they did *not* reject them *without scientific investigation*, trusting to rhetorical warrants like authority, emotional commitment to "the scientific method," and pure hunch. On the other hand, all scientists accept dozens of new developments annually in fields outside their specialties on grounds that can only be called rhetorical: the strength of personal and communal warrants that have nothing to do with scientific proof. Since such warrants never yield certainty, the people who make these choices sometimes turn out to have been wrong; occasionally a "wild" scheme later establishes itself, and an established truth is overthrown. But most of what we think of as scientific life would simply disappear if such uncertainties led scientists to insist on scientific proofs for every belief on which they act.

Perhaps I can appeal here to your *own* expertise. Simply think of the last article you read in your own field, one not addressed to the general public, and then ask, what proportion of the propositions in it that you accept could *you* yourself prove or disprove according to the standard of proof set by Karl Popper's test of falsifiability.[6] My guess is that the figure will run as low as 5 percent. There is absolutely nothing wrong in that—except when poor education in the intellectual procedures needed for that remaining 95 percent leads people to poor performance with their rhetoric.

I can do even less justice to the fourth kind of sharing—our connections with all cultures, all of humankind. It is perhaps self-evident that rhetoric in some form will be found in all cultures. The capacity to engage in symbolic exchange, the capacity to use statements about the world rather than mere pointing or brute force, is recognized by all anthropological schools as a distinctive feature—perhaps the essential feature—of human cultures. Though what constitutes a good reason, a genuine warrant, will vary considerably from culture to culture, I can be sure in advance of studying any new culture that people in it will have their own way of distinguishing good argument from bad, and that they will recognize a difference between those who are good at finding the right words and those whose words mislead or destroy. I can be equally sure that any chance we have of building understanding among cultures will depend on a rhetoric of discovery. What do we share beneath our surface differences? Let us inquire together, in symbolic exchange. There is no other way except to eliminate differences by forceful domination.

So I must assume, without further argument, that rhetoric is a universally needed and practiced art, if there is any such thing as a universally needed and practiced art, and hurry on to the fifth and most implausible of all my claims today. Most traditional educational systems have sought to study and instill understanding of some kind of ultimate good, some supreme standard against which all of our interests and endeavors can be measured. In America today we can rely on no such standard. Our culture has no publicly acknowledged and universally accepted ultimate standard of that kind. Our question then becomes, Can rhetoric in any sense fill a gap that is left when theology, philosophy, the idea of scientific progress, faith in ultimate political revolution, and all other gods have failed?

To show how it might do so would be a tall order.[7] I can only suggest that when we ask the question, "What warrants for assent are *really* good ones?" we are forced to practice rhetoric-A at the highest possible level—one that indeed we may want another name for: "metarhetoric" or, perhaps better, "rhetorology." We are then asking the kind of question that the Carnegie essay calls for when it asks us to think about the "issues of values that we share in common." We are pushing ourselves to reflect not just on the warrants for assent in particular cases, but on the ultimate ways of grounding assent, the varieties of modes of assenting, modes of warranting. And we are likely here to engage in a good deal of comparison across fields and cultures.

The rhetorologist will be interested not so much in whether Mr. A or Mr. B wins in a particular debate as in the structures of assumption and proof that both share, and in how these structures might differ from the structures found in neighboring disciplines or in the same discipline a decade before or a decade after. You can see immediately that there are a lot of rhetorologists around, traveling under other names. Indeed, in most disciplines these days one finds people who are reopening "settled" questions about what constitutes good warrants for assent in that discipline—they are exploring the ways we think about the ways we think. One sees efforts everywhere to rehabilitate proofs that earlier thinkers tried to reject: "telling a good story" as one form of validation in history; analogy as one form of genuine argument in science; metaphor as inescapable in all inquiry; the persuasive force of a speaker's ethos; appeals to tradition or precedent; even a legitimated and controlled reliance on emotional stirrings.

Even more important than the critical rehabilitation of these warrants rejected by earlier positivisms is the critical probing of basic assumptions within and among the disciplines. Suddenly everyone seems to be aware that human thought does not have to be either strictly deductive or strictly empirical but can be "topical," rhetorical. If you look at any statement that purports to be proof, in any discipline, you find that it relies on "unprovable" assumptions, sometimes stated, often left tacit: assumptions about what makes a fact in that subject, about the purpose of inquiry, about the self-evidency of certain principles and definitions, about the proper methods of moving back and forth between "unquestioned" principles and "undeniable" facts. The work of the rhetorologist is precisely to pursue the comparative worth of different warrants in different persuasive enterprises, and to invent—or if you prefer, discover—improved ways for minds to meet within disciplines and among seemingly different or conflicting disciplines.

To the rhetorician—though not to most other people—it has been clear for more than two thousand years that none of the individual disciplines provides a method for examining the basic assumptions necessary to the practice of that method. The lawyer does not use legal argument to establish the validity of legal argument; to do that requires some kind of political philosophy—either one derived from an established authority or an assumed good, like the divine right of kings, or one discovered in symbolic intercourse among those who choose to think about such matters—that is, by rhetorology. The physicist cannot prove, using the methods of physical science, even that nature exists, or that the proofs of physics are any more than game playing, or that evidence should not be fudged, and so on. Rhetorologists cannot "prove" such matters either, and they welcome what might be called the "Gödel bandwagon," that new growth industry that has convinced even the mathematicians that *ultimate, certain* proofs are not to be had.[8] The rhetorologist has always known what popularizers of Gödel are saying, that "truth" is a larger concept than "proof," that there are many truths that are "uncertifiable." For rhetorology, this has never presented a crisis but simply a challenge to find new topics, new shared places from which any given rhetorical community can move, trusting to various degrees of warranting in the search for livable truths, not certainties.

As I said earlier, most philosophies have hoped to school the vagaries of various rhetorics, to rein in the immensely frisky pony of mankind's free-ranging symbols, by discovering some supreme single substance or method that all could—or should—adhere to; some metaphysics or meta-*some*thing that could determine which first principles are *really* first and then establish the others in relation to them. Many thinkers today still pursue that kind of hope for a supreme monistic view of all knowledge. But I don't have to tell you that they move in many different paths to many different ultimate principles. And as soon as they offer to take us with them to their heights, as soon as they attempt to meet those of us who do not share a self-evident vision of some single ordered truth, they perforce must enter the domains of rhetoric—either the lower forms, attempting to win converts; or rhetorology, attempting to discover common ground between their programs and ours. Thus even those who hold to a faith that someday, somehow, a unified language of all knowledge will be discovered, with a universally accepted supreme substance or concept to validate it, are forced to work here and now in a pluralistic world of differences that are found not just on the surface but very deep, a messy world of dispute, of lines of reasoning that are only probable, not certain, of major questions about which there seem to be not just two sides but many sides.

In that world some people become skeptical and even cynical: If nothing can be finally demonstrated, everything is equally doubtful, and all claims to knowledge are spurious. But the rhetorologist has learned, from practicing the less comprehensive kinds of rhetoric, that to be uncertain is not the same as to be cognitively helpless. Having learned to use symbolic exchange to test the "maybes" in everyday affairs, the rhetorologist is not afraid to use such exchange to test the maybes that we dispute "at the top," as it were. The faith required to do so is not a blind faith, because it is perpetually rewarded with islands of clarity that make human life not only possible but rewarding. It will look like blind faith only to those who insist that there is only one kind of serious inquiry—the pursuit of certainty—and that all the rest is mere guesswork, or mere rhetoric.[9]

## IV

Clearly, I have thrown caution to the winds and allowed my imperialism to run riot. My claim is not of course that those other good things on the Carnegie list should be discarded; in any college curriculum I could respect, all would be pursued vigorously. But I do fear that the Carnegie essay's careful rhetorology, its search for what we share beneath our differences of expression, may become quickly corrupted when it gets into the hands of curriculum committees, corrupted into a list of six or eight required courses. Then, when the committee report is manhandled by the faculty council, the final new plan, to be hailed in the *New York Times* or *Time* magazine as the product of the Carnegie Foundation study, will cut the eight courses to four: one called Freshman English, the rest turned into distribution requirements in history, the social sciences, and the natural sciences. Category six, our shared values, the study of ethics, will simply be dropped, as it almost always is, as too hot to handle.

If we are to forestall that mutilation, we must push ourselves into thinking hard about what specific priorities we share and about how to answer when some Ned Snyder pronounces, "Gentlemen, we are already the best men's college in the country. Why on earth should we change ...?"

When Matthew Arnold was about to go to Oxford, his father, Thomas, wrote to the university to ask whether Aristotle's *Rhetoric* was required study there. "I could not," he said, "consent to send my son to [a] University where he would lose it altogether." Many, perhaps most, of our students "lose it altogether," and I rather doubt that many parents have threatened to withdraw them because of the lack. What they may complain about, these days, is the failure of the college to teach "the basics." Obviously, then, our problem is in one sense quite simple. Just teach the public the truth: namely, that what they mean when they cry "Back to the basics!" is "Back to rhetoric!"

With such an effort at a resounding peroration I dramatize that my program is circular: We must use a corrupted medium to improve that medium. But the circularity does not alarm me, because it need not be vicious. A vicious circle is actually a spiral, moving downward. It is true that rhetoric, especially political rhetoric, does sometimes work like that. But we have all experienced moments when the spiral moves upward, when one party's effort to listen and speak just a little bit better produces a similar response, making it possible to try a bit harder—and on up the spiral to moments of genuine understanding.

# Notes

## Introduction

1. Though unable to do justice to Booth's life and works here, I can at least refer inquiring minds to James Phelan's entry on Wayne C. Booth in the *Dictionary of Literary Biography*, vol. 67, *Modern American Critics since 1955*, ed. Gregory Jay (Detroit: Gale Research Company, 1988), 49–66. Phelan is one of Booth's former students and an exemplary, Booth-inspired scholar of rhetoric and narrative. In particular, Phelan gives excellent accounts of the first four of Booth's major books: *The Rhetoric of Fiction* (Chicago: University of Chicago Press, 1961; 2nd ed., 1983); *A Rhetoric of Irony* (Chicago: University of Chicago Press, 1974); *Modern Dogma and the Rhetoric of Assent* (Chicago: University of Chicago Press, 1974); and *Critical Understanding: The Powers and Limits of Pluralism* (Chicago: University of Chicago Press, 1979). There is also *Rhetoric and Pluralism: Legacies of Wayne Booth*, ed. Frederick J. Antczak, yet another Booth student (Columbus: Ohio State University Press, 1995), with its fifteen essays about or galvanized by Booth's work, its introduction to Booth's life and writings, and, not least, Booth's characteristically insightful (and playful) afterword, sifting the sifters of his thought. That book includes a helpful bibliography on Booth compiled by Lee Artz, including a section entitled "Works about Wayne Booth" that is current through 1995.

2. To mention just two of the more judicious readers of Derrida, see the work of Rodolphe Gasché and Christopher Norris.

3. See Wayne C. Booth, *The Rhetoric of Rhetoric: The Quest for Effective Communication* (Oxford: Blackwell, 2004): "[T]oo few have recognized the way in which the shrewder deconstructionists were actually reviving the necessity of pluralistic rhetorical inquiry: truths are multiple, and most truths are uncovered only by methods available when we give up the quest for absolute certainty.... My anti-deconstructionist colleagues are sure to be annoyed with this defense of Derrida as a heroic rescuer. I can only ask them to re-read Derrida, especially his later works like *The Gift of Death*, and acknowledge how he is probing our rhetoric in a quest for the grounds, however shaky, for our deepest human values" (79).

4. See note 3 above.

5. Jacques Derrida, quoted in Giovanna Borradori, *Philosophy in a Time of Terror: Dialogues with Jürgen Habermas and Jacques Derrida* (Chicago: University of Chicago Press, 2003), 106. For some of the limitations of Booth's willingness to address himself to overt political issues, see Barbara Foley, "Wayne Booth and the Politics of Ethics," in Antczak, *Rhetoric and Pluralism* (see note 1), 135–52, as well as his own concessions to and moderations of her and others' assessments in his afterword in Antczak, *Rhetoric and Pluralism*, 284 and passim, and in his afterword to the second edition of *The Rhetoric of Fiction* (1983).

6. Toril Moi, *What Is a Woman?* (Oxford: Oxford University Press, 1999), esp. chap. 2, "'I Am a Woman': The Personal and the Philosophical."

7. In chapter 7 of this book, in his essay on his teacher and colleague Richard McKeon, Booth writes, "Some have chosen . . . to harmonize [McKeon's] various selves under the general term *rhetorician* or *architectonic rhetorician*. I can understand that, but I fear that the term *rhetoric* has for most current readers misleading connotations; besides, it implies a neglect of the sense in which he was a metaphysician or even theologian: that's why we perhaps need a new term like *rhetorologist*." For a fuller account of the term, see *The Rhetoric of Rhetoric*.

8. Wayne C. Booth, "My Life with Rhetoric: From Neglect to Obsession," in *A Companion to Rhetoric and Rhetorical Criticism*, ed. Walter Jost and Wendy Olmsted (Oxford: Blackwell, 2004), 499.

9. Booth, *Rhetoric of Rhetoric*, xi.

10. Booth, *Rhetoric of Fiction*, 2nd ed., 105.

11. "I am not one of those who loves knowledge for its own sake. . . . [M]y goal is practical: how to improve the practice of controversy by increasing the chances of understanding" (*Critical Understanding*, 341–42); "Most rhetoricians, like me, have elevated political or ethical or social effect [Goodness] over the other two grand values [Truth, Beauty]. . . ." (afterword to Antczak, *Rhetoric and Pluralism*, 283); "Rhetorical study is of *use*, of purposes pursued, targets hit or missed, practices illuminated for the sake not of pure knowledge but of further (and improved) practice" (*Rhetoric of Fiction*, 2nd ed., 441). Booth's position can be usefully compared and contrasted to that of another narrative rhetorician, Peter Brooks, who speaks of the Freudian drive to know, or "epistemophilia," in *Psychoanalysis and Storytelling* (Oxford: Blackwell, 1994) and elsewhere. For such a useful discussion of Brooks, see James Phelan, *Reading People, Reading Plots: Character, Progression, and the Interpretation of Narrative* (Chicago: University of Chicago Press, 1989).

12. Wayne C. Booth, *The Company We Keep: An Ethics of Fiction* (Berkeley and Los Angeles: University of California Press, 1988).

13. Booth, *Rhetoric of Fiction*, 2nd ed., 151. Subsequent references to this book are to the second edition (1983), cited parenthetically in the text. In the afterword, Booth writes, "I think of it now [his own later typologies of implied authors and audiences given in the afterword] as a radically incomplete checklist of rhetorical topics (in the traditional sense of *places*, or perhaps we could call them *openings*)—a list of 'leads' to be explored in thinking about a particular tale, not (as in too many recent similar efforts) a list of entities fixed in some linguistic object or ideal structure" (428).

14. Ibid., 419.

15. Throughout almost all of his works from *Modern Dogma and the Rhetoric of Assent* on, Booth elaborates in new ways George Herbert Mead's (and many others') recognition that, rather than some determinate, preformed entity, the self is, in

Booth's phrase, "a field of selves." In his poem, "Ars Poetica?" the Lithuanian-born poet Czeslaw Milosz gives a memorable image of the kind of thing Booth is pointing to:

> The purpose of poetry is to remind us
> how difficult it is to remain just one person,
> for our house is open, there are no keys in the doors,
> and invisible guests come in and out at will.
> (*New and Collected Poems: 1931–2001* [New York: HarperCollins, 2003], 241)

In other formulations familiar to modernity, or modernism(s), or postmodernism(s), the individual is a "divided self" (Hegel), an "absence-in-presence" (Derrida), whose "unconcealment" is always at the same time and necessarily a "concealment" (Heidegger), a "selection and deflection" (Burke) as well as a "repression" (Freud), an unconscious discourse (Lacan), and so on. In the gap or space between "inside" and "outside" of the concept of the self (indeed, in that "between" belonging to all concepts as such) lies the opportunity for invention, and it is precisely here that Booth has operated from the beginning.

16. Booth, *Modern Dogma*, 126.

17. This might be usefully compared and contrasted to Peter Brooks's metaphor that the relationship between text and reader is that of transference (acting-out within the reading experience) of trauma—itself arguably one further kind of friendship; see Peter Brooks, *Reading for the Plot: Design and Intention in Narrative* (Cambridge, MA: Harvard University Press, 1984), chap. 8, and *Psychoanalysis and Storytelling*. In several of his books Stanley Cavell pursues a similar Freudian metaphor for reading.

18. Again, see Brooks on desire in *Reading for the Plot*.

19. Wayne C. Booth, ed., *The Knowledge Most Worth Having* (Chicago: University of Chicago Press, 1967), and *Now Don't Try to Reason with Me: Essays and Ironies for a Credulous Age* (Chicago: University of Chicago Press, 1970); Wayne C. Booth and Marshall W. Gregory, *The Harper & Row Reader: Liberal Education through Reading and Writing* (New York: Harper & Row, 1984; 2nd ed., 1988), and *The Harper & Row Rhetoric: Writing as Thinking, Thinking as Writing* (New York: Harper & Row, 1987; 2nd ed., 1990); Wayne C. Booth, Gregory G. Colomb, and Joseph M. Williams, *The Craft of Research* (Chicago: University of Chicago Press, 1995); Booth, *Modern Dogma*, and *Critical Understanding*.

20. Moi, *What Is a Woman?* 211; emphasis added. "What we would say when," that is, in facing a given situation, is a formulation framed by J. L. Austin.

21. Booth, *The Company We Keep*, 70–71.

22. Booth, *Critical Understanding*, 220–32.

23. Moi, *What Is a Woman?* 232.

24. Wayne C. Booth, ed., *The Art of Growing Older: Writers on Living and Aging* (Chicago: University of Chicago Press, 1992); *For the Love of It: Amateuring and Its Rivals* (Chicago: University of Chicago Press, 1999); and *The Vocation of a Teacher: Rhetorical Occasions, 1967–1988* (Chicago: University of Chicago Press, 1988).

## Chapter 1

1. This scene illustrates again what I am saying about the importance of Shakespeare's willingness to give himself difficulties that are worth surmounting. Give yourself a man who has no real objections to an act, and then throw somebody at him

to persuade him to that act: the conflict is insignificant, the tension slight, the drama weak. Give yourself an extremely good man and set someone to persuade him to do the most horrible of deeds; inevitably, if you rise to the occasion, you must create a true giant of a rhetorician to accomplish the almost impossible persuasive task: you must create Lady Macbeth.

## Chapter 2

1. Henry James, *The Question of Our Speech: The Lesson of Balzac; Two Lectures* (Boston: Houghton Mifflin, 1905), 63. A fuller quotation can be found in R. W. Chapman's indispensable *Jane Austen: A Critical Bibliography*, 2nd ed. (Oxford: Clarendon Press, 1969). Some important Austen items published too late to be included by Chapman are (1) Ian Watt, *The Rise of the Novel* (Berkeley and Los Angeles: University of California Press, 1957); (2) Stuart M. Tave, review of *Jane Austen: Irony as Defense and Discovery*, by Marvin Mudrick, *Philological Quarterly* 32 (July 1953): 256–57; (3) Andrew H. Wright, *Jane Austen's Novels: A Study in Structure* (London: Chatto & Windus, 1953), 36–82; (4) Christopher Gillie, "*Sense and Sensibility*: An Assessment," *Essays in Criticism* 9 (January 1959): 1–9, esp. 5–6; (5) Edgar P. Shannon Jr., "*Emma*: Character and Construction," *PMLA* 71 (September 1956): 637–50.

2. See, for example, Marvin Mudrick, *Jane Austen: Irony as Defense and Discovery* (Princeton, NJ: Princeton University Press, 1952), 91, 165; Frank O'Connor, *The Mirror in the Roadway* (London: Hamish Hamilton, 1957), 30.

3. As Austen says in the second chapter epigraph, Emma is "a heroine whom no one but myself will much like" (quoted in James Edward Austen-Leigh, *A Memoir of Jane Austen* [London: R. Bentley, 1870; reprint, Oxford: Clarendon, 1926], 157).

4. The best discussion of this problem is Reginald Farrer's "Jane Austen," *Quarterly Review* 228 (July 1917): 1–30; reprinted in William Heath's *Discussions of Jane Austen* (Boston: Heath, 1961). For one critic, the book fails because the problem was never recognized by Jane Austen herself: Mr. E. N. Hayes, in what may well be the least sympathetic discussion of *Emma* yet written, explains the whole book as the *author's* failure to see Emma's faults. "Evidently Jane Austen wished to protect Emma. . . . The author is therefore in the ambiguous position of both loving and scorning the heroine" ("*Emma*: A Dissenting Opinion," *Nineteenth-Century Fiction* 4 [June 1949]: 18, 19).

5. A. C. Bradley, for example, once argued that Jane Austen intended Jane Fairfax to be as interesting throughout as she becomes at the end, but "the moralist in Jane Austen stood for once in her way. The secret engagement is, for her, so serious an offence, that she is afraid to win our hearts for Jane until it has led to great unhappiness" ("Jane Austen," in *Essays and Studies*, vol. 2, by Members of the English Association [Oxford: J. Murray, 1911], 23).

6. I know of only one full-scale attempt to deal with the tension between sympathy and judgment in modern literature, Robert Langbaum's *The Poetry of Experience* (New York: Random House, 1957). Langbaum argues that in the dramatic monologue, with which he is primarily concerned, the sympathy engendered by the direct portrayal of internal experience leads the reader to suspend his moral judgment. Thus, in reading Browning's portraits of moral degeneration—for example, the duke in "My Last Duchess" or the monk in "Soliloquy of a Spanish Cloister"—our moral judgment is overwhelmed "because we prefer to participate in the duke's power and freedom, in his hard core of character fiercely loyal to itself. Moral judgment is in fact important as the thing to be suspended, as a measure of the price we pay for

the privilege of appreciating to the full this extraordinary man" (83). While I think that Langbaum seriously underplays the extent to which moral judgment remains even after psychological vividness has done its work, and while he perhaps defines "morality" too narrowly when he excludes from it such things as power and freedom and fierce loyalty to one's own character, his book is a stimulating introduction to the problems raised by internal portraiture of flawed characters.

7. Mary Lascelles, *Jane Austen and Her Art* (Oxford: Oxford University Press, 1939), 204.

8. It seems to be difficult for some modern critics, accustomed to ferreting values out from an impersonal or ironic context without the aid of the author's voice, to make use of reliable commentary like this when it is provided. Even a highly perceptive reader like Mark Schorer, for example, finds himself doing unnecessary acrobatics with the question of style, and particularly of metaphor, as clues to the norms against which the author judges her characters. In reading *Persuasion*, he finds these clues among the metaphors "from commerce and property, the counting house and the inherited estate" with which it abounds ("Fiction and the Matrix of Analogy," *Kenyon Review* [autumn 1949]: 540). No one would deny that the novel is packed with such metaphors, although Schorer is somewhat overingenuous in marshaling to his cause certain dead metaphors that Austen could not have avoided without awkward circumlocution (see esp. p. 542). But the crucial question surely is this: What precisely are these metaphors of the countinghouse doing in the novel? Whose values are they supposed to reveal? Accustomed to reading modern fiction in which the novelist very likely provides no direct assistance in answering this question, Schorer leaves it really unanswered; at times he seems almost to imply that Jane Austen is unconsciously giving herself away in her use of them (e.g., p. 543).

But the novel is really very clear about it all. The introduction, coming directly from the wholly reliable narrator, established unequivocally and without "analogy" the conflict between the world of the Elliots, depending for its values on selfishness, stupidity, and pride—and the world of Anne, a world where "elegance of mind and sweetness of character" are the supreme values. The commercial values stressed by Schorer are only a selection from what is actually a rich group of evils. And Anne's own expressed views again and again provide direct guidance to the reader.

9. The first two quotations are from Edmund Wilson's "A Long Talk about Jane Austen," in *A Literary Chronicle: 1920–1950* (Garden City, NY: Doubleday, 1956). The third is from Mudrick, *Jane Austen*, 206.

10. It has lately been fashionable to underplay the value of tenderness and good will in Jane Austen, in reaction to an earlier generation that overdid the picture of "gentle Jane." The trend seems to have begun in earnest with D. W. Harding's "Regulated Hatred: An Aspect of the Work of Jane Austen," *Scrutiny* 8 (March 1940): 346–62. While I do not feel as strongly aroused against this school of readers as does R. W. Chapman (see his *Critical Bibliography*, 52, and his review of Mudrick's work in the *TLS* [*Times Literary Supplement*, September 19, 1952]), it seems to me that another swing of the pendulum is called for: when Jane Austen praises the "relenting heart," she means that praise, though she is the same author who can lash the unrelenting heart with "regulated hatred."

11. Edd Winfield Parks, "Exegesis in Austen's Novels," *South Atlantic Quarterly* 51 (January 1952): 117.

12. Katherine Mansfield, *Novels and Novelists*, ed. J. Middleton Murry (New York: A. Knopf, 1930), 304.

## Chapter 3

1. [*From my present perspective, this sentence is nonsense. Almost everything one writes can be considered rhetorical—in the sense of "hoping to produce some effect on a fellow creature." (Throughout the essays in this volume, bracketed comments in italic type are my current—2004—interpolations. Bracketed material in roman type appeared in the original essay.)*]

2. [*Why was he reluctant? Well, because he was aware of how many readers would take the word* rhetoric *in a pejorative sense.*]

3. [*Re-reading in 2004, I must intrude my sense of how much harm is now result-ing from the emphasis on standardized tests. When the challenge of rhetorical binding is ignored, the* point *of education gets lost, along with the fun of it.*]

4. [*Here again I cringe at the sexism. But—to repeat—I think it important not to pretend that "back then" I had any problem with masculine discourse.*]

## Chapter 4

1. Critical comments by two of my friends have made me think that this claim is not only difficult to prove but quite probably mistaken. Mr. Ronald Crane suggests that it reflects plain ignorance of just how low controversy sank in previous centuries. "Have you read the attacks on Bentley?" Mr. Laurence Lerner reminds me of the stan-dards, if they can be called that, of political controversy in the seventeenth century. And I remind myself, now, of what public debate could be like in nineteenth-century England and America.

Clearly the sweeping historical claims that run throughout this first section of my talk are in no way demonstrated by my examples. They might, in fact, be taken as illustrations of the very thing I am claiming to oppose: the use of mere assertion (the more extreme the better) in place of careful argument. Fortunately, my argument that we need more and better rhetorical theorizing does not depend on the extreme claim that we are the *most* rhetorical age: it is enough that our lives are permeated by rhetoric, good or bad, and nobody doubts that.

I still suspect, *pace* Mr. Crane, that we are *quantitatively* the most rhetorical age in history—and not only in the undeniable sense that more men are living by rhetoric than ever before. Surely the *proportion* of rhetorical activities to nonrhetorical (like plowing, shearing, or building) is higher now than ever before. But this modified claim, a radical retreat from my original assertions, may be unimportant, and it is certainly one that would be hard to prove (Crane might intrude again: "Can you think of any previous age with as much pure science or pure music? These two areas are less rhetorical than ever before").

2. [*Clear back in 1936, I. A. Richards labored to revive rhetoric, in the good sense, by defining it as "the art of removing misunderstanding"* (The Philosophy of Rhetoric, *long out of print but recently reprinted, edited by John Constable [London: Routledge, 2001]).*]

## Chapter 5

1. John Middleton Murry, "Metaphor," in *John Clare and Other Studies* (1927; reprint, London and New York: P. Nevill, 1950), 85–97. Reprinted in Warren Shibles, comp., *Essays on Metaphor* (Whitewater, WI: Language Press, 1972), 27.

2. For evidence, see the table of contents of Sack's *On Metaphor* or leaf through Shibles's immense compendium *Metaphor: An Annotated Bibliography and History* (Whitewater, WI: Language Press, 1971).

3. See, for example, Demetrius, *On Style*: "When the metaphor seems daring, let it for greater security be converted into a simile. . . . [By adding 'like'] we obtain a simile and a less risky expression."

4. H. W. Fowler, *The King's English*, 3rd ed. (Oxford: Oxford University Press, 1931), 218.

5. Norman Mailer, *The Armies of the Night* (New York: New American Library, 1968), 320.

6. My colleague Ted Cohen has shown me an emphatic restatement by E. L. Doctorow of this claim that metaphorists are the unacknowledged legislators of the world: "And I am led to an even more pugnacious view—that the development of civilizations is essentially a progression of metaphors" ("False Documents," *American Review* 26 [1977]: 231–32).

7. I have argued this point many times elsewhere. Otherwise, see also Alan Donagan's *The Theory of Morality* (Chicago: University of Chicago Press, 1977). I think it is fair to say that most professional philosophers in 1978, in contrast with the world of, say, 1958, would claim that to repudiate ethical argument as necessarily irrational is to contradict reason.

8. Stephen Pepper, *World Hypotheses: A Study in Evidence* (Berkeley and Los Angeles: University of California Press, 1942). In *Concept and Quality: A World Hypothesis* (Lasalle, IL: Open Court, 1966), Pepper suggests that "the purposive act" is a fifth root metaphor.

9. See my "M. H. Abrams: Historian as Critic, Critic as Pluralist," *Critical Inquiry* 2 (spring 1976): 411–45. In Abrams's other great work of "metaphoric criticism," *The Mirror and the Lamp: Romantic Theory and the Critical Tradition* (New York: W. W. Norton, 1953), he engages in very little explicit judging of metaphors as he marshals diverse historical descriptions of poets as mirrors, fountains, instruments, makers of objects, teachers, lamps, and whatnot. He lets history do the judging for him as the useful, enduring metaphors are brought forth in quotation from those whose lives were energized by thinking through or with them. Another excellent example of criticism disguised as history is Arthur Lovejoy's *The Great Chain of Being* (Cambridge, MA: Harvard University Press, 1933). The power of a metaphor like the "great chain" to survive Lovejoy's sustained historical scrutiny does not, in our usual way of thinking, say anything about its truth. But once we begin to take seriously the task of criticizing metaphor, we must reopen the question of whether the metaphors that have recently replaced God's plenum—mechanistic evolution, for example—have not sacrificed a good deal of general truth for what they have gained in local validity.

10. Marshall Sahlins, *Culture and Practical Reason* (Chicago: University of Chicago Press, 1976).

## Chapter 7

1. I am indebted to Eugene Garver and Richard Buchanan for critical suggestions incorporated here.

2. I later learned that many an ordinary-language and analytical philosopher had been attacking these proofs more solemnly, even insisting that Plato was really not

worth bothering about. The current scene tends to overlook, or even to forgive, the absurd reductionisms of many mid-century philosophers.

3. For some of his students, the punches were destructive, and for some, like the angry Robert Pirsig who attacked McKeon as "The Professor" in *Zen and the Art of Motorcycle Maintenance*, the destruction was felt as deliberate. My own view is that McKeon never intended to destroy the arguer, only the fallacious argument or reading. His profound probing did, however, produce some personal tragedies.

4. See *Selections from Medieval Philosophers*, ed. and trans. (with introductory notes by) Richard McKeon, 2 vols. (New York: Scribner's, 1929-1930), 1:142-84.

5. He "covers" these three dimensions of his career—the scholarly philosopher, the educator, and the pursuer of international justice and understanding—in his essay entitled "Spiritual Autobiography," in *"Freedom and History" and Other Essays*, ed. Zahava McKeon (Chicago: University of Chicago Press, 1990), 3-36.

It is hard sometimes to avoid a sense of gloom as one thinks about the fate of McKeon's three grand projects. His philosophical work is still largely ignored, in spite of many who share my sense that he was their strongest intellectual influence. His educational project, both for graduate and undergraduate education, is in most institutions and minds fragmented beyond recognition, both at home and abroad. His visions for UNESCO and for the world political dialogue seem even more hopeless than they could have seemed in his own time. So what do we gain by attempting to keep "him" alive? We keep those hopes alive, in a world that has always made such hopes questionable.

6. George Kimball Plochmann, *Richard McKeon: A Study* (Chicago: University of Chicago Press, 1990), 57-59. For a variety of charts illustrating his own search for a comprehensive view, see Richard McKeon, *On Knowing: The Natural Sciences*, ed. David Owen and Zahava McKeon (Chicago: University of Chicago Press, 1994), especially the list on pp. ix-x. For his posthumous—much more complicated chart—see *Selected Writings of Richard McKeon*, vol. 1, *Philosophy, Science, and Culture*, ed. Zahava McKeon and William Swenson (Chicago: University of Chicago Press, 1998), 218.

7. Plochmann, *Richard McKeon*, 93.

8. There does seem to be some agreement among many that "operationalist" or "rhetorician" is the best single label. My original intention for this essay was to explore how McKeon-the-rhetorical-theorist jibed or clashed with McKeon-the-rhetorician and McKeon-the-universalist. But as Kenneth Burke has God say, in the wonderful dialogue with Satan at the end of *The Rhetoric of Religion: Studies in Logology* (Boston: Beacon Press, 1961), "It's more complicated than that."

9. Plochmann, *Richard McKeon*, 91.

10. For McKeon, a favorite "monist" target was Rudolf Carnap, with his pursuit of a unified language of all the sciences. I think today he would have fun exhibiting the flaws in E. O. Wilson's recent totalizing effort in *Consilience: The Unity of Knowledge* (New York: Knopf/Random House, 1998).

11. Richard Rorty, *Contingency, Irony, and Solidarity* (New York: Cambridge University Press, 1989).

12. For a full development of the "reciprocal" relations of philosophies—in the McKeon view—both their inevitable capacity to refute one another, each of them claiming fundamental priority in a different way, and their inescapable dependence on one another, see Walter Watson's excellent account in *The Architectonics of Meaning* (Albany, NY: SUNY Press, 1985; 2nd ed., Chicago: University of Chicago Press, 1993).

13. His accounts, in "Spiritual Autobiography" (see note 5 above) of his youthful arrogance about ultimate mastery are amusing: "The three chief ingredients of which it [my youthful "system"] was composed were a scientific basis in behaviorism, . . . a normative criterion in pragmatism, . . . and a symbolic system. . . . It was a highly satisfactory philosophy, because it could be applied to a succession of subject matters and problems with little need for adjustment and with only a minimum of knowledge of the particular subject matter to which it was to be accommodated. I have never since been able to achieve comparable scope of system or convenience of method" (7).

14. Of course it remains true, as revealed later here, that McKeon's pluralism is itself a kind of "system" that claims to refute at least the exclusivist claims of each philosopher he admires and thus could be accused of being a very special version of "bias."

15. G. E. Moore, *The Philosophy of G. E. Moore*, ed. Paul Arthur Schilpp (New York: Tudor, 1952), 676.

16. Alan D. Sokal, "Transgressing the Boundaries: Toward a Transformative Hermeneutics of Quantum Gravity," *Social Text* (spring/summer 1996): 338–46.

17. Ibid., introduction. The great historian Arnoldo Momigliano once met with a group of us professors who had been influenced by McKeon—long before "postmodernism"—and there was a terrific and unresolved battle with him over our assertion that even historical and scientific facts are "constructed": "real" enough—some of them at least—but always depending, in our formulations of them, on the McKeonite fourfold scheme: our first principles (whether comprehensive, reflexive, simple, or actional); our methods (whether dialectical, operational, logistic, or problematic); our interpretations (whether ontological, entitative, existentialist, or essentialist); and our selections (whether of hierarchies, of matters, of types, or of kinds). We could hardly provide in two hours a "McKeon-education" for that highly learned traditionalist, Momigliano, and he left seeming to feel—as many who read Derrida leave feeling—that the rational store has been sold to the barbarians. (As I think of it now, I wonder whether we really listened honestly to his arguments, even as he failed to grasp ours.)

18. From Richard McKeon, "World Community and the Relations of Cultures," in *Perspectives on a Troubled Decade: Science, Philosophy, and Religion, 1939–1949*, tenth symposium, ed. Lyman Bryson, Louis Finkelstein, and R. M. MacIver (New York: Harper and Bros., 1950), 801–5.

19. Were there serious violations of the four? That's hard to determine. We can assume so—he was a human being. There were certainly violations of value placements that others would insist on—such as mercy-over-justice, or toleration-over-truth. But were they violations of his own code? It's a complicated and unanswerable question—at least until some probing biographer studies his entire life. Here we pursue mostly the "publishing" McKeon.

20. You'll search in vain in his works for favorable references to Nietzsche as a real philosopher. Descartes fares somewhat better. He was embraced by the young McKeon seeking full certainty and mastery ("Spiritual Autobiography," 8); later, as the product of his placement in history and culture, Descartes nicely exemplifies "the logistic method with reflexive principles and existentialist interpretation" (Richard McKeon, "Philosophic Semantics and Philosophic Inquiry," in *"Freedom and History,"* 254).

21. Richard McKeon, "A Philosopher Meditates on Discovery," in *Selected Writings*, 1:44–60; emphasis added.

22. Richard McKeon, "Dialogue and Controversy in Philosophy," in *Entretiens philosophiques d'Athène* (Athens: Institut international de philosophie, 1955), 161–78.

23. McKeon, "Spiritual Autobiography," 14–25.

24. Ibid., 20.

25. See especially the conclusion of McKeon's "Philosophy and the Diversity of Cultures," *Ethics* 60 (1950): 233–60. For a much celebrated current effort to grapple with similar problems raised by the "hybridity" of cultures, and what would-be thinkers can do about it, see Homi Bhabha, *The Location of Culture* (London: Routledge, 1994). I wish that I could wave a magic wand and produce a dialogue between McKeonites and Homi Bhabha and other "postcolonial discourse" scholars. They would be surprised by the great overlap, and they could learn from one another.

26. McKeon, "World Community," 810.

27. Richard McKeon, "Philosophy and Freedom in the City of Man," *Ethics* 59, no. 3 (April 1949): 161.

28. See my "Individualism and the Mystery of the Social Self; or, Does Amnesty Have a Leg to Stand On?" in *Freedom and Interpretation: The Oxford Amnesty Lectures, 1992,* ed. Barbara Johnson (New York: Basic Books, HarperCollins, 1993), 69–102.

29. Perhaps the clearest account of this history is that given in McKeon's "A Philosopher Meditates on Discovery." See also his "Philosophy and Method," *Journal of Philosophy* 48 (1951): 653–82. If he were writing in the late 1990s, I'm pretty sure he would note—along with all other postmodernists—that we are at a new turn, with struggles about where the turn from language-as-center should go: back toward "pragmatics" and "action" or even "further back" to "substance" or even nature itself.

30. McKeon, "A Philosopher Meditates on Discovery," 220.

31. Aristotle, *Politics*, bk. 1, chaps. 4–5. A cogent argument that Aristotle's explanation of slavery cannot easily be excised from his full philosophical position can be found in Eugene Garver, "Aristotle's Natural Slaves: Incomplete *Praxeis* and Incomplete Human Beings," *Journal of the History of Philosophy* 32 (1994): 1–22.

32. Of several recent works reviving interest in casuistry, the only ones I've read with real profit are Albert Jonsen and Stephen Toulmin's *The Abuse of Casuistry: A History of Moral Reasoning* (Berkeley and Los Angeles: University of California Press, 1988), and James Chandler's *England in 1819: The Politics of Literary Culture and the Case of Romantic Historicism* (Chicago: University of Chicago Press, 1998), esp. 39–41 and chaps. 3, 4, and 9.

33. Except perhaps for one: "Thou shalt always try to adjust your universally valid values to the case at hand."

34. McKeon, "Spiritual Autobiography," 35–36.

35. See McKeon, *Selections from Medieval Philosophers*, especially (from my perspective) the accounts of Augustine, Anselm, Abailard, and Aquinas.

## Chapter 8

1. Northrop Frye, *The Educated Imagination* (Bloomington: Indiana University Press, 1964), 55.

2. Mikhail Bakhtin, *Problems of Dostoevsky's Poetics*, ed. and trans. Caryl Emerson, with an introduction by Wayne C. Booth (Minneapolis: University of Minnesota Press, 1984), 56–57. This work is subsequently cited by page number in parentheses in the text.

3. See especially *The Dialogic Imagination: Four Essays by M. M. Bakhtin*, ed. Michael Holquist, trans. Caryl Emerson and Michael Holquist (Austin: University of Texas Press, 1981).

## Chapter 9

1. William Ellery Channing, *Self-Culture* (Boston: Dutton and Wentworth, 1838), 40.

2. For what in my view is the best celebration of friendship as a life-goal, see book 8 of Aristotle's *Nicomachean Ethics*.

3. I assume here the distinction that I made originally in *The Rhetoric of Fiction* (Chicago: University of Chicago Press, 1961) and elaborated recently in *Critical Understanding: The Powers and Limits of Pluralism* (Chicago: University of Chicago Press, 1979), chap. 7. For now, the important point is that we are here putting to one side all questions about the flesh-and-blood author in order to attend to the author implied by the total acts of telling *this* story in *this* way. In a work in progress on ethical criticism from which this present article is extracted, I have been forced into a more complicated analysis of various "authors" and "readers" than is necessary at this point.

4. The metaphor of "friendship with implied authors" is, as I have already suggested, only one of several that could profitably be pursued once we agree to think of texts as persons. We might ask, for example, how the books coming our way qualify as *gifts*, friendly or unfriendly, ritualized or spontaneous, loaded with obligation or free. A whole ethics of fiction might be built entirely on the beautiful "theory of gifts" that Lewis Hyde developed earlier in this journal ["Some Food We Could Not Eat: Gift Exchange and the Imagination," *Kenyon Review* (fall 1979)].

5. It also throws us into the immense problem of the "authority" of the author. I discuss the authority of five different "authors"—all of them discoverable in every work, if we look hard enough—in chapter 7 of *Critical Understanding*. For the fullest account of how moral beliefs can serve as the basis of fictional form, see Sheldon Sacks, *Fiction and the Shape of Belief: A Study of Henry Fielding with Glances at Swift, Johnson, and Richardson* (1964; reprint, Chicago: University of Chicago Press, 1980). See also *The Rhetoric of Fiction*, chap. 5.

## Chapter 10

1. The responses varied from the most perceptive and sympathetic, by Thomas M. Conley, in "Booth's *Company* and the Rhetoric We Keep," *Rhetorica* 8, no. 2 (spring 1990): 161–74, to one of the least sympathetic, by Joseph Epstein, "Educated by Novels," *Commentary* (August 1989): 36–38.

2. See Wayne C. Booth, *The Company We Keep: An Ethics of Fiction* (Berkeley and Los Angeles: University of California Press, 1988), 28 n. 3, for a brief summary of some attempt to question a dogma that, as Hilary Putnam says, prefacing his own refutation, has become a "cultural institution," a "received answer" that will continue to live despite cogent underminings (*Reason, Truth and History* [Cambridge: Cambridge University Press, 1981], 127). See also, for a more recent further disproof of the dogma, Charles Taylor, *Sources of the Self* (Cambridge and Cambridge, MA: Cambridge University Press and Harvard University Press, 1989), 53–62.

3. And indeed it was attacked: "This [book] is a bloated monument to the bankrupt tradition of critical humanism," wrote one "DTO" in the *Journal of Modern Literature* 16 (1990), after making clear that the whole book was invalidated by

one major fault: I failed to "engage in any systematic substantial debate" with Paul de Man.

4. Martin Green, "Recantations and Equivocations," *Commonweal*, February 10, 1989.

5. The best of these by far is Barbara Foley's "Wayne Booth and the Politics of Ethics," in *Rhetoric and Pluralism: Legacies of Wayne Booth*, ed. Frederick J. Antczak (Columbus: Ohio State University Press, 1995).

6. Mark A. R. Facknitz, *The Ethics of Fiction*, University of Hartford Studies in Literature 21 (Hartford, CT: University of Hartford Press, 1989).

7. One or two reviewers expressed a full-fledged, self-confident, uncompromising aestheticist denunciation: "Both for literature's and morality's sake, it is probably better to separate the two the way Wallace Stevens supposedly did in his, possibly apocryphal, remark: 'Ezra Pound deserves a Nobel prize for his poems, and to be hanged for his politics'" (Carl Rudbeck, in *Svenska Dagbladet*, May 7, 1989; trans. Blaine H. Boogert).

8. For example, see Hazard Adams, "The Dizziness of Freedom: Or, Why I Read William Blake," *College English* 48 (September 1986): 431–43; George Anastaplo, *The Artist as Thinker: From Shakespeare to Joyce* (Athens, OH: Swallow Press, 1983); Max Apple et al., "A Writers' Forum on Moral Fiction," *Fiction International* 12 (1980): 5–25; Warner Berthoff, *Literature and the Continuances of Virtue* (Princeton, NJ: Princeton University Press, 1986); Christopher Clausen, *The Moral Imagination: Essays on Literature and Ethics* (Iowa City: University of Iowa Press, 1986); and—skipping down through the alphabet—"Literature and/as Moral Philosophy," special issue, *New Literary History* 15 (autumn 1983); J. Hillis Miller Jr., *The Ethics of Reading: Kant, de Man, Eliot, Trollope, James, and Benjamin* (New York: Columbia University Press, 1986); Irving Massey, *Find You the Virtue: Ethics, Image, and Desire in Literature* (Fairfax, VA: George Mason University Press, 1987)—I resist the impulse to go on.

9. See, for example, Tobin Siebers, *The Ethics of Criticism* (Ithaca, NY: Cornell University Press, 1988); J. Hillis Miller, *Versions of Pygmalion* (Cambridge, MA: Harvard University Press, 1990); Robert Coles, *The Call of Stories: Teaching and the Moral Imagination* (Boston, MA: Houghton Mifflin, 1989).

10. Stephen Pepper, *World Hypotheses: A Study in Evidence* (Berkeley and Los Angeles: University of California Press, 1942).

11. The dangers of dealing in great lumps can be seen in Allan Bloom's effort, in *The Closing of the American Mind* (New York: Simon and Schuster, 1987), to describe the ethical disasters caused by rock music (68–81). He is entirely justified in reviving Plato's claim that different musical modes have different potential powers to move the soul. But when he lumps all rock together, he simply denies what is obvious to all aficionados: some rock poisons the soul; some rock elevates it. It is a pity that Bloom's lumping will drive most devotees of music away from a kind of improved "Platonic" musical criticism that we need.

12. Our sense of the craftsman's skill, of course, can also be considered under ethical categories: conscientiousness, free creativity, and so on. See *The Company We Keep*, chap. 4, and my "*Poetics* for a Practical Critic," in *Essays on Aristotle's "Poetics,"* ed. Amélie Oksenberg Rorty (Princeton, NJ: Princeton University Press 1992).

13. In fact many philosophers of science are now acknowledging that the old dichotomies between self and other, subjective and objective, value-based and fact-based, always did great injustice to the actual ways in which even the "hardest"

scientists think. And specialists in given "scientific" fields are recognizing that the ways in which scientists in fact convince one another of new scientific truth simply do not fit these old dichotomies. See, as a representative attack, Donald McCloskey, *The Rhetoric of Economics* (Madison: University of Wisconsin Press, 1985).

14. Anthony Adler, "Vanity, Vulgarity, and Vapidity at Steppenwolf Theatre," *Chicago*, September 1990, 91–93.

15. See Stuart M. Sperry's review in *Modern Fiction Studies* 35 (winter 1989): 846.

16. Conley, "Booth's *Company* and the Rhetoric We Keep"; subsequent citations are given parenthetically in the text. See also Thomas M. Conley, *Rhetoric in the European Tradition* (London: Longman, 1990), the most penetrating one-volume history we have of major rhetorical theorists.

17. This claim is empirically verifiable by anyone who will ask friends to think of "some book that has changed my life." See Booth, *The Company We Keep*, 278–79.

18. See, for one of the best of these, John Dewey, *The Quest for Certainty: A Study of the Relation of Knowledge and Action* (New York: Minton, Batch, 1929).

19. The two philosophers who have most fully articulated such a possibility are Stephen Pepper, in *World Hypotheses* and later works, and Richard McKeon—see his *"Freedom and History" and Other Essays: An Introduction to the Thought of Richard McKeon*, ed. Zahava K. McKeon, with an introduction by Howard Ruttenberg (Chicago: University of Chicago Press, 1990). For a systematic exposition and development of McKeon's views, see Walter Watson, *The Architectonics of Meaning: Foundations of the New Pluralism* (Albany, NY: SUNY Press, 1985; 2nd ed., Chicago: University of Chicago Press, 1993).

## Chapter 11

1. [*Henry James*, The Wings of the Dove *(1902; reprint, ed. J. Donald Crowley and Richard A. Hocks, New York: W. W. Norton, 1978). I refer to the Norton edition by page number only (when appropriate); otherwise, I cite James's divisions of the novel by book and section numbers, along with the Norton page number as necessary. Subsequent citations are given parenthetically in the text, with the Norton edition identified for clarity in citations of page numbers alone (e.g., Norton, 458; otherwise, bk. 10, sec. 1, 323). I have not cited the volume numbers of the novel because the book numbers run consecutively across the two volumes.*] Many readers have found *The Wings of the Dove* exasperatingly difficult. In this matter, though not in his rather lukewarm final evaluation, William James speaks for us all when he says, in a letter to Henry in the autumn of 1902, that he had to read "many pages, and innumerable sentences twice over to see what the dickens they could possibly mean" (Norton, 458). I myself must have encountered fifty moments when I had to stop, puzzled, and then choose for some pronoun the most likely antecedent.

2. My pages here could be filled with quotations about "making use of" versus "living with." Milly's story is in large part her gradual discovery of how Kate Croy, Merton Densher, Lord Mark, and Mrs. Lowder would use her. As she begins, for example, to experience the lionizing of the clever but vulgar socialite, Mrs. Lowder, "it came up for Milly that Aunt Maud [Mrs. Lowder] had something particular in mind. . . . Mrs. Lowder made use of the moment: Milly felt as soon as she had spoken that what she was doing was somehow for use" (Norton, 161).

3. In James's works it's not easy to say which is worse, reducing people to objets d'art, as Gilbert Osmond in *The Portrait of a Lady* uses the wonderful Isabel, finding her "as smooth to his general need of her as handled ivory to the palm," or exploiting

others for financial gain, as Kate and Densher use Milly here. I wonder whether my "use" of this novel would be more blameworthy, for James, if I were being paid a fortune for it. If the payment entailed my saying what I knew would harm someone, I would become one of his worst villains.

4. Gérard Genette, *Narrative Discourse: An Essay in Method*, trans. Jane Levin (Ithaca, NY: Cornell University Press, 1972).

5. Martha G. Nussbaum, "Flawed Crystals: James's *The Golden Bowl* and Literature as Moral Philosophy," in *Love's Knowledge* (New York: Oxford University Press, 1990).

6. [*In the previously published essay, this summary was reserved for the appendix.*]

7. James Phelan, *Reading People, Reading Plots: Character, Progression, and the Interpretation of Narrative* (Chicago: University of Chicago Press, 1989).

8. Wayne C. Booth, *The Company We Keep: An Ethics of Fiction* (Berkeley and Los Angeles: University of California Press, 1988).

9. In chapter 4 of *The Company We Keep* I present a detailed case for the inescapable potential powers of works themselves. In practice not even the most aggressive theorist denies those powers, just as I of course do not deny that a novel's powers will fail with readers not prepared to discover them.

10. See Peter J. Rabinowitz, "Truth in Fiction: A Re-examination of Audiences," *Critical Inquiry* 4 (1977): 121–41, and "Against Close Reading," in *Pedagogy as Politics: Literary Theory and Critical Teaching*, ed. Maria-Regina Kecht (Urbana: University of Illinois Press, 1992); as well as Janice Radway, *Reading the Romance: Women, Patriarchy, and Popular Literature* (Chapel Hill: University of North Carolina Press, 1984). The qualities and dangerous powers of popular fiction, when millions in a given culture "read-with" it, are explored by Claudia Roth Pierpont, in "A Study in Scarlett" (*New Yorker*, August 31, 1992, 87–103). Her chief subject is *Gone with the Wind*, but she helps explain why other blockbusters—*Uncle Tom's Cabin* and *Ivanhoe*, for example, get themselves "read-with" by so many, while yet others, aimed equally at a popular market, fail.

11. By far the most devoted and persuasive reading of this kind (re-reading for structure) I've encountered, addressed to one novel alone, is Gérard Genette's tracing of Proust's maneuverings, in *Narrative Discourse*. To me it is unfortunate that Genette for the most part protects himself from the task of direct evaluation, but implicit in his loving attention is one grand judgment: *Remembrance of Things Past* [*In Search of Lost Time*] is a great achievement. Even though his kind of detailed tracing is not today in the forefront of criticism, a fair number of "narratologists" are practicing the sympathetic attention to structural choices that it requires. I find even more interesting a variety of efforts to combine ideological interests—Marxist, Freudian, feminist, ethical—with the closest possible attention to authors' achieved forms; in other words, these studies have combined reading-with and reading-against without destroying the works considered. I document several of these—Barbara Foley's, James Phelan's, Peter Rabinowitz's, David Richter's—in the notes (esp. nn. 15 and 29) to my "*Poetics* for a Practical Critic," in *Essays on Aristotle's "Poetics,"* ed. Amélie Oksenberg Rorty (Princeton, NJ: Princeton University Press, 1992), 387–409. But others are emerging, especially Mary Doyle Springer's work on the "feminist" prophecies of Wallace Stevens (in a book forthcoming); see also her "Closure in James: A Formalist Feminist View," in *A Companion to Henry James Studies*, ed. Daniel Mark Fogel (Westport, CT: Greenwood Press, 1993), 265–82. Another group of scholars is moving from what might be called the opposite side: starting with ideological questions and finding them best answered

by close reading. The most impressive volume I've found pursuing this direction, published since completing this essay, is *Famous Last Words: Changes in Gender and Narrative Closure*, ed. Alison Booth (Charlottesville: University Press of Virginia, 1993). All of the "feminist" essays Booth commissioned attend closely to intended forms, most of them in ways that might well have impressed James. The one most relevant here, however, is Stephen D. Arata, "Object Lessons: Reading the Museum in *The Golden Bowl*," 199–229. Many of Arata's points about the ethical effects of reading that great book could be incorporated here. But of course he does not mention the ethical effects on him of pursuing his critical task, or on us of reading the results.

12. A first-class introduction to the conflicts between the ethical demands of given genres and the ethical interests of implied authors is given by Peter Rabinowitz in "'Reader, I blew him away': Convention and Transgression in Sue Grafton," in Booth, *Famous Last Words*.

13. [*Now (in 2004), having just re-read and lectured on* Emma, *I have to add it to the "Henry James" list: it is a novel whose structure can only be fully understood when read twice.*]

14. All quotations here are from Henry James, *The Complete Notebooks of Henry James*, ed. Leon Edel and Lyall H. Powers (New York: Oxford University Press, 1987), 102–7, 114–16. This first quotation is from the entry for November 3, 1894. The work is subsequently cited in the text by date of entry.

15. Henry James, "The Younger Generation," quoted in *Henry James and H. G. Wells: A Record of Their Friendship, Their Debate on the Art of Fiction, and Their Quarrel*, ed. Leon Edel and Gordon N. Ray (Urbana: University of Illinois Press, 1958), 190–92. An excellent brief defense of James's silence in the palazzo scene is given by Mary Doyle Springer in *A Rhetoric of Literary Character: Some Women of Henry James* (Chicago: University of Chicago Press, 1978), 162–63, 165–66.

## Chapter 12

1. Dinesh D'Souza, *Illiberal Education: The Politics of Sex and Race on Campus* (New York: Free Press, 1991); Gertrude Himmelfarb, *The De-Moralization of Society: From Victorian Virtues to Modern Values* (New York: Alfred Knopf, 1995).

2. Jacques Derrida, "Beyond: Giving for the Taking, Teaching and Learning to Give, Death," in *The Gift of Death*, trans. David Wills (Chicago: University of Chicago Press, 1995), 35–52.

3. Lee Ann Carroll, "Pomo Blues: Stories from First-Year Composition," *College English* 59, no. 8 (December 1997): 916–33.

4. Elizabeth Anne Leonard, "Assignment #9—A Text Which Engages the Socially Constructed Identity of Its Writer," *CCC* 48, no. 2 (May 1997): 215–30; hereafter cited by page number parenthetically in the text.

5. Aristotle, *Nicomachean Ethics* (innumerable editions). For his treatment of *habit* (what he sometimes labels *ethos*), see especially book 2.

6. Alasdair MacIntyre, *After Virtue* (Notre Dame, IN: University of Notre Dame Press, 1984); Charles Taylor, *Sources of the Self: The Making of the Modern Identity* (Cambridge, MA: Harvard University Press, 1989).

7. William Bennett, *The Book of Virtues* (New York: Simon and Schuster, 1993).

8. For a good introduction to casuistry, see Albert R. Jonsen and Stephen Toulmin, *The Abuse of Casuistry: A History of Moral Reasoning* (Berkeley and Los Angeles: University of California Press, 1988); for a deeper probing, with special reference to the

romantic period, see James Chandler, *England in 1819: The Politics of Literary Culture and the Case of Romantic Historicism* (Chicago: University of Chicago Press, 1998).

9. John Dewey, *Democracy and Education: An Introduction to the Philosophy of Education* (1916; reprint, New York: Free Press, 1966).

10. Patrick White, ed., "Symposium: Is Morality a Non-Aim of Education?" *Philosophy and Literature* 22, no. 1 (April 1998): 136–99.

11. As I mentioned earlier, the word *useful* is itself deeply ambiguous. As a "pragmatic pluralist" who considers William James almost a saint, I do cringe when he succumbs to the phrase "cash value" to cover usefulness. When the useful is reduced to the free-market kind of utilitarianism, I go beyond cringing to passionate refutation. So did John Stuart Mill; throughout much of his later work he insisted that for Utilitarianism to work, it must depend on the dominant presence of "men of noble character"—human beings judging the "useful" in genuinely ethical terms. See his chapter "Infirmities and Dangers" in John Stuart Mill, *Utilitarianism, Liberty, and Representative Government*. Of the many editions, the one I prefer, because of its introduction by A. D. Lindsay, is the Everyman Library edition (London: J. M. Dent & Sons, 1910).

12. Wayne C. Booth, *The Company We Keep: An Ethics of Fiction* (Berkeley and Los Angeles: University of California Press, 1988); hereafter cited by page number parenthetically in the text.

13. Stephen R. Covey, *Seven Habits of Highly Effective People: Restoring the Character Ethic* (New York: Simon and Schuster, 1989). This simplistic book, translated into twenty-eight languages, has sold more than ten million copies. For an excellent exposé of the dangers in such coding, see Alan Wolfe, "White Magic in America: Capitalism, Mormonism, and the Doctrines of Stephen Covey," *New Republic*, February 23, 1998, 26–34.

14. Peter Rabinowitz, *Before Reading: Narrative Conventions and the Politics of Interpretation* (Ithaca, NY: Cornell University Press, 1987).

15. Mikhail M. Bakhtin, *The Dialogic Imagination: Four Essays*, ed. Michael Holquist, trans. Caryl Emerson and Michael Holquist (Austin: University of Texas Press, 1981).

16. Lionel Trilling, "On the Teaching of Modern Literature," in *Beyond Culture: Essays on Literature and Learning* (New York: Viking Press, 1965), 3–30.

17. Peter Rabinowitz and Michael Smith, *Authorizing Readers: Resistance and Respect* (New York: Teachers College Press/NCTE, 1997).

## Chapter 13

1. The American Civil Liberties Union (to which I belong) often goes too far in opposing *all* objections to any public expression. But as Cass Sunstein argues, there are almost no full "free-speech absolutists" who would accept no limits whatever on public "speech," however defined. He shows how we have committed absurd extensions of the "free speech" defense. See his *Democracy and the Problem of Free Speech* (New York: Free Press, 1993), 56, 121–24.

2. On May 31, 1995, then-senator Bob Dole's televised attack on violent movies prompted an amazing outburst of angry responses, pro and con, including visibly self-serving attempts at rebuttal by Hollywood producers. See *New York Times*, June 2, 1995.

3. Wendy Steiner, *The Scandal of Pleasure: Art in an Age of Fundamentalism* (Chicago: University of Chicago Press, 1995), 211.

4. See, for developments of this claim, the works by Robert Coles, Bruno Bettelheim, and Marina Warner in the appendix to this chapter.

5. On the subject of how philosophical fashions, like the oversimplified reliance on separation of fact and value, resist rational disproof and persist even after being thoroughly refuted, see Hilary Putnam's cogent chapter "Fact and Value," in *Reason, Truth, and History* (Cambridge: Cambridge University Press, 1981), 127–49, and his more recent book, *"The Collapse of the Fact/Value Dichotomy" and Other Essays* (Cambridge, MA: Harvard University Press, 2002). As long ago as 1974 I had listed, in *Modern Dogma and the Rhetoric of Assent* (Chicago: University of Chicago Press, 1974), more than two score refutations of the fact-value split—all of them by "philosophers" and many of them carefully reasoned. Those scores are by now raised to hundreds. See also Bernard Williams, *Ethics and the Limits of Philosophy* (Cambridge, MA: Harvard University Press, 1985), esp. chap. 5, and *Morality* (Cambridge: Cambridge University Press, 1972). For a neglected earlier turn on the question, see A. E. Taylor's "Actuality and Value," chap. 2 of *The Faith of a Moralist* (London: Macmillan, 1930). Any "absolutist" supporting the distinction will simply cast aside these claims to engage in real inquiry about values.

6. They tended to ignore just how passionately Auden could argue for the moral and ethical "happenings" that good literature *must* achieve. "Poetry," he wrote, "can do a hundred and one things, delight, sadden, disturb, amuse, instruct—it may express every possible shade of emotion, and describe every conceivable kind of event, but there is only one thing that all poetry *must* do; it must praise all it can for being and for happening." See W. H. Auden, "Making, Knowing and Judging," in *The Dyer's Hand* (London: Faber and Faber, 1962), 60. Readers who are not aware of the intense rejection of morality-centered criticism by most prominent critics by mid-century should have a look at the controversy over the Bollingen Prize awarded to Ezra Pound in 1949. See Noel Stock, ed., *Ezra Pound: Perspectives* (Chicago: University of Chicago Press, 1965), esp. the essay by Allen Tate, "Ezra Pound and the Bollingen Prize" (1959).

7. Many of the art-for-art's-sakers were, like Oscar Wilde, actually passionate moralists, preaching a new set of standards. But many of their followers lost that point, talking as if moral reasoning about anything was a thing of the past.

8. Kenneth Burke, *The Philosophy of Literary Form: Studies in Symbolic Action*, 3rd ed. (Baton Rouge: Louisiana State University Press, 1973).

9. This post-1960s avalanche is too huge for adequate footnoting. In the appendix, I list, with some annotation, a crude selection that includes mainly those works that actually use the words *moral* or *ethical* in their titles. If you doubt my claim about the avalanche, go to your library's computer and call up not just "morality and literature" or "ethics and literature" but such pairings as "religion and literature," "Christianity and literature," "Judaism and literature," or "literature and culture." The most careful critique of the ideological excesses and careless distortions of literary works exhibited by too many in the "avalanche" has been a series of essays by the Shakespearean scholar Richard Levin. The angry responses of those he has criticized (to me, almost always justly) demonstrate both the complexity and importance of the issues raised by "moral inquiry," especially when extended as broadly as I have done here. See, for example, Levin's "The New and the Old Historicizing of Shakespeare," in *The Historical and Political Turn in Literary Studies*, ed. Winfried Fluck (Tübingen: Gunter Narr Verlag, 1995).

10. David Hume, "Of the Standard of Taste," in *Selected Essays*, ed. Stephen Copley and Andrew Edgar (Oxford: Oxford University Press, 1963), 133–54; hereafter cited by paragraph number and page number parenthetically in the text. The essay, first published in 1742, has been reprinted hundreds of times. Until quite recently it appeared in almost every anthology of literary criticism.

11. It could be argued, perhaps even proved statistically, that people in America these days spend a larger portion of their time with stories, both obviously fictional and purportedly "real," than has been true in any other culture. Consider their access to TV, radio, movies, gossip, newspapers (including the tabloids inventing "real" stories), audiotapes, rap records, best-selling mysteries, Ann Landers, and the flood of anecdote-filled therapy books. We may long for a culture in which people sat around the fire in the evenings and told "real" stories or read Dickens to one another. But more Americans now live more hours in *that* story-world than would have been found in any older culture. [*Sad addition, 2004: A recent study claims to offer hard proof that the percentage of Americans who read* anything *is falling rapidly. The claim is that more and more just watch TV.*]

12. Dole, in his outburst about violence and sex in movies, praised and blamed works that he later admitted he had never experienced. More scandalous, in my view, are the "trained" academics who discourse about novels or works of criticism without reading more than the fragments that happen to offend.

13. The rhetorical notion of reading as a transaction between reader and author has been around for a long time—starting with the ancient rhetoricians. In this century it was dramatized most tellingly by the much-neglected but groundbreaking work of Louise Rosenblatt. See *Literature as Exploration* (1938; 5th ed., New York: Modern Language Association, 1995), and *The Reader, the Text, the Poem: The Transactional Theory of Literary Work* (Carbondale: Southern Illinois University Press, 1978). Rosenblatt avoids the relativistic notions pushed by some reader-response critics. For her, both readers and texts have powers that must be respected.

14. In *A Rhetoric of Irony* (Chicago: University of Chicago Press, 1974), I report on a large number of such cases, including the claim by ironic columnists like Mike Royko and Art Buchwald that they never write an ironic column without having many "straight" readers respond angrily in defense of the very positions the columnists are advocating.

15. One fashionable version of this relativism, "All values are contingent," is advocated by Barbara Herrnstein Smith in *Contingencies of Value: Alternative Perspectives for Critical Theory* (Cambridge: Cambridge University Press, 1988).

16. This doesn't mean that I have any confidence about where I'll come out. And what about Amis's own contributions outside a given work? Can he be the final authority? I don't know how Amis thinks about the morality of what seems to me his deeply nihilistic and potentially destructive novel. But having just read his morally rich encomium of Jane Austen's moral effects (*New Yorker*, January 8, 1996, 31–35), I'm flooded with doubts about my moral indictment of his novel. The "author" who praises Austen in this way could not have written the novel as I read it. Did I simply miss the author's implied moral clues?

17. A term more accurate here than *practical* might be *rhetorical* in the classical sense—a sense standard in Hume's time. But modern connotations would make it seem pejorative. For Hume's wonderfully moving and carefully reasoned discussion of how the thinker is to live after proving, as he believes, that "reason" has nothing to

say about it, see his conclusion to book 1, "Conclusion of This Book," in *A Treatise of Human Nature*, 2 vols. (London, 1738).

18. In practice, I would add one more: the critic's hidden motives other than the pursuit of critical truth. I turn to this point in my conclusion.

19. In his conclusion Hume at last moves openly into our territory by risking some moral judgments against specific works. He freely reveals strong convictions about how certain moral beliefs will mar fictions and ought to be judged negatively by the kind of critic he has set up as a model. I do wish that he had employed a few paragraphs of serious argument about such conclusions. As they stand, they sound like the exercise of prejudice.

20. The best recent account I have seen dealing with revenge violence in the "real" world is Sister Helen Prejean's *Dead Man Walking: An Eyewitness Account of the Death Penalty in the United States* (New York: Random House, 1993).

21. Yet for Sunday school purposes, which are not to be sneezed at, they will still be morally superior to some children's books that these days make harmful and dangerous behavior look unqualifiedly "cool"—and radically imitable. I'm thinking, for example, of some of Roald Dahl's clever enticements in works like *Charlie and the Chocolate Factory* (1964), made into the even more questionable movie *Willy Wonka and the Chocolate Factory* (1971).

22. An outstanding example is Austin Wright's *Tony and Susan* (New York: Baskerville, 1983), a gut-wrenching page-turner that implicates the reader in strong moral judgments from beginning to end: one emerges having been not just thrilled and torn but educated about the meaning of violence itself. Many a violent movie, like Sam Peckinpah's *The Wild Bunch*, gives attentive spectators a clear sense of the director's strong disapproval of what goes on. There is often an ironic contrast, of course, between the expressed disapproval and the actual exploitation: crime does not pay—except when portrayed enticingly.

23. Or we would know that, as implied dramatist, he wants us to see it as unforgivable; as I suggest in my conclusion, tellers can and do create works that imply authors far better, on this or that scale, than their everyday selves.

24. This ending seems to me utterly, deliberately empty, but, as I noted earlier, I may have missed moral clues.

25. For a brilliant celebration of the role of "shattering," see Walter A. Davis, *Get the Guests: Psychoanalysis, Modern American Drama, and the Audience* (Madison: University of Wisconsin Press, 1994). His critique of the traditional view that tragedy's gift is catharsis is especially challenging. He argues that genuinely powerful tragedy does not purge our pity and fear but probes our deepest consciousness so that we can "enter the Crypt, know the power death-work and soul-murder have in the constitution and regulation of the psyche, and begin to seek out the possibility of the dialectic that could attempt their reversal. . . brought face to face with the existential imperative which drama inserts directly into the deepest places of our psyche" (263). That case resembles, in ways that might surprise Davis himself, my claim that the best moral effect is not just placement but inquiry.

26. I borrow this phrase from a wonderfully inquiring current novel, *The Good Husband*, by Gail Godwin (New York: Ballantine Books, 1994). A central character, on her deathbed, makes the claim that the key task in life is "ordering one's loves," determining not just which loves we care about but which loves we *ought* to care about most.

27. James Baldwin, interview by Mel Watkins, *New York Times Book Review*, September 23, 1979, 3.

## Chapter 14

1. This chapter borrows some from my essay in a volume honoring David Tracy: *Radical Pluralism and Truth*, ed. Werner G. Jeanrond and Jennifer L. Rike (New York: Crossroad, 1991), 62–80. I also quote from various published versions of an essay on the rhetorics of science and religion.

2. Thomas M. Lessl, "Gnostic Scientism and the Prohibition of Questions," *Rhetoric and Public Affairs* 5, no. 1 (spring 2002): 133–58. See also "Lessl on Gnostic Scientism: Four Responses," *Rhetoric and Public Affairs* 5, no. 4 (winter 2002): 709–40.

3. I don't like that word *religionist*, but it's hard to find a better one. Call them the believers? Well, scientists are believers too. The faithful? Well, scientists are pursuing their faith. The devout? Sounds pejorative. The theologians? Sounds too exclusive. So it will have to be religionists—even though one of my dictionaries says that that word sometimes means simply "bigots."

4. One of the best treatments of rhetoric in scientific study is Alan G. Gross's *The Rhetoric of Science* (Cambridge, MA: Harvard University Press, 1990; 2nd ed., 1996). By "going a bit too far" in intruding rhetoric onto every scientific moment, he has offended many, but he ought to be read by everyone. My bibliography of books and articles on the subject has about 250 titles.

5. For a good (though no doubt by now somewhat outdated) summary of "theories of everything," speculations about how this or that scientific pursuit will explain it all, see Timothy Ferris, *The Whole Shebang: A State-of-the Universe(s) Report* (New York: Simon and Schuster, 1997).

6. For an amazingly revealing exploration of dogmatic, violent excesses on both sides, I can't resist recommending Dan Brown's *Angels and Demons* (New York: Atria Books, 2000)—set mainly in the Vatican and much more than a mere "murder mystery." It implicitly "argues" for a genuine union between science and religion. The heroine, a particle physicist, says: "Faith is universal. Our specific methods for understanding it are arbitrary. Some of us pray to Jesus, some of us go to Mecca, some of us study subatomic particles. In the end we are all just searching for truth, that which is greater than ourselves," and "we are grateful for the power that created us" (110).

7. Fritjof Capra, *The Tao of Physics: An Exploration of the Parallels between Modern Physics and Eastern Mysticism* (New York: Bantam Books, 1975). Here is a painfully reduced list of other key works in the controversy: Peter J. Bowler, *Reconciling Science and Religion: The Debate in Early Twentieth-Century Britain* (Chicago: University of Chicago Press, 2001); Jacob Bronowski, *Science and Human Values* (New York: Harper & Row, 1956; rev. ed., 1965); Paul Davies, *God and the New Physics* (London: Dent, 1983); John William Draper, *History of the Conflict between Religion and Science* (New York: D. Appleton, 1875); Amos Funkenstein, *Theology and the Scientific Imagination: From the Middle Ages to the Seventeenth Century* (Princeton, NJ: Princeton University Press, 1986); Langdon Gilkey, *Naming the Whirlwind: The Renewal of God-Language* (Indianapolis: Bobbs-Merrill, 1969); Stanley L. Jaki, *Science and Creation: From Eternal Cycles to an Oscillating Universe* (Edinburgh: Scottish Academic Press, 1974; rev. ed., Washington, DC: University Press of America, 1986); W. Warrant Richardson and Wesley J. Wildman, eds., *Religion and Science: History, Method, Dialogue* (London: Routledge, 1996). Finally, though Iris Murdoch rejects the term *God* and most religious terms from her inquiry, I see her *Metaphysics as a Guide*

to Morals (London: Chatto and Windus, 1992; New York: Penguin, 1993) as a marvelous candidate for this list; I wish every scientist would read it, following its echoing of Anselm's ontological proof.

8. John Polkinghorne, *The Faith of a Physicist: Reflections of a Bottom-Up Thinker*, Gifford Lectures, 1993–94 (Minneapolis: Fortress Press, 1996). See also his *Belief in God in an Age of Science* (New Haven, CT: Yale University Press, 1998).

9. Ian Barbour, *Religion and Science: Historical and Contemporary Issues* (San Francisco: HarperCollins, 1997), a rev. ed. of his *Religion in an Age of Science*, Gifford Lectures, 1989–1990 (San Francisco: Harper & Row, 1990).

10. The word *relativism* is almost as ambiguous as *religion*. What I have here called "utter" relativism is a synonym for complete skepticism. But for some the term comes closer to the "pluralism" that I've been defending for decades: Not "There is no truth," but "There are many genuine truths, truths that only seem to refute each other." For a splendid questioning of utter cultural relativism, probing the religious issues it raises, see Richard Shweder's "Post-Nietzschean Anthropology: The Idea of Multiple Objective Worlds," in *Relativism: Interpretation and Confrontation*, ed. Michael Krausz (Notre Dame, IN: University of Notre Dame Press, 1989), 99–139.

11. Robert Wuthnow, "Is There a Place for 'Scientific' Studies in Religion?" *Chronicle of Higher Education*, January 24, 2003.

12. I wonder how Leibniz would respond to that, as he worked out his theory of "the best of all possible worlds." But of course his whole project was based on the acknowledgment that when judged from the human perspective, a very great deal "went wrong" in creation.

13. By "purest" I mean those who are not in it for money or fame. For too many, it boils down to "Not enough people are accepting, or paying enough, for my research" or "I didn't get my proper share of scholarly citations this year." Even their egotistical worries confirm the claim that "something is wrong with the world."

14. Matthew Arnold, *Literature and Dogma: An Essay Towards a Better Apprehension of the Bible* (London: Smith, Elder, 1883), chap. 1.

15. Thomas Merton saw as the turning point in his life the moment when he realized he had been ignoring Warrant Four: his "religion" before that had never acknowledged his own need for repair. See Robert Inchausti, *Thomas Merton's American Prophecy* (Albany: State University of New York, 1998), chap. 2.

16. See Alan Lightman and Roberta Brawer, *Origins: The Lives and Worlds of Modern Cosmologists* (Cambridge, MA: Harvard University Press, 1990).

17. See Rudolf Otto, *The Idea of the Holy: An Inquiry into the Non-Rational Factor in the Idea of the Divine and Its Relation to the Rational*, trans. John W. Harvey (London: Oxford University Press, 1923), 1–30. See also Jacques Derrida, *The Gift of Death* (Chicago: University of Chicago Press, 1995), 25–34.

18. See the deeply informative book by John T. Noonan Jr., *Bribes: The Intellectual History of a Moral Idea* (Berkeley and Los Angeles: University of California Press, 1988).

## Chapter 15

1. Ford Madox Ford, *Parade's End* (four "Tietjens" novels: *Some Do Not...* [1924], *No More Parades* [1925], *A Man Could Stand Up—* [1926], and *The Last Post* [1928]), ed. Robie Macauley (New York: Alfred A. Knopf, 1950), 19, 170.

2. Jacques Derrida, "Genesis and Structure of the Essay 'On the Origin of Languages,'" in *Of Grammatology*, trans. Gayatri Chakravorty Spivak (Baltimore: Johns Hopkins University Press, 1976), 165.

3. Note that the "area" classification into three rhetorics that I am building here cuts across the "quality" classification into subrhetoric, "mere" rhetoric, rhetoric-B and rhetoric-A that I found essential in "Mere Rhetoric, Rhetorology, and the Search for a Common Learning" [*chapter 17 in this volume*]. Rhetoric-1 and rhetoric-A overlap, but they are by no means identical.

4. George Stigler, *"The Economist as Preacher" and Other Essays* (Chicago: University of Chicago Press, 1982).

5. After the Ryerson Lecture a biologist friend said, "You know, Arnold Ravin could not have *really* understood Wright's work; it was beyond him." "Do you mean," I asked, "that we were wrong in listening to him?" "Oh, no; you were right, because he was right. But he was himself depending more on rhetorics-2 and -3 than you realized."

6. Michael Polanyi, *Personal Knowledge: Towards a Post-Critical Philosophy* (Chicago: University of Chicago Press, 1958; rev. ed., New York: Harper & Row, 1962); Rom Harré, "Science as a Communal Practice," in *Varieties of Realism: A Rationale for the Natural Sciences* (Oxford: Blackwell, 1986).

7. "[W]hat earlier philosophers have alluded to by speaking of coherence as the criterion of truth is only a criterion of *stability*. It may equally stabilize an erroneous or a true view of the universe. The attribution of truth to any particular stable alternative is a fiduciary act which cannot be analysed in non-committal terms [that is, it depends on prior commitment to some enterprise shared with others].... [T]here exists no principle of doubt the operation of which will discover for us which of two systems of implicit beliefs is true—except in the sense that we will admit decisive evidence against the one we do not believe to be true, and not against the other. Once more, the admission of doubt proves here to be as clearly an act of belief as does the non-admission of doubt" (Polanyi, *Personal Knowledge*, 294).

8. Donald T. Campbell, "Ethnocentrism of Disciplines and the Fish-Scale Model of Omniscience," in *Interdisciplinary Relationships in the Social Sciences*, ed. Muzafer Sherif and Carolyn W. Sherif (Chicago: Aldine, 1969), 328–48. I thank Marvin Mikesell for this reference.

9. Anxiety about the ethnocentrism of experts was not invented in recent decades. As early as 1902, Alexander R. Hohfield, summarizing a central session of the annual meeting of the Modern Language Association, lamented "the increasing specialization of the papers" and claimed that it was "rapidly decreasing the number of occasions when a considerable proportion of those present are capable of joining in a discussion." Many a scholar has been hard-pressed to find proper analogies for our plight. Just after World War II John Erskine, describing how scholars claim to "cover" jointly fields that no one of them has mastered, recalled an ancient Irish legend: "[T]here was a tower so high that it took two persons to see to the top of it. One would begin at the bottom and look up as far as sight could reach, the other would begin where the first left off, and see the rest of the way." I owe these quotations to Gerald Graff, *Professing Literature: An Institutional History* (Chicago: University of Chicago Press, 1987), 111.

Chapter 17

1. This essay was prepared for presentation at the original conference sponsored by the Carnegie Foundation, a series of public lectures and discussions at the University of Chicago.

2. Four of the following five kinds of generality, and the notion of distinguishing the four kinds, I borrow from that great student of rhetoric, Richard McKeon; see Richard McKeon, "The Battle of the Books," in *The Knowledge Most Worth Having*, ed. Wayne C. Booth (Chicago: University of Chicago Press, 1967), 188–89.

3. Morris Kline, *Mathematics: The Loss of Certainty* (New York: Oxford University Press, 1980).

4. See James D. Watson, *The Double Helix: A Personal Account of the Discovery of the Structure of DNA* (New York: Scribners, 1968); and Donald Johanson and Maitland Edey, *Lucy* (New York: Simon and Schuster, 1981). For a fine, semipopular account of both the scientific problems and the rhetorical exchanges involved in the development of microbiology, see Horace Freeland Judson, *The Eighth Day of Creation: Makers of the Revolution in Biology* (New York: Simon and Schuster, 1979).

5. Michael Polanyi, *Personal Knowledge: Towards a Post-Critical Philosophy* (Chicago: University of Chicago Press, 1958; rev. ed., New York: Harper & Row, 1962); see especially chap. 9, "The Critique of Doubt."

6. Karl R. Popper, *The Logic of Scientific Discovery* (London: Hutchinson, 1959; rev. ed. 1968); see especially chaps. 4–6.

7. I am currently trying to address the problem in a largely unwritten work about the rhetoric of religion—especially the rhetoric of various surrogate religions that travel in secular guise. For a sample of the problems such inquiry raises, see my "Systematic Wonder: The Rhetoric of Secular Religions," *Journal of the American Academy of Religion* 53 (1985): 677–702.

8. The best account I have seen of the revolution effected by Gödel's famous paper of 1931 is offered by Ernest Nagel and James R. Newman in *Gödel's Proof* (New York: New York University Press, 1958).

9. It is not appropriate to my argument to lay down the principles that I expect to be found by rheterologists who think together long and hard about the grounds of their discourse. But one thing is clear from recent probings in various fields: Metaphysical questions that many modernists thought settled once and for all, settled with firm answers like "God is dead" or "Values are man-made and therefore nonrational," are now reopened. The ancient "proofs for the existence of God," for example, have often been "shown" to carry no rigorous "scientific force." But they are coming alive again, sometimes in traditional vocabulary, sometimes in entirely new terms. See, for example, Iris Murdoch's *The Sovereignty of Good* (London: Routledge and Kegan Paul, 1970). She claims to be proving only the reality of the good, not of God. But her proof exactly parallels one version of the traditional ontological proof.

# Index

Abrams, M. H., 16, 94, 341n9
accommodation: justified vs. preconceived, 61; of metaphor to audience, 83
Addison, Joseph, 248
Adler, Anthony, 186
adventure stories, 166–67
advertising: image building and propaganda in, 66; role of metaphor in, 95
Aesop's fables, 163, 201, 241, 255, 258
affective fallacy concept, 226
amateuring, pursuit of, 306–12
American Academy of Arts and Letters, 2
American Civil Liberties Union, 350n1
Amis, Martin: on Austen, 352n16; works: *The Information*, 231, 249, 250, 251, 257–58
Amnesty International, 133
Anselm of Canterbury, 123
Antczak, Frederick, 335n1
anthropology, understanding of, 287
anti-Semitism, in *Merchant of Venice*, 186
apocalyptic protest, writing about, 93–94
appraisal and appraising concept, 323. *See also* warrants, shared
Arata, Stephen D., 348–49n11
Aristotle: on action, 205; comprehensiveness of, 72; defense of, 122; on desire to know, 17; on friendship, 10, 158, 159; on habits, 222; as influence, 70; on mastery of subject, 61; on metaphor, 80, 90; on

pleasure, 11; pluralistic approach to, 124, 191–92; on poetry vs. history, 96; on rhetoric, 65, 281, 291, 320, 321; on slavery, 135–36, 344n31; on tragedy, 259; on values, 145; works: *Poetics*, 145; *Rhetoric*, 57, 320, 333
Arnold, Matthew: on critic's task, 242; education of, 333; on poetry, 96, 185; on religion, 272–73; on stories, 244
Arnold, Thomas, 333
art and aesthetics: approaches to, 155–56; for art's sake, 243; comparative discussion of, 186–87; dogmatic judgment of, 181–82; ethical task in, 97, 215–16; forms and meanings of, 141–47; moral effects of, 239–40, 242; moral obligation vs. ethical quality of, 189–90; persuasion as, 56–57, 65; polyphonic voices and, 148–53; violence in, 255
*Art of Growing Older, The* (Booth), 17
Artz, Lee, 335n1
assent concept, 5, 323. *See also* warrants, shared
Auden, W. H., 226, 243, 351n6
audience: consideration of, 70, 260; decorum expected by, 89; metaphor's success and, 80–81, 83, 98; narrative and authorial types of, 230; particularities of character and, 30–31; regrets of, for Macbeth's fall, 28–29; in rhetorical stance, 16, 55,

audience (*cont.*)
  58–63; university members as,
  282–83. *See also* author-reader
  relationship; readers
Augustine (saint), 191–92, 266, 321
Austen, Jane: comprehensive view of, 49;
  critical re-reading of, 204; desire to
  read more of, 167–68; on *Emma*,
  35–36; illusion of her presence as a
  character, 51–52; ironic English
  history by, 109, 111–12; moral effects
  of works of, 352n16; teaching works
  of, 234; value of tenderness and good
  will in, 339n10; works: *Mansfield
  Park*, 49. See also *Emma*; *Persuasion*;
  *Pride and Prejudice*
author-reader relationship: friendship as
  metaphor for, 10–11, 157–60, 345n3;
  irony's effect on, 110, 111–12; as
  partnership and dialogue, 8–9;
  qualities of experience in, 157; as
  transaction, 246, 352n13
authors: always-present voice of, 147–48;
  "authority" of, 345n5; changing
  predilections for, 253; classification of
  pleasures offered by, 160–69;
  disappearance of, 151; ideal type of,
  209; implicated in work's ideology,
  146–47; "intentions" of, 8; multiple
  versions of, 9; polyphonic voices and,
  148–53, 211–12; profound probing by,
  233; as "purified" friends, 259–61.
  *See also* author-reader relationship;
  implied author; voice/speaker

Babbitt, Irving, 156
Baker, Russell, 110
Baker, Sheridan, 61
Bakhtin, Mikhail: on author, 233;
  challenge of, 147–48; critique of
  individual, 116; on heteroglossia, 9;
  on ideology and ideological
  formalism, 145–46; on polyphonic
  voices, 148–53, 211–12; as vague *and*
  suggestive, 153; Western criticism at
  time of, 141–47; works: *Problems of
  Dostoevsky's Poetics*, 140
Baldwin, James, 260
Barbour, Ian, 269–70
Barthelme, Donald, 107, 110, 111, 112

Barthes, Roland, 4
Bartlett's *Familiar Quotations*, 158
Barzun, Jacques, 60–61
Bateson, Gregory, 116
beauty: capacity to discern, 247;
  connecting with, 276; reduced to
  market value, 196; of
  well-constructed story, 206–7, 211,
  215–16
Beauvoir, Simone de, 13, 155
Beckett, Samuel, 115
Bellow, Saul, *Herzog*, 97
Benchley, Peter, *Jaws*, 166–67, 201
Bennett, William, 222
Bentley, A. C., *Trent's Last Case*, 203–4
Bhabha, Homi, 344n25
Bible: stories of, 240–41; teaching of, 230;
  violence in, 255. *See also* God
Blackmur, R. P., 244
Bloom, Allan, 346n11
Bollingen Prize, 351n6
books as friends metaphor: authors as
  "purified" in, 259–61; description of,
  10–11, 157–60, 345n3; identification
  of two minds in, 111–12; moments of
  creative intensity fostered in, 215–16;
  revival of, 190; usefulness and, 158,
  160, 169. *See also* friendship
Boorstin, Daniel, 66
Booth, Alison, 348–49n11
Booth, Phyllis, 307, 309
Booth, Wayne: background of, 2, 335n1;
  breadth of interests, 1–2, 3; career
  choice of, 305–6; character-as-activity
  preoccupation of, 3, 11–14, 17–18; as
  implied author, 314; journal
  cofounded by, 74; lifelong
  commitment to rhetoric, 3–7;
  relativism and dogmatism negotiated
  by, 15–16; scientific and religious
  beliefs of, 121, 270; student writing
  by, 57. *See also specific works*
Bourdieu, Pierre, 13
Bradley, A. C., 338n5
Brain, Robert, 157
brokenness of cosmos: emotions
  connected to, 276–78; humans as all
  part of, 274; responsibility for fixing,
  275–76; shared recognition of,
  271–72, 274

*Harper & Row Reader, The* (Booth, coauthor), 12
*Harper & Row Rhetoric, The* (Booth, coauthor), 12
Harré, Rom, 297
Hartshorne, Charles, 269
Haverford College, 315
Hayes, E. N., 338n4
Hegel, G. W. F., 337n15
Heidegger, Martin, 16, 17, 337n15
Heiserman, Arthur, 74
Hemingway, Ernest, 29
Hildebrand, Roger, 286–87
Himmelfarb, Gertrude, 221
history: Austen's ironic English, 109, 111–12; of controversy over moral inquiry, 242–45; in general education, 316; of ideas and of thought, 125–27, 134; poetry as more philosophical than, 96; standards of controversy in, 67, 340n2; understanding of, 287; of writing about apocalyptic protest, 93–94
Hobbes, Thomas, 92
Hoekema, David, 220
Hohfield, Alexander R., 356n9
Homer: appreciation for, 248; changing views of, 187; Plato on, 185; pleasure of reading, 165; useful information of, 169; on violence, 255; works: *Iliad*, 255; *Odyssey*, 169, 234
Horace, 242, 253
"How Bakhtin Woke Me Up" (Booth): comments on, 140, 153; text of, 141–53
Hugo, Victor, *Les Misérables*, 231
human beings: as always comparative, 186–87; limits of, 113–18, 282–89; meaning of life and, 152–53; metaphors in discussing behavior of, 94; relations among things and, 157; as rhetoric-endowed species, 318–19; stories' effects on, 254–55
human character: as controversial term, 224; ethical teaching and, 223; general rhetoric in appraising, 291–92
human rights, 130–33, 135, 342n5
Hume, David: challenge of, 184; defense of, 122–23; dogmatism and, 15; on literary judgment, 245–53, 259, 261;

pluralistic approach to, 191–92; on specific works, 353n19; works: "Of the Standard of Taste," 245–53
humor: maintaining sympathy with character through, 37–40; in metaphors out of context, 86. *See also* comedy
Hyde, Lewis, 345n4

ideology, form intertwined with, 141–47
implied author: Booth as, 314; concept of, 7–9; critical engagement with, 230–31, 232–33; ethical effects of genres vs., 349n12; everyday selves vs., 353n23; fictions as gifts from, 159, 345n4; metaphor of friendship with, 50–52, 345n3; norms of *Emma* and, 45–49; patterns of desires and gratification that reveal, 168–69; reasoning of, 251; virtuousness of, 11
*Independence Day* (film), 233
indirect discourse, vitality of, 150
infanticide, 133
information theory, 72–73
intellectual arguments: conflicting claims in, 317–18; diminishment of, 67; evaluation of, 70; lack of listening in, 5–6; lack of training in constructing, 71; productive, critical conversation about, 234–35; relocation of standards of, 185–89; rhetorical evaluation in, 295–97, 322–24; in rhetorical stance, 58–63; tools as openings in, 12–14, 16; understanding in, 285–86; "warrantable assent" in, 5. *See also* dialogue
interdisciplinarity: commitment to, 299–300; communication in, 289; rhetoric as proper term for, 4–5
International Society for the History of Rhetoric, 318
intrigue, plot as synonymous with, 145
"ironic, ironical, irony" (family of terms): current misuses of, 112–18; distinctions of, 105–6; synonyms for, 103–4; uncritical uses of, 101–3
irony: cosmic, metaphysical, 112–18; critics' talk about, 104; declared dead, 100; as efficient communication,

realism, 7–8

reciprocal refutation, 190–91

relativism: ambiguity of term, 355n10; avoidance of, 184; coduction distinguished from, 187; Hume's refutation of, 247–53; in literary judgment, 246; McKeon distinguished from, 123, 127, 130; pluralism and, 191–92; of truth, 270; of values, 352n15

religionists: questions for, 278; rhetoric utilized by, 266; use of term, 354n3

religions: ambiguity of term, 355n10; attacks on, 265–66; blessings neglected in, 277; definitions of, 270–71, 272–73; "the Fall" in, 274; metaphors of, 96–97; rhetoric's relationship to, 266–67, 357n7; science as rival to, 269–70; science's similarities with, 267–69; science's warrants shared with, 270, 271–77; self-reproach and responsibility in, 275; spending time in, 305; stories of, 235–36, 240–41; theology, cosmic irony, and, 113–18

relocations: from lumping to particulars, 185; from monism to pluralism, 190–91; from moral obligation to ethical quality, 189–90; overview of, 184; of standards of arguments, 185–89

"representative anecdote" concept, 154

re-reading: concept of, 202–3, 250; mystery of first vs. ironic intensities of second, 44; for structure, 204–5, 348–49n11, 349n13

res/verba distinction, 144

rhetoric: ambiguities of, 281; centrality of, 320, 327–34; commitment to, 3–7, 147–48; definition of, 6–7, 55–56, 62, 65–66, 68, 320, 340n3; ecumenical type of, 281; frontline, general, and academy kinds of, 291–97, 320, 322–24; in general education, 316, 333–34; "mere," 318–19, 333; metaphor as figurative device of, 75–77; opprobrium attached to, 4–5, 55, 66–68, 134, 292, 318; practical approach to, 336n11; religion's relationship to, 266–67; revival of

study of, 67–73; science's relationship to, 267; teachability of, 56–58; techniques and consequences of, 9; topical method of, 12–14; understanding and evaluation based in, 289–97

rhetorical age: concept of, 67, 340n2; persuasion as way of life in, 70, 71–73

rhetorical stance: advertiser's stance vs., 61–62; balance in, 62–63; definition of, 58; entertainer's stance vs., 62; pedantic stance vs., 58–61

Rhetoric of Fiction, The (Booth): afterword of, 10; on implied author, 7–9; on objectivity, 152; reading and research for, 3–4; title of, 61–62, 72; chapter of: "Control of Distance in Jane Austen's Emma," 34, 35–52

Rhetoric of Irony, A (Booth): adjectives and definitions in, 104; inductive theorizing in, 4; on intended irony, 110; on irony's function, 9–10; on misreading irony, 352n14

Rhetoric of Rhetoric, The (Booth): earlier echoes of, 64; on listening-rhetoric, 5; rhetoric defined in, 7; chapter of: "Rhetoric, Science, Religion," 264, 265–78

rhetorologists and rhetorology: application of, 317–18; hopes for, 278; McKeon as, 125, 134, 336n7; questions reopened in, 330–31, 357n9; science's vs. religion's approach in, 267–70; testing "maybes" in, 332–33

rhetrickery, use of term, 4, 266

"Richard McKeon's Pluralism" (Booth): comments on, 14–15, 120, 336n7; text of, 121–38

Richards, I. A., 4, 340n3

Richardson, Samuel, 82

Richter, David, 348–49n11

Ricoeur, Paul, 76, 79

Riesman, David, 67–68

Roanoke College, 302

Robbe-Grillet, Alain: Jealousy, 55; Project for a Revolution in New York, 97

Rockefeller grant, 2

rock music, 346n11

romantics, ironic principle of, 113–15